Profiles of
KENTUCKY'S
UNITED STATES
SENATORS
1792–Present

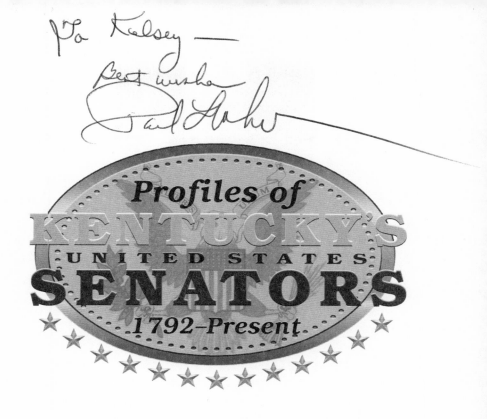

Profiles of KENTUCKY'S UNITED STATES SENATORS

1792–Present

Biographical essays of all who have represented Kentucky in the US Senate

PAUL L. WHALEN

Acclaim Press
— *Your Next Great Book* —

P.O. Box 238
Morley, MO 63767
(573) 472-9800
www.acclaimpress.com

Book Design: Ron Eifert
Cover Design: Frene Melton

Library of Congress Control Number: 2020940564
ISBN: 978-1-948901-65-9 / 1-948901-65-X

First Printing 2020
Printed in the United States of America
10 9 8 7 6 5 4 3 2 1

This publication was produced using available information.
The publisher regrets it cannot assume responsibility for errors or omissions.

Contents

To my wife Teena,
my partner
for going on four decades!

Acknowledgments

There are many people who encouraged me with the writing of this book and offered their suggestions and constructive criticism. They include Dr. James Claypool, NKU Professor of History, Emeritus, who made some initial suggestions on style and organization; my friend and fellow DOE Attorney, Jay Jalovec, Esq., who was always willing to provide an initial proof reading and grammar critique; my daughter Lucy Whalen, who was not hesitant to mark up a chapter that she reviewed if it was needed; Ms. Hayley Kirley, NKU graduate student who helped prepare the manuscript for the publisher; Ms. Madelyn Newman, my intern from the University of Tennessee at Martin, who assisted with editing and critiquing the rough first half of the book; and Mr. Alan Wild and Ms. Chelsie Stover, who also assisted with initial proof reading.

I would like to thank the Filson Historical Society in Louisville for its research assistance, in particular, Jennie Cole and Johna Picco. Also, many thanks to the staff at the Covington Branch at the Kenton County Library for their assistance and not shaming me when returning overdue books.

Finally, I am grateful to the staff at Acclaim Press for publishing the book.

Firsts and Onlys
for Kentucky
United States Senators

- **John Brown** was Kentucky's first US senator.
- **Humphrey Marshall** was the first member of the Federalist Party to serve as US senator from Kentucky.
- **John Breckinridge** was the first to resign to become US attorney general.
- **Buckner Thruston** was the first Kentucky US senator to resign to become a federal judge.
- **John Adair** was the first general to serve as US senator from Kentucky.
- **Henry Clay** was the youngest person to serve as US senator from Kentucky. (Age twenty-nine when he assumed office on December 29, 1806.)
- **George M. Bibb** was the first Kentucky US senator to serve as secretary of the treasury.
- **Henry Clay** was the first Speaker of the House to serve as US senator from Kentucky.
- **Henry Clay** was the first and only US secretary of state to serve as US senator from Kentucky.
- **Henry Clay** was the first Kentucky US senator to run for president.
- **John J. Crittenden** was the only Kentucky US senator to be nominated for a seat on the Supreme Court.
- **Richard Johnson** was the first US senator from Kentucky to be elected vice president.
- **Richard Johnson** is the first and only US senator from Kentucky to acknowledge having biracial children.
- **John Breckinridge** (grandson) was the first and only Kentucky US senator to be expelled from the Senate.
- **James Beck** was the only foreign-born US senator from Kentucky. (Scotland)

- **John Stuart Williams** was the only person to serve as a Confederate general prior to election to the US Senate from Kentucky.
- **Willis Machen** was the only Kentucky US senator to serve as a member of the Congress of the Confederacy prior to serving as a US senator.
- **William J. DeBoe** was the first medical doctor to be elected US senator from Kentucky.
- **William J. DeBoe** was also the first Republican elected US senator from Kentucky.
- **Joseph C.S. Blackburn** was the only US senator whose brother served as Kentucky governor.
- **Joseph C.S. Blackburn** is the only Kentucky US senator with a mountain peak in Alaska named for him. (Mount Blackburn, the fifth highest peak in the US)
- **John C.W. Beckham** was the first popularly elected US senator.
- **William O. Bradley** was the only Kentucky US senator to die of injuries sustained in a streetcar accident.
- **Alben W. Barkley** was the only US senator to serve in Congress during both World War I and World War II. (He served in the House of Representatives during World War I and the Senate during World War II.)
- **Albert Benjamin "Happy" Chandler** was the only US senator to resign to become Commissioner of Major League Baseball.
- **Virgil Munday Chapman** was the only Kentucky US senator killed in a car accident.
- **John Sherman Cooper** was the only Kentucky US senator to serve on the Warren Commission, which investigated the assassination of President Kennedy.
- **Wendell Ford** was the only person to serve without a break in services as state senator, lieutenant governor, governor, and US senator.
- **Mitch McConnell** is the first Kentucky US senator to have his spouse serve as a cabinet secretary.
- **Mitch McConnell** is the longest-serving Kentucky US senator.
- **Jim Bunning** is the only member of the Major League Baseball Hall of Fame to be elected to the US Senate.
- **Rand Paul** is the only Kentucky US senator to be sworn in on the same day his father was sworn in as a member of the US House of Representatives.

Kentucky's
United States Senators

Many political giants have served Kentucky as its US senators since Kentucky's admission to the Union in June 1792. Because of their political stature, the political giants in the US Senate from Kentucky have overshadowed the achievements of their lesser known predecessors or colleagues.

As of 2019 a total of sixty-six men have served in Kentucky's two Senate seats. Senators from Kentucky have been leaders in that body for a significant period of the nineteenth, twentieth, and twenty-first centuries. In the nineteenth century, Henry Clay and John J. Crittenden were leaders without portfolio for much of the time between 1830 and 1860. Senator Stevenson was Democratic caucus chair in the 1870s, and Senator Beck was Democratic caucus chair during the 1880s. Senator Alben Barkley was Senate Democratic majority leader during the 1930s and 1940s. Senator Earle Clements was Lyndon Johnson's deputy in the 1950s. Senator John Sherman Cooper was an early leader of the Vietnam anti-war movement in the Senate. Senator Wendell Ford was Democratic whip. Senator Mitch McConnell has dominated Senate Republican leadership since the turn of the twenty-first century. He has served as minority leader and now as majority leader.

The purpose of this book is to profile the Senate services of these individuals and shine a light on the lives and contributions of these men, particularly those who are not as well-known as Clay, Barkley, Ford, and McConnell, all of whom have been political giants during their long tenures in the Senate.

While there are sixty-six men who have served as US senators from Kentucky, some have served at two, three, or even four different periods of time. For example, Henry Clay served a partial term from 1806 to 1807 and another partial term from 1810 to 1811.

Then he served for a third period from 1831 to 1842 and finally a fourth period from 1849 to his death in 1852. John J. Crittenden was elected to serve a term from 1817 to 1823 but resigned in 1819. He then returned to serve from 1835 to 1841 with a brief time out only to return in 1842 to

1848, when he resigned to run for governor. Then Crittenden was reelected to the Senate to serve from 1855 to 1861. The same situation exists for John Sherman Cooper, who served unexpired terms from 1945 to 1949 and 1952 to 1955 and a final period of three full elected terms from 1956 to 1973. Because these senators' contributions were significant, they are given a section or chapter for each Senate term or period.

There is not currently a complete history or profiles of Kentucky's US senators. The purpose of this book is to introduce the reader and historian to each of the men who have been sent to Washington to represent Kentucky in the Senate from the beginning of statehood in 1792 to the present. There are many biographies of Henry Clay, who served as both US senator from Kentucky and Speaker of the House of Representatives. There are biographies of John J. Crittenden and John G. Carlisle. There are recent biographies published Joseph Blackburn of Barkley and McConnell. Many other senators were just as colorful, such as James Beck and Ollie James, yet the stories of many of these men are unknown to most Americans and Kentuckians. Contributions from this group include four who served as vice president, two who served as attorney general, three who served as secretary of the treasury, several who served as postmaster general, one US secretary of state, and ambassadors to Spain, Weimar Germany, India, and East Germany.

The nation, and perhaps the world, knows the names of Henry Clay, John J. Crittenden, Alben Barkley, Happy Chandler, and Mitch McConnell. Many of the remaining sixty senators made important contributions. Using the *Senate Journal*, newspapers of the time, and personal papers, this book will examine the lives of these men to shed more light on them and their time in the Senate.

Kentucky senators have served in important leadership roles. In the early years of the Senate, Senators John Brown and John Pope served as president pro tempore of the Senate. Brown served during two sessions of the Eighth Congress (October 17, 1803 to February 26, 1804). John "One Arm" Pope served during the last session of the Eleventh Congress (February 23, 1811 to November 3, 1811). Former Senator Richard M. Johnson presided over the Senate as vice president under Martin Van Buren. Johnson is the only vice president elected by the Senate under the Twelfth Amendment to the Constitution.

Following the stories of Kentucky's senators, one can see how the US Senate has grown in importance and power. During the first two decades of the nineteenth century, many senators resigned to go back to Kentucky and take "lesser" positions as state court judges or in law practices. After the 1840s, that did not happen.

In telling the individual stories of individual Kentucky senators, one of the reasons for the enactment of the Seventeenth Amendment to the

Constitutions can be seen. The 1896 election of Republican William DeBoe took a specially called session of the General Assembly because the legislature had failed to elect a senator during the regular session. With the election of Republican President William McKinley, Senator DeBoe was able to reward some of the legislators who supported his election. The state representative from Newport was made postmaster of Newport.

Political eras are reflected in the elections of groups of senators. From 1792 to 1824, most of Kentucky's senators were Jeffersonian Democrats. After 1824, senators reflected the policies of Henry Clay and, after 1834, the Whig Party. The Whig Party died soon after Clay did in 1852. The last two senators elected as Whigs from Kentucky were Archibald Dixon, who served from September 1852 to March 1855, and John J. Critten-den, who was elected as a Whig in 1855. With the Civil War, one sees the end of the Clay legacy and a new era of Democrats dominating Kentucky politics and Senate elections until the 1890s.

Earle Clements literally sacrificed his Senate career, filling in as the Democratic majority leader while Democratic Majority Leader Lyndon Johnson recovered from a heart attack in 1956. John G. Carlisle fought the Republican tariff in 1888, voting against it in the House, and, after being appointed to fill a vacancy, voted against it again in the Senate.

There were several senators whose careers were cut short. Ollie James, who served from 1913 to 1918, was President Woodrow Wilson's go-to guy in the Senate during the first years of his administration. James was the chairman of the Democratic National Convention that nominated Wilson in 1912 and re-nominated him in 1916. James was chosen by the administration to administer federal patronage in Kentucky over nota-bles such as Watterson and Bingham.

There were many men appointed to serve a few months because of death or resignation. Robert Humphreys was appointed by Governor Chandler to fill the vacancy caused by the sudden death of Senator Alben Barkley. Humphreys was a personal friend of Chandler's who, as president pro tem-pore of the Kentucky Senate in 1935, helped Chandler change the nomi-nating procedure for the Democratic Party from a convention to a primary. Under the primary system, Chandler was able to secure the Democratic nomination for governor and, thus, his first term as Kentucky's governor.

Research to date indicates that Kentucky governors who became US Sen-ators (with the exception of Ford, Crittenden, and Clements) were under-achievers as senators. Governors who were underachievers as senators would include Adair, Metcalfe, Morehead, Stevenson, Bradley, and Beckham.

Unlike the House of Representatives, in which all members are stand-ing re-election every two years, only a third of the US senators are stand-ing for re-election every two years. The purpose of the three classes of senators is to determine which Senate seats are up for election every two years. Kentucky's two senators are members of "Class Two of Three" and "Class Three of Three."

Class Two of Three

John Brown (Frankfort) • Democratic-Republican
   June 18, 1792 to March 4, 1805
Buckner Thruston (Lexington) • Democratic-Republican
   March 4, 1805 to December 18, 1805
Henry Clay (Second term) (Lexington) • Democratic-Republican
   January 10, 1810 to March 4, 1811
George M. Bibb (First term - Frankfort) • Democratic-Republican
   March 4, 1811 to August 23, 1814
George Walker (Jessamine) • Democratic-Republican
   August 30, 1811 to December 16, 1814
William T. Barry (Lexington) • Democratic-Republican
   December 16, 1814 to May 1, 1816
Martin D. Hardin (Frankfort) • Federalist
   November 3, 1816 to March 4, 1817
John J. Crittenden (First term - Russellville) • Democratic-Republican
   March 4, 1817 to March 3, 1819
Richard M. Johnson (Scott County) • Democratic-Republican
   December 10, 1819 to March 4, 1829
George M. Bibb (Second term - Frankfort) • Jacksonian
   March 4, 1829 to March 4, 1835
John J. Crittenden (Frankfort) • Whig
   March 4, 1835 to March 4, 1841
James T. Morehead (Warren) • Whig
   March 4, 1841 to March 4, 1847
Joseph R. Underwood (Bowling Green) • Whig
   March 4, 1847 to March 4, 1853
John B. Thompson (Mercer) • Know-Nothing
   March 4, 1853 to March 4, 1859
Lazarus W. Powell (Henderson) • Democratic
   March 4, 1859 to March 4, 1865
James Guthrie (Louisville) • Democratic
   March 4, 1865 to February 7, 1868
Thomas C. McCreery (First term - Richmond) • Democratic
   February 19, 1868 to March 4, 1871
John W. Stevenson (Covington) • Democratic
   March 4, 1871 to March 4, 1877

James B. Beck (Lexington) • Democratic
March 4, 1877 to May 3, 1890
John G. Carlisle (Covington) • Democratic
May 26, 1890 to February 4, 1893
William Lindsay (Frankfort) • Democratic
February 15, 1893 to March 4, 1901
Joseph Blackburn (Second term - Woodford County) • Democratic
March 4, 1901 to March 4, 1907
Thomas H. Paynter (Greenup County) • Democratic
March 4, 1907 to March 4, 1913
Ollie M. James (Crittenden County) • Democratic
March 4, 1913 to August 28, 1918
George B. Martin (Ashland) • Democratic
September 7, 1918 to March 4, 1919
Augustus O. Stanley (Henderson) • Democratic
May 19, 1919 to March 4, 1925
Fred M. Sackett (Louisville) • Republican
March 4, 1925 to January 9, 1930
John M. Robsion (Barbourville) • Republican
January 11, 1930 to November 30, 1930
Ben M. Williamson (Ashland) • Democratic
December 1, 1930 to March 4, 1931
Marvel M. Logan (Edmondson/Warren Counties) • Democratic
March 4, 1931 to October 3, 1939
A.B. "Happy" Chandler (Versailles) • Democratic
October 10, 1939 to November 1, 1945
William A. Stanfill (Hazard) • Republican
November 19, 1945 to November 5, 1946
John Sherman Cooper (First term - Somerset) • Republican
November 6, 1945 to January 3, 1949
Virgil Chapman (Paris) • Democratic
January 3, 1949 to March 8, 1951
Thomas R. Underwood (Lexington) • Democratic
March 19, 1951 to November 4, 1952
John Sherman Cooper (Second term - Somerset) • Republican
November 5, 1952 to January 3, 1955
Alben W. Barkley (Second term - Paducah) • Democrat
January 3, 1955 to April 30, 1956
Robert Humphreys (Mayfield) • Democratic
June 21, 1956 to November 6, 1956
John Sherman Cooper (Third term - Somerset) • Republican
November 7, 1956 to January 3, 1973

Walter "Dee" Huddleston (Elizabethtown) • Democratic
January 3, 1973 to January 3, 1985
Mitch McConnell (Louisville) • Republican
January 3, 1985 to present

Class Three of Three

John Edwards (Bourbon County) • Anti-Administration
June 18, 1792 to March 4, 1795
Humphrey Marshall (Frankfort) • Federalist
March 4, 1795 to March 4, 1801
John Breckinridge (Lexington) • Democratic-Republican
March 4, 1801 to August 7, 1805
John Adair (Mercer County) • Democratic-Republican
November 8, 1805 to November 18, 1806
Henry Clay (First term - Lexington) • Democratic-Republican
December 19, 1806 to March 4, 1807
John Pope (Springfield) • Democratic-Republican
March 4, 1807 to March 4, 1813
Jesse Bledsoe (Lexington) • Democratic-Republican
March 4, 1813 to December 24, 1814
Isham Talbot (First term - Frankfort) • Democratic-Republican
February 2, 1815 to March 4, 1819
William Logan (Shelby County) • Democratic-Republican
March 4, 1819 to May 28, 1820
Isham Talbot (Second term - Frankfort) • Democratic-Republican
October 19, 1820 to March 4, 1825
John Rowan (Bardstown) • Democratic
March 4, 1825 to March 4, 1831
Henry Clay (Third term - Lexington) • Whig
November 10, 1831 to March 31, 1842
John J. Crittenden (Second term - Frankfort) • Whig
March 31, 1842 to June 12, 1848 (Second Term)
Thomas "Stonehammer" Metcalfe (Carlisle) • Whig
June 23, 1848 to March 4, 1849
Henry Clay (Fourth term - Lexington) • Whig
March 4, 1849 to June 24, 1852
David Meriwether (Louisville) • Democrat
July 6, 1852 to August 31, 1852
Archibald Dixon (Henderson) • Whig
September 1, 1852 to March 4, 1855

John J. Crittenden (Third term - Woodford) • Whig
March 4, 1855 to March 4, 1861
John C. Breckinridge (Lexington) • Democratic
March 4, 1861 to December 4, 1861
Garrett Davis (Bourbon County) • Unionist
December 10, 1861 to September 22, 1872
Willis B. Machen (Eddyville) • Democratic
September 27, 1872 to March 4, 1873
Thomas C. McCreery (Second term - Daviess County)
Democratic • March 4, 1873 to March 4, 1879
John Stuart Williams (Mt. Sterling) • Democratic
March 4, 1879 to March 4, 1885
Joseph C.S. Blackburn (First term - Woodford County) • Democratic
March 4, 1885 to March 4, 1897
William J. Deboe (Crittenden County) • Republican
March 4, 1897 to March 4, 1903
James B. McCreary (Richmond) • Democratic
March 4, 1903 to March 4, 1909
William O. Bradley (Garrard County) • Republican
March 4, 1909 to May 23, 1914
Johnson N. Camden (Woodford County) • Democratic
June 16, 1914 to March 4, 1915
John C.W. Beckham (Bardstown) • Democratic
March 4, 1915 to March 4, 1921
Richard P. Ernst (Covington) • Republican
March 4, 1921 to March 4, 1927
Alben W. Barkley (First term - Paducah) • Democratic
March 4, 1927 to January 19, 1949(1st)
Garrett L. Withers (Webster County) • Democratic
January 20, 1949 to November 26, 1950
Earle C. Clements (Madisonville) • Democratic
November 27, 1950 to January 3, 1957
Thruston Morton (Louisville) • Republican
January 3, 1957 to December 16, 1968
Marlow Cook (Louisville) • Republican
December 17, 1968 to December 27, 1974
Wendell H. Ford (Owensboro) • Democratic
December 28, 1974 to January 3, 1999
Jim Bunning (Fort Thomas) • Republican
January 3, 1999 to January 3, 2011
Rand Paul (Warren County) • Republican
January 3, 2011 to present

Part I
1792–1809
Early Period

The years 1787–1800 have been termed the "Formative Years of the Senate" by Senate Historian Richard A. Baker in his *Senate Stories—200 Notable Days.*[1] For Kentucky, the formative years do not begin until the admission of Kentucky in June 1792. Politics in the first decades of statehood were dominated by Isaac Shelby and his associates.

As Kentucky had been part of Virginia, its leaders were influenced by "Anti-Federalists" or by supporters of Thomas Jefferson and James Madison. This is seen in the legislature's election of veteran Congressman John Brown.

You will read that the legislature elected Kentucky's only Federalist US senator, Humphrey Marshall, to replace John Edwards for the term beginning 1795 to 1801. As a Federalist, Marshall voted for the Jay Treaty, which almost resulted in him being lynched on a return visit to Kentucky.

The lack of Kentucky politicians' importance to the Senate is reflected in part by the fact that between 1801 and 1819, only Senator John Pope served a full six-year term.

Important legislative events during this period included the disputed presidential election of 1800.

JOHN BROWN
(1757-1837)

- Class Two of Three
- Senate Service: June 18, 1792–March 4, 1805
- Political Affiliation: Democratic-Republican
- Residence at time of election: Frankfort
- Served with Presidents Washington, Adams, and Jefferson
- Served with Governors Shelby, Garrard, and Greenup

Kentucky's first US senator, John Brown, was one of the brightest individuals elected to represent Kentucky. While at the College of William & Mary with future Supreme Court Chief Justice John Marshall and future Justices Bushrod Washington and William Short, Brown was admitted to the parent chapter of Phi Beta Kappa on December 4, 1778. Prior to attending William & Mary, Brown had attended Princeton. After leaving William & Mary, he studied law under Thomas Jefferson and George Wythe.

Brown arrived in Kentucky in 1783 as a young lawyer who came to the district as the executor of the estate of his uncle, Captain William Preston. Preston had received a land grant in Kentucky in exchange for his Revolutionary War military service.

Before becoming Kentucky's first US senator, Brown had represented Virginia in the Continental Congress (1777–1778) and the US Congress

(1789–1791). He sponsored the legislation that granted Kentucky statehood.

As a member of the Virginia Assembly, Brown brought petitions and resolutions before the body for the establishment of a separate independent state of Kentucky as early as 1786.

Brown was appointed by the Virginia Assembly on October 23, 1787 to be the Kentucky representative of the Virginia delegation to the Continental Congress, which was then meeting in New York City. As a representative in Congress, he had regular contact with James Madison, a fellow member of the Virginia Delegation, and they lodged at the same place in New York.[1] During 1788, Brown brought Kentucky's application for statehood before the Congress. It was turned down due in part to the fear the northeastern states had of Kentucky's potential support of Southern views toward the formulation of what would become the US Constitution in 1789.

As the congressman who represented the District of Kentucky, he was involved with the debate and compromise that established the location of the nation's capital on the banks of the Potomac.

The Federal Judiciary Act was passed in September 1789. Hundreds of office seekers were in New York applying for jobs in the new government. Congressman Brown's friend and former law partner, Harry Innes, was appointed federal judge for the District of Kentucky.[2]

On January 28, 1791, Congressman John Brown of Virginia's District of Kentucky moved for an act that would separate Kentucky from Virginia and make Kentucky a separate state. President George Washington signed the act on February 4, 1791, which enacted the formation of Kentucky as a state effective June 1, 1792, "when it should be received into this Union, as a new and entire member of the United States."[3]

In June 1792, the Kentucky legislature elected Brown as one of the two US senators from Kentucky along with John Edwards to be seated at the Senate's November 1792 session. Edwards's term would end in March 1795.[4]

As a US senator, Brown was sympathetic to the French in their disputes with Britain. He continued to work for open navigation of the Mississippi River, whose ownership changed several times between France and Spain.

His writings reflect that he was in Philadelphia during the yellow fever plague of 1793. The yellow fever epidemic in Philadelphia from July through October 1793 killed approximately 5,000 people out of a population of 45,000 in one of the most cosmopolitan cities in North America at the time.

By 1796, Brown was so impressed with Frankfort that he made it his home that year and began the building of his home, Liberty Hall, for his parents, who came to Kentucky. It is an outstanding example of Georgian architecture and is said to have been designed by Thomas Jefferson.[5]

He denounced the Alien and Sedition Acts in 1798.[6] The Alien and Sedition Acts were a series of four pieces of legislation signed into law by President John Adams that made it more difficult for immigrants to become citizens and be granted the right to vote. They also made it easier to deport immigrants and made it difficult to criticize government officials.

In 1799, Senator Brown married Margaretta Mason, the daughter of the Rev. John Mason, a Presbyterian minister from New York City. Margaretta Brown is best known for founding the first Sunday school west of the Alleghenies.[7]

One of the most important votes of Brown's career as an US senator involved the vice presidency of Aaron Burr in the disputed election of 1800.

It was the vision of western politicians such as Brown that encouraged the Jefferson administration to send Robert Livingston and James Monroe to France to negotiate the treaty for New Orleans, which culminated in the Louisiana Purchase on March 1, 1803.

Brown was the first of two Kentuckians to serve as president pro tempore of the Senate. He served during the Eighth Congress from October 17 through December 6, 1803, and January 23 through February 26, 1804. He was elected to that position with twenty-four of the possible twenty-nine votes on Monday, October 17, 1803.

Brown's defeat at reelection in 1804 has been said to have been due to the "machinations of his opponent and future senator" Buckner Thruston.[8] Rumors were spread that Brown was using his office to profit from a canal project around the "Falls of the Ohio" at Louisville.

After his retirement from the Senate, Brown resumed a lucrative law practice and land speculation. At the time of his death in 1837, the Franklin County tax rolls indicated that Brown owned about 10,000 acres.

JOHN EDWARDS
(1748–1847)

- Class Three of Three
- Senate Service: 1792–1795
- Political affiliation: Democratic-Republican
- Residence at time of election: Bourbon County
- Served with President George Washington
- Served with Governor Isaac Shelby

The 2004 Democratic nominee for vice president was not the first "John Edwards" elected to serve in the US Senate. That honor goes to John Edwards of Bourbon County, Kentucky, the second US senator elected by the Kentucky legislature on June 18, 1792, in Lexington.

Edwards was born in Stafford County, Virginia, in 1748. Stafford County is also the location of George Washington's boyhood home of Ferry Farm. This was where he attended the common schools.

In 1780, Edwards moved to Kentucky. Soon after, he became involved in electoral politics. He was one of the Kentucky County delegates to the Virginia House of Delegates from 1781 to 1783 and 1785 to 1786. He was a delegate to the convention called to define the limits of proposed Kentucky statehood that met at various times from 1785 to 1788. He was a member of the Constitutional Convention in Danville, which wrote Kentucky's first constitution in 1792.

According to the *Proceedings of The Senate of the United States*, John Brown and John Edwards were present on Monday, November 5, 1792.

As Vice President John Adams was absent, John Langdon was duly elected president pro tempore. It was Langdon who administered the oath of office to both Brown and Edwards.

As that session of Congress ended at noon on Monday, March 4, 1793, the members of the US Senate met for most of the day on Saturday, until 7 p.m., when the Senate adjourned until Monday, March 4, 1793, for a "Spécial Session" for the presidential inauguration began. Edwards and Brown were both present when the Honorable John Langdon, president pro tempore, read the summons of the president of the United States to the Senate Chamber in Philadelphia.

Edwards had the honor of witnessing the second inauguration of President George Washington in the Senate Chamber. Before taking the oath of office, Washington addressed the Senate Chamber, which was open for guests from the House of Representatives, foreign dignitaries, and other visitors. Washington was brief:

> FELLOW-CITIZENS: I am again called upon, by the voice of my country to execute the functions of Chief Magistrate. When the occasion proper for it shall arrive, I shall endeavor, to express the high sense, I entertain of this distinguished honor, and of the confidence which has been reposed in me by the people of the United States of America. Previous to the execution of any official act of the President, the Constitution requires an oath of office. This oath I am now about to take, and in your presence; that, if it shall be found, during my administration of the Government, I have, in any instance, violated, willingly or knowingly, the injunction thereof I may (besides incurring Constitutional punishment) be subject to the upbraiding of all who are now witnesses of the present solemn ceremony.[1]

After the administering of the oath by Judge Cushing, Washington and the spectators left. The Senate acted on nominations from the president and adjourned, *sine die*.

Senator Edwards missed voting on the Jay Treaty, as his term had ended in March 1795. The vote was not taken up until June 1795.

After his service in the US Senate, he became a legislative leader in Kentucky. According to H.E. Everman in his chapter on James Garrard (1796–1804) in *Kentucky's Governors*, Edwards is characterized as Garrard's "closest friend and legislative leader."[2] He was a state representative in 1795 and a member of the State Senate from 1796 to 1800.

He died in 1837 and is buried in a family cemetery near Paris, Kentucky.

HUMPHREY MARSHALL
(1760–1841)

- Class Three of Three
- Senate Service: March 4, 1795–March 4, 1801
- Political Affiliation: Federalist
- Residence at time of election: Lexington
- Served with Presidents Washington and Adams
- Served with Governors Shelby and Garrard

Humphrey Marshall was one of the few Federalists to experience success in Kentucky politics. Just before his election, the Federalist administration of George Washington had experienced success in quashing the Whiskey Rebellion and winning victory over the native Americans comprising the Western Confederacy [Miami, Miami and Lenape] at Fallen Timbers in August 1794. Later in 1794, Federalists in the legislature nominated Marshall for the Senate seat held by John Edwards. Perhaps because he was the only Federalist, he garnered eighteen votes on the first ballot compared with sixteen for John Breckinridge, eight for John Fowler, and seven for incumbent Senator John Edwards. On the final ballot, he defeated Breckinridge twenty-eight to twenty-two.

Senator Marshall was born in Orlean, Fauquier County, Virginia. He was a member of the Marshall family that included John Marshall. According to Humphrey Marshall's Congressional biography, he pursued classical studies before becoming a surveyor. He served in the Virginia militia during the Revolutionary War. After the war, he moved to Kentucky in 1782 and studied law there. Upon his admittance to the bar, he practiced in Fayette County.

He also became involved in politics. He was a delegate to the Danville convention in 1787 to consider the separation of Kentucky from Virginia, which he opposed. He was a delegate to the Virginia convention that ratified the Constitution of the US. Upon statehood, he was elected as a member of the Kentucky House of Representatives, where he served from 1793 until 1794, when the legislature elected him to the US Senate.

Humphrey Marshall appeared with Senator John Brown at the Tenth Session of the Senate of the United States, which began Monday, June 8, 1795. The first order of business was the receipt of the treaty entered into by the US and Great Britain under the auspices of John Jay, Envoy Extraordinary to His Britannic Majesty. That day, the secretary of the Senate ordered thirty-one copies of the treaty printed. On Tuesday, June 9, 1795, three more senators appeared, and the secretary ordered three more copies to be printed.[1]

Though Kentucky was very "anti-Federalist," Marshall was a very partisan Federalist. He voted for the Alien and Sedition Acts, as well as the Jay Treaty. As a result of his vote in favor of the Jay Treaty, a group of angry citizens in Frankfort threw stones at him. Another group attempted to throw him into the Kentucky River. In order to avoid that dunking, Marshall appealed to the Baptists in the group. He is thought to have said, "Now allow me to say that according to Baptist rules, it is irregular to administer baptism before the receiver gives his experience. If you are determined to proceed, let the exercise be performed in decent order. Let me give my experience first." As Marshall was a noted agnostic, if not atheist this was so humorous to the mob that it disbanded in a fit of laughter.

Humphrey Marshall's work exploits after his time in the Senate are worthy of mention. During the summer of 1806, with John Wood, he established a Federalist newspaper in Frankfort called the *Western World*. Marshall filled that paper with allegations concerning Kentucky Republicans and their involvement with Aaron Burr. It was alleged that Burr had come to Kentucky to raise an army and separate the western United States and join it with Spain's southwestern empire.[2]

In addition to stirring things up with his newspaper, Marshall was elected to serve in the Kentucky House from 1807 to 1809. It was there he came into conflict with the young Henry Clay.

On January 4, 1809, Clay challenged Marshall to a duel after a scrimmage on the floor of the Kentucky House involving an argument over trade with Britain.[3] Peace had dissolved in December 1808 when Clay introduced a resolution calling for all members of the General Assembly to wear "homespun" garments as a means of encouraging local manufacturing and reducing British imports. Although Clay typically wore finer garments than Marshall, for the duration of the debate on his motion, Clay wore simple, homemade clothes. Marshall regarded the measure as demagoguery and employed a tailor to make him a suit of British broadcloth to wear on the House floor. The two men exchanged insults on the House floor. The insults escalated until Clay challenged Marshall to a duel, which Marshall quickly accepted. The duel took place in Indiana on January 19, 1809, just across the Ohio River from Shippingport, Kentucky. On the first shot, Marshall missed, and Clay lightly grazed Marshall's stomach. Marshall missed again on the second shot, and Clay's pistol misfired. Marshall's third shot lightly wounded Clay in the thigh, while Clay missed Marshall entirely. Clay insisted that the two each take another shot, but Marshall declined on grounds that Clay's injury put him on unequal footing with his adversary, and the matter was ended.

Marshall continued his literary pursuits. He wrote the first history of Kentucky, *The History of Kentucky: Exhibiting an Account of the Modern Discovery; Settlement; Progressive Improvement; Civil and Military Transactions; and the Present State of the Country*, which was published in 1812.

He died near Lexington, Kentucky, on July 3, 1841, and was buried on his farm, Glen Willis, in Leestown, Kentucky.

JOHN BRECKINRIDGE
(1760–1806)

- Class Three of Three
- Senate Service: March 4, 1801–August 7, 1805
- Political affiliation: Democratic-Republican
- Residence at time of election: Lexington
- Served with President Jefferson
- Served with Governor Garrard

John Breckinridge was successful in his second attempt to secure a seat in the US Senate when he defeated incumbent Federalist Humphrey Marshall in a vote of the Kentucky legislature in March 1801.

Breckinridge began his political career when he was elected to the Virginia legislature at age nineteen while a student at the College of William & Mary. He was the second son of Colonel Robert Breckinridge of Augusta County, Virginia, and was born on December 2, 1760, on a farm on which a part of the city of Staunton now stands. In 1785, he married Mary Hopkins Cabell, a daughter of Colonel Joseph Cabell. Together, the Breckinridges had nine children. He was the grandfather of John Cabell Breckinridge, who would become vice president under Buchanan and a Confederate general.

Breckinridge served in the Virginia militia during the Revolutionary War. After the war, he studied law and began his practice in Charlottesville, Virginia. He was elected to Congress as an "Anti-Federalist," or Democratic-Republican, but resigned in 1792 before the commencement of the congressional term.

He moved to Kentucky in 1793 and resumed the practice of law in Lexington. He was appointed by Governor Isaac Shelby as the second attorney general of Kentucky in 1795 and served until November 30, 1797, when he resigned. He was a member of the state House of Representatives from 1798–1800, serving as Speaker in 1799 and 1800. He was a member of the State Constitutional Convention in 1799 for Kentucky's second constitution.

Some have speculated that he was the author of the Kentucky Resolutions of 1798 and 1799, protesting Adams' Alien and Sedition Acts. While many believe that Jefferson actually wrote the Kentucky Resolutions, as well as the Virginia Resolutions, due to Breckinridge's position as Speaker of the Kentucky House, he had a hand in passing the Kentucky Resolutions.

Breckinridge was sworn in as a US senator on Monday, December 7, 1801, by Senate President Pro Tempore Abraham Baldwin (a senator from Georgia) because Vice President Aaron Burr was absent.[1]

One of the perks of being a Senator beginning that session was the eligibility for an annual subscription to any three newspapers published anywhere in the US.

In this day and age of government transparency or C-SPAN, the fact that a vote was taken on whether the Senate would allow stenographers is unusual, to say the least. Kentucky's Senators Brown and Breckinridge were on opposite sides of the issue on the first vote. Breckinridge voted "yea" and Brown "nay."[2]

When the vote was to allow "stenographers and note takers," Breckinridge and Brown both voted with the "yeas."

On Wednesday, January 6, 1802, Breckinridge took the floor sponsoring the repeal of the Judiciary Act of February 1801,[3] which was sponsored and passed in the last three weeks of the Adams administration. Breckinridge's work on the floor took more than two months of floor debate. Because of his work on the floor of the Senate for President Jefferson, he is considered one of the first-floor leaders of that body. While he was not attorney general at the time, it is thought that he believed that President Thomas Jefferson's purchase of the Louisiana Purchase was constitutional, even though the Constitution did not cover this specific issue.

He is probably best known for serving as US attorney general for Jefferson and as the scion of the Breckinridge family, which spawned at least three Kentucky congressmen and a US vice president.

He resigned to become US attorney general in August 1805. He was serving as attorney general when it is thought he caught tuberculosis and died at age forty-six at his estate, Cabell's Dale, near Lexington, Kentucky, on December 14, 1806. He was buried in Lexington Cemetery in Lexington.

He was a mentor to Henry Clay and one of the founding fathers of Transylvania University and the city of Lexington. Breckinridge County, Kentucky, was named in his honor.

BUCKNER THRUSTON
(1763–1845)

- Class Two of Three
- Senate Service: 1805–1809
- Political affiliation: Democratic-Republican
- Residence at time of election: Lexington
- Served with Presidents Jefferson and Madison
- Served with Governors Garrard and Greenup

Buckner Thruston became the fourth US senator from Kentucky in 1805. He was born in Petsoe Parish, Gloucester County, in southeast Virginia, on February 9, 1763. According to his congressional biography, he pursued preparatory studies and graduated from the College of William & Mary at Williamsburg, Virginia. In 1788, he moved to Lexington, Kentucky, where he studied law and was admitted to the bar. As Lexington was part of Virginia at the time, he was elected to represent Lexington in the Virginia Assembly in 1789. When Kentucky became a state in 1792, he was elected clerk of the first state senate. He served as one of the three commissioners appointed to settle the boundary dispute that came with the separation of Kentucky from Virginia.

In addition to practicing law, Thruston served as a federal district judge for Kentucky in 1791 and as a judge of the circuit court from 1802 to 1803. In 1804, President Jefferson appointed him US judge for the court of the Territory of Orleans, but he declined. He was elected as a Democratic-Republican to the US Senate and served from March 4, 1805, to December 18, 1809.

Thruston was elected to succeed Kentucky's first senator, John Brown, by the Kentucky legislature on November 26, 1804. He was elected on the seventh ballot over John Adair. Brown dropped out after the sixth ballot.[1]

During Thruston's Senate tenure (1805–1809), important events included the American military involvement in Tripoli (April 1805), Lewis and Clark reaching the Pacific Ocean (November 1805), an embargo of certain products from Great Britain (April 1806), and the US banning the slave trade (March 1807). Americans in 1806 and 1807 paid little attention to these events; they were focused on the accusations of treason against former Vice President Aaron Burr and Napoleon's wars in Europe.[2]

In respect to an Amendment to the June 4, 1805, Treaty with Tripoli ("Concerning ransom of hostages"), to amend the treaty (8 STAT L. 214) concluded at Tripoli "which was before the Senate on April 12, 1806, between the U.S. the Bashaw of Tripoli and the subjects of Tripoli," Thruston and his colleague split.[3] Thruston voted against the amendment and Adair voted for it. The amendment was defeated nine for and twenty against.[4]

At the time of the founding of the nation, slavery was protected. Article 1, Section 9, of the US Constitution protected the slave trade for twenty years. Only starting January 1, 1808, would laws become effective in entirely abolishing the international slave trade.

> The Migration or Importation of such Persons as any of the States now existing shall think proper to admit, shall not be prohibited by the Congress prior to the Year one thousand eight hundred and eight, but a tax or duty may be imposed on such Importation, not exceeding ten dollars for each Person.[5]

The two most important votes Senator Thruston made were held on December 17, 1805, voting for the legislation to "Prohibit the Importation of Slaves after January 1, 1808, into any port of the U.S. Territory after January 1, 1808." Thruston voted for the legislation; his Kentucky colleague John Adair voted against it. The legislation passed the Senate 16–11; seven did not vote.[6]

In April 1806, Thruston voted for the partial embargo against Great Britain. Adair voted against it. In February 1806, Thruston, as a member of Congress, received reports from President Jefferson on the success of the Lewis and Clark Expedition, which included finding the mouth of the Missouri River.[7]

On December 14, 1809, Thruston was nominated by President James Madison to serve as a judge on the Circuit Court for the District of Columbia. He was confirmed by the Senate on December 14, 1809, and served in that position for almost thirty-four years. As a judge, he lived in an area of Washington known as Glover Park.

Thruston died in Washington, D.C., on August 30, 1845, and was buried in the Congressional Cemetery. Thruston's wife, Jeannette, with whom he had eight children, had died on March 28, 1835.

JOHN ADAIR
(January 9, 1757–May 19, 1840)

- Class Three of Three
- Senate Service: November 8, 1805–November 18, 1806
- Political Affiliation: Democratic-Republican
- Residence at time of election: Mercer County
- Served with President Jefferson
- Served with Governor Greenup

John Adair was elected to the US Senate by the Kentucky legislature on his third try. He was successful in being elected to fill the balance of the term left vacant when Senator John Breckinridge resigned to become attorney general of the US under President Thomas Jefferson.

Adair's life was much more significant out of Washington than in it.

According to the *Proceedings of The Senate of the United States*, Adair spent only a short session in Washington from December 1805 through April 1806. That session confirmed President Jefferson's recess appointments, in addition to dealing with multiple treaties with the Indian nations and Tripoli. Of those under consideration, Adair was one of three senators who considered the treaty signed at Vincennes between the US and the Piankashaw Nation (they were members of the Miami who lived separate from the rest of the Miami) and were to report back to the Senate.[1]

On Tuesday, December 17, 1805, Adair split with his Kentucky colleague Thruston on the issue of further "importation of slaves into any port or place within the jurisdiction of the United States after the first day of January 1808." Thurston voted for the legislation, and Adair voted against the legislation. The legislation passed the Senate 16–11.[2]

One of the most interesting votes made by Senator Adair was on whether West Florida was part of the Louisiana Purchase. Adair voted with the minority of eight that believed West Florida was part of the Louisiana Purchase. Kentucky's other senator, Thruston, voted with the twenty-three in the majority.[3]

He was the seventh person and third general to serve as Kentucky governor. A native of South Carolina, he was in the South Carolina Militia in the American Revolution before moving to Kentucky in 1786. During the Northwest Indian War (a/k/a Ohio War, Little Turtle's War etc.) Northwest in the 1790s, Adair served in the Kentucky Militia and rose to brigadier general. He was a delegate to the Kentucky Constitutional Convention of 1792. He was elected thirteen times by the voters of Mercer County to the Kentucky House of Representatives beginning in 1793, including two years as Speaker. In 1804, Adair was Governor Garrard's compromise appointment for registrar of the State Land Office.

Adair had been a candidate in 1800 for the same seat for which Breckinridge defeated him in a legislative vote of 68–13. However, Adair became Speaker of the Kentucky House in 1802. In 1804, he sought a Senate seat held by John Brown but was defeated as a result of Henry Clay's support of Buckner Thruston. In August 1805, with the vacancy caused by Breckinridge's resignation, the legislature elected Adair to the remaining two years of Breckinridge's Senate term, which ended in March 1807.

Unfortunately, Adair was tainted by the Aaron Burr conspiracy and trial of December 1805. This resulted in the legislature rejecting Adair in November 1806 for a full six-year term. Rather than serve out the final months of his existing term, Adair resigned on November 18, 1806. Henry Clay was appointed for the three-and-a-half months left on Adair's term.

Elected governor in 1820 during the economic panic, Adair emphasized better state funding for education and prison reform. The major concern of his administration was "debtor relief." Part of his plan was the state's creation of the Bank of the Commonwealth, which issued $3 million in paper money.

After leaving office, Adair was elected to one term (1831–1833) in the US House. His sole term was unexceptional, due in part to high absenteeism.

Adair counties in Kentucky, Missouri, and Iowa are named for John Adair.

HENRY CLAY
(1777–1852)
First Term

- Class Three of Three
- Senate Service November 19, 1806–March 4, 1807
- Democratic-Republican
- Lexington
- Served with President Jefferson
- Served with Governor Greenup

Henry Clay was elected as a stand-in after Senator John Adair resigned when the legislature elected John Pope instead of Adair for the full term, beginning March 4, 1807. Clay was elected 68–10 over George Bibb.[1]

During the first month, Clay was one of the attorneys defending Aaron Burr in Federal Court in Frankfort for conspiracy and treason.[2] Clay was technically three months short of his thirtieth birthday, thus too young to be a senator, but he was sworn in anyway.

His defense of Burr in Kentucky cast a cloud over his tenure in Washington.

On his third day in the Senate, Clay made his first speech, "a demand that the West be given its due with the creation of a federal circuit court for Ohio, Kentucky and Tennessee." Clay headed the committee that considered this proposal. The committee also drafted the legislation

37

creating the new circuit court. The creation of a new circuit required the appointment of an additional justice to the US Supreme Court. With the passage of this legislation, Clay's political friend Thomas Todd received the associate justice appointment.[3]

Despite knowing that he was only going to be in the Senate for less than three months, he sponsored legislation for a canal around the Falls of the Ohio at Louisville, a toll bridge across the Potomac, and a canal to connect the Delaware and Chesapeake Bays.

He also made an impassioned speech advocating the end of the importing of slaves, which impressed many, including Senator John Quincy Adams.

Clay would briefly return to the Senate to fill a vacancy caused by the resignation of Buckner Thruston, serving from January 4, 1810, to March 3, 1811. On that date, Clay began his career in the US House, where he would serve as Speaker before returning to the Senate in 1831.

JOHN POPE
(1770–1845)

- Class Three of Three
- Senate Service 1807–1813
- Democratic-Republican
- Washington County
- Served with Presidents Jefferson and Madison
- Served with Governors Greenup, Scott, Shelby

John Pope succeeded Henry Clay in March 1807 as a Democratic-Republican member of the US Senate from Kentucky, in his second attempt to be elected to the Senate. On Nov. 9, 1805, Pope was a candidate before the Kentucky legislature as a US senator. He was defeated 45–35 by John Adair to fill the seat vacated by John Breckinridge when he became Jefferson's US attorney general. On Nov. 20, 1806, he was elected on the fourth ballot 45–37 over John Adair to a six-year term beginning March 3, 1807. At the time of his election, he was a resident of Lexington.

Following his senate service, he moved to Springfield, and studied and practiced law there and throughout the Central Kentucky region of Washington, Shelby, and Fayette Counties. Pope married three times. His first wife, Ann Henry, died on March 1, 1806; this marriage produced no children. Eliza Pope, whom he married in Lexington on February 11, 1810, was the sister-in-law of future President John Quincy

Adams. This marriage produced two daughters, Elizabeth and Florida; Florida Pope died young. Following the death of Eliza on April 24, 1818, he married a widow, Frances Walton, on May 1, 1820, in Washington County, Kentucky.

Before his election by the legislature as US senator, Pope was elected twice to the Kentucky House of Representatives, where he served during 1802 and from 1806 to 1807. It should be noted that he was serving in the Kentucky House when he was elected to the US Senate.

The First Session of the Tenth Congress began on Monday, October 26, 1807, and Pope appeared on the first day with Buckner Thruston without the paperwork; his reason was that the governor and secretary of state were absent when he left, and it would be forwarded to him shortly. The *Senate Journal* states:

> The Honorable John Pope, appointed a Senator by the state of Kentucky, for the term of six years, commencing on the fourth of March last, stated that the governor and secretary being absent when he left home, he came to the seat of government without his credentials; but that he expected they would be speedily forwarded to him: Whereupon, he took his seat in the Senate, and the oath was administered to him as the law prescribes.[1]

A few months after he took office in Washington, he wrote to a friend, "I have embarked in political life and mean to make a business of it. I occupy much higher ground here both on the scale of talents and republicanism than either you or myself expected; except Breckinridge no man from the West ever had more popularity in Congress."[2]

In respect to legislative matters that made a mark on the nation, Pope did not make much of a national impact in his single term, unless his influence on the appointments to offices in the Illinois Territory is considered. These appointments were created on February 3, 1809. Senator Pope's brother, Nathaniel Pope, was appointed by President Madison as secretary of the Illinois Territory. Pope's cousin, Ninian Edwards, was appointed as governor of the Illinois Territory. Nathaniel later became an Illinois Territory delegate to Congress and was appointed by President Monroe as a federal judge when Illinois became a state.

Whether due to Pope's popularity or his ability as a legislator, his colleagues elevated him to the position of president pro tempore in 1811—an honor rare for first-term senators.

Pope served in the Senate with Henry Clay from 1810 to 1811. Clay was elected to finish Buckner Thruston's term.

When the Twelfth Congress convened in November 1811, Clay entered a new career in the House. Pope found his former senatorial colleague now firmly ensconced as Speaker, a position seldom given to first-term representatives, and Pope was president pro tempore of the Senate.

Pope was not reelected to the Senate. Reasons that he did not receive a second term included his voting against the instructions of the legislature that elected him. He voted for the re-chartering of the Bank of the United States in 1811. He also voted against declaring war on Britain in 1812.

In fact, Pope was responsible for delaying the Senate vote on war. Pope and Thomas Worthington from Ohio attempted to halt the bill by proposing that France be included as a belligerent and that the Non-Importation Acts be repealed. Pope also tried to stall the declaration by amending its phraseology. Nevertheless, on June 18, the Senate passed the war declaration 19–13, with Pope on the side of the minority.

The news of war was hailed as a second declaration of independence in Kentucky, and Pope's vote was hailed as a second declaration of war on his constituents. In 1811 he had defied instructions and favored an unpopular bank; in 1812, he had again defied instructions and opposed a popular war. For this, he received an immediate censure by his fellow citizens. While cannons boomed in Lexington and Frankfort to help celebrate the war declaration, Pope's effigy burned in Nicholasville and Mount Sterling. On two successive nights, irate Lexingtonians paraded an effigy of Pope through the streets and then burned it in "unrestrained indignation."

In 1816, he unsuccessfully ran against Henry Clay's Lexington-based congressional seat. Following that election, Governor Gabriel Slaughter appointed Pope as Kentucky's secretary of state where he served from 1816 to 1819.

Pope's most lasting record of achievement is found in his service as third territorial governor of Arkansas. In 1829, President Andrew Jackson appointed Pope governor of Arkansas Territory. He was one of the first territorial governors to bring his family with him. He was responsible for organizing Arkansas for statehood and organized road and river transportation between Little Rock and Memphis. He continued a program of land sales and selected the site for the Arkansas Capitol, now known as the Old State House. Pope dictated that it be Greek revival style. It was completed in 1842, and it is the oldest surviving state capitol building west of the Mississippi River.

At the end of his tenure in Arkansas in March 1835, Pope returned to Kentucky and won election to the US House of Representatives. He served in that capacity from 1837 to 1843 and died on July 12, 1845, at the age of seventy-five. He is buried on Cemetery Hill in Springfield.

Pope County, Arkansas, was named in his honor.

Part II
1810–1820

Senators of this period of history were preoccupied with war with Britain and the recovery from the War of 1812. John Pope finished a six-year term during this period. Both Henry Clay and John J. Crittenden served partial terms during this time. Clay's second partial term from 1810 to 1811 was his last until after service in the House as Speaker when he made a national name for himself as leader of the "War Hawks." This was in contrast to John Pope, who continued to serve in the Senate. Pope was vocally against war with Britain and worked with others in an attempt to keep the nation out of the War of 1812.

It was during this period that the Capitol, along with the White House, was burned by British troops. The Senate had to meet in other quarters until 1820.

After the Capitol was burned by the British during the War of 1812, on August 24, 1814, Congress met in what was known as the "Old Brick Capitol," a building on the site of the present Supreme Court Building. Kentucky senators who used the "Brick Capitol" are Senator William T. Barry (1814–16), Senator Martin D. Hardin (1816–17), Senator Isham Talbot 1815–1819, and Senator John J. Crittenden (1817–1819).

In 1820, political rancor was at an all-time low. James Monroe was reelected to the presidency with minimal opposition.

HENRY CLAY
(1777–1852)
Second Term

- Class Two of Three
- Senate Service: 1810–1811
- Political affiliation: Democratic-Republican
- Residence at time of election: Lexington
- Served with President Madison
- Served with Governor Scott

This was the second time Clay was elected to fill the term of a Kentucky US senator who had resigned. He was elected as a Democratic-Republican to the US Senate to fill the vacancy caused by the resignation of Buckner Thruston and served from January 4, 1810, to March 3, 1811.

During his second time as a member of the Kentucky General Assembly, Clay was elected by his colleagues to fill the fourteen months left in the term of Senator Buckner Thruston, who resigned to accept a judicial appointment. Henry Clay defeated Kentucky House Speaker William Logan 63–31 in this election to the Senate.

The Senate received Clay's certificate of appointment or election on Thursday, February 1, 1810. Clay was sworn in on Monday, February 5, 1810.

The major issue before Congress when he entered the Senate was the renewal of the Non-Intercourse Act. In the last days of President Thomas

43

Jefferson's presidency, the US Congress had replaced the Embargo Act of 1807 with the almost unenforceable Non-Intercourse Act of March 1809. This Act lifted all embargoes on American shipping except for those bound for British or French ports. The intent was to damage the economies of the United Kingdom and France. Like its predecessor, the Embargo Act, it was mostly ineffective and contributed to the coming of the War of 1812. In addition, it seriously damaged the economy of the US due to a lack of markets for its goods.

"The House sent a bill to the Senate that would close U.S. ports and French vessels."[1] In a fiery voice, Clay's first speech argued that the nation had tried peaceful resistance to European arrogance. "Clay shouted, "when this, is abandoned, without effect, I am for resistance by the sword".[2] He preferred "the troubled ocean of war, demanded by the honor and independence of the country, with all its calamities, and desolations, to the tranquil, putrescent pool of ignominious peace."

Clay scoffed at those who argued that the economy could not sustain a war. He also bragged that the US had the military might to conquer British territory unaided. He is credited with saying, "The militia of Kentucky are alone competent to place Montreal and Upper Canada at your feet." But Clay was alone in his opinion. This would change when he went to the House the following year and became leader of the "War Hawks."

During this time in the Senate, Clay would be a proponent of "internal improvements." This would include the protection of infantry manufacturing concerns. On March 22, 1810, Clay and his Kentucky colleague Senator John Pope proposed an amendment to naval appropriations that would require the secretary of the Navy to favor the purchase of domestic naval supplies. Pope specifically wanted to help Kentucky hemp farmers. Hemp could be made into rope that could rig the sails of ships.

Clay was unhappy with the constraints of the rules of the Senate. He instead stood for election for the House from the Lexington area.

Clay supported the annexation of West Florida. He claimed it was part of the Louisiana Purchase. He opposed the re-chartering of the Bank of the United States in 1811, claiming it was unconstitutional. Later in Clay's political career he would favor a national bank. The vote on the re-chartering of the bank was tied in the Senate at 17–17. The speech by the elderly Vice President George Clinton was thought to have been either written or dictated by Clay when Clinton voted "nay."

Congress adjourned on March 3, 1811. Clay and his pregnant wife, Lucretia, returned home to Ashland in Lexington, where she would give birth to Henry Clay Jr.[3] Henry Clay would not return to the Senate for twenty years, after his service as Speaker of the US House of Representatives and US secretary of state for President John Quincy Adams.

GEORGE M. BIBB
(1776–1859)

- Class Two of Three
- Senate Service: 1811–1814 and 1829–1835
- Political affiliation: Democratic-Republican
- Residence at time of election: Frankfort
- Served with Presidents Madison, Jackson
- Served with Governors Scott, Metcalfe, Breathitt, and Morehead

George Mortimer Bibb was a nineteenth-century Kentucky statesman who served two stints in the US Senate, 1811–1814 and 1829–1835. He served in numerous state judicial positions, as well as John Tyler's secretary of the treasury from 1844–1845.

Like Henry Clay, Bibb was born in Virginia and moved to Kentucky in the 1790s.

Bibb's younger brother, John Bibb, of Frankfort was an amateur horticulturist who developed Bibb lettuce.

Bibb was active in the Masonic Order in Kentucky. He was a Worshipful Master of Lexington Lodge No. 1, like Clay. Bibb was also the first Worshipful Master of the Russellville Lodge No. 17 and Hiram Lodge No. 4 in Frankfort. In 1804, Bibb was elected by Masons as Grand Master of Kentucky.

Bibb was a candidate considered by the Kentucky legislature in 1806 for the US Senate. He had been elected to the Kentucky House in 1806 but resigned after serving only a few days.

Bibb was serving in the US Senate during the Foster negotiations in 1811. The US was attempting to negotiate its difference with Britain through the British minister to the US, Augustus J. Foster. It was the conclusion of Americans that the British would not repeal the "Orders of Council" short of force. Senator Bibb is quoted as saying to Governor Charles Scott in the *Lexington, Ky. Reporter* from March 7, 1812, "I do not expect any substantial benefit from negotiation—and look to a war or most base and disgraceful submission as the only alternatives."

After leaving the US Senate in 1814, he resumed practicing law in Lexington. He moved to Frankfort in 1816. In 1817, he was elected to the Kentucky House of Representatives. He was again appointed chief justice of the Kentucky Court of Appeals from 1827 to 1828.

He was reelected to the US Senate in 1829 and served as a Jacksonian-Democrat through 1835. During the Twenty-First Congress, he was chairman of the US Senate Committee on Post Office and Post Roads. Later in his term, he served as chair of the Senate Committee on the Judiciary.

During Bibb's second term, he saw many important historical events. He saw the resignation of Vice President John Calhoun of South Carolina as a result of the "nullification crisis," the passage of the Indian Removal Act, and the passage of the Maysville Road Bill, only for the latter to be vetoed by President Andrew Jackson.

Bibb is said to have voted against the Indian Removal Act, which passed the Senate and the House with the support of President Jackson. Both he and Tennessee's Felix Grundy voted on the removal of Native Americans from lands east of the Mississippi, in the series of removals or removals which resulted in the Native Americans trips west as the "Trail of Tears."

The Maysville Road Bill was one in which Bibb showed his true colors as a pro-Jacksonian partisan and against the interests of his state. The political battle over funding internal improvements came to the national forefront in 1830, when Congress passed a bill sponsored by Jackson's bitter political foe Henry Clay, though Clay was not a member of Congress at the time. The bill authorized a $150,000 federal purchase of stock in the Maysville, Washington, Paris, and Lexington Turnpike Road Company. The company proposed a sixty-mile road from Maysville, an inland port on the Ohio River, to Clay's hometown of Lexington. The project lay entirely within Kentucky. The Senate voted 24–18 on May 15, 1830, to approve the bill. Senator Bibb, being a Jacksonian, voted against it, while fellow Kentucky Senator John Rowan voted for it.

On May 27, Jackson vetoed the bill, alleging that the road had no connection with any existing improved transport system and that it was fully within a single state. Jackson argued that the proposed bill required an unconstitutional use of federal dollars. The veto decision was highly unpopular with many in the newly established Democratic Party, which Jackson led, including those in the Ohio Valley who supported federal aid for canals and roads. Jackson's veto was instrumental in establishing a long-term federal policy limiting the use of federal transportation funds to interstate projects as well as harbors and river improvements serving foreign trade. From that point, Congress no longer provided sizable federal expenditures for intrastate canals and roads until the 1930s.

However, a few days after his veto, President Jackson signed appropriations for the Portland and Ohio Canal on the Ohio River and to finish the Cumberland Road from Cumberland, Maryland, to Illinois. During the fall of 1832, Senator Bibb suffered a personal loss. The nation was in the midst of a cholera epidemic. Bibb's son, Charles S. Bibb, the newly named US district judge for Arkansas, was one of its victims. According to the *Niles Weekly Register* for November 10, 1832, Louisville was losing an average of eight people a week to cholera, and upriver in Cincinnati, a third of the people abandoned their homes.[1]

During the 1830s, Kentucky's legislature and politics were dominated by Henry Clay's Whigs. Throughout Bibb's tenure, he would vote contrary to his Whig colleagues, as seen with his vote on the Maysville Road Bill.[2]

The Kentucky General Assembly elected John J. Crittenden, a leading Whig and Kentucky statesman, to replace Bibb for the term beginning March 4, 1835.

When Bibb was sixty-eight in 1844, President John Tyler, a Whig, appointed him secretary of the treasury to replace John C. Spencer, who had resigned. He was an aged man when he assumed his treasury position, dressing "in antique style, with knee breeches." Bibb's Annual Report on the State of the Finances for 1844 consisted of an elaborate compilation of statistics detailing the financial history of the nation since 1789. In addition, he presented a solid argument for the establishment of a "sinking fund," accumulated through regular deposits and used to pay the interest and principal on the national debt. Bibb advocated using treasury surplus revenue from customs and internal revenue collection to supply the sinking fund. Such a fund had been used effectively to reduce the deficit from 1789 to 1835, but Bibb was unable to revive it.[3]

Following his service as secretary of the treasury, Bibb continued to live in Washington, D.C., where he practiced law until his death on April 14, 1859. He was originally buried in Congressional Cemetery in Washington. He was removed from that location on June 18, 1859, with his final interment location unknown.

In 1937, Senator Bibb was honored with the naming of a Treasury-class Coast Guard cutter in his name. The Treasury-class cutters were named in honor of former secretaries of the Treasury Department, which Bibb headed from 1844 to 1845.

JOHN ROWAN
(1773–1843)

- Class Three of Three
- Senate Service: 1825–1831
- Political affiliation: Jacksonian-Democratic
- Residence at time of election: Nelson County
- Served with Presidents John Quincy Adams and Andrew Jackson
- Served with Governors Desha and Metcalfe

John Rowan is probably best known for being the founder of "Federal Hill," the estate that has become My Old Kentucky Home State Park in Bardstown. It was said to be the inspiration for composer Stephen Foster's "My Old Kentucky Home." Foster, a relative of Rowan, visited the estate on many occasions.[1]

Senator John Rowan was born in York, Pennsylvania, in 1773. He was the middle child of five children of Captain William Rowan and Elizabeth Rowan. He had two older brothers and two younger sisters. The family moved to Kentucky in 1783 after Captain Rowan had spent all he had supporting the American Revolution. In 1784, the family settled in what is present-day McLean County at Fort Vienna now Calhoun, Kentucky. At that time, it was over 100 miles from the nearest white settlement. At a dinner given for him in Louisville in 1829, Rowan recounted the move from Pennsylvania to Kentucky.

49

Gentlemen—You have justly designated me as 'a son of the wilderness.' My father at the close of the Revolutionary war, under the illusive hope of repairing the ravages which his devotions to the cause of liberty had made to his patrimonial estate, emigrated from Pennsylvania his native state, to the wilderness of Kentucky. He arrived at this place in the month of March 1783. In the spring of the following year he took with him five families, and made a settlement in the country. The Subject of your present kindness was then about 11 years of age. Of the hard privations endured by that little colony, of the dangers they encountered, and of the fortitude which they encountered, and met them, it does not behove [sic] me to speak. I cannot, however, forbear to mention an incident which took place in one of the many incursions made upon them by the savages. It is illustrative of the times, and relates to my Mother; and I am led to the recital of it by the affectionate veneration with which I cherish her memory.

She had walked out with Mrs. Barnett to a place where a company of young people were pulling flax, at the extremity of a large field which adjoined the fort. Mrs. Barnett had taken with her, her infant son about two years of age. Very soon after they had joined the flax pulling company, a band of savages burst from their ambuscade, and rushed upon them, discharging their guns at them and yelling almost hideously. My mother, who was an atheletic [sic] woman started to run, but recollecting that Mrs. Barnett was a delicate and weakly woman, unable to carry her child, turned and ran back in the face of the Indians, under the fire of their guns, snatched the child from the arms of its feeble mother; and bore him in safety to the fort, although she was closely pursued, shot through the clothes with an arrow, and twice burned with the powder of guns which were shot at her. Mrs. Barnett and her infant were both saved. He is now a respectable citizen of Ohio country, and there are still living three persons besides myself, who witnessed the scene and shared in its dangers.[2]

In about 1790, the Rowan family moved to the Bardstown-Nelson County area, which provided better educational opportunities for the Rowan children. While in Nelson County, Rowan was a close friend of Felix Grundy, who served as a senator from Tennessee and attorney general of the US. According to Grundy's biography, they attended Salem Academy in Bardstown from about 1790 to 1792. Rowan and Grundy were rivals in the study of Greek and Latin. Following their studies at Salem Academy, both studied law under George Nicholas in Lexington.

After statehood in 1792, Nicholas became Kentucky's first attorney general. Rowan, Grundy, and future Senator John Pope were considered the first lawyers trained in Kentucky. It should also be noted that the three were admitted together to the bar. They also were delegates to the second Kentucky Constitutional Convention in 1799.[3]

Rowan was considered an inveterate gamester due to his love of cards and gambling.[4]

As an attorney, Rowan established himself as a criminal defense attorney. He was described as "Tall and fearsome." Rowan personified the dominant culture of honor. In addition to being fond of cards, he liked to drink. In January 1801, Rowan and a young doctor, James Chambers, had an argument in a Bardstown tavern over which of the two was the finest scholar of Greek and Latin. They exchanged physical blows, and Rowan challenged Chambers to a duel. In the resulting duel, Rowan killed Chambers. At the same time, it almost cost him his political career.[5]

To exemplify the close relationship between leading politicians of the day, the case of *Cunningham v. Caldwell* comes to mind. Argued before the Kentucky Court of Appeals in February 1807, all four counsel were to become US senators. Isham Talbot and Jesse Bledsoe represented the successful appellant. John Rowan and Henry Clay represented the appellee. The chief judge of the Kentucky Court of Appeals was Felix Grundy, who would become an US senator from Tennessee.[6]

Prior to his election to the Senate, Rowan was appointed by Governor Greenup as Kentucky secretary of state. He served as secretary of state from 1804 until 1806 when he was elected to the US House of Representatives. He served in that post for only one term, from 1807–1809. He was later elected to the Kentucky state House of Representatives where he served from 1813–1817 and again from 1822–1824. He was judge on the Kentucky Court of Appeals from 1819–1821.

Rowan was sworn in on March 4, 1825, just prior to the inauguration of John Quincy Adams.[7]

The most historical memorable of Rowan's record as a senator was his 1828 "no vote" on the extension of the "National Road" from Zanesville, Ohio, to Maysville, Kentucky, and "therein through the states of Kentucky, Tennessee, Alabama and Mississippi to New Orleans."[8] In February 1828, the Kentucky legislature had sent a resolution to all of Kentucky's federal representatives to vote for the extension. It passed the House and would have passed the Senate except it came up one vote short. Senator John Rowan voted against the extension of the "National Road" through Kentucky to New Orleans. This was in part due to his Jacksonian view that states should take care of their own "internal improvements" such as roads and canal. In 1828, President John Quincy Adams would have signed the measure into law. In 1830, the measure passed the Senate with Rowan voting for it and his colleague, Senator Bibb, voting against it. In 1830, it was vetoed by President Jackson.[9]

Rowan maintained two residences in Kentucky most of his life: one in Nelson County and one in Louisville. In December 1830, Rowan was indicted by a Jefferson County grand jury for voting in the August 1830 election while a resident of Nelson County at the time of voting.[10]

A saying attributed to Rowan concerns the office of the Vice President of the United States. "He (the v p) is politically embalmed in the chair of the senate, awaiting the resurrection which the death, political or natural, of the president has been ordained by the constitution to produce."[11]

Senator Rowan must have supported the doctrine of "nullification."[12] This is reflected in the resolution of a public meeting held in Henderson, Kentucky. Paragraph 6 of the resolution is:

> Resolved, that our senator in Congress, John Rowan by advocating said doctrine of nullification, has forfeited the confidence of his constituents, and all claim to their suffrages in a future election.[13]

As most of Kentucky's legislators were favorable to Clay, the defeat of Rowan for reelection was considered certain.[14]

In the presidential election of 1840, Rowan announced his support for the reelection of Martin Van Buren. One newspaper noted that this announcement coincided closely with his appointment as a commissioner to carry into effect the claims with Mexico.[15]

Rowan died on July 13, 1843. Most newspapers referred to the cause of death as cholera and some as influenza. Here is one obituary from the *Vicksburg Whig* (Vicksburg, Mississippi).

> DEATH OF JUDGE ROWAN—The *Louisville Journal* of the 14th makes the following announcement of the death of Judge Rowan of that city: —'We announce with no ordinary regret, that the Hon. John Rowan died last evening a little before sunset. He died of cholera morbus, of a sickness of two or three days. —His professional and political career was a long and brilliant one. We hope that the pen of one of his few peers will do justice to his memory.'—*Vicksburg Whig*[16]

Rowan was buried in Bardstown at his Federal Hill Estate.[17]

JESSE BLEDSOE
(1776–1836)

- Class Three of Three
- Senate Service: 1813–1815
- Political affiliation: Democratic-Republican
- Residence at time of election: Bourbon County
- Served with President James Madison
- Served with Governor Isaac Shelby

Jesse Bledsoe was elected by the legislature to serve a full six-year term from 1813 to 1819, succeeding John Pope. During this period, the nation was involved in the War of 1812. Two years into the war, the British invaded Maryland, Virginia and the District of Columbia. British troops sacked and burned many of the government buildings in Washington D.C. including the White House and Capitol, in August 1814. Then, less than two years into his term, he resigned with little explanation.

Bledsoe was thought to be volatile [or had a temper], earning him the nickname "hot-headed" Jesse Bledsoe. He was considered an outstanding lawyer. He was uncle to Robert Emmett Bledsoe Baylor, who studied law with him; Thomas Chilton, who likewise represented Kentucky in Congress; and William Parish Chilton, who would rise to political prominence in Alabama and the Confederacy.[1]

53

Jesse Bledsoe was born in Culpeper County, Virginia, on April 6, 1776. His father was a Baptist minister. When Bledsoe was very young, his family migrated with a Baptist congregation through the Cumberland Gap into Kentucky. Many of the adults in this traveling congregation were property, including a number of enslaved persons.

Bledsoe attended Transylvania Seminary and Transylvania University in Lexington, where he studied law. He was admitted to the bar about 1800 and commenced the practice of law in the Bourbon County area.

In 1808, he was appointed secretary of state by Governor Scott. He was elected to the Kentucky House of Representatives, where he served in 1812. Bledsoe was elected as a Democratic-Republican to the US Senate and served from March 4, 1813, until his resignation on December 24, 1814.

The *Senate Journal* has the following references for Senator Bledsoe:

Bledsoe first appeared in the Senate on Monday, May 24, 1813, to begin a term of six years having been elected by the Legislature of Kentucky.[2] On the same day Bledsoe was sworn in as a senator, the record reflects that Henry Clay, Esquire of Kentucky was elected Speaker of the House of Representatives.[3]

One of the most important resolutions presented by Bledsoe concerned Captain Oliver Hazard Perry. On Wednesday January 5, 1814,[4] Bledsoe reported from committee, that "they found duly enrolled the resolutions expressive of the sense of Congress of the gallant conduct of Captain Oliver H. Perry, the officers, seaman, marines and infantry acting as such on board his squadron: also a resolution relative to the brilliant achievement of Lieutenants Burrows and M'Call."[5]

He was last recorded present as seen on Saturday, January 7, 1815.[6]

Although the governor of Kentucky hoped he would change his mind, the Senate received a letter from Bledsoe confirming that he had resigned his seat effective December 24, 1814.

The president laid before the Senate the letter from the Honorable Mr. Bledsoe, essentially vacating his Senate seat on Friday, January 20, 1815.[7]

It should also be noted that in January 1815—right after Bledsoe left Washington—Barton W. Stone, the famous Restoration preacher, opened a school in Lexington. Stone later baptized Bledsoe—a decision that later had significant influence for Bledsoe.

He became judge of the Lexington Circuit Court in 1822 by appointment by Governor Adair. He also practiced law and taught at Transylvania, his alma mater. He was apparently quite a person—known for his skill in classical languages—and was regarded by Henry Clay as the strongest advocate he ever opposed. Eventually, Bledsoe gave all this up to become a minister in the Restoration Movement, moving to Mississippi in 1833 and to Texas in 1835. He died at Nacogdoches on June 25, 1836.

GEORGE WALKER
(1763–1819)

- Class Two of Three
- Senate service: August 30, 1814–February 2, 1815
- Political affiliation: Democratic-Republican
- Residence at time of election: Jessamine County
- Served with President James Madison
- Served with Governor Isaac Shelby

George Walker, a state senator, was appointed by Kentucky Governor Isaac Shelby on or about August 30, 1814, to serve in the US Senate to fill the vacancy caused by the resignation of George M. Bibb, who returned to private life in Lexington.

Walker was the brother of David Walker, a Congressman from Kentucky who served as major on the staff of Governor Isaac Shelby of Kentucky in the Battle of the Thames during the War of 1812. He was also the uncle of Florida's eighth governor, Governor David Shelby Walker, who served from 1866 to 1868.

George Walker was thought to have been born in Culpeper County, Virginia. He attended the common schools, though his brother David's biography says he (David) attended private schools.

Walker served in the Revolutionary War. He served under Generals Nathaniel Greene and Daniel Morgan at the Battle of Cowpens on June

17, 1781, and the Battle of Guildford Courthouse on March 15, 1781. He was also at the Battle of Yorktown when the British surrendered on October 19, 1781.[1]

He moved to Jessamine County, Kentucky, in 1794. His brother, David, had previously moved to Logan County, Kentucky, where he was elected to several positions that included state representative during the meeting of the first Kentucky Legislature.

Upon arriving in Kentucky, George Walker studied law. He was admitted to the bar and commenced practice in Nicholasville. In 1801, he was appointed commissioner of the Kentucky River Company. He was elected to the Kentucky Senate, where he served from 1810 to 1814.

Walker was appointed to the Senate within days after the British burned the White House and the Capitol Building itself, including the Chambers of each house of Congress, the Supreme Court (which met in the Capitol), and the Library of Congress.

When Walker was sworn into office on Monday, September 19, 1814, it was done in the temporary quarters of the Post Office and Patent Building, otherwise known as Blodgett's Hotel. Walker was one of the few members of Congress in Washington to serve his senatorial career in temporary quarters. It was not until December 1815 that Congress moved to a new temporary building referred to as the "Brick Capitol." It is the site of today's Supreme Court Building, and Congress stayed there until 1820.[2]

Walker served with Jesse Bledsoe until Bledsoe resigned. A review of the record indicates that Walker voted with Bledsoe most of the time. One example includes the vote on Wednesday, October 19, 1814, to increase the membership of the Mississippi Territorial Legislative Council. Both men voted to increase the number of members in the legislative council.

Walker caught the attention of President James Madison. *The Journal of the Executive Proceedings of the Senate* for Monday, December 12, 1814, has the president submitting Walker's name for the position of principal assessor for the Second Collection District of Kentucky. This was a position that involved the collection of revenue for the federal government. Walker may have changed his mind; as the record indicates on December 28, 1814, President Madison withdrew Walker's name. Madison instead nominated Thomas B. Scott for the position.

Walker was present on Saturday, December 17, 1814, when they voted nay in the first reading of a bill that would give the widow of Vice President Elbridge Gerry the balance of his salary should he have lived to complete his term. On Monday, December 19, 1814, the bill giving widow Gerry the balance of the late vice president's salary was passed.

Walker was in the Senate on Wednesday, February 1, 1815. That Wednesday was his last day as a US senator. On that day, the Senate considered the purchase of Thomas Jefferson's library for the Library of Congress and appropriations for repairing of the building in Washington that had been damaged by the British.

On Thursday, February 2, 1815, William T. Barry was sworn in to replace Walker, and Isham Talbot was sworn in to replace Jesse Bledsoe. Both had been elected by the Kentucky legislature.

Walker died in Nicholasville in 1819. He was buried on his estate nearby.

WILLIAM TAYLOR BARRY
(1784–1830)

- Class Two of Three
- Senate Service: 1814–1816
- Political affiliation: Democratic-Republican
- Residence at time of election: Lexington
- Served with President James Madison
- Served with Governor Isaac Shelby

William T. Barry served briefly as US Senator from Kentucky. He was elected by the Kentucky legislature in December 1814 to succeed George Walker, Governor Isaac Shelby's appointee, until the election by the legislature. He did not take his seat until Thursday, February 2, 1815. From his swearing-in until December 1815, Barry served in the Post and Patent Office Building as the city of Washington, DC was burned by the British and most government office buildings and their contents including the Capitol and White House was destroyed the previous August.

Barry's service as a US Senator was one of many positions he served. Some of his positions ranged from state representative to postmaster general of the US to US minister to Spain.

He was born in Lunenburg County, Virginia, on February 5, 1784. He moved to Fayette County, Kentucky, at age twelve in 1796 with his parents. He attended the common schools of the day, as well as the Pisgah Academy and Kentucky Academy in Woodford County, located near the present-day Versailles Road.

He attended Transylvania University in Lexington and graduated from the College of William & Mary at Williamsburg, Virginia, in 1803. Returning to Kentucky, he studied law, was admitted to the bar in 1805, and commenced practice in Lexington. He was appointed commonwealth's attorney and later elected as a member of the state House of Representatives in 1807. He was elected as a Democratic-Republican to the Eleventh Congress to fill the vacancy caused by the resignation of Benjamin Howard, and he served from August 8, 1810, to March 3, 1811.

He served in the military during the War of 1812. He was re-elected as a member of the state House in 1814 and was chosen as Speaker. Barry was elected as a Democratic-Republican to the US Senate to fill the vacancy caused by the resignation of George M. Bibb and assumed office December 16, 1814.

He resigned from the Senate on May 1, 1816, after he was appointed judge of the Circuit Court for the Eleventh District of Kentucky and served from 1816 to 1817. He then was reelected to the Kentucky Senate and served from 1817 to 1821.

He was elected lieutenant governor of Kentucky in 1820 with Governor John Adair and simultaneously served as a professor of law and politics at Transylvania University in 1822. He served in appointive offices, of secretary of state of Kentucky in 1824, and chief justice of the State Court of Appeals in 1825. He was an unsuccessful Democratic candidate for governor of Kentucky in 1828.

Barry's crowning achievement was his appointment as postmaster general by President Andrew Jackson on March 9, 1829. He served until April 10, 1835. He was the only member of Jackson's original cabinet not to resign as a result of the *Petticoat Affair*, which involved the social ostracism of Margaret O'Neill Eaton, the wife of Secretary of War John H. Eaton, by a group of cabinet members' wives. It was led by Second Lady Florida Calhoun, the wife of Vice President John Calhoun. It started when Florida Calhoun and certain wives of Jackson's cabinet members refused to socialize with John and Peggy Eaton, accusing them of dubious morality. Rumors were circulating that the couple had an adulterous affair while Peggy's first husband was still living. (These rumors were similar to accusations previously raised against Jackson's wife, Rachel.) Though many might think it harmless gossip among the members of Jackson's cabinet, the *Petticoat Affair* turned into a serious feud between Andrew Jackson, Calhoun, and their respective supporters. Andrew Jackson had to devote a considerable amount of energy to manage the effects of the scandal and eventually was forced to dismantle most of his cabinet to settle the issue.

Barry resigned upon his appointment as envoy extraordinary and minister plenipotentiary to Spain on May 1, 1835.[1]

He died in Liverpool, England, on August 30, 1835, while in route to Madrid, Spain. He was originally interred in England, but his body was brought back for reinternment in the State Cemetery at Frankfort, Kentucky, in 1854.

Barry was the uncle of Luke Blackburn, who became governor of Kentucky, and Joseph Blackburn, future three-term US senator from Kentucky.

MARTIN D. HARDIN
(1780–1823)

- Class Two of Three
- Senate Service: 1816–1817
- Political affiliation: Federalist
- Residence at time of election: Franklin County
- Served with President James Madison
- Served with Governor Gabriel Slaughter

On November 13, 1816, Governor Gabriel Slaughter appointed Martin D. Hardin to the US Senate seat vacated when William T. Barry resigned. The appointment was only effective until the General Assembly convened later that year. When the Kentucky legislature convened, it elected him to serve out the remainder of Barry's term. The legislature ratified the governor's appointment by giving Hardin seventy-four votes. His opponents Samuel Woodson received thirty votes, Norborn Beall twelve, and Matthew Lyon two.[1] Hardin did not seek reelection for a full term at the expiration of the term. He was appointed on November 13, 1816, and was sworn in during the Second Session of the Fourteenth Congress on Thursday, December 5, 1816.[2] Hardin served in the "Old Brick Capitol," which was a temporary meeting place for Congress until 1817 because the Capitol Building had been burned by the British in 1814.

Hardin was born along the Monongahela River in western Pennsylvania on June 21, 1780. He was the eldest son of Colonel John and Jane (Davies) Hardin. Named for his grandfather, he adopted the middle initial "D." to distinguish between them. He was a cousin of Benjamin Hardin and father of John J. Hardin. As a six-year-old, he moved to Kentucky with his parents. The Hardin family settled near the present-day city of Springfield in Washington County, Kentucky, in April 1786.

He attended Transylvania Seminary, now known as Transylvania University, in Lexington. He studied law with George Nicholas, Kentucky's first attorney general. He was admitted to the bar in 1801 and practiced law in Richmond. Among those who read law in his office were his cousin, US Representative Benjamin Hardin and future Kentucky Governor and Postmaster General Charles A. Wickliffe.

He won election to the Kentucky House of Representatives while still in his twenties (1805–1806), representing Madison County. He was appointed clerk of the Kentucky Court of Appeals in 1808. In 1810, he published *Reports of Cases Argued and Adjudged in the Court of Appeals of Kentucky*, covering the proceedings of the court between 1805 and 1808.

On January 20, 1809, he married Elizabeth Logan, daughter of famed Kentucky pioneer Benjamin Logan. Their eldest son, John J. Hardin, represented Illinois in the US House of Representatives and was killed in the Battle of Buena Vista during the Mexican-American War.

In April 1812, as the War of 1812 became more imminent, Hardin wrote to Isaac Shelby, Kentucky's first governor and a hero of the Revolutionary War, urging him to be a candidate in the upcoming gubernatorial election. Shelby went on to win the election, and Hardin, who had by this time relocated to Frankfort, was elected to represent Franklin County in the Kentucky House. In August 1812, shortly after the election, Shelby appointed Hardin secretary of state.

Hardin volunteered for service in the War of 1812. Hardin's unit pursued the legendary Shawnee warrior Tecumseh through northern Ohio and Michigan and participated in the Battle of the River Raisin.

One of the most important votes that Hardin was a participant of took place on Friday, December 6, 1816, the third reading of legislation admitting Indiana Territory as a state.[3] Indiana officially became a state on December 11, 1816. He was sworn in again on Tuesday, December 24, 1816, when the vote of the Kentucky legislature was reported electing Hardin to the balance of William T. Barry's term.[4]

On Tuesday, January 7, 1817, Hardin presented a motion requiring attorneys who collected debts on behalf of the federal government to post bond.[5]

On Tuesday, February 11, 1817, Hardin's resolution to the Post Office and Post Road Committee was to consider the feasibility to establish a postal route from Port William to Bedford to New Castle, Kentucky, in Henry County.[6] Establishment of a postal route in addition to mail delivery could mean federal financial assistance for the roads that were part of a postal or mail route.

On Wednesday, February 12, 1817, the Senate jointly met with the House for the opening of the electoral votes for president and vice president.[7] James Monroe and Daniel D. Thompkins were declared duly elected on Thursday February 13, 1817, with 183 votes over Rufus King (New York) and John Howard (Massachusetts), who had 34 and 22 votes, respectively.[8]

Politically, Hardin favored the construction of internal improvements at federal expense and adhered to a loose interpretation of the US Constitution. His entry in the 1936 *Dictionary of American Biography* notes that while some of his fellow Kentuckians believed he was a Federalist, Hardin was actually a national Democrat who probably would have associated with the Whig Party had he lived long enough to see its formation.

According to Shelby's executive journal, Hardin resigned on or before February 3, 1813. The next day, Shelby nominated Hardin's assistant, former Governor Christopher Greenup, to replace him. Greenup served only a month, resigning on March 11, 1813, and Hardin was reappointed to serve the remainder of Shelby's term.

In 1818, Hardin returned to the Kentucky House, serving until 1820 and acting as Speaker of the House from 1819 to 1820.

Hardin died in Frankfort on October 8, 1823. He was originally buried on his farm in Franklin County but was reinterred in the State Cemetery in Frankfort.

JOHN JORDAN CRITTENDEN
(1786–1863)
First Term

- Class Two of Three
- Senate Service: 1817–1819 (First Term)
- Political affiliation: Democratic-Republican
- Residence at time of election: Russellville
- Served with President Monroe
- Served with Governor Slaughter

From 1817 to 1819, John J. Crittenden served the first of four separate terms in the US Senate. Crittenden was elected to the Senate on December 10, 1816, while he was serving as Speaker of the Kentucky House of Representatives.

Crittenden was born near Versailles in Woodford County, Kentucky, on September 10, 1787. He completed preparatory studies at home, then attended Pisgah Academy in Woodford County before going to boarding school in Jessamine County, most likely Bethel Academy. After Bethel, he briefly attended Washington College in Lexington, Virginia. He later attended and graduated from the College of William & Mary in Williamsburg, Virginia. This is where he studied law in 1806. It was at William & Mary that Crittenden met the young John Tyler, whom he would later serve for five months as attorney general of the United States.

He was admitted to the Kentucky Bar and commenced practice in Versailles in Woodford County just prior to his twenty-first birthday. Within a few months, Crittenden decided the practice of law would be more lucrative in the Green River country in southwest Kentucky. By the end of 1807, Crittenden had moved to Russellville, the seat of Logan County. He had a thriving legal practice in the area of disputed land claims. It was in Russellville that he met Ninian Edwards, the chief justice of the Kentucky Court of Appeals.

In 1809, President Madison appointed Edwards governor of the newly created Illinois Territory. When Ninian Edwards left for Illinois, he made the twenty-three-year-old Crittenden his aide and appointed him the first attorney general of the Illinois Territory. On May 27, 1811, after a three-year courtship, Crittenden married Sarah Lee at her family home in Woodford County. He took her back to Russellville, and they lived in a house on the southwest corner of Ninth and Main streets. Sarah would be the first of Crittenden's three wives.

During the War of 1812, he served as aide to Governor Isaac Shelby, who led the Kentucky militia into Ontario and Michigan.

Following his service during the war, he returned to Russellville and resumed practicing law. At the same time, he served in the Kentucky House of Representatives. When he was elected by the legislature to the US Senate, he was serving as Speaker.

Crittenden was elected by the legislature on the second ballot by a 72–47 vote over John Adair.

On Monday, December 1, 1817, Crittenden was sworn into office.[1] During the proceedings, senators found how much senators could spend on newspapers during the session. According to the *Senate Journal,* "That each Senator, be supplied, during the present session, with three such newspapers, printed in the United States, as he may choose, provided the same be furnished at the usual rate, for the annual charge of such papers; and provided, also, that if any Senator, shall choose to take any newspapers, other than daily papers, he shall be supplied with as many such papers, as shall not exceed the price of three daily papers."[2]

On Thursday, December 11, 1817, Crittenden was appointed to the Committee on Naval Affairs.[3]

As Crittenden's time in the Senate during this first stint was brief, he did not create a significant legislative record. However, he made friends and found admirers. He was first given the opportunity to address the Senate in late January 1818. The subject concerned a Revolutionary War soldier's pension bill. The speech was never recorded, but the speaker's style was captured in a letter from John H. Todd to Thomas Speed on

February 4, 1818; a copy of this letter is found in Crittenden Papers. The following is an excerpt from the letter:

> He did note that Crittenden seemed a little nervous when he began, but that as he proceeded, his voice became 'clear and sonorous,' and his language 'rich, chaste and nervous.' He held his audience from beginning to end by his 'impassioned' manner, his 'terrible' invective, and his "irresistible' arguments. His eloquence, wrote his friend, 'puts a spell upon our senses, and makes our very blood run cold.' Admitting that this picture might sound exaggerated, he nevertheless concluded that 'of all the speakers I have ever heard, he is unquestionably the most powerful and efficient in debate'.[4]

He was not the only person who was impressed with Crittenden's speaking abilities on the floor of the Senate. A reporter from the *Richmond Enquirer* was similarly impressed.[5]

During this first time in the Senate, Crittenden attempted to obtain compensation for Matthew Lyon, a Vermont editor who had been fined and imprisoned in 1798 for violating the Sedition Act for his criticism of President John Adams. When Crittenden's attempt to obtain compensation for Lyon was voted down by the Judiciary Committee in 1818, Crittenden offered substitute legislation that would offer compensation for all who were imprisoned as a result of the Sedition Act as it was declared unconstitutional. That effort failed as well.

At this time, he also attempted to resolve a boundary dispute between Kentucky and Tennessee. The boundary was the extension of the 36⁰ 30' north latitude of the line, which was the boundary between Virginia and North Carolina. It was discovered after Kentucky and Tennessee became states that the boundary surveyor, Thomas Walker, made an error in his survey. As a result, it was discovered that about 2,500 square miles south of the Tennessee border should have been in Kentucky. Crittenden attempted to remedy this by adding land from unsettled portions of west Tennessee to Kentucky. This effort was unsuccessful as well. However, after Crittenden left the Senate in 1819, he played a major role during the 1820s in resolving the boundary dispute.

On March 3, 1819, Crittenden's last act as senator was voting on February 22, 1819, in favor of the ratification of the convention between the US and the chiefs and headmen of the Cherokee Nation.

While Crittenden enjoyed his time as a senator, he had financial needs. He had a wife and three children. A fourth child (Thomas Leonidas) was due in May 1819. Members of Congress were earning $5 per day each day Congress was in session. Congress was usually in session for three months during the winter. When Congress was not in session, members were not paid. Unfortunately, to sustain a long career in Congress, a man had to be independently wealthy or, like Daniel Webster, have friends who would subsidize him; this is theoretically illegal in the late twentieth and early twenty-first Century.[6]

John Jordan Crittenden would not return to the US Senate until 1835. During this fifteen-year period, he would be reelected several times to the Kentucky Legislature and become an even closer political ally of Henry Clay. Under President John Quincy Adams, he was appointed US Attorney for Kentucky in 1827. In December 1828, he was nominated by Adams to replace Kentuckian Robert Trimble on the US Supreme Court. Unfortunately for Crittenden, the Senate blocked his nomination so that Andrew Jackson would make the appointment.

ISHAM TALBOT
(1773–1837)

- Class Three of Three
- Senate service February 2, 1815–March 3, 1819; October 19, 1820–March 3, 1825
- Political affiliation: Democratic-Republican
- Residence at time of election: Franklin County
- Served with Presidents Madison and Monroe
- Served with Governors Slaughter, Adair and Desha

Senator Isham Talbot was selected twice to fill a Senate vacancy for the same Senate seat. The first was to fill the vacancy caused by the resignation of Jesse Bledsoe in in December 1814. The second was to fill the vacancy in the same seat when his successor Senator William Logan decided to resign after only a year-and-a-half.

Isham Talbot was born in Bedford County, Virginia in 1773. Records are not available as to the month and date of his birth. His family moved to Harrodsburg, Kentucky. He studied law and was admitted to the bar and initially practiced law in Versailles prior to moving to Frankfort. He served in the Kentucky Senate from 1812–1815 until his election to the US Senate.[1]

Talbot's legislative accomplishments were few in number. For example, on Friday, December 29, 1815, he introduced legislation to assist

Mr. John Bate in renewing his Saline lease with the US on government property in Illinois.[2]

On January 9, 1816, Talbot presented a memorial request from the Kentucky legislature requesting compensation for horses lost by Kentuckians during the War of 1812.[3]

Talbot was the only Kentucky senator present on Tuesday, March 4, 1817, at James Monroe's first inauguration as president of the US.[4]

Senator Talbot, with his colleague Senator Richard Johnson, voted for the bill to establish a uniform system of bankruptcy throughout the US. Talbot made the motion that the bill be read for a third time on February 15, 1822.[5] However, it did not become law.

Talbot was a practicing attorney most of his adult life. His hometown newspaper, *The Argus of Western America*, has many notices concerning his legal practice during the 1820s. It is interesting to note that while serving in the Senate, Talbot seemed to have an active law practice in Frankfort.[6] In an article about a contested real estate case *Green v. Biddle*, it notes at the end of the article that Talbot and Ben Hardin were counsel for the Greens' heirs.

In a notice published in the *The Argus of Western America* on May 16, 1822, but with a date in the notice of November 12, 1821, Talbot writes:

> The Subscriber being about to set out for the City of Washington, in fulfillment of the duties of his public station, has committed to the charge of Terrence Cooney, Esq. the custody of all the papers of his Clients as well the transaction of all his business in a private, as well as professional character, during his absence. He will be found at all times in my office opposite the Tavern of Capt. Weisinger in Frankfort.[7]

In 1824, he acquired a new law partner. According to a "Law Notice," Isham Talbot and J.D. Garrard had an office "opposite of Capt. Weisingers' Tavern."[8] The same notice was in the *The Argus of Western America* from February 25, 1824:

After leaving the Senate, he continued to be active in politics. In 1827, he was appointed to the Central Committee of what would become the Whig Party when General Thomas Metcalfe was the candidate for Governor and Joseph R. Underwood, Esq. was candidate for Lt. Governor. It should be noted that both Metcalfe and Underwood were later elected to the Senate.[9]

Additionally, it was noted that he and two others signed a letter defending a Colonel John Speedsmith on January 15, 1831, for allegedly criticizing Henry Clay. Many supporters of Andrew Jackson were of the opinion that Clay urged his supporters in the US House of Representatives to support John Quincy Adams in the disputed presidential election of 1824. Clay, who became US secretary of state, allegedly made a "corrupt bargain" with Adams to have his supporters vote for Adams over Jackson in exchange for becoming Adams' Secretary of State. It said:

> We were present during the wholetime [sic] Colonel John Speedsmith was addressing the Jacksonian Convention and heard nothing escape him like the charge of 'bargain, sale and corruption' between Messrs. Adams and Clay.

JAS. LOVE
CLIFTON RODES
ISHAM TALBOT[10]

Talbot died near Frankfort on September 25, 1837. He was survived by his son William Garrard Talbot (1813–1837) and daughter Elizabeth Garrard "Eliza" Talbot Dudley (1806–1860). They were children from his first marriage with Margaret Garrard Talbot (1788-1815), the daughter of Kentucky's second governor, James Garrard, and his wife Elizabeth Montjoy). He was survived by his second wife Adelaide Thomason Talbot (1800–1873), whom he married when she was seventeen. They had three or four children. She is buried in Mt. Olivet Cemetery in Washington, D.C.[11]

Part III
1820–1834
Growing Pains

The period 1820–1834 for the Senate and Kentucky is a period of coming into its own. A second generation (after statehood and the Revolution) are coming into their own. Henry Clay was a dominant political figure not only in Kentucky but also nationally and would remain so for the next thirty years.

While Clay was not in the Senate in 1820, he was the Speaker of the US House of Representatives. He was responsible for the Compromise of 1820, which would regulate the expansion of slavery in the United States for the next thirty years. As Speaker, Clay would not allow the admission of Maine as a "free state" without the admission of Missouri as a "slave state." In addition, the opponents of slavery gave up prohibiting slavery in the territories in exchange for a prohibition of slavery in those parts of the Louisiana Purchase north and west of Missouri and north of latitude 36° 30.° The only territories that had slavery were Arkansas and Oklahoma. It should be noted that Texas would not become part of the United States until 1845.

With the exception of William Logan, the other five senators completed their designated term. Johnson, Bibb, and Clay were recognized beyond Kentucky. Richard Johnson was elected vice president alongside President Martin Van Buren. George Bibb later served as secretary of the treasury under President Tyler. Henry Clay was an unsuccessful candidate for president in 1824 and served as secretary of state under President John Quincy Adams from 1825–29. After his Senate service, John Rowan served on a commission to adjust land claims against Mexico.

WILLIAM LOGAN
(1776–1822)

- Class Three of Three
- Senate Service: March 4, 1819–May 28, 1820
- Political affiliation:Democratic-Republican
- Residence at time of election: Shelby County
- Served with President Monroe
- Served with Governor Gabriel Slaughter

William Logan was elected by the Kentucky legislature for a six-year term that began March 4, 1819. He was sworn in as a US Senator on Monday, December 6, 1819, in the Senate Chambers in Washington, D.C.[1] Logan served less than a year.

Logan was born within the fort at Harrodsburg; he spent his early childhood in St. Asaphs Fort, which is also known as Logan's Station near present-day Stanford, Kentucky.[2] He was educated by his parents and tutors.

He was a delegate to the 1799 Kentucky Constitutional Convention.

Before his election to the US Senate, Logan was a member of the Kentucky House of Representatives from 1803 to 1806 and again in 1808 and served as Speaker for two terms. He was a judge of the court of appeals from 1808 to 1812. He was also a presidential elector in 1808, 1812, and 1816. Logan was elected as a Democratic-Republican to the

US Senate and served from March 4, 1819, to May 28, 1820, and he resigned to run for governor in 1820. "*Mr. Logan* [emphasis added] obtained leave of absence for the remainder of the session." That is the last mention of Logan in the *Senate Journal*.[3] A review of the Senate's activities of the previous three days indicates the Logan was present.

Based on his letter on January 9, 1820, to his wife, he said of his month in the Senate — "I go where I am invited and eat when it suits me. I have been at the President's (Monroe) at levees and dinner. I have been at Mr. Crawford's and going this week to dinner to MM Adams' as I have a card from Mr. & Mrs. Adams."[4]

In the same letter he writes about being governor and chief magistrate of Kentucky. In his letter on March 3, 1820, he writes about coming home.

In the handwritten obituary, William Logan, Esquire, died at his residence near Shelbyville on Thursday, August 8, 1822, of prevailing fever. The obituary talks of his failed bid to become governor. It also adds that despite his loss, "his character was unaffected and his honor untarnished." Then further on in the obituary, "A large portion of the people of Kentucky looked upon him as their next Chief Magistrate; and it is probable had his life been spared, he would have attained to this summit of ambition."[5]

He was buried in the Logan family cemetery near Shelbyville.

RICHARD M. JOHNSON
(1780–1850)

- Class Two of Three
- Senate Service: 1819–1829
- Political affiliation: Democratic-Republican
- Residence at time of election: Scott County
- Served with Presidents Monroe and John Quincy Adams
- Served with Governors Slaughter, Adair, Desha, and Metcalfe

Prior to his election as a US Senator, Richard M. Johnson was a war hero of the War of 1812, a Central Kentucky planter, and a Congressman. After leaving the Senate, he is best remembered as a vice president of the US and the father of two black daughters, Imogene and Adaline.

As *Courier-Journal* columnist Billy Reed wrote, Richard Johnson's life "was distinguished by his unconventional habits and his military adventures."[1] His service in Congress may be considered above average, as he was nominated by the Democratic Party for vice president and elected to serve with President Martin Van Buren.

Johnson was born at Beargrass in Jefferson County, Kentucky, on October 17, 1780. His family soon moved to Bryan Station near Lexington in Fayette County. His family then moved to Great Crossing near Georgetown in Scott County.

He studied Latin in his youth and attended Transylvania University in Lexington, where he studied law. He was admitted to the bar at age nineteen and practiced law in Scott County. He was elected to the Kentucky Legislature just prior to his twenty-first birthday. In 1806, Richard Johnson was elected to the US Congress, where he served until March 3, 1819.

While Johnson was in Congress, he voted to declare war on Great Britain. In support of the war effort, he went back to Kentucky and took command of a battalion of volunteers in the militia. Under the command of Governor Isaac Shelby, Johnson was a hero in the Battle of the Thames in lower Canada. It was there Johnson was given credit for killing the great Chief Tecumseh while being severely wounded himself. It was said the he had wounds from at least twenty-five-gun balls [musket balls].[2]

Upon returning to Congress, Johnson was a champion of veterans' rights. He was active in sponsoring pension legislation for veterans of the Revolutionary War and the War of 1812, as well as pensions for widows and orphans of both wars. He left the US House of Representatives when his term ended in March 1819.

Upon leaving the US House of Representatives, he was immediately elected to the Kentucky House of Representatives. During that session of the legislature, he was elected to fill the vacancy in the US Senate caused by the resignation of John J. Crittenden.

Johnson appeared on Monday, January 3, 1820, to present his credentials and take the oath of office.[3] In respect to what would be the Missouri Compromise, Johnson was one of the five senators appointed on Saturday, February 24, 1820, to the select committee to decide the procedure for the admission of Missouri Territory to the Union.[4]

During his tenure as a US Senator, he sponsored legislation that would prevent imprisonment for debtors. As chair of the Committee on Post Offices and Post Roads, he opposed the elimination of mail delivery on Sundays. He believed that it would be a violation of "church and state" to stop delivery on Sundays.[5] It was interesting to note that during this period of history, this committee was responsible for funding the building of "post roads" in order to transport mail throughout the nation.

He was on the Select Committee, which prepared a report on "A Bill to Abolish Imprisonment for Debt." He presented the second reading of the bill on March 23, 1826.[6] Johnson sponsored legislation to abolish imprisonment for debt on a national level every session he served in the Senate. Unfortunately, such legislation was not passed until Johnson left the Senate. One such bill was signed into law on January 18, 1841, when Johnson was within six weeks of leaving office as vice president of the United States.[7]

Although Johnson himself was not formally educated, he was support-
ive of education. He sponsored legislation for the support of Columbian
College, now George Washington University, during his tenure in the Senate. He helped establish the Choctaw Academy in Scott County, which
educated Native Americans from 1825 until 1848. During this time, over
600 Native American men and boys from seventeen tribes were educated at
this school. (Some of the buildings are now being restored).[8]

Richard Johnson spent most of his time from 1820 through 1829 in
Washington, attending to Senate duties. His mixed-race mistress, Julia
Chinn, ran his home and farm known as "Blue Spring" in Scott County.
It was there, in 1824, that Johnson and his family entertained the Mar-
quis de Lafayette. In addition to dinner, there was a 500-pound cheese
made by the neighbor women for the occasion.[9]

Unable to win another term in the Senate, Johnson returned to the US
House of Representatives. During his tenure in the House, he became a
close ally of President Andrew Jackson. It was his unwavering support
of Jackson that helped Richard Johnson obtain Jackson's support as the
Democratic candidate for vice president in 1836.

The issue of Johnson's family was raised during the campaign of 1836.
During the campaign, the *Louisville Journal* of September 14th reprinted
an article from the *Bangor Republican* concerning Johnson's relationship
with his mixed-race mistress and children. As printed in the *Journal*:

From the Bangor Republican
COL. RICHARD M. JOHNSON

This exemplary Christian and distinguished statesman, warrior and
philanthropist, after 30 years uninterrupted service of his country,
in the field of battle and in the Halls of Congress, is now brought
forward, and with great unanimity by the democratic party of the
United States as their candidate for the Vice Presidency—and who
is Richard Johnson?—a planter of Kentucky, a civilian and soldier.
What has he done? In early life, yielding to the great laws of nature,
which, in the warm and genial regions of the south, vindicate and
accomplish in superior grace and attractions of the sable female race
the inevitable destiny of the colored population sooner or later to
triumph in full domination over the sultry glebe and sunny clime;
but abhorring the licentious lives of such men as Clay and Poindex-
ter, Richard M. Johnson turned to the sacred volume, which has
been his guide and trust through life, and finding that 'God made
of one flesh all the nations of the earth,' he took a Creole for a wife.
His is now a widower, having lived in honest wedlock with the
woman of his choice, and raised and educated a family of children,

the heirs of his estate; intelligent and respectable, but slightly tinged with their African origin. So much for his domestic relations.[10]

At that time, the balloting for president and vice president were separate. Due in part to many folks not approving of Johnson openly providing for his mixed-race children, he did not receive enough electoral votes to become vice president. This is even though Martin Van Buren received the needed number of electoral votes to become president. Richard Johnson became vice president because of a vote of the US Senate on February 8, 1837. Johnson remains the only vice president of the US to be elected by the US. Senate As vice president, he served under Van Buren from March 4, 1837 until March 3, 1841.

Johnson returned to private life in Kentucky after the election of 1841, running his farm and tavern. He served in the Kentucky legislature from 1841 to 1843 and was again elected in 1850, but he never took office. He died of a stroke on November 19, 1850. There are Johnson Counties in Kentucky, Illinois, Iowa, and Nebraska named for Senator Richard Johnson.

HENRY CLAY
(1777–1852)
Third and Fourth Terms

- Class Three of Three
- Senate Service:1831–1843
- Political affiliation: National Republican (Anti-Jacksonian) and Whig
- Residence at time of election: Lexington-Fayette County
- Served with Presidents Jackson, Van Buren, Harrison, and Tyler
- Served with Governors Metcalfe, Breathitt, Morehead, Clark, Wickliffe, and Letcher

Prior to joining the Senate for his third stint, Henry Clay had completed service as President John Quincy Adams' secretary of state. Clay served about fifteen years in the US House of Representatives —most of that time as Speaker. In 1814, he was selected to serve as one of the commissioners who went to Ghent, Belgium, to negotiate the end of the War of 1812. John Quincy Adams served as a commissioner as well. The two negotiated the treaty that ended the War of 1812 on December 24, 1814. In 1820, as Speaker of the US House of Representatives, Clay was responsible for the Missouri Compromise of 1820. During this Senate stint, Clay was responsible for his second of three compromises that staved off civil war.

Until the election of Andrew Jackson, those who were elected president had previously served as secretary of state. Presidents who previously had served as secretary of state included Jefferson, Madison, Monroe, and John Quincy Adams. It is likely that Henry Clay hoped that he would serve two terms as John Quincy Adams' Secretary of State and be his designated successor in the election of 1832. Unfortunately for Clay, Adams was defeated in 1828.

One of the reasons Clay wanted to return to the Senate was to have a national platform in order to be visible for a run for president as a candidate for the National Republicans or those opposed to the policies of Andrew Jackson.[1] Those included Jackson's policies concerning the federal government funding internal improvements, as seen in his veto of the extension of the National Road from Zanesville, Ohio, to Maysville, Kentucky to Lexington and points south. This was called the veto of the Maysville Road bill. Incumbent Senator John Rowan, whose seat Clay would take, voted against it, despite its potential benefit to Kentucky.

On November 9, 1831, Henry Clay was elected by the Kentucky legislature over former US Senator and future Vice President Richard Johnson 55–45.[2]

One of Clay's goals as a senator was to establish Congress as the "the wheel of government." Clay was concerned that President Andrew Jackson, in less than three years, had extended executive power at the expense of the legislative.[3]

As a senator and presidential candidate for the National Republicans in 1832, Clay stated his views to Senator Johnston of Louisiana in four general points:

1. 'Tariff protection in both theory and practice must be preserved.
2. Duties on foreign products can be reduced or repealed when not competing with domestic industries but must be maintained when they do compete.
3. Taxes ought not be levied specifically for internal improvements, but surpluses of revenue should be applied to the promotion of public works.
4. The Charter of the Bank of the United States should be renewed with any modifications suggested by experience'.[4]

This emphasis on "internal improvements" was the primary focus of Clay's American Plan, which advocated federal financing of roads, bridges, and canals.

In addition to his political philosophy, Clay was a person who brought a sense of theater with him when he spoke:

"for Clay rising from his desk in the Senate was comparable to the curtain going up in a first-rate theater. He used props for stage business, such as the little silver snuffbox that he absentmindedly rolled from one hand to the other, creating a near hypnotic spell while he spoke. He pulled his snow-white handkerchief from his coat with a flourish and polished his spectacles as though lost in thought, the pause lengthening and listeners' expectations swelling until he again broke the silence with 'his unequaled voice, which was equally distinct and clear, whether at its highest key or lowest whisper—rich, musical, captivating".[5]

During this period, Clay was nominated by the short-lived National Republican Party at its May 1832 convention in Washington, D.C. Its platform contained points from Clay's American System.[6]

In many respects, Clay's beliefs in the role of government were implemented 100 years later by President Franklin D. Roosevelt. David and Jeanne Heidler wrote, "he also foreshadowed the future by extolling the virtue of planned progress, the idea that the government was not only empowered but obligated to perform economic functions that individuals could not or that private corporations would not."[7]

In the summer of 1832, Congress considered renewal of the charter for the Bank of the United States (BUS), which was to expire in 1836. President Jackson wanted to dissolve the bank when its charter expired. Jackson disliked the Bank of the US and all banks. Jackson disliked the Bank of the US due to its independence from the executive. The new president of Bank of the US was Nicholas Biddle, who instituted policies to control credit nationally. When Congress passed legislation in 1832 to renew the charter for Bank of the US, President Jackson vetoed it. Clay led the charge to override the veto but was unsuccessful.[8]

With the presidential election of 1832, Clay and the National Republicans underestimated the popularity of Andrew Jackson. In November 1832, Clay received 49 electoral votes to Jackson's 219 electoral votes.[9]

In his return to the Senate after the election of 1832, Clay rescued President Jackson in the Nullification Crisis. South Carolina protested the federal government's tariffs of 1828 and 1832. (It should be noted at that time there was no federal income tax.) John Calhoun, Jackson's first vice president, believed that states had a right to nullify federal tariffs and other laws. In November 1832, South Carolina passed legislation (Ordinance of Nullification) that said the imposition of federal tariff legislation was "null and void" in the state of South Carolina.

As a compromise, Clay proposed that all existing tariffs remain in effect until March 3, 1840. At that time, all existing tariff laws would be repealed. After March 3, 1840, all duties collected would be equal and laid for the purpose of providing only such revenue as the government needed to operate "without regard to the protection or encouragement of any branch of domestic industry whatever."[10]

Congress debated several bills to alleviate the crisis with South Carolina from December 1832 through February 11, 1833. On February 12, 1833, Clay introduced his Compromise Tariff, and Senator John Calhoun announced his support of Clay's bill. On March 2, 1833, President Andrew Jackson signed Clay's legislation.[11] Almost at the same time, South Carolina repealed its Ordinance of Nullification. It should also be noted that President Jackson pocket vetoed Clay's public lands bill after Congress had adjourned.

During the Twenty-Third Congress from March 4, 1833, until March 4, 1835, Clay would speak almost every day the Senate was in session. He was described in the following way:

> He pleaded, cajoled, coaxed and flattered colleagues in long, powerful speeches that excoriated the chief executive [Jackson] and his misuse of presidential power. All of a sudden, the quiet, sedate, drab, patrician and uninteresting Senate of the United States became the arena for one of the greatest cockfights in American history. Crowds appeared daily and filled every place to watch the bloody encounters between the President's maddened opponents and his equally agitated supporters. Just as he transformed the House when he served as Speaker, so Clay now converted the Senate into an exciting, sometimes raucous forum for full-scale airings of every important national issue.[12]

With Clay, Daniel Webster and John Calhoun joined the verbal assault on President Jackson.

The National Republican Party morphed into the "Whig Party" in 1834, with Clay considered its leader. The Whigs were united in their support of the BUS and a Second Bank of the United States. They believed that a national bank would stabilize the nation's currency. Most supported a high tariff, distribution of money from sale of public lands to the states, and government assistance to help overcome economic downturns.[13]

In 1837, the Panic or Depression hit the nation. President Van Buren called a special session of Congress to consider an independent treasury system to replace the BUS. Clay opposed Van Buren's independent treasury, blaming the depression in part on the failure to keep funds in the BUS and to renew its charter. He also blamed the depression on the fact the Jackson Administration had for the first time in history paid off the national debt, drying up the money supply.

Clay sought the Whig nomination for President in 1840. However, he was defeated by General William Henry Harrison.

In order to prepare for the presidential election of 1844, Henry Clay thought he needed time to campaign. Clay submitted his resignation from the Senate to take effect on March 31, 1842. In addition to taking care of his personal affairs and getting some rest, the North Carolina Whigs were meeting and were going to name him as their candidate for President in 1844.[14]

Part IV

1832–1852

Domination by Henry Clay

Henry Clay and the Whigs dominated Kentucky politics for twenty-plus years following his service as secretary of state for President John Quincy Adams. Crittenden served as US attorney general for three presidents.

The influence of the Whig domination of Kentucky and Clay's leadership is seen in Whig majorities in the legislature. The legislature displaced incumbent Jacksonian Democrat John Rowan with Clay and subsequent election of Whigs to the Senate until 1852. Clay served continuously from 1831 until 1843 when he resigned to prepare to run again for President in 1844. Unfortunately for Clay, he was defeated by James K. Polk in 1844.

The six senators who were elected by the legislature during this period were Whigs. Three were Whig governors. One, Thomas "Stonehammer" Metcalfe, served in the House with Clay when the contested presidential election of 1824 was decided by Congress in favor of John Quincy Adams over Andrew Jackson. As members of the House, Clay and Metcalfe voted for Adams.

John J. Crittenden was also a towering figure during this period. In addition to serving as US senator, Crittenden briefly served as US attorney general for Presidents William Henry Harrison and John Tyler. He was elected governor of Kentucky before serving as attorney general for President Millard Fillmore.

Clay and the Whigs advocated his American System, which included the involvement of federal and state governments in providing internal improvements. Clay envisioned a diversified American economy in which agricultural interests and manufacturers would exist side by side. Clay and the Whigs saw beyond the argument of whether the US would be an industrial or agricultural nation. It could be both, he insisted. The ideas put into practice included building the National Road, America's first major highway; chartering the Second Bank of the United States, a new national bank in 1816; and passing the first protective tariff the same year. For Kentucky it included federal funding of the Portland Canal at Louisville to provide better navigation of the Ohio River and for the system of Marine Hospitals to provide medical care for injured sailors on America's waterways.

Clay's major legacy of this period was the Compromise of 1850, which may have said staved off the Civil War for another ten years.

One of the legacies of Clay's American System was Abraham Lincoln's founding of Land Grant Colleges in 1865. (Lincoln was a former Whig.)

JOHN J. CRITTENDEN
(1787–1863)
Second and Third Terms

- Senate Service: 1835–1841 (Second Term); 1842–1848 (Third Term)
- Political affiliation: Whig
- Residence at time of election: Franklin County
- Served with Presidents Jackson, Van Buren, Harrison, Tyler, Polk, and Harrison
- Served with Governors Morehead, Clark, Wickliffe, Letcher, and Owsley

John J. Crittenden served two almost back-to-back periods in the US Senate. In 1835, he succeeded Bibb, a Jacksonian. He served in that seat until 1841, when he was appointed attorney general by President William Henry Harrison. Crittenden was succeeded by James Turner Morehead. Then in 1842, he was appointed and elected to Henry Clay's seat when Clay resigned. He resigned in 1848 after being elected governor of Kentucky in the August 1848 election.

As a senator who served with Henry Clay, Crittenden was compared favorably to his colleague. An excerpt from *The Courier-Journal* said:

'From the Commonwealth.' Hon. John J. Crittenden. It will be seen, by the following extracts from the correspondence of the *Baltimore Chronicle,* that Mr. Crittenden has again distinguished himself on the floor of the Senate. No man is more rapidly rising in public estimation than the newly elected Senator from Kentucky. His eloquence is universally admired, and the estimation of his countrymen already ranks him as the fit colleague of Henry Clay. In our own state he is beloved by every good man in it, and the day is not far distant when his fame will extend throughout the length and breadth of this great nation, as a citizen of irreproachable private life, and as a statesman of the first order of talent and the purest public virtue.[1]

During this period, both Crittenden and Clay were national leaders within the National Republicans and the Whig Party. Crittenden served as attorney general under three Whig Presidents. Clay seemed to be the opposition leader to the Jacksonians and later the Democrats. Clay seemed focused upon being elected president. At one time, he imagined serving eight years in the administration of John Quincy Adams followed by eight years as President. Crittenden supported Clay's candidacy as a National Republican in the 1832 election, in which President Jackson defeated Clay. Clay did not seek the presidency in 1836 but with Crittenden's support sought the Whig nomination in 1840, only to be defeated by eventual winner William Henry Harrison at the Whig Convention. In 1844, Clay won the Whig nomination only to be defeated by dark horse Democrat James K. Polk. In 1848, Clay decided to seek the Whig nomination for president after Crittenden had endorsed General Zachary Taylor. Clay expected Crittenden to withdraw his endorsement of Taylor and did not do so. Clay's disappointment resulted in a personal estrangement between the two men until shortly before Clay's death in 1852.

An anti-Jackson candidate was sought to succeed incumbent Senator John Rowan for the term ending in March 1831. Rowan had become unpopular due to his vote against the "Maysville road bill."[2] When the election for Rowan's successor began on January 1830, Crittenden received sixty-eight of the sixty-nine votes needed for election. Crittenden was a member of the legislature as Speaker of the House of Representatives. However, Crittenden refused to vote. Due to Crittenden's refusal to vote for himself, there was a deadlock.[3]

The Senate election was not decided until after a new legislature was elected in August 1830, which met in November 1830. Though Crittenden was again elected Speaker, he stepped aside for the election of Clay by a nine-vote margin over former Senator Richard Johnson.[4]

In August 1834, the Whig Party captured a majority of seats in the Kentucky legislature. When the legislature met, Crittenden was elected to the Senate seat held by Bibb, whose term expired in March 1835, by a vote of ninety-four to forty over James Guthrie.[5]

During this period, Crittenden and most Whigs followed the lead of Henry Clay, the leader of the Jackson opposition in the Senate. Crittenden supported Clay on the protective tariff to protect American manufacturers. Crittenden was an advocate of proceeds of public land sales being distributed to the states. Crittenden joined Clay in opposing the Seminole war and Indian removals, as well as the Jackson-Van Buren anti-Bank of the National Bank program. A review of Senate votes during the period that Crittenden and Clay served together indicate they rarely differed on important issues.[6]

In 1841, Crittenden resigned from the Senate to take an appointment as attorney general in President William Henry Harrison's administration. After the sudden death of President Harrison, Crittenden resigned with the rest of the cabinet, with the exception of Secretary of State Daniel Webster, on September 11, 1841.[7] President John Tyler (who succeeded Harrison) failed to support the agenda of the Whigs in Congress on many issues. The breaking point came when Tyler vetoed the establishment of a second Bank of the United States in the form of legislation called "The Fiscal Corporation of the United States."[8]

When Crittenden returned to the Senate in 1842, Kentucky hemp growers and manufacturers were facing competition from producers in India and Russia. Rope and bag prices were the lowest in years due to foreign competition. The House passed a higher tariff than Crittenden wanted. However, the Senate and Crittenden went along. But President Tyler vetoed the tariff legislation. Then there was a third tariff bill that Crittenden and his colleague Senator Morehead joined with Democrats in passing by one vote. However, Tyler pocket vetoed this tariff legislation, and the Kentucky hemp industry failed to get the protection it needed.[9]

Crittenden voted with the Senate majority against President Tyler's "Treaty of Annexation Between the United States and the Republic of Texas" on June 8, 1844. He was the eleventh vote against. Kentucky Senator Morehead was the twenty-third vote against.[10] It was voted down 39–16.

On February 27, 1845, Crittenden (as did Morehead) voted "for" the joint resolution requesting that the President enter into negotiations with the Republic of Texas for Texas to become part of the US. The first vote was tied 26–26.

Crittenden spoke about the acquisition of Texas in March 1845. Crittenden brought up the question of whether "…has Congress the power, in its legislative capacity to propose terms and make negotiations for admitting Foreign States into this Union?"[11]

In May 1846, Crittenden and his colleague Senator Morehead voted with the majority (40–2) to go to war with Mexico.[12]

Although Crittenden voted for the declaration of war with Mexico, he thought it unnecessary. He did not agree with President Polk's acquisition of new territory as a result of the war.[13]

Crittenden had taken Clay at his word when he indicated after his 1844 defeat for the Presidency that he would not be a candidate in 1848. In 1847, Clay still seemed unavailable as a presidential candidate in 1848. There were some who thought Crittenden should be the Whig presidential candidate in 1848. The *Nashville Republican Banner* newspaper, as early as 1846, endorsed Crittenden candidacy in 1848.[14] Crittenden, eager to elect a Whig President, endorsed and worked for General Zachary Taylor.[15]

In 1848, Crittenden became the Whig candidate for Governor of Kentucky. In past elections the margin of the Whig candidate for governor were growing smaller. Crittenden, whose popularity in Kentucky was second only to Clay's, ran for Kentucky governor in order to help ensure a Kentucky victory for Whig Zachary Taylor in 1848.

John J. Crittenden was elected governor in August 1848. Zachary Taylor carried Kentucky in November 1848. Crittenden resigned as governor in 1850 after accepting an appointment from President Millard Fillmore as US General.

Crittenden would return in 1854 to the US Senate.

JAMES TURNER MOREHEAD
(1797–1854)

- Class Two of Three
- Senate Service: March 4, 1841–March 3, 1847
- Political affiliation: Whig
- Residence at time of election: Warren County
- Served with Presidents Van Buren, Harrison, Tyler, and Polk
- Served with Governors Letcher and Owsley

Former Kentucky Governor James T. Morehead was elected by the legislature to the Senate for the term beginning in March 1841. He succeeded John J. Crittenden, who held this seat from 1835 to 1841.

According to the *Senate Journal*, Morehead's credentials were presented to the Senate by Senator Henry Clay on Wednesday, March 1, 1841. After a brief address by newly elected Vice President John Tyler, Clay presented the credentials of Morehead, chosen as a senator by the legislature, and Morehead took his seat in the Senate. Following his swearing-in, Morehead had the opportunity to see President William Henry Harrison give the longest presidential inaugural address in US history.

A special session that began on March 4, 1841, for the inauguration of President William Henry Harrison was in response to a summons from President Van Buren, dated January 6, 1841.

Senator Morehead was born near Shepherdsville in Bullitt County on May 24, 1797. His family moved to a farm near Russellville in Logan County. He attended the public schools. At age sixteen, he left Logan County to attend Transylvania University in Lexington.

He studied law with Judge Henry P. Broadnax and John J. Crittenden in Russellville before being admitted to the bar in 1818. He moved to neighboring Warren County and commenced practice in Bowling Green, Kentucky. He was elected to the Kentucky House from Warren County, where he served from 1828 to 1831. He was elected lieutenant governor in 1832 with Democratic Governor James Breathitt. When Breathitt died in 1834, Morehead became governor and served until 1836. He returned to the Kentucky House from 1837 to 1838.[1]

Morehead was appointed president of the State Board of Internal Improvements by Governor James Clark in 1838 and served until 1841. The Board of Internal Improvements was an important state institution from 1835 until 1850. The board helped develop financial support for financing roads, locks, and dams for Kentucky's transportation system.

Morehead was elected by the legislature as a Whig to the US Senate and served from March 4, 1841, to March 3, 1847. During his Senate career, he served as chairman of the Committee on Indian Affairs, Twenty-Seventh Congress, and Committee on Retrenchment, Twenty-Seventh and Twenty-Eighth Congresses. He also served as a member of the Foreign Relations Committee. During his service in the Senate, he defended a federal bank bill and opposed the annexation of Texas, although he supported the war with Mexico after it began.

Specific references to Morehead and proposed legislation in the *Senate Journal* are found on:

Tuesday, April 5, 1841 when — Mr. Morehead presented a preamble and resolution passed by the General Assembly of the State of Kentucky, requesting the Senators and Representatives of that State in Congress to use their exertions to procure the establishment of an agency within the State of Kentucky for the manufacture and inspection of water-rotted hemp, intended for the use of the navy; which were referred to the Committee on Naval Affairs.

Mr. Morehead presented the memorial of the representatives of James Trabue, deceased, late an officer in the revolutionary war, praying an allowance of bounty land, for his military services; which was referred to the Committee on Revolutionary Claims.

On Thursday, December 30, 1841, the *Journal* reflects that the Senator was busy as seen with the following: Mr. Morehead presented the petition of William P. Duval, late Governor of the Territory of Florida, praying the payment of a sum of money ascertained to be due to him for extraordinary expenses and sacrifices in the discharge of his duties, upon a suit instituted by the United States against him in the federal court of the middle district of Florida, for the recovery of an alleged deficit in his accounts with the Government; which was referred to the Committee of Claims.

Mr. Morehead presented the petition of the administrator of Richard C. Allen, deceased, praying that he may be allowed to enter, in any land district in Florida, a quantity of land equal in value to other lands of which the said Allen was a purchaser at public sale, but to which the United States had no title; which was referred to the Committee on Private Land Claims.

On motion by Mr. Morehead,

Ordered, That the petition of Edward Graham, on the files of the Senate, be referred to the Committee on Indian Affairs. [Note that Morehead was chair of that Committee]

Agreeably to notice, Mr. Morehead asked and obtained leave to bring in a bill (S. 109) for the relief of James Sympson's heirs, which was read the first and second times, by unanimous consent, and referred to the Committee on Private Land Claims.

Friday, January 1842 when — Mr. Morehead presented the memorial of a number of citizens of Hardin County, Kentucky, praying the repeal of the bankruptcy law.

On Tuesday, December 6, 1842, it is interesting to note the Senators from Kentucky and one from Connecticut were the only Senators present.

The honorable John J. Crittenden and the honorable James T. Morehead, from the State of Kentucky, and the honorable Perry Smith, from the State of Connecticut, attended. The number of Senators present not being sufficient to constitute a quorum, on motion by Mr. Kerr, The Senate adjourned.[2]

The previous day, Monday, December 5, 1842, there was not a quorum either, since only twenty-four senators were present. Neither Morehead nor Crittenden was present on Monday.

The *Louisville Morning Courier*, on March 12, 1847, quoted an article from the *New York Tribune* on Whig senators leaving in March 1847. It was titled "Ex-Senator Morehead."

James T. Morehead never served in Congress until he took his seat in the Senate at the opening of the Extra Session of 1841; but he had previously been elected Lt. Governor of Kentucky and we think he acted for some time as Governor. He is a tall, grave, plain, spare, dark thoughtful man of some fifty years of age, probably a lawyer by profession, but more like a planter in appearance—one who would be recognized at a glance as eminent or honesty, truth and sound judgment. Mr. Morehead seldom addresses the Senate but always impressively, and there are few men in it who labor more earnestly or successfully to be thoroughly informed of every public question, so as to vote exactly and uniformly right. The more brilliant and versatile talents of his eminent colleague, Mr. Crittenden, have tended to obscure his merits, but the nation loses not sounder or truer man from her Councils at the close of the XXIX Congress.[3]

During Morehead's time in the Senate, he was overshadowed by Henry Clay, who served with him during the first years of his Senate service, and by John J. Crittenden during the second half of his term.

After his time in Congress, he practiced law in Covington. He made at least one campaign speech during the 1852 presidential election for the Whigs at the Cerro Gordo Club in Newport, Kentucky, in September 1852.[4]

He died in Covington on December 28, 1854. He was buried in the state lot at the Frankfort Cemetery in Frankfort. The city of Morehead was named in his honor.

JOSEPH R. UNDERWOOD
(1791–1876)

- Class Two of Three
- Senate Service: 1847–1853
- Political affiliation: Whig
- Residence at time of election: Warren County
- Served with Presidents Polk, Taylor, and Fillmore
- Governors Owsley, Crittenden, Helm, and Powell

According to the record left behind, Joseph R. Underwood left a legacy similar to his predecessor James T. Morehead (brother of Congressman Warner Lewis Underwood and grandfather of Oscar Wilder Underwood, a congressman and senator from Alabama).

Underwood was born in Goochland County, Virginia, on October 24, 1791. He moved to Barren County, Kentucky, in 1803 and lived with his uncle, Edmund Rogers. He attended the common schools in the area.

Underwood went to Lexington, where he attended and graduated from Transylvania College in 1811. Upon graduation, he studied law in Lexington and was admitted to the bar in 1813. He also served in the War of 1812 as a lieutenant in the Thirteenth Regiment, Kentucky Infantry.

He practiced law in Glasgow, Kentucky, where he served as town trustee and county auditor until 1823. He was elected to the Kentucky

House, where he represented Barren County from 1816 to 1819. He moved south to Bowling Green in 1823. He was elected to represent Warren County as a member of the state House from 1825 to 1826. He was an unsuccessful candidate for lieutenant governor in 1828. He was a judge of Kentucky's highest court, the Court of Appeals, from 1828 to 1835 following the Old Court-New Court controversy.[1]

He was elected as a Whig to the Twenty-Fourth Congress and to the three succeeding Congresses from March 4, 1835, to March 3, 1843. He served as chairman of the Committee on the District of Columbia, Twenty-Seventh Congress. He was not a candidate for re-nomination or re-election in 1842.

He resumed the practice of law and served as a presidential elector for the Whig ticket in the 1844 presidential election. He was elected to the Kentucky House, where he served in 1846 and as speaker.

He was elected by the legislature as a Whig to the US Senate and served from March 4, 1847, to March 3, 1853. He served as a member of the Senate during the Mexican War.

Underwood first appeared in the Senate on Monday, December 6, 1847. Senator John J. Crittenden presented his credentials from the governor and the General Assembly. Underwood was sworn in by the president of the Senate, Vice President George M. Dallas.

Underwood's most significant legislation was the amendment that helped establish a railroad from Louisville to St. Louis via New Albany, Indiana, and Alton, Illinois. The following comes from the *Senate Journal* on Friday, January 24, 1851:

> The Senate proceeded to consider, as in Committee of the Whole, the bill (S. 393) granting the right of way and making a grant of lands to the States of Louisiana and Mississippi in aid of the construction of a railroad from Madisonville, in the State of Louisiana, to Jackson, in the State of Mississippi.
>
> On motion by Mr. Underwood to amend the bill by adding the following as additional sections (7, 8, 9, 10, 11 and 12): Sec. 7. And be it further enacted, That there be, and is hereby, granted to the States of Indiana and Illinois, in aid of the construction of a railroad from Louisville, in the State of Kentucky, by New Albany, in Indiana, and Mount Carmel, on the Wabash river, to Alton, with a branch to a point on the Mississippi river opposite St. Louis, in Missouri.[2]

He was not a candidate for re-election to the Senate. He was a member of the Kentucky House from 1861 to 1863. He also resumed the practice of law and engaged in farming.

During the Civil War, Underwood was a Unionist. His Warren County plantation, Mount Air, was described in the *New York Times*:

Mount Air was as much an anchor for the region as the limestone beneath its auburn soil. Josie's father, Warner, was until only two years earlier a congressman, and his older brother, Joseph, was a former State Supreme Court justice and United States senator who had just returned to the State Legislature. Both men were lawyers, Virginia-born and college-educated, and Whig devotees of Henry Clay. They were also owners of some 35 slaves between them. Yet they were unconditional Unionists, an unflinching political position the secession crisis had only further strengthened.[3]

Underwood died near Bowling Green in 1876 and was buried in Fairview Cemetery.

THOMAS "STONEHAMMER" METCALFE
(March 20, 1780–August 18, 1855)

- Class Three of Three
- Senate Service: June 23, 1848–March 3, 1849
- Political affiliation: Whig
- Residence at time of election: Nicholas County
- Served with President Polk
- Served under Governors Owsley and Crittenden

Thomas "Stonehammer" Metcalfe, a former Kentucky governor, was appointed to the Senate by Governor William Owsley. As one of the few stonemasons to serve in public life, he delighted in being called "Old Stonehammer." A vacancy occurred when Senator John J. Crittenden resigned to run for governor. Crittenden believed that by running for governor, he would assist Zachary Taylor in winning Kentucky as well as the presidency in 1848.

Owsley's appointment of Metcalfe was described by the *Louisville Morning Courier* as follows: "The appointment does Gov. Owsley much credit. Gov. Metcalfe is one of the truest, staunches and most reliable men in the Commonwealth, and we know of none who could better fill Mr. Crittenden's place or more worthily represent old Kentucky, in that most august and dignified body, the U.S. Senate."[1]

Metcalfe had served as a member of the US House from March 4, 1819, until his resignation June 1, 1828. One of the most important decisions he made as a House member concerned the 1824 presidential election, which had four candidates: Andrew Jackson, John Quincy Adams, William Crawford, and Henry Clay. None of the four candidates won a majority of the electoral votes, although Jackson received a majority of the popular vote. When the election was to be decided by Congress, Clay dropped out of the running and threw his support to Adams. On February 9, 1825, as a member of the US House, Metcalfe voted for John Quincy Adams.

Metcalfe had served as Kentucky's tenth governor from 1828 to 1832. He continued to be an ally of Henry Clay. He was nominated for governor as a National Democrat, which is what Clay's allies were called before the Whig Party formed in 1834. In 1848, as well as 1828, Metcalfe filled in for John J. Crittenden when Crittenden decided not to run for governor.

Metcalfe is ranked as one of the better governors of his time. He signed into law an Act for the Establishment of Uniform Schools in 1830. It was one of the first efforts to establish "common" or public schools throughout Kentucky. His administration knew that only a third of Kentucky's children were being educated; legislation left the establishment of local schools to the counties. As a good Whig, he sided politically with Henry Clay. While he supported Andrew Jackson regarding nullification, he opposed the "spoils system" as espoused by Jackson for his political cronies. Following Metcalfe's service as governor, he served as a state senator and president of Kentucky's Board of Internal Improvements.[2]

After his appointment to the Senate, he was sworn in on Monday, July 3, 1848.

During his brief tenure, Metcalfe served on the Committee on Military Affairs. When he served in the House, he served on the Committee on the Militia. Metcalfe was a veteran of the War of 1812, in which he served as a captain.

As his tenure in the Senate was less than nine months, Metcalfe did not leave much of a mark. As a Whig, he was often on the opposite side of a vote from Mississippi's Democratic Senator Jefferson Davis—the future president of the Confederacy.

He voted for ending the slave trade in the District of Columbia and excluding slavery in the territory acquired from Mexico as a result of the Mexican War. This may be surprising, given that Kentucky was a slave state and that, as a member of the House, Metcalfe had opposed restrictions on slavery in the Louisiana Purchase. Here is the excerpt from the *Senate Journal* concerning the 1848 vote:

> In respect to slavery in the land acquired from Mexico by treaty from the Mexico after the war, Metcalfe voted for legislation

which would have prevented the spread on slavery into those territories.

Mr. Dix presented resolutions of the Legislature of the State of New York, instructing the Senators and requesting the Representatives of that State in Congress to use their best efforts to procure the enactment of laws for the establishment of governments for the territory acquired by the late treaty of peace with Mexico, and that, by such laws, involuntary servitude, except for crime, be excluded from such territory; to use their best efforts to preserve the territory thus acquired as common property, protect it from the claims of Texas, and prohibit the extension over it of the laws of Texas, or the institution therein of domestic slavery; and to use their strenuous efforts to procure the passing of a law to protect slaves from unjust imprisonment, and put an end to the slave trade in the District of Columbia; which were read.

> On motion by Mr. Dix, that they be printed,
> It was determined in the affirmative,
> Yeas ... 45
> Nays ... 6
> On motion by Mr. Dickinson, The yeas and nays being desired by one-fifth of the Senators present,
> Those who voted in the affirmative are,
> Messrs. Allen, Atchison, Atherton, Badger, Baldwin, Bell, Benton, Berrien, Bradbury, Breese, Butler, Cameron, Clarke, Clayton, Corwin, Davis, of Massachusetts, Dayton, Dickinson, Dix, Dodge, of Iowa, Douglas, Felch, Fitzgerald, Foote, Green, Hamlin, Houston, Hunter, Johnson, of Maryland, Johnson, of Louisiana, Johnson, of Georgia, Jones, King, Mason, Metcalfe[emphasis added], Miller, Niles, Pearce, Phelps, Rusk, Sebastian, Spruance, Turney, Underwood, Upham.
> Those who voted in the negative are,
> Messrs. Borland, Davis, of Mississippi, Downs, Fitzpatrick, Hannegan, Yulee.[3]

Upon leaving the Senate, Metcalfe returned to his farm, Forest Retreat, in Nicolas County. He died in 1855 and was buried in his family cemetery on Forest Retreat. Metcalfe County was named in his honor.

HENRY CLAY
(1777–1852)
Fifth Term

- Class Three of Three
- Senate Term: 1849-1852
- Political affiliation: Whig
- Residence at time of election: Fayette County (Lexington)
- Served with Presidents Taylor and Fillmore
- Served with Governors Letcher and Powell

This was Clay's last term and perhaps his most notable in the Senate when he crafted the "Compromise of 1850." He was in the House of Representatives when he crafted the Missouri Compromise in 1820. Clay had left the Senate in 1844 to prepare his campaign for the Presidency as a Whig. He narrowly lost that election to James K. Polk of Tennessee. He had sought the Whig nomination for President in 1848 but had lost out to eventual winner Zachary Taylor. It was at that time that his friendship and alliance with John J. Crittenden had dissolved due to Crittenden's support of Taylor.[1]

In 1848, with Crittenden's resignation from the Senate to become Kentucky's governor, Governor William Owsley offered to appoint Clay to Crittenden's seat. Clay refused the appointment, and Owsley appointed to the seat former Governor Metcalfe, who was later elected for the balance of the term ending at noon on March 3, 1849.

On a trip to New Orleans in February 1849, Clay received word that the Kentucky legislature had elected him to the Senate to succeed Metcalfe at noon on March 3, 1849. With the support of Governor Robert Letcher, Clay had won election by a 92–45 vote over former Senator and Vice President Richard M. Johnson, a Democrat.[2] Clay did not attend the session that began on March 4, 1849, which was held to confirm newly inaugurated President Taylor's cabinet appointments. Clay had recently been ill and was also recovering from a fall. In the late 1840s, Clay had been going to points south including New Orleans. On December 20, 1848, he had left Lexington to go to New Orleans via the Ohio and Mississippi Rivers to "escape Kentucky and its wintry blasts" and recuperate from his long and debilitating illness.[3]

Clay did not appear in the Senate until Monday morning, December 3, 1849. He received an ovation as he entered the Senate Chamber. One description has it—

> Seated in his usual place, Clay looked old and worn. He coughed a great deal. His head was partially bald on top, his hair fringed with iron gray streaks; his cheeks were shrunken, his nose look pinched, but his wide mouth was 'wreathed in genial smiles,' just as in years past. He always dressed in black with a white shirt, the collar of which stood high, covering his long neck and reaching to his ears. Nearly seventy-three years of age, Clay was back where he belonged, and little of importance seemed to have changed during his absence. He 'generally kissed the prettiest girls wherever he went,' played cards in his room, and enjoyed a large glass of bourbon whenever he relaxed.[4]

Upon Clay's arrival in Washington, he found himself in the midst of a government dealing with the fallout of winning the Mexican War. Territory in the form of California and New Mexico (New Mexico included the present states of New Mexico and Arizona) had been acquired as a result of the war. In the interim since the war, gold had been discovered in California and its population had swelled. Now the people of California were asking Congress for admission as a state without a period of territorial status. Under Mexican rule, these areas prohibited slavery. Southerners were opposed to admitting two more free states, thereby shifting the balance of power to the free states. Additionally, Texas claimed much of the New Mexico territory up to and including the city of Santa Fee. Then Texas had over $11 million in debt that it wanted the federal government to pay. The President at the time, Zachary Taylor, was unable to provide any leadership on these issues.[5] Then there were also the issues of the Mormons and the Utah Territory and the Fugitive Slave Act.

On April 13, 1850, the Senate approved the creation of a Committee of Thirteen that was comprised of six free state and six slave state senators, with Clay as Chair. On May 8, 1850, Clay presented the report to the Senate. It included three bills or pieces of legislation. The first was an amended Fugitive Slave Act, the second was to eliminate the District of Columbia slave market, and the third was called Clay's Compromise. It bundled all the legislation from the Committee on Territories concerning Mexican Cession. It admitted California as a "free state," established New Mexico and Utah Territories on the basis of popular sovereignty and adjusted the Texas boundary by having Texas give up the Rio Grande for $10 million.[6]

Unfortunately for Clay, President Zachary Taylor threatened to veto the compromise when it was first announced in May. However, President Taylor died in July. His successor Millard Fillmore supported the compromise and was an admirer of Clay. This is seen is Fillmore's consultation with Clay in reorganization of the president's cabinet. As there was bad blood between Clay and Crittenden at the time, Fillmore asked Clay if he would not hold it against him if he appointed Crittenden as attorney general. Clay gave Fillmore his assurances that making Crittenden his attorney general would be fine with him.[7]

Clay carefully guided the package of legislation through legislative debates for several weeks. However, Maine's Democratic senator proposed removing New Mexico from the legislative package. The removal of New Mexico threatened the Texas boundary settlement. Clay's work seemed to have been ruined. So, on August 5, 1850, he left Washington, D.C., for the cooler climes of Newport, Rhode Island.[8]

Fortunately, Senator Stephen A. Douglas, Democrat of Illinois, shifted strategies in getting Clay's package passed in Clay's absence by the end of August 1850.[9]

It is interesting to note the extent of Clay's celebrity. On December 16, 1850, Clay attended a performance of the renowned "Swedish Nightingale," Jenny Lind, with Daniel Webster. After the performance, Webster made a point of going backstage to see Miss. Lind. However, it was Henry Clay that Ms. Lind wanted to meet. Miss. Lind had heard Clay argue a case before the Supreme Court of the United States. She found his voice in speech "captivating." So, Clay made a special point to meet her.[10]

During late 1851, Clay's health worsened. In December, he submitted his resignation from the Senate, effective September 1, 1852. Unfortunately, his health became so bad that by May, he was unable to return to Kentucky. Henry Clay died in his rooms at the National Hotel with his son Thomas, his servant James Marshall, and Senator James C. Jones (a Whig from Tennessee who had rooms above his) at his side.[11]

Clay's death marked the first time in American history and one of the first times in history due to the telegraph and the railroad that mourning was instantaneous across thousands of miles. Clay died in Washington, D.C., at 11:17 a.m. of tuberculosis. By noon, his wife Lucretia in Lexington received the news by telegram from their son Thomas. Lucretia had heard the church bell throughout Lexington prior to receipt of the telegram. By 12:30 p.m., President Fillmore had closed all federal offices and that afternoon shops in Lexington closed in honor of Clay.

Henry Clay had a state funeral in Washington. He was the first person to lie in state in the Capitol rotunda.[12] His body was returned to Lexington with much ceremony for final services and burial in the Lexington Cemetery.

At the time of his death, Clay and his wife Lucretia had been married for more than fifty-three years. They had eleven children.

In his last will and testament, in addition to taking care of his family, he arranged for the gradual emancipation of his slaves.[13]

Clay's memory has been honored in many ways over the years. Many streets and even a few cities and towns have been named for him. There has been the submarine, the USS Henry Clay. Henry Clay High School in Lexington was named in Clay's honor.

Counties in the following sixteen states were name "Clay" in honor of Senator Henry Clay—Alabama, Florida, Georgia, Illinois, Indiana, Kansas, Kentucky, Minnesota, Mississippi, Missouri, Nebraska, North Carolina, South Dakota, Tennessee, Texas, and West Virginia.

Clay County, Iowa, was named for Henry Clay Jr., who was killed in the Mexican War.

DAVID MERIWETHER
(1800–1892)

- Class Two of Three
- Senate Service: July 6, 1852–August 31, 1852
- (Territorial Governor of New Mexico 1853–1857)
- Political affiliation: Democratic
- Residence at time of election: Louisville
- Served with President Fillmore
- Served with Governor Powell

Kentucky Secretary of State David Meriwether was appointed by Kentucky Governor Lazarus Powell, a Democrat, to serve the two months following the death of Henry Clay.

Meriwether was born in Louisa County, Virginia, on October 30, 1800. He was a cousin of Meriwether Lewis of Lewis and Clark fame. As a child, he moved with his family from Virginia to Kentucky.

In February 1823, Meriwether married Sarah H. Leonard, who lived directly across the Ohio River from his home in Kentucky. The newly married couple settled on land given to them by Meriwether's father in Jefferson County, Kentucky, where Meriwether farmed and practiced law. He began a long career in state politics and served in the Kentucky House of Representatives from 1832 to 1845. In 1846, he was an unsuccessful Democratic candidate for the US Congress. In

1849, he was a delegate to the State Constitutional Convention and served as secretary of state of Kentucky from September 3, 1851, until July 5, 1852.

Henry Clay had submitted his letter of resignation from the US Senate dated December 17, 1851, to be effective September 1, 1852. Clay submitted his resignation in December 1851 so that the Whig majority in the legislature would be able to elect his successor. If he had submitted during the summer of 1852, Kentucky's Democratic governor would have been able to appoint his successor.

Henry Clay died in Washington, D.C., on June 29, 1852. The legislature was not in session at the time of Clay's death, and the commission of Clay's designated successor, Whig Archibald Dixon, was not effective until September 1, 1852. Governor Powell appointed Kentucky Secretary of State David Meriwether, a Democrat.

A review of the *Senate Journal* during his tenure indicates that the most significant legislation or resolution sponsored by Meriwether concerned the canal in Louisville. On Friday, August 6, 1852, it stated:

> Mr. Meriwether submitted the following resolution; which was considered by unanimous consent, and agreed to: Resolved, That the Committee on Roads and Canals be requested to inquire into the propriety of making an appropriation sufficient to purchase the remainder of the stock in the Louisville and Portland canal, owned by individuals, and thereafter reducing the tolls on said canal to a sum sufficient to cover all necessary repairs and the working thereof.[1]

Meriwether's congressional biography indicates that he was not appointed to serve on any Senate committees during his two-month tenure.

Even though Meriwether's term ended in September, he was paid until December 20, 1852, per the following resolution, which was read on December 21, 1852, and passed on January 5, 1853:

> Mr. Rusk submitted the following resolution; which was read: Resolved, That the honorable David Meriwether, late a member of the Senate from the State of Kentucky, be paid his mileage and per diem up to the 20th day of December, inclusive. While only a 'benchwarmer' in his Congressional career, he impacted the history of New Mexico more than Kentucky.[2]

David Meriwether was the third governor of New Mexico Territory, serving from 1853 to 1857, and served as superintendent of Indian affairs for New Mexico. He had a colorful early career as a would-be trader in Spanish-colonial New Mexico, which figured into his 1853 appointment, along with his family relationship with President Franklin Pierce.

President Pierce, a cousin by marriage of Meriwether, appointed him governor of New Mexico Territory. Meriwether's experience in the fur trade required dealings with Native Americans. His early experiences in New Mexico was an important factor in justifying his appointment. In his first interview with Pierce, Meriwether demonstrated his grasp of issues concerning the Mexican border. Pierce was concerned that new hostilities between the US and Mexico were likely to break out, and one of Meriwether's first duties as governor was to help in the resolution of the border issues and achieve better relations between the two countries. On his way to New Mexico, an encounter with a party of Kiowa Indians resulted in the release of two captured Mexican girls. When he reached Santa Fe, Meriwether quickly sent the girls down to El Paso and then to their homes in Chihuahua, thereby winning the support of Chihuahua Governor Angel Trias. After the signing of the Gadsden Purchase between the US and Mexico on December 30, 1853, Meriwether successfully negotiated with Governor Trias to transfer the disputed territory in southern New Mexico from Mexico to the US's possession.[3]

Governor Meriwether played a large role in the treaty negotiations with the Utes, Apaches, and Navajos, which produced at least a brief period of relative peace in New Mexico.

He resigned as governor in 1857 and returned to his family in Kentucky, where he spent the rest of his long life. In 1858, he was elected to the Kentucky House of Representatives, where he served as its Speaker in 1859. He served several terms over the next twenty-seven years, the last one at age eighty-five. He died at home in 1892 at age ninety-two. He is buried in Cave Hill Cemetery in Louisville, Kentucky.

Part V
1852–1861
Pre-Civil War Tensions

When Henry Clay died in June 1852, Kentucky was without a dominant political leader for the first time since statehood. Prior to Clay and his Whig Party, the dominant political leadership had centered on Kentucky's first and fifth governor, Isaac Shelby and his associates. John J. Crittenden would have been the logical choice to assume the mantel of Clay. However, Crittenden was of the same generation as Clay, and new generation politicians born in the nineteenth century were competing with Crittenden, who was sixty-five (born in 1787) when Clay died.

During this time, the nation faced tensions over slavery and westward expansion, as well as the authority of the federal government. One of the first tests of the authority of the federal government came from Brigham Young and the Mormon settlement of Utah. Former Kentucky Governor and future US Senator Lazarus Powell was sent to Utah to negotiate with Brigham Young in order to bring federal law to Utah Territory.

In 1854, Congress, under the leadership of Senator Stephen Douglas of Illinois, essentially repealed Clay's work by passing the Kansas-Nebraska Act. Prior to the Kansas-Nebraska Act, Kansas was designated as a territory that would be "free." The Kansas-Nebraska Act allowed the voters of the territories to vote on whether they would become "free" or "slave" states. Consideration of the admission of Kansas and Nebraska as states brought civil war to Kansas as early as 1856. In May 1856, pro-slavery activists sacked and burned the city of Lawrence, Kansas, where many abolitionists had settled. Additionally, there was heated debate in Congress. Prior to admission, a state had to have its proposed constitution approved by Congress. In Kansas, a group of citizens had a convention in Topeka and created a constitution that prohibited slavery. A rival group met in the town of Lecompton and wrote a constitution that would allow slavery in Kansas should it become a state. President Buchanan endorsed the Lecompton Constitution. Congress and Kansas voters rejected the Lecompton Constitution. However, prior to the rejection of the Lecompton Constitution, there was much bloodshed in Kansas. Kansas voters rejected the Lecompton Constitution, and Kansas was finally admitted to the Union in 1861.

Anti-immigrant sentiment was seen in this period, reflected in the anti-immigrant No Nothing and American Parties. Following the 1840s, Catholic immigrants from Ireland (fleeing the Great Potato Famine) and Germany (fleeing the Revolutions of 1848) seemed unsettling to many Americans.

Senator Archibald Dixon, a supporter of the Kansas-Nebraska Act, convinced Stephen Douglas to include language that repealed the prohibition on slavery north of 36° 30'.

John J. Crittenden attempted to avoid civil war by uniting moderates in the Senate. He authored a series of amendments to the US Constitution known as the Crittenden Compromise, which, had they been passed by Congress, may have averted Civil War.

ARCHIBALD DIXON
(1802–1876)

- Class Three of Three
- Senate Service: September 1, 1852–March 3, 1855
- Political Affiliation: Whig
- Residence at time of election: Henderson County
- Served with Presidents Fillmore and Pierce
- Served with Governor Powell

Archibald Dixon was born April 2, 1802, in Caswell County, North Carolina. Most sources say he was born near Red House. A North Carolina paper of the period reported that he was born in a log house three miles from Yanceyville.[1] His father, Captain Wyn Dixon, and grandfather, Colonel Henry Dixon, were military officers in the American Revolution. His mother, Rebecca Hart Dixon, was a relative of Henry Clay's wife Lucretia Hart. The family moved from North Carolina to the Henderson area due a loss of his family's assets. Dixon attended the common schools in Henderson County and read law.[2]

Dixon was elected to represent Henderson County in the Kentucky House of Representatives in 1830, serving three consecutive one-year terms through 1833. Following this, he returned to his law practice and, in 1835, partnered with Lazarus W. Powell. From 1836 to 1840, he represented Henderson, Daviess, and Hopkins Counties in the Kentucky Senate. The next year, he returned to the Kentucky House, serving from 1841 to 1843. In 1844, Dixon was chosen as the Whig nominee for lieutenant governor on a ticket with William Owsley. Dixon defeated his opponent, William S. Pilcher, by more than 11,000 votes. At the expiration of his term, the Whig party considered nominating Dixon for governor but instead chose the more prominent and experienced John J. Crittenden, who defeated Dixon's former law partner, Lazarus Powell.

Dixon was married twice. In 1834, he married Elizabeth Pollitt. Elizabeth and Archibald had six children. One of his daughters, Rebecca, married Governor John Young Brown (1891–1895) of the nineteenth century.[3] Elizabeth died in 1852. In 1853, he married Susan Peachy Bullitt.

The voters of Henderson County chose pro-slavery Dixon to represent them at the Constitutional Convention of 1849. He was narrowly defeated by future Senator James Guthrie as President of the Convention. However, Guthrie appointed him to one of the ten standing committees—"The Committee on the Executive for the State at Large."[4] During the deliberations, Dixon made speeches in favor of preserving slavery, with the emphasis that slavery was a property matter. He was also outspoken about the need for judges to be elected by popular vote of the people.[5] Prior to the Constitution of 1850, judges were appointed in Kentucky.

In 1851, he unsuccessfully ran for governor as a Whig. He was defeated by Lazarus Powell, his former law partner and a resident of Henderson.

Henry Clay submitted his resignation from the Senate on December 17, 1851. Less than a month later, Dixon was elected by the legislature on the seventh ballot on December 30, 1851, to replace Clay.[6] He was the last Whig elected by the Kentucky legislature.

There was a snag in getting Dixon seated. Clay issued his resignation on December 17, 1851, to be effective on September 1, 1852. Unknown to Clay, he would die on Tuesday June 29, 1852. Kentucky's Democratic governor, Lazarus Powell, took the opportunity to appoint Kentucky Secretary of State David Meriwether to the vacancy for July and August.

When the Senate resumed business on December 6, 1852, Archibald Dixon, with his credentials, was escorted by Tennessee Senator Jones. As Dixon prepared to take the oath of office, an objection was made by California Senator Gwin. As a result, the proceedings to seat Dixon were suspended.[7] After investigation and discussion, a vote was taken to seat Dixon. The vote was passed 27–16. His senate colleague Underwood voted for him. His future friend Stephen Douglas of Illinois voted against him being seated.[8]

As a senator who strongly believed in the institution of slavery, Archibald Dixon is remembered most for his Senate tenure as the man who gave Illinois Senator Stephen Douglas the language that repealed the Missouri Compromise in the Kansas-Nebraska Act of 1854.[9] In 1854, Douglas, with Dixon's suggestion, repealed the provision that required all states above latitude 36°30' to be "free" states. In 1820, Henry Clay had put together the Missouri Compromise, allowing Missouri to be admitted as a slave state if Maine was admitted as a free state at the same time. Then every state above 36°30' would be admitted as free, and most states below that latitude would be slave states. In 1854, there were those who wanted Kansas to be admitted as a slave state. The Kansas-Nebraska Act put the decision to the vote of the settlers of the territory seeking to become a state. Dixon spent a significant part of February 4, 1854, speaking in favor of repealing the Missouri Compromise of 1820 in favor of "Popular Sovereignty" in the Kansas-Nebraska Act.[10] The repercussions included pre-civil war bloodshed in Kansas Territory prior to the Civil War.

On June 28, 1854, Dixon[11] spoke in response to the Committee on the Judiciary considering a petition of 2,900 citizens praying for the repeal of the "Fugitive Slave Act." It is interesting to note his words regarding abolitionists:

> I know from my friend from Tennessee (Senator Jones), in his denunciation of Abolitionism—and which I agree, with him, 'is a curse to the country, and will continue to be so until it is utterly eradicated from all political associations—'[12]

By 1855, the Whig Party was essentially no more. He cooperated more with his Democratic colleagues in the Senate. It was reported in the Raleigh N.C. paper, "His old party—the Whig—no longer exists."[13] The reaction in Kentucky was not nearly so favorable:

> Hon. Archibald Dixon, the nabob of Henderson, the man who began a race with Lazarus Powell 10,000 in his favor, and came out 800 behind, has declared his intentions to act with the Democratic Party. The Ohio river still runs on—[14]

During the infamous Illinois Senate election of 1858, Dixon publicly endorsed Douglas over Lincoln.[15]

In 1861, Dixon joined Kentuckians John J. Crittenden, James Guthrie, and Charles Wickliffe in the border state peace conferences.[16] Though Dixon believed in slavery, he still believed in keeping Kentucky as part of the Union.

Dixon died on Sunday, April 23, 1876, at 11:00 p.m., at the age of seventy-four. His funeral was at the Presbyterian Church of Henderson on April 25, 1876. It was said the cause of death was "complication of disorders and softening of the brain." In addition to reviewing his civic contributions, his obituary said Dixon was "Southern in every instinct and sympathy of his being, he was a devotee to the union of the States."[17]

The Webster County seat of Dixon, Kentucky, was named in honor of Senator Archibald Dixon.

JOHN BURTON THOMPSON
(1810–1874)

- Class Two of Three
- Senate Service: 1853–1859
- Political affiliation: Know-Nothing/Whig
- Residence at time of election: Mercer County
- Served with Presidents Pierce and Buchanan
- Served with Governors Powell and Charles Morehead

The lone "Know-Nothing" Party member elected to the Senate from Kentucky was John Burton Thompson of Mercer County. With the decline of the "Whig" Party and the death of Henry Clay in 1852, many Whigs became associated with the Know-Nothing or American Party. In the statewide election held in 1855, the Commonwealth elected its only "Know-Nothing" governor, Governor Charles Slaughter Morehead. The Know-Nothing Party was an anti-immigrant party. It opposed the increased immigration of foreign-born Roman Catholics.[1]

Senator Thompson was born in Mercer County near Harrodsburg on December 14, 1810. He was named for his father, and his mother was Miss Nancy Robards. He was the second of ten children. He attended the common schools of the area before studying law. He was admitted to the bar and practiced law in Harrodsburg and Mercer County, Kentucky. He served as the commonwealth (prosecuting) attorney. He was elected by his community to both houses of the legislature. He served a term in the Kentucky Senate from 1829 to 1833 and a term in the state House in 1835 and 1837.

He was elected as a Whig to fill the unexpired term of Congressman Simeon H. Anderson, beginning in December 1840. He was later re-elected, serving until March 3, 1843, as the congressman of the old Fifth Congressional District. He was reelected to that seat and served from 1847 to 1851.

Thompson was elected lieutenant governor as a Whig in 1851 with Democratic Governor Lazarus Powell. The following year, the legislature elected him to the Senate seat held by Joseph Underwood, a fellow Whig.

According to the *Daily Nashville Union*, in Thompson's election by the legislature, he defeated Stone73–65.[2]

He was administered the oath of office by Michigan Senator Lewis Cass on Friday, March 4, 1853. Following the administration of the oath to Thompson and other new senators, the Senate reelected Senator David R. Atchison of Missouri as president pro tempore of the Senate. Then the senators joined the rest of Washington outside to watch the inauguration of President Franklin Pierce.[3]

In April 1854, he spoke in favor of the Homestead Bill.[4]

In December 1854, Mr. Adams of Mississippi brought forth legislation to amend the naturalization process. Mr. Adams was concerned with the influx of foreigners. His concern was that they would vote with "one mind." An article in the *Louisville Daily Courier* pointed out that Mr. Adams did not associate with those who called themselves "Know-Nothings." It also criticized Kentucky's Know-Nothing Senator Thompson, whose "sentiments are unpalatable to foreign population of our country."[5]

In 1858, he broke with his Kentucky colleague Senator John J. Crittenden in voting to admit Kansas into the Union under the LeCompton Constitution. The LeCompton Constitution would have admitted Kansas as a "slave" state.[6] Kansas would not be admitted until the presidency of Abraham Lincoln as a "free state."

Senator Thompson died in Harrodsburg on January 7, 1874. He was buried in Spring Hill Cemetery. According to his obituary, five years prior to his death, he married Mrs. Mary Hardin Bowman, daughter of Judge Chinn, who survived him.[7]

JOHN JORDAN CRITTENDEN
(1787–1863)
Fourth Term

- Class Three of Three
- Senate Service: 1855–1861
- Residence at time of election: Woodford County
- Served with Presidents Pierce and Buchanan
- Served with Governors Powell, Morehead, and Magoffin

In measuring a Senator's accomplishments, John J. Crittenden's last term in the Senate was the one in which he made the biggest impact upon Kentucky and the nation.

After leaving the Senate in 1848, John J. Crittenden served as Kentucky governor and then as US attorney general for President Millard Fillmore. Crittenden had sought the governorship in 1848 in order to help Zachary Taylor win Kentucky's twelve electoral votes. Taylor's Democratic opponent, Lewis Cass of Michigan, ran with General William Orlando Butler of Carrollton, Kentucky.

As an early Taylor supporter, Crittenden sacrificed his longstanding friendship and political alliance with Henry Clay. Crittenden supported General Zachary Taylor prior to Clay getting into the race on April 10, 1848. Crittenden stayed with Taylor even after Clay's announcement.[1] In a note responding to Clay's note to him about the announcement, Crittenden replied that he hoped that "it may turn out for the best."

Once Taylor became the Whig nominee, Crittenden played a major role managing Taylor's campaign in Kentucky and other states.[2] This rupture in the relationship between Clay and Crittenden was never the same after 1848. Prior to Clay's death in 1852, the pair tentatively reconciled, though their relationship was never the same.[3] Crittenden visited Henry Clay for the last time in May 1852. After the attorney general left, Clay turned to his son Thomas and said, "Treat him kindly."[4]

During this interlude, Crittenden's personal life changed. His second wife, Maria Todd, whom he married in 1826, died in 1851. A month after Crittenden returned to Kentucky in July 1851 after participating in a tour by Fillmore's cabinet commemorating the completion of the Erie Railroad to Buffalo, Maria became seriously ill. On September 6, it was thought that her illness was on the mend. As Crittenden was getting ready to go back to Washington and resume his duties as US attorney general, Maria took a turn for the worst and died at about 10:30 a.m. on September 8, 1851. Maria had been his constant companion and had been one of the few congressional wives to accompany her husband to Washington.[5]

However, by 1853, the twice-widowed Crittenden married Elizabeth Ashley, a widow.

Just prior to leaving the Senate in 1848, Crittenden had split with Clay over the 1848 Whig nomination for President.

When Crittenden returned to the Senate in 1855, it was for the first time that he was not under the shadow of Henry Clay. Crittenden's road back to the Senate had been filled with uncertainty.

In November 1851, the General Assembly had convened to elect a successor to Senator Joseph Underwood, whose term would expire in 1853. Crittenden was interested in succeeding Underwood because his term as attorney general for the Fillmore administration would be over in March 1853. However, his candidacy for the Senate seat for 1853 to 1859 did not receive the support as it might have in the past. In addition to the incumbent Senator Underwood, Archibald Dixon and George Robertson, the House Speaker and a friend of Clay's, also wanted the seat.

Upon Crittenden's public announcement as a candidate, Democrats desirous of defeating Crittenden and embarrassing the Whigs pledged to vote against him at all costs, even if it meant electing Dixon. The legislature cast its first two ballots on November 17, 1851. Crittenden's allies held back his name from nomination to spare him almost certain defeat for those two days. Balloting deadlocked for several days, with

Clay supporters throwing their support to Dixon, Robertson, and Lieutenant Governor John B. Thompson, a compromise candidate. Another compromise was proposed whereby Clay, his health failing, would resign his Senate seat, creating two Senate vacancies and allowing both Dixon and Crittenden to be elected. The legislature postponed the election until December 11, 1851, in order to give Clay time to respond. However, Clay did not respond. On the evening of December 11, the Whigs knew that neither Crittenden nor Dixon had the votes to be elected. Therefore, Lieutenant Governor John B. Thompson was elected as the compromise candidate.[6] Though this was a compromise, it was considered a disappointment. It was noted that Thompson's election had cost the state $12,500 in legislative expenses. Many wondered if Thompson's service would be worth that much to Kentucky.[7]

A week after the Thompson's election, Clay announced that he would resign effective in September 1852. This would allow the Whig-dominated legislature to select Clay's successor rather than the Democratic Governor Powell. Crittenden declined the opportunity to be elected by the legislature to succeed Clay in 1852. As a result, Archibald Dixon was elected to serve in the remainder of Clay's term, effective in September 1852. However, Clay died on June 24, 1852, a little over two months prior to the effective date of his resignation and the effective date of Dixon's term as specified by the legislature. In the meantime, Kentucky's Democratic Governor Lazarus Powell appointed Kentucky Secretary of State David Meriwether to represent Kentucky for the less than two months before Dixon was to assume the seat on September 1, 1852.

Three weeks before Clay's death in June 1852, Clay sent for Crittenden, and the two were reconciled; Crittenden delivered a eulogy for Clay in September 1852, publicly dispelling the feud. After Clay's death, Crittenden became the most prominent Whig leader in Kentucky.

In 1853, the legislature was to elect a successor to Senator Dixon. Now satisfied that the feud between Clay and Crittenden had ended, Dixon did not seek reelection, leaving Crittenden with no Whig opposition. On a joint vote of the two houses of the General Assembly, Crittenden was elected 78–59 over Governor Lazarus Powell.

Archibald Dixon, who was elected by the legislature to serve the final two years of Clay's original term ending in March 1855, decided not to seek reelection. On January 10, 1854, the Whig-controlled legislature elected Crittenden 78–59 over Governor Lazarus Powell.[8]

Though the terms for newly elected members began on March 3, 1855, the first session did not begin until December. In the meantime, the nation was consumed with violence and political intrigue in Kansas. Kansas elected its first territorial delegate to Congress in November 1854.

Crittenden was sworn in on Monday, December 3, 1855.[9] On December 12, 1855, Crittenden was appointed to the Committee on Finance and the Committee on Retrenchment.[10] This new Congress was the first one elected since the formation of the Republican Party in the summer of 1854. Due to political flux, it was difficult—if not impossible—to determine the political affiliation of each member. In the House, no party had a majority. The makeup was thought to be about a hundred Republicans, eighty-Democrats, and about forty-five Americans or Know-Nothings.[11] The Senate had ended the Thirty-Fourth Congress with thirty-five Democrats, nine Republicans, two members of the Free-Soil Party, eight Whigs and seven vacancies. Crittenden was still considered a Whig at this time.

On or about March 17, 1858, Senator John J. Crittenden delivered what has been transcribed as a sixteen-page speech on the floor of the Senate regarding the admission of Kansas to the Union.[12]

Crittenden begins his speech doubtful about the support (from the residents of Kansas) of the constitution submitted with Kansas' application for statehood. Crittenden alleges that there was fraud not only in the vote on the proposed constitution but also in the election of the territorial legislature. His speech was considered one of the most important statements on the subject of the issue. He reiterated throughout the speech that he did not believe the Lecompton Constitution and the territorial government that sponsored it represented the "will and voice" of the people of the territory of Kansas.[13]

On the vote on the Kansas Bill in May of 1858, Crittenden voted no.[14]

Crittenden had proposed a compromise on Kansas's Lecompton Constitution. Senator Crittenden received criticism for his opposition to the admission under the Lecompton Constitution.[15] Because of this speech, Crittenden was accused of contracting "Black Republican Malaria" which ended his career. Then it goes on to imply that perhaps his actions were those of someone who might be trying to unite North and South in order to lead a new party in the 1860 presidential election.

On his return home to Kentucky, he was warmly greeted in Cincinnati before going over to Covington and his home state of Kentucky.[16]

Beginning in the fall of 1858, Senator Crittenden began to systematically attack both Democrats and Republicans. It was his belief that the leaders of both the Republican and Democratic parties were selfish and intolerant and working to break up the nation that he had worked so hard to preserve. He had reluctantly become part of the "American Party," despite the religious prejudices of many of its leaders as he saw it as the only to preserve the nation.

On January 4, 1859, Crittenden was one of two Kentuckians who spoke at the opening of the new Senate Chamber. The other was Vice President John Breckinridge.[17]

Crittenden was part of the Constitutional Union Party. As a former Whig, Crittenden had begun to openly criticize both Democrats and Republicans in the fall of 1858.[18] It was his belief that the leadership of both parties of the day were leading the nation into a breakup of the union due to their constant agitation about slavery. He met with fifty members of the "Opposition" in Congress. He laid out his concerns about slavery and related agitation as well as radical.

After the election of Republican Abraham Lincoln of Illinois in November 1860, the most important work of Crittenden's career began. On December 18, 1860, Senator Crittenden proposed to amend the Constitution of the United States by introducing six amendments (see Appendix 5). These amendments included the banning of slavery above the 36° 30 line from the East Coast to the West Coast. It also stated in Article Two that Congress would not have power to abolish slavery in the District of Columbia. Then finally, it would "shore" up the enforce of the Fugitive Slave Act. It was introduced by Crittenden as SB 50 and held over for a second reading.[19]

On December 31, 1860, the Senate unanimously agreed to consider SB 50 for Wednesday January 2, 1861, at one o'clock.[20] The Senate adjourned on January 2 without hearing SB 50.[21] On January 3, Pennsylvania Senator William Bigler brought two petitions from citizens of Philadelphia in support of Crittenden's amendments. The Senate voted to allow the legislation "lie on the table".[22] On January 9, Senator Bigler brought sixty-six petitions from the citizens of Philadelphia supporting Crittenden's compromise.[23]

On January 11, 1860, Senator Bigler introduced three more petitions from citizens of Philadelphia and one petition from the citizens of Lancaster County, Pennsylvania. His colleague Senator Cameron brought in eleven more petitions in support of Crittenden's legislation from Philadelphia.[24] On Friday January 12, Senators Cameron and Bigler submitted more petitions from citizens of Philadelphia and Lancaster County in support of Crittenden's compromise.

On January 14, 1861, Crittenden voted with the majority 27–24 against admission of Kansas into the Union as a state.[25] His colleague Senator Dixon voted no as well. On the same day, Crittenden presented a petition from the citizens of Annapolis, Maryland, in support of the compromise.

On January 16, Senator James A, Bayard, Jr. presented a petition from the citizens of Wilmington, Delaware, in support; Senator Anthony Kennedy also presented a petition from citizens of Frederick County, Maryland. Senator Bigler presented more petitions from Philadelphia, Port Clinton, and Lehigh, Pennsylvania.[26]

Crittenden's last term in the Senate ended on the day Lincoln was sworn into office. However, the Kentucky Senate requested that he remain and continue his work of conciliation as long as he judged it worthwhile. At the same time, there was a possibility that he would be joining the US Supreme Court as an associate justice. Justice John A. Campbell was considering resigning after his home state of Alabama seceded. President Lincoln had decided to appoint Crittenden to the vacancy. However, Campbell reconsidered and decided not to resign.[27]

Crittenden spent the last weeks of his Senate term attempting to save the Union and avoid civil war with what would be known as the Crittenden Compromise. In some newspapers, there was the reflection of hope that Crittenden's efforts would bear fruit. In the *Summit County Beacon* (Akron, Ohio), there were at least two articles on Crittenden's meetings.[28] Crittenden's Compromise would include six amendments to the US Constitution. Provisions would include slavery would be prohibited above latitude 36 degrees; 30 minutes as agreed in the Missouri Compromise. Fugitive slave laws were to be enforced and if not, the federal government would reimburse slave owners for rescued slaves. One of the proposed amendments would prohibit interference with slavery in any of the existing slave states.

Even after the election of Abraham Lincoln as president in 1860, Crittenden rejected the idea that secession was inevitable and continued to work for the preservation of the Union.

The compromise proposal was referred to a special committee proposed by Crittenden's fellow Kentucky senator, Lazarus Powell. Though it was believed that Republicans in general, including their representatives on the committee, were disposed to accept Crittenden's compromise or one substantially similar to it, President-elect Lincoln had already instructed his trusted allies in Congress to resist any plan to extend slavery into the territories. Consequently, when the committee held its first meeting, the Republican members blocked Crittenden's proposed compromise. However, they were finally voted on by the Senate soon after dawn on the last hours of the Thirty-Sixth Congress on March 4, 1861. They were defeated 19–20.[29]

Having failed to secure compromise at the federal level, Crittenden returned to Kentucky in early 1861, attempting to persuade his home state to reject the overtures of fellow southern states and remain in the Union. In May 1861, a conference was held to decide Kentucky's course in the war. The conference failed to produce a united course of action but adopted the policy of armed neutrality.

In April, the General Assembly called a convention of border states to be held in Frankfort in May. On May 27, 1861, Crittenden was chosen chair of the convention and called it to order. With war having largely precluded any good the meeting could have accomplished, only nine of Kentucky's twelve delegates were present, along with four from Missouri (out of seven elected), and one from Tennessee; Virginia, Maryland, and Delaware sent no delegates. The convention accomplished little beyond calling on the southern states to reconsider their secession and on the northern states to moderate their demands.[30]

President Lincoln called a special session of Congress to begin on July 4, 1861. Kentucky's elections were not scheduled until August 1861.[31] This resulted in a special election being set on June 20, 1861. Even before Crittenden had left Washington, a movement started to have him run for Congress from Henry Clay's former Ashland District, which was centered in Lexington. Crittenden agreed to run because the incumbent was William E. Simms, a southern sympathizer. Even though he was in his mid-seventies, Crittenden campaigned aggressively throughout the district. He and other Unionist candidates won nine of Kentucky's ten congressional districts.[32]

Crittenden died July 26, 1863 in Frankfort. At the time of his death, he was preparing to run for reelection to the US House of Representatives.

The inscription on Crittenden's tomb says:

For fifty years he devoted himself with inflexible integrity, consummate wisdom, and patriotic zeal, to the course and service of his native state, and his whole country.[33]

LAZARUS W. POWELL
(1812–1867)

- Class Two of Three
- Senate Service: 1859–1865
- Political affiliation: Democratic
- Residence at time of election: Henderson County
- Served with Presidents Buchanan and Lincoln
- Served with Governors Morehead, Magoffin, Robinson, and Bramlette

In January 1858, the Kentucky legislature elected former Governor Lazarus Powell to the seat held by John B. Thompson, whose term expired in March 1859. During the year between his election to the US Senate and his assumption of office, President Buchanan appointed Powell as an emissary or commissioner with Major Benjamin McCulloch to negotiate with the Mormons in Utah. In 1856, Powell had campaigned for the Buchanan and Breckinridge ticket.[1]

Lazarus Powell was born near Henderson, Henderson County, Kentucky, on October 6, 1812. He attended the public schools of Henderson County. He graduated from St. Joseph College in 1833. He studied law at Transylvania; he was admitted to the bar and commenced practice at Henderson in 1835 while farming at the same time. He was a member of the State House of Representatives in 1836. He served as a presidential elector for the Democratic ticket in 1844. He was an unsuccessful candidate for governor in 1848. He was elected governor of Kentucky in 1851 and served until the end of 1855.

During the 1860 presidential campaign, Powell appeared at meetings with John C. Breckinridge, one of the two Democratic candidates for president. He appeared at one such meeting in Louisville on July 14, 1860.[2] Powell was listed fourth on the list of seven speakers at the Jefferson County Courthouse.

Powell's association with Breckinridge and the "Peace Democrats" caused him to come under suspicion in the Unionist Kentucky legislature. On October 1, 1861, the Kentucky Senate passed a resolution 20–5 asking both Powell and Breckinridge to resign their seats. If they did not resign their seats, the resolution requested an investigation of their loyalty to the national government. It was sent to the Kentucky House, which adjourned without acting on the resolution.[3]

Senator Powell and fellow border state Democratic Senator Willard Saulsbury of Delaware tended to the extreme in their denunciation of Lincoln and his policies. They repeatedly condemned his anti-slavery policies and his authorization of the arrests of war opponents as tyrannical and certain to reduce support for the Union cause in their states. These Democrats professed loyalty to the Union — a loyalty that Republicans questioned, with good reason in the cases of Senator and former Vice President John C. Breckinridge of Kentucky and two Missouri senators as all three were expelled from the Senate after they joined the Confederacy. Union Democrats supported southern rights and claimed that Lincoln's real purpose in the war was first to end slavery then impose black equality upon the South.[4]

It can also be said that Powell's home state colleague Garrett Davis was just as opposed to Lincoln. With this in mind, one wonders about Davis' role in the Senate expulsion case of Powell. As the story of Powell's expulsion case is one of the few that merited a report of the Office of the Historian of the US Senate, it is reproduced below.

The Expulsion Case of Lazarus W. Powell of Kentucky (1862)

Issues
 Alleged disloyalty to the Union

Chronology
 Resolution introduced: Feb. 20, 1862
 Referred to committee: Feb. 20, 1862
 Committee report: March 12, 1862
 Senate vote: March 14, 1862

Result: Not Expelled

Background

At the onset of the Civil War, Peace Democrats, who advocated neutrality in the clash between the states, looked to Kentucky Senator John C. Breckinridge as their titular head. By the summer of 1861, however, Breckinridge had fled Washington to accept a position with the Confederacy. Left behind in the Senate was his Kentucky colleague and good friend, Lazarus Powell. A Democrat and a former governor of the state, Powell continued to insist that Peace Democrats were not merely Confederates in disguise, despite the actions of many who deserted to the South. As the war escalated and emotions heightened, Powell's position became increasingly awkward, especially among Unionists in Kentucky.

Statement of the Case

On February 20, 1862, Morton Wilkinson (R-MN) submitted a passionately worded resolution calling for Powell's expulsion. The resolution turned out to have been written by Powell's Kentucky colleague, Garrett Davis, who had been elected as a Unionist to fill Breckinridge's vacant seat. The lengthy list of charges concluded with the contention that 'Under the false and delusive cry of neutrality and peace, he has doubtless assisted to seduce hundreds and hundreds from loyalty and duty into rebellion and treason. He has not supported the Constitution of the United States, but he has sounded the charge to his recruits, and they have made the overt attack upon it.' The Senate referred the matter to the Committee on the Judiciary.

Response of the Senate

On March 12, 1862, the committee, chaired by Republican Lyman Trumbull of Illinois, recommended that the resolution not pass. Although the committee disapproved of Powell's former activities aimed at keeping Kentucky neutral, it found no clear evidence that Powell favored the rebellion.

Garrett Davis took immediate exception to the recommendation. Announcing that he acted at the insistence of the Kentucky legislature, Davis bitterly assailed Powell for attending pro-Confederate political rallies in June and September of 1861. Davis, although gracious to Powell personally, told the senators that their colleague traveled to Henderson, Kentucky, where Powell presided over a states' rights convention that adopted resolutions encouraging Kentucky to resist troops from either army. A Republican senator charged: 'This was long after the Battle of Bull Run. . ... It was when the Federal troops were marching upon Kentucky for the purpose of rescuing the State. . ... We had the solemn, stern, bloody fact of the existence of civil war; and even then, we find a Senator counseling his people to resist the Government in crushing out that rebellion.'

Republican Lyman Trumbull, however, eloquently defended the Democrat Powell. He reminded the Senate that, unlike Breckinridge and other secessionists who joined the Confederacy, Powell 'came to the Government of the United States to discharge his duties here.' 'He does not agree with me in sentiment,' Trumbull continued, 'his opinions are not my opinions; I do not agree with the views that he has so often announced here; but he is entitled to his own opinions; and no man is to be expelled from this body because he disagrees with others in opinion."

Powell himself, however, stated his case most effectively. Although he had not intended to speak after the committee recommended in his favor, he decided that Davis' virulent assault required a response. Addressing the Senate on March 14, Powell admitted attending the Kentucky rallies, which were sponsored by long-time friends and political acquaintances. Regarding the Confederacy, he observed, 'Breckinridge went there; I did not.' He insisted that he had attempted to use his position in the Senate to resolve national difficulties through conciliation and compromise, rather than coercion. While acknowledging that his efforts had been doomed to failure, Powell defied the senators to find any speech in which he did not call for a constitutional Union. 'If it comes to that, that a senator cannot speak and vote as he thinks proper and right without expulsion,' he concluded, 'then the majority are masters and the minority are slaves, and a seat in the American Senate would no longer be desired by an honest man or a patriot.' Convinced of his innocence, the Senate on March 14 voted down the resolution, 11 yeas to 28 nays, and permitted Powell to retain his seat.

Conclusion

Amid the confusing currents of sectional and party factionalism that swirled about his case, Powell probably benefited most from the Senate's growing wariness about defining loyalty and treason. Even clearly drawn partisan lines could alter quickly. By 1864, for example, both Garrett Davis and the Kentucky legislature had shifted their political sympathies to the South. Powell remained in the Senate until 1865, when he returned to his law practice in Kentucky, reconciled with both Davis and the state assembly. He died in 1867.

At the 1864 Democratic Convention in Chicago, the delegation for Delaware nominated Senator Lazarus Powell in nomination for the presidency. Powell withdrew his name from nomination, believing that the nominee should be from a non-slave state.

Powell left the US Senate in March 1865 and returned to the practice of law in Henderson.

Powell was a candidate for the US Senate in 1867 for the Senate seat that would be open effective in March 1869. Delegations from Washington County were lined up to vote for him at the state convention in 1867.[6]

Powell died on July 3, 1867, at 4:00 p.m. of apoplexy in Henderson, and his death was announced by future Governor John Young Brown.[7] He was buried in Fernwood Cemetery in Henderson. Powell County was named in Powell's honor.

JOHN C. BRECKINRIDGE
(1821–1875)

- Class Three of Three
- Senate Service: March 4, 1861–December 4, 1861
- Political affiliation: Democratic
- Residence at time of election: Lexington
- Served with President Lincoln
- Served with Governor Magoffin

Senator John C. Breckinridge remains the only member of the US Senate from Kentucky expelled from the Senate for treason. The Kentucky legislature elected Breckinridge while he was still vice president on December 12, 1859. All the Democratic members of the legislature voted for Breckinridge for the six-year senate term beginning on March 4, 1861. He succeeded Senator Crittenden. The opposition voted for Joshua Bell. In the House, the vote was 58– 38 for Breckinridge. In the Kentucky Senate, the vote was 23–14 for Breckinridge. The votes totaled 81–52.[1]

Prior to being elected to the US Senate by the Kentucky legislature, John C. Breckinridge served as President James Buchanan's vice president. During the Buchanan presidency, it seems there was very little contact between the two men. Because of this lack of interaction, Vice President Breckinridge barely had any influence with the president.

In June 1860, the national Democratic Party had split. In its first convention at Charleston, South Carolina, it was unable to come to a resolution as to its presidential nominee for 1860 until most of the southern delegates had bolted. Once the southern delegates left Stephen Douglas of Illinois, a former close friend of Breckinridge, had the necessary two-thirds of the votes of those present to secure the nomination. The southern delegates had a Democratic Convention at Baltimore. There, on June 23, 1860, Democrats nominated then-Vice President John C. Breckinridge.[2]

On March 4, 1861, John C. Breckinridge appeared in the Senate Chamber to be sworn into office with fourteen other new senators. He was sworn in by Vice President Hannibal Hamlin of Maine. Following his swearing-in, the Senate adjourned for the inauguration of Abraham Lincoln on the South Portico of the Capitol.[3]

His brief career as a US senator marked him early as a southern sympathizer.

In April 1861, the senator also called "Major" Breckinridge gave a rousing speech in Versailles before thousands. The article on the speech sounds as if Breckinridge is inciting the crowd to the Southern Cause. The articles say:

> Often as we have heard our gallant Senator he has never presented his ideas so clearly, nor has he given utterance to arguments so convincing so patriotic, so truthful, and so much like the man himself, as he did in his speech yesterday. His allusions to the war news was most apropos-like himself a soldier, he is anxious to know *whether Kentucky will be coerced into the support of a traitorous, treacherous, and treasonable administration.*[4] [Emphasis added]

The *Louisville Daily Courier* on August 9, 1861, marked him as the "leader of the Secessionists in the Senate and mouth-piece of disunion sentiment in Congress."

The *Senate Journal* of December 4, 1861, contains the resolution expelling Breckinridge from the Senate. It states as follows:

> *Mr. Chandler submitted the following resolution for consideration:*
> Resolved, That John C. Breckinridge be, and he hereby is, expelled from the Senate. The Senate proceeded, by unanimous consent, to consider the resolution; and the same having been amended, on the motion of Mr. Trumbull, to read as follows:
> Whereas John C. Breckinridge, a member of this body from the State of Kentucky, has joined the enemies of his country, and

is now in arms against the government he had sworn to support: Therefore—

Resolved, That said John C. Breckinridge, the traitor, be, and he hereby is, expelled from the Senate. On the question to agree to the resolution as amended,

- It was determined in the affirmative,
- Yeas . . . 37
- Nays . . . 00

On motion by Mr. Trumbull,

The yeas and nays being desired by one-fifth of the senators present, those who voted in the affirmative are,

Messrs. Anthony, Browning, Carlisle, Chandler, Clark, Collamer, Cowan, Dixon, Doolittle, Fessenden, Foot, Foster, Grimes, Hale, Harlan, Harris, Howe, Kennedy, King, Lane, of Indiana, Lane, of Kansas, Latham, McDougall, Morrill, Nesmith, Pomeroy, Rice, Sherman, Simmons, Sumner, Ten Eyck, Thomson, Trumbull, Wade, Wilkinson, Wilmot, Wilson.

So, the resolution as amended was agreed to—two-thirds of the senators present having voted in the affirmative.[5]

It should be noted that Breckinridge's colleague from Kentucky, Lazarus Powell, was not present for the vote.

Following his expulsion from the Senate, Breckinridge became a noted general and secretary of war for the Confederates. He served with General Jubal Early in the Battle of Monocacy outside of Washington, D.C. in July 1864. They were defeated by Union General Lew Wallace. Following the Civil War, he spent time in exile in Canada and France. He eventually returned to Kentucky, where he practiced law.

Breckenridge, Minnesota, and Breckenridge, Texas, even with the spelling difference, were named in his honor while he was vice president. Breckenridge, Colorado, was originally Breckinridge in his honor. When he joined the Confederacy, the "i" was changed to an "e."

His funeral in May 1875 was attended by most of Kentucky's statewide officeholders, former Confederate and Mexican War veterans, and at least one Union general, General George Pendleton of Ohio.[6]

Part VI

1861–1877

The Civil War and Reconstruction

While Kentucky stayed in the Union during the Civil War, most of its senators had southern sympathies and favored slavery. At the end of the Civil War, most opposed Reconstruction policies.

Perhaps the most controversial or newsworthy during their Senate tenure was Garrett Davis. Davis, a Central Kentucky slave owner, got frustrated when the federal government failed to act at the beginning of the Civil War. As a result of this frustration, Davis began to run guns to other Union sympathizers in Kentucky.

Guthrie's Senate tenure had potential but was cut short due to his age and health. Stevenson also had potential but was denied a second term due to a public view of his "aloofness" and an aggressive opponent in Bernie Beck.

McCreery served two terms. Some of McCreery's words and actions reflected a racist nature.

In many respects, the attitudes of Kentucky' post-Civil War senators reflect the idea that Kentucky became part of the Confederacy after the war.

GARRETT DAVIS
(1801–1872)

- Class Three of Three
- Senate Service: 1861–1872
- Political affiliation: Unionist and Democratic
- Residence at time of election: Bourbon County
- Served with Presidents Lincoln, Johnson, and Grant
- Served with Governors Magoffin, Robinson, Bramlette, Helm, Stevenson, and Leslie

Garrett Davis was an outspoken US Senator from Kentucky during the Civil War and Reconstruction. He was born in Mount Sterling, Kentucky, on September 10, 1801. He was the younger brother of Congressman Amos Davis.

He was educated in the common schools of the area. His first employment was in the office of the county clerk of Montgomery County and then with the clerk of neighboring Bourbon County. He studied law and was admitted to the bar in 1823. He practiced law in Paris, the county seat of Bourbon County. He was elected and served in the Kentucky House of Representatives from 1833 to 1835.

In 1838, he was elected as a Whig to the Twenty-Sixth Congress and to the three succeeding Congresses from March 4, 1839 to March 3, 1847. As a congressman, he served as chairman of the Committee on Territories in the Twenty-Seventh Congress. He served briefly with Democrat Jefferson Davis of Mississippi. Davis was not a candidate for reelection in 1846. Had Davis been reelected in 1846, he would have served with a new Whig congressman from Illinois—Abraham Lincoln.

Garrett Davis left electoral politics for almost a decade and resumed the practice of agricultural law. Though he was approached for electoral office, he declined the nomination for lieutenant governor in 1848. When the Whig Party fell apart in Kentucky, he was approached by some for the American Party for nomination for governor in 1855. After he declined, the American Party nominated his future Senate colleague Lazarus Powell, who was then elected. He was also approached by the same party for the nomination for the presidency in 1856 and was third in the American Party's convention voting, receiving eight votes. The eventual nominee, former President Millard Fillmore, received 1,779 votes. Although a slave owner and proponent of states' rights, he was opposed to secession and supported the Constitutional Union ticket in 1860.

Davis was elected as a Unionist to the US Senate to fill the vacancy caused by the expulsion of John C. Breckinridge in December 1861. Mr. Davis was elected after several ballots, in which he defeated James Guthrie and Joshua Bell. On the final ballot, Bell dropped out, and Mr. Beeman of Louisville switched his vote to Davis, which was surprising, as Guthrie was from Louisville. Davis won by one vote, 46–45. James Guthrie would be elected to the Senate about five years later.

While Davis took the seat of Breckinridge due to Breckinridge's disloyalty to the Union, Kentucky Senator Powell's loyalty was being called into question as set forth in the *New York Times* on December 17, 1861:

> Mr. Guthrie, or some other unflinchingly loyal Louisvillian, may soon be called on to take the place of Mr. Powell. Mr. Powell is generally suspected. He may deserve arraignment before the bar of the Senate. If he cannot there render a satisfactory account of his recent antecedents, associations, whereabouts, and whatabouts, and of his recent status, motives and designs, let him be expelled, and consigned to the disposal of the Executive for safe keeping.
>
> Mr. DAVIS will honor his State and his country. It is truly said of him that he has labored with wonderful perseverance and fearlessness to arm the loyal men of Kentucky, and place them in a condition and position to defend themselves and he fully represents the sentiments of his native commonwealth, that secession is no remedy for evils, but rather an aggravation, and that the surest guarantee for the protection of the rights of the South is to be found in the Union under the Constitution.[1]

Prior to his election to the Senate, Garrett Davis was suspected of assisting in the procuring of arms for Union sympathizers in Kentucky. There was a great frustration that many favoring the Confederacy were publicly arming themselves while Governor Magoffin did nothing. It was estimated that in the spring of 1861, Davis was responsible for the distribution of arms to Mason and Fleming, as well as to Boyd, 200; to Greenup, 200; to Montgomery, 100; to Bath, 100; to Clark, 100; to Madison, 100; to Fayette, 200; to Scott, 200; to Bourbon, 300; and to the city of Covington, 500.[2]

An opinion article in a 2011 *New York Times* may best describe why many pro-slavery Kentuckians such as Davis supported the Union:

> Social, racial, economic and political order—slavery and Union—depended upon a spirit of national comity and mutual respect. The makeup of Kentucky society, with its growing urban centers of Louisville, Lexington, Paducah and the northern towns near Cincinnati, along with mixed labor relationships in the countryside where resident slaves, hired slaves, free laborers and family farmers often toiled together in the fields, reinforced this sentiment. Slow and natural change was fine for Kentuckians. Political or social revolution, which Civil War would undoubtedly portend, was not.[3]

While Davis supported the Union, he also supported slavery and was a harsh critic of President Lincoln and his administration.

In April 1862, Davis was the most outspoken of the border state members of Congress who criticized the administration's freeing slaves in the District of Columbia and the order that forbid the Union Army from returning fugitive slaves. He was compared to the Confederacy's President Jefferson Davis.[4]

Senator Davis was also a critic of the Buchanan administration for its failure to act between the November 1860 election and Lincoln's inauguration in March 1861. These failures included,

> ... disproportionate share of Federal muskets and rifles found their way South, that "quantities of money lay ready for seizure at southern mints and "the Navy was scattered in distant seas, leaving but a very small part of it within immediate reach of the Government.

On December 15, 1862, Garrett Davis introduced a resolution set forth below.

Resolved, That after it became manifest that an insurrection against the United States was about to break out in several Southern States, James Buchanan, then President, from sympathy with the conspirators and their treasonable project, failed to take necessary and proper measures to prevent it; wherefore he should receive the censure and condemnation of the Senate and the American people.

The measure did not pass.[5]

Newspaper headlines during Davis's time in the US Senate indicated his outspokenness against the Lincoln administration and, later, Reconstruction. Examples include "The Change that is Going on Against the War—Garrett Davis" and "The Suit for Damages of the Hon. Garrett Davis against General Palmer."

Senator Davis filed suit in Bourbon County Circuit Court against General Palmer and Brisbie, the Kentucky Central Railroads, and others for enticing and carrying away some of his slaves.

Senator Fessenden of Maine—When Senator Henry Wilson of Massachusetts introduced a resolution to expel Senator Garrett Davis of Kentucky for disloyalty, Fessenden stated that he would vote neither to expel nor to censure the senator. Though garrulous Garrett said 'many violent and unreasonable things about the administration,' Fessenden argued: 'It was easy to imagine a state of things in any country when its government has become so obnoxious to the people that it was the duty of the senator to rise in his place and say, "I call upon the people to resist this outrageous exercise of authority."'[6]

After William Pitt Fessenden's remarks, Wilson withdrew his resolution.

On January 14, 1865, the *New York Times* described the January 13 encounter between Davis and Wilson as, "Garret Davis wasted three hours to-day abusing Henry Wilson in particular, and Massachusetts generally. The reply of the Bay State Senator was severe and triumphant. Applause in the densely packed galleries could not be repressed, and the effect of the speech was as observable on the crowded floor of the Senate."[7]

The *New York Times* published an editorial about the Senator on January 28, 1864. It was titled "The Proposed Expulsion of Senator Davis." The editorial begins:

—Without wishing to be at all intrusive, we venture to express the opinion that the Senate of the United States is wasting a good deal of valuable time and zeal in discussing the proposal to expel Mr. GARRETT DAVIS, of Kentucky, for words used in certain resolutions offered by him a few days since. The proposition seems to us to smack a good deal more of personal or party passion than zeal for the public good . . . to expel a Senator, and disfranchise his State, for words spoken in debate, would be an extraordinary stretch of power, only to be justified by the most extraordinary circumstances.[8]

The *Louisville Daily Journal* on April 29, 1867 references Davis's letter about Sumner, Wade, and Stevens, who were Congressional Radicals. They would not accept Democrats elected from Kentucky in 1866.

Following the impeachment trial of President Andrew Johnson, Davis filed his own opinion of the trial. "Hon. Garrett Davis' Opinion Filed in Connection with the Impeachment Trial" tells that Mr. Davis did not propose to believe the violence against blacks in the South as seen in the story about his debate with the Senator Wiley from West Virginia. Mr. Wiley has implied violence against blacks in Texas.[9]

During the summer of 1872, Davis traveled the state. He spoke on behalf of the Democratic Party for the election of November 1872. However, his health was not good, and he sat in a chair while giving a speech before the Democratic faithful in Covington.

On September 7, 1872, the *Courier Journal* reprinted a report from the *Mt. Sterling Sentinel* that Senator Davis had been stricken with paralysis at the home of his son-in-law, Wm. McGowan. It stated there was no hope of recovery.

He died in Paris, Bourbon County, Kentucky, on September 22, 1872. His funeral was held on September 26, 1872, at his home in Paris.[10] He was buried in the Paris Cemetery.

Davis County, Iowa, was named in his honor.

The Honorable Willis B. Machen was appointed by the governor and then elected by the legislature on January 21, 1873, to the vacancy caused by Davis's death. The January 21 results were announced by Lieutenant Governor Carlisle and Speaker McCreary.

JAMES GUTHRIE
(1792–1869)

- Class Two of Three
- Senate Service: 1865–1868
- Political affiliation: Democratic
- Residence at time of election: Louisville
- Served with Presidents Lincoln and Johnson
- Served with Governors Bramlette, Helm, and Stevenson

James Guthrie was born near Bardstown, Nelson County, Kentucky on December 5, 1792. He attended McAllister's Academy in Bardstown, engaged in transporting merchandise to New Orleans in 1812, studied law with Judge John Rowan, and was admitted to the bar in 1817.[1] He practiced in Bardstown. He was appointed commonwealth attorney in 1820 and moved to Louisville. He was a member of the State House of Representatives from 1827 to 1831, a member of the State Senate from 1831 to 1840, an unsuccessful candidate for election to the US Senate in 1835, a delegate of and president of the Kentucky Constitutional Convention in 1849, a road and railroad builder, and the founder and president of the University of Louisville.

In 1827, Guthrie succeeded in becoming a state legislator, served in Kentucky's lower house until 1831, when he was elected to the state Senate. During the nine years he was in that body, Guthrie served twice as Speaker pro tempore.

In 1828, Guthrie mustered enough support to secure city status for Louisville; it was the first time a town in Kentucky had achieved city status. He was elected to the new city council and quickly became chair of its most powerful committee, the finance committee. Guthrie served in the House until 1831, when he was elected to the Kentucky Senate. He was twice chosen president pro tempore of that body. He served on the Finance and Education Committees. In 1834, he co-founded the State Bank of Kentucky and served as one of its directors.

Back in Louisville, Guthrie called for the construction of a new building to house both city and county government offices. Secretly, he hoped Kentucky's capital would be moved to Louisville and the building would become the state's capitol building, but the courthouse and two other projects proposed by Guthrie—a waterworks and a bridge over the Ohio River connecting Louisville to Indiana—were halted by the Panic of 1837. The unfinished courthouse came to be known as "Guthrie's Folly," but it was still touted to bring the capital to Louisville in 1842. All three projects were eventually completed, and Guthrie's Folly became the Jefferson County Courthouse.

In 1836, a dispute arose among the medical faculty at Transylvania University. Guthrie encouraged some of the disgruntled faculty members to relocate to Louisville and start the Louisville Medical Institute, a precursor to the University of Louisville. In 1843, Guthrie became the third president of Louisville Medical Institute. In 1846, the Kentucky General Assembly chartered the University of Louisville, which subsumed the Louisville Medical Institute. Guthrie became president of the university on December 7, 1847 and served until his death. Working with the trustees of the common schools, Guthrie established a high school that met in the university's academic building, which eventually became Louisville Male High School.

Among the other projects Guthrie promoted were the creation of a Board of Health and free public schools in Louisville. He encouraged the city to purchase the turnpike between Louisville and Portland and purchase stock in the Louisville and Ohio Railroad. He also convinced the city to buy the land that would become Cave Hill Cemetery, his final resting place. Guthrie served on the Louisville City Council until 1839. In 1845, he was a delegate to a convention on internal improvements held in Memphis, Tennessee, and chaired by John C. Calhoun.

He was appointed secretary of the treasury by President Franklin Pierce from 1853 to 1857.

President Franklin Pierce recognized Guthrie's financial acumen and appointed him secretary of the treasury in 1853. Soon, he became the most influential member of Pierce's cabinet. A hard-money Democrat,

Guthrie was opposed to a national bank and to the issuance of small distinctive notes by free and charter banks. He advocated for the adoption of a universal currency that would be convertible to gold on demand. In his first report, he was critical of his predecessor, Thomas Corwin, because he had made private arrangements for debt repurchases. He also accused Corwin of conspiring with a New York port master to underreport duties collected and deposit them into a trust. Guthrie caused a brief public uproar by removing the port master from his post.

During Guthrie's tenure, the treasury had large budget surpluses due to the discovery of gold in California. He used much of these surpluses to pay down the national debt, which shrank from over $60 million in 1853 to $30 million in 1857.[2] He also purchased silver bullion for coinage, which aided struggling banks by returning money to circulation and increasing their depleted reserves. He encouraged more efficient processes in the Treasury Department as a whole and required monthly (rather than quarterly) reports from customs agents. In 1853, he employed Captain Alexander Bowman of the US Army Corps of Engineers to begin construction of an extension to the Treasury Building's south wing. Many considered Guthrie to be the ablest secretary of the treasury since Alexander Hamilton.[3]

After leaving the Treasury, Guthrie served as vice president and then president of the Louisville Nashville Railroad Company and president of the Louisville-Portland Canal Company He was a member of the peace convention of 1861 held in Washington, D.C., to devise means to prevent the impending war.

Kentucky delegates to the 1860 Democratic National Convention in Charleston, South Carolina, favored Guthrie for the office of president. A two-thirds majority of delegates was required to secure the nomination. On the first of many ballots, Guthrie received thirty-five votes; by the thirty-sixth, he was up to sixty-five and a half- but still trailed the leading vote-getter, Stephen Douglas, by eighty-six votes. With no candidate able to secure the needed votes, the meeting adjourned and reconvened in Baltimore, Maryland, a month later.

At the Baltimore meeting, Guthrie garnered ten votes on the first ballot. He received five-and-a-half on the second ballot, which finally saw Douglas attain the necessary majority. Douglas was defeated by Abraham Lincoln in the presidential election. Guthrie was offered the job of secretary of war by President Lincoln, but he declined because of age and failing health.

The impending Civil War found Guthrie a delegate to the Washington Peace Conference in February 1861, where he chaired the committee that wrote the convention's proposal for peace. The peace conference failed, but while in the capital, Guthrie and other peace delegates met with President-elect Lincoln. The meeting proved contentious, and at its close, Lincoln voiced concern regarding the language of his guests. Guthrie reportedly told Lincoln, "Mr. President, if General Washington occupied the seat that you will soon fill, and had it been necessary to talk to him as we have to you to save such a Union as this, I, for one, should talk to him as we have to you."[4]

The Kentucky legislature narrowly chose Guthrie over a fellow Louisville native, Lovell H. Rousseau, for a seat in the US Senate in 1865. Guthrie served in the US Senate from March 4, 1865 to February 7, 1868.

In that body, he opposed the Republican Party's Reconstruction efforts. A supporter of President Andrew Johnson, he opposed the Freedmen's Bureau and the passage of the Fourteenth Amendment.

On January 23, 1866, in a two-sentence statement under "The News," the *Louisville Daily Journal* said, "We are glad to see that our worthy Senator, Hon. James Guthrie, has taken ground, in reference to the bill in Congress enlarging the powers of the Freedmen's Bureau, against, including Kentucky with the States lately in rebellion. The Senator, in this, faithfully represents the wishes of his constituents."[5]

In respect to the Freedmen's Bureau, Senator Guthrie made an extensive speech on the floor of the Senate on Saturday, January 20, 1866, during the pendency of legislation reorganizing the Freedmen's Bureau. In that speech, Guthrie said the legislation should not apply to Kentucky, as Kentucky was not a state in rebellion.[6] In closing, Guthrie said, "but the cause of the Union prevailed with the people of Kentucky, and Kentucky has been true to the Union always. I hope gentlemen will consent to strike Kentucky out the bill. We can take care of ourselves, and we pledge you that Kentucky will do what is right toward these people."[7]

The article in the *Louisville Daily Courier* of February 11, 1868, presents an interesting tribute to the senator, titled "The Resignation of Senator Guthrie." It states:

> Hon. James Guthrie yesterday returned his commission as United States Senator to the Governor of the State, and retired finally, we presume from public life. It is generally known that for the last year he has been so enfeebled by disease that he has been debarred from occupying his seat in the Senate, and the consciousness that he cannot do so now, and that the public interests require that his seat be filled by someone capable of opposing the mad and ruinous schemes of the Radical party, no doubt prompted his resignation. In doing he has acted with an unselfish spirit and a self-denying patriotism, which will secure for him the gratitude of his constituents.[8]

On February 7, 1868, Guthrie resigned his position due to ill health. He suffered a stroke on April 8, 1868, which left him paralyzed and bedridden for the rest of his life. On June 11, 1868, he resigned as president of the Louisville and Nashville Railroad and recommended General William Tecumseh Sherman to be his successor.

Governor Stevenson was interested in the vacancy. However, there was a significant number of Kentuckians who wanted him to finish his service as governor.[9]

Guthrie died in Louisville, Kentucky, on March 13, 1869. He was buried in Cave Hill Cemetery. The city of Guthrie, Kentucky, and Guthrie Street in downtown Louisville are named in his honor.

THOMAS CLAY MCCREERY
(1816–1890)

- Class Three of Three
- Senate Service:1868–1871, 1873–1879
- Political affiliation: Democratic
- Residence at time of election: Daviess County
- Served with Presidents A. Johnson, Grant, and Hayes
- Served with Governors Stevenson, Leslie, and McCreary

Thomas Clay McCreery was first elected to the US Senate as a result of the resignation of Senator James Guthrie in 1868. McCreery first appeared in the Senate on Thursday, February 27, 1868, to present his credentials to the president pro tempore of the Senate. He took the oath of office the next day.

McCreery was born in Daviess County in the community of Yelvington, about twelve miles east of Owensboro on present-day US Route 60, near the Daviess-Hancock County line. He was educated in the local common schools and attended Centre College in Danville, Kentucky, from which he graduated in 1837. He studied and briefly practiced law in Frankfort.

In his first election, the *Louisville Daily Courier* described him as a distinguished gentleman and veteran Democrat.

Thomas McCreery has in him all the materials for leadership. No man could more successfully marshall his party to victory. No man could efficiently organize and systemize their columns. He is a just, fair, fearless man, a bold thinker, a thorough lawyer, a pure patriot, and 'old-fashion (sic)' Democrat" of the old-style type. He is no gala-time Democrat—no summer day recruit. He was neither 'drafted' or whipped into the ranks, nor called there by the fact of the recent successes of the party. He has not just moulted his Democratic feathers and put on Democratic colors. He is a scarred soldier in the faith. He is from the section of Kentucky that is building up Louisville, whilst other sections were pouring their wealth and trade into the full lap of Cincinnati.[1]

McCreery's maiden speech was March 2, 1868, when he made an amendment to one the rules of impeachment of President Andrew Johnson. He moved to amend the 20th rule of impeachment concerning "All preliminary or interlocutory questions and motions may be argued by counsel on both sides."[2] He was critical of the radicals in their pursuit of impeachment of Johnson. He said they closed the prison doors on anyone who could say anything on behalf of President Johnson.[3] It should be noted that he voted to acquit President Andrew Johnson in the impeachment trial.

McCreery was considered an exceptional orator. He was described in the *Louisville Daily Journal* as follows: "No man in the State speaks with more vigor beauty and grace; he has a livelier style of delivery of his opinions; is as always impressive and entertaining. We shall not attempt to repeat what he said or try to imitate him. That would be impossible. He is one of those speakers who must be heard to be appreciated."[4]

His most memorable outspoken event was one where he should have kept his mouth shut even if he was an anti-Reconstruction Democrat. McCreery made his biggest mark around December 13, 1870, two months after the funeral of Robert E. Lee, when he tried to introduce a resolution concerning the legal status of Arlington. He was said to have done this to provide financial relief to Lee's wife, Mary. He thought that the wave of southern sympathy for the Lee family reflected the national mood.

Senator McCreery made headlines around the nation as a result of his resolution. As the vote in the Senate reflected, many of the reports were not favorable. Some were personally insulting to the senator as seen in Topeka, Kansas's *The Daily Commonwealth* of Friday December 16, 1870.

The article on page 2 was headlined— "**AN INSULT TO THE NATION**." It said:

> Our dispatches bring us an account of the motion made by Senator McCreery of Kentucky, in the senate on Wednesday, of which it is difficult to speak as temperately as newspaper discussion of the merits of the legislative motions, by whomsoever proposed deserves. Senator McCreery, who has been two years in the United States senate without leaving the impress of anything about him, save his heavy footfall on the yielding carpet of the chamber, on anything appertaining to national affairs, had like Senator Sprague, determined at length to make a sensation, and he did it. He woke suddenly to his matutinal tea and muffins to-day, to find himself famous, or rather we would speak more by adding the card in adding a prefix to the above epithet. ...

One sentence accuses him of doing this in order to prepare for a run for Kentucky governor—

> 'must do something that would canonize him in the hearts of his constituents, and at the same time bring him before the majority of the people of Kentucky as an eligible candidate for governor, and as we before remarked, he did it, and at the same time he insulted the nation and spat upon the grave of sixteen thousand (the number of Union soldiers buried at Arlington) soldiers of the Union.
>
> Mr. McCreery on Saturday last tried to get a resolution before the United States senate, asking for an investigation into the title deeds of Arlington Heights, which had been confiscated by the government as the property of General Lee, to see if it was not the property of his wife, and if so, to provide for the removal of the hecatomb of slain patriots reposing there, and its restoration to Mrs. Lee. . . .
>
> His speech proceeded amidst an unutterable calm—all listening with bated breath to what were not his calm front and carefully weighed utterances, might have been deemed the ravings of a mad man.
>
> At its conclusion, Edmunds, of Vermont, leaped indignantly to his feet and objected to the reception of such an outrageous proposition'.

At least four other senators spoke in opposition of McCreery's proposed resolution and it was defeated.

McCreery served two non-consecutive terms, due in part to an ambitious Kentucky governor and fallout from the Civil War. He served from February 19, 1868, to March 3, 1871. However, McCreery faced many accusations from Governor John W. Stevenson, an aspirant for his Senate seat. One of those unfounded accusations was from helping hated former Union General Stephen G. Burbridge obtain a position as a revenue collector. Burbridge had been a disliked military governor of Kentucky beginning in June and lasting through February of 1865. He was hated due to his Order No. 59, which said: "Whenever an unarmed Union citizen is murdered, four guerillas (alleged confederates) will be selected from the prison and publicly shot to death at the most convenient place near the scene of the outrages."[5] Due to a whispering campaign that the senator was helpful to Burbridge in obtaining a federal job, he lost to Stevenson in the following election.

He was able to return to the Senate after two ballots of the legislature on December 19, 1871.[6] He defeated Republican J.M. Harlan, who would later become an associate justice of the US Supreme Court, 112–20. It was rumored that after his election, McCreery delivered to the crowd "from the top of the counter in the lobby of the Capitol Hotel (Frankfort) . . . the most magnificent piece of oratory to which he had listened. The crowd went wild with delight."[7]

McCreery's second term failed to point to much achievement. He was part of the majority of senators who refused a seat to a duly elected black senator, Pinkney Benton Stewart Pinchback from Louisiana. In the matter of seating Pinkney Benton Stewart Pinchback, or PBSP, McCreery said in an interview, "He will give that n*****?___ [Pinchback] some sleepless nights before he gets his seat."[8] On March 8, 1876, the full Senate voted 32–29 not to seat Pinchback. The fact that five Republicans voted along with the Democrats was a clear signal Reconstruction was losing steam, as evidence by the end of formal Reconstruction in 1877.[9]

As a senator, McCreery showed no interest in the social circles of Washington. He lived in a rented room in Georgetown. He took frugal meals in his room and was indifferent to his appearance.[10]

McCreery was not a candidate for re-election. After retiring from the Senate, he lived on his farm in Daviess County before moving to Owensboro. His obituary spoke highly of his oratory skill, stating, "His speeches delivered in the Senate read like classics though few in number."[11]

He died in Owensboro on July 10, 1890. He was buried in Elmwood Cemetery.

JOHN W. STEVENSON
(1812-1886)

- Class Two of Three
- Senate Service: 1871–1877
- Political affiliation: Democratic
- Residence at time of election: Covington
- Served with President Grant
- Served with Governors Leslie and McCreary

Governor John White Stevenson was elected by the Kentucky Legislature to succeed Democratic Senator Thomas McCreery in 1870 in a bitter campaign that is more memorable than his six years of service in the US Senate.

John White Stevenson was born in Richmond, Virginia. His mother, Mary White Stevenson, died while giving birth. His father, Andrew, was a Virginia congressman and minister to Great Britain during Martin Van Buren's administration. The younger Stevenson graduated from the University of Virginia in 1832, studied law and practiced briefly in Vicksburg, Mississippi, before moving to Covington, Kentucky, in 1841.

On June 15, 1843, Stevenson married Newport resident Sibella Winston. They eventually had five children, three daughters and two sons.

Before his election as lieutenant governor, Stevenson was elected to the Covington City Council, then served two terms in the state

House and was a delegate to the Kentucky Constitutional Convention of 1850. With Madison C. Johnson and James Harlan (father of US Supreme Court Justice John Marshall Harlan), he served on the commission that revised Kentucky's civil and criminal code from 1850 to 1854. They produced the Code of Practise in Civil and Criminal Cases in 1854.

Stevenson was elected to the US House in 1856 for Kentucky's Tenth District, where he served from 1857 to 1861. He was defeated in the 1860 general election as the Unionists won nine of Kentucky's ten congressional seats. Stevenson was defeated in that election by John W. Menzies. During his two terms in Congress, Stevenson supported the admission of Kansas under the pro-slavery Lecompton Constitution.

As a Southern sympathizer and a leading lawyer in Northern Kentucky, John Stevenson kept out of the public spotlight during the Civil War. He did this in order to avoid arrest and imprisonment during the uncertain times.

He was elected lieutenant governor in the summer of 1867. He became governor upon the sudden death of John L. Helm on September 8, 1867.[1] He was subsequently elected as governor in 1868. He served until 1871, when he resigned, having been elected as a Democratic US Senator.

During his term as governor, mob violence and civil unrest were problems in post-Civil War Kentucky. Within a month of becoming governor, Stevenson sent the state militia to Mercer County to quell the violence. In 1869, he had to send the militia to Boyle, Garrard, and Lincoln counties to put down mob violence.

In respect to supporting the rights of newly freed blacks, he was rather ambivalent. He would warn that violence against blacks would not be tolerated but would rely on local authorities to enforce the law. He was silent when the legislature refused to ratify the Fifteenth Amendment to the US Constitution and passed legislation that would not allow the testimony of a black person against a white person in the courts of the Commonwealth.

As governor, Stevenson was active in promoting public education. He supported a successful referendum that raised additional taxes for school purposes on a segregated basis. He also established a State Bureau of Education.

When Senator Guthrie resigned in 1868 for health reasons, there was some discussion about Governor Stevenson running for that seat.[2]

Stevenson was not above getting into the mud when going after something he wanted. In 1869, he became embroiled in a political controversy in which he charged contenders for a Senate seat he coveted with endorsing former Union General Stephen G. Burbridge for a position with the Grant administration.

Some of that is reflected in the following excerpt from the article, "Recollections and Reminiscences of Senator Thomas C. McCreery," published in *The Courier-Journal*, Sunday, August 15, 1897, Section 2:

Briefly stated the charge was made that McCreery had indorsed the application of Burbridge—a name almost universally hated in Kentucky—for some position under the Government. It was said that Thomas L. Jones made the statement at a banquet given by Stevenson on January 8, Jackson's Day. Stevenson as Lt. Governor, had succeed to the Governorship on the death of Helm, and was a candidate to succeed McCreery in the Senate. It was understood that Stevenson had used this information imparted by Jones to his opponent's prejudice and had given Jones the authority. Jones denied having made the statement, and not only denounced Stevenson, but declared his willingness to meet him on the dueling ground anywhere between the two oceans. Stevenson summoned other witnesses to sustain his recollection as to what Jones had said; and if my memory is not at fault, their testimony tended to strongly to sustain his recollection as to what Jones had said; and if it did not fully corroborate it. Jones was very fiery and anxious to fight Stevenson, who in a manly statement, giving what he believed were the facts and what a great many others believed were the facts, declined to accept Jones' challenge, bearing the denunciation bravely, but was greatly worried and distressed. McCreery denied with emphasis the accusation against himself and demanded the proof, which could not be produced. The result was, however, that McCreery was defeated and Stevenson elected.[3]

Stevenson appeared with his colleague Senator Garrett Davis on March 4, 1871. With seventeen other new senators, he was sworn in by Vice President Schuyler Colfax.[4]

As a US Senator, Stevenson was not known for any particular piece of legislation or cause. He was a fiscal conservative and watchdog of Southern rights. He opposed the spending of federal dollars on internal improvements.

In 1872, Stevenson campaigned locally for the Democratic presidential/vice presidential ticket. In July 1872, Stevenson appeared at rally called a "Ratification Meeting" at the courthouse in Newport for the Democratic nominees, Horace Greeley for president and Benjamin Gratz Brown for vice president.[5]

When Congress attempted to move the Newport Barracks and arsenal to Columbus, Ohio, Stevenson presented petitions from Kentuckians to reverse that action.[6] The senator was ultimately successful in his efforts, although the barracks and arsenal were moved to high ground in the nearby District of the Highlands (now Fort Thomas) due to the occasional flooding in Newport by the Ohio River.

During Stevenson's tenure, the Democrats were in the minority in the Senate. From December 1873 until he left the Senate on March 3, 1877, Stevenson served as chair of the Senate Democratic Caucus.[7] As chair of the Democratic Caucus during the period immediately after the disputed presidential election of 1876, it is interesting to note Stevenson's lack of a role in setting up the commission in deciding the winner of that election.

The senator did make a statement about the disputed election of 1876 to a *Cincinnati Enquirer* reporter upon arriving home to Covington on the evening of December 22, 1876, for the Christmas holidays. Though he was reluctant to speak about the issue he is quoted as saying:

> I shall be called upon soon to act in the United States Senate, and for that reason there are phases of the outlook as I see it of which I might not be proper to speak—that is, I do not wish to forestall my action. I want to enter upon my duty uncommitted and untrammeled.

In response to a question about the Senate Committee, Stevenson responded, in part:

> If there is any significance to the Senate Committee it is that desperate leaders mean to crowd matters in the extreme to put Mr. Hayes in. I have the most unshaken confidence that Mr. Tilden has been elected President, and this will still be more incontestably shown by the work of the Investigating Committees in the South.[8]

Stevenson sought reelection to the Senate in 1876. During a joint session of the General Assembly in July 1876, when it failed to elect a senator on the fifth ballot, Stevenson's name was withdrawn from further consideration. This narrowed the race down to James Beck, the eventual winner, and John Stuart Williams, who eventually was elected to the Senate in 1879. Governor Preston Leslie was still under consideration after the fifth ballot.[9]

Following his service as a US Senator, Stevenson served as one of Kentucky's representatives to the Southern Exposition in 1883 along with Kentucky notables Senator James Beck, Publisher Henry Watterson,

Congressman and future Governor Proctor Knott, and Speaker and future US Senator John G. Carlisle.[10]

He also practiced law and was a professor at the Cincinnati Law School. It should be noted that during his years as an attorney, he was associated with John G. Carlisle and William Goebel, the future Kentucky governor who would die from an assassin's bullets. He was elected president of the American Bar Association in 1884–1885.

Stevenson died at his home at Fourth and Garrard in Covington, Kentucky. His funeral was held at Trinity Episcopal Church in Covington.[11]

On the day of his funeral, Governor Proctor Knott ordered state offices closed. Knott attended the funeral along with State Treasurer Richard Tate ("Honest Dick") and State Auditor Hewitt. Future Kentucky US Senator Judge William Lindsay was also present at the funeral.[12]

He was buried in Spring Grove Cemetery in Cincinnati, Ohio.

WILLIS BENSON MACHEN
(1810–1893)

- Class Three of Three
- Senate Service: September 27, 1872 to March 3, 1873
- Political affiliation: Democratic
- Residence at time of election: Lyon County
- Served with President Grant
- Served with Governor Preston Leslie

On September 22, 1872, Governor Preston H. Leslie appointed Willis Benson Machen to the US Senate to fill the vacancy caused by the death of Garrett Davis on that same day. When the Kentucky legislature reconvened, he was formally elected to the seat on January 21, 1873, and defeated Republican Tarvin Baker 104–18. He was formally sworn in on December 2, 1872, by Vice President Schuyler Colfax. He was accompanied by Senator Stevenson.

Machen was born the son of Henry and Nancy Tarrant Machen on April 10, 1810, in Caldwell County, Kentucky. He attended the common schools of the area and became a farmer. Machen attended Cumberland College in Princeton, Kentucky. Upon graduation, Machen engaged in farming near Eddyville. In addition to farming, Machen worked at the Livingston iron forge. Soon, he and a partner opened their own business, but it failed and nearly led Machen to financial ruin. Eventually, he was able to repay his debts, and he began building turnpikes. An injury forced him to abandon that course as well, so he turned to the practice of law. He was admitted to the bar in 1844 and quickly built a large clientele.

He married Lizzie Machen, who died at age twenty in February 1859.[1] Machen later married Margaret A. Lyon, daughter of US Representative Chittenden Lyon and granddaughter of US Representative Matthew Lyon.

As early as 1858, Machen had been considered for the position of lieutenant governor.[2] With the advent of the Civil War, Machen was a delegate to the Confederate Convention at Russellville. Machen was chosen on November 20, 1861, as a committeeman from the First Congressional District of Western Kentucky to help organize Kentucky into a Confederate state.[3]

Before his appointment to the Senate, Machen was an announced candidate for governor in 1871, prior to Preston Leslie receiving the Democratic nomination.

According to the *Senate Journal* on December 6, 1872, Machen presented a petition of merchants requesting the removal of taxes on state and national banking institutions, which was referred to the Committee on Finance.

Just before he left office, Machen asked for, and by unanimous consent obtained, leave to bring in a bill (S. 1579) for the erection of a public building for the use of the US in Paducah, Kentucky. It was read the first and second times by unanimous consent referred to the Committee on Public Buildings and Grounds and ordered to be printed on February 12, 1873. Unfortunately, it would be another twenty years before a new federal building would be built in Paducah.

Following his brief congressional tenure, he returned to farming. He also jointly owned several iron furnaces in Lyon County. In 1880, Machen was appointed to the Kentucky Railroad Commission and served one full term.

Following his term on the railroad commission, Machen retired to Mineral Mound, his 1,000-acre estate on the Cumberland River near Eddyville. Eddyville is where he raised tobacco.

On September 9, 1893, the newspapers reported "Ex-United States Senator W.B. Machen of Eddyville, Taken to the Hopkinsville Asylum." The article explained that Machen "had a severe attack of the grippe last winter, which affected his mind greatly, and it has gradually giving away ever since family and friends deemed it advisable to send him where he could receive medical treatment. He is about eighty-two years old and was for years one of the most active and prominent men in the State."[4]

He died September 29, 1893, at the Western Asylum in Hopkinsville. He was interred in Riverview Cemetery in Eddyville. Today, Machen's former estate is the site of Mineral Mound State Park.

Part VII
1877–1902
Tariffs and Growing Importance
of the Senate

Reconstruction ended when the Congressional Commission decided the 1876 presidential election between Republican Rutherford Hayes and Democrat Samuel Tilden. After the November 5 election, Tilden had 184 electoral votes to Hayes' 165 electoral votes. Additionally, Tilden had more than 260,000 more popular votes than Hayes. At that time, it took 185 electoral votes to win the presidency, making Tilden short one electoral vote. Nineteen electoral votes were contested in South Carolina, Florida, and Louisiana. The Congressionally-appointed Commission on March 2, 1877, declared Hayes the winner. A deal was made so that that if the Commission decided the election in favor of Hayes, federal troops in the former Confederate states would be withdrawn.[1]

This is a twenty-five-year period of six American Presidents between Ulysses Grant and Theodore Roosevelt that few Americans can name. It is a time of economic debate over tariffs as well as the gold standard.

Senators Beck, Blackburn, and Carlisle were active in the debates over using gold and silver standard. Both Beck and Carlisle were considered experts in the issue. In fact, Carlisle's expertise in monetary issues resulted in his appointment as secretary of the treasury in the second Cleveland administration.

JAMES BURNIE BECK
(1822–1890)

- Class Two of Three
- Senate Service: 1877–1890
- Political affiliation: Democratic
- Residence at time of election: Lexington
- Served with Presidents Hayes, Garfield, Cleveland, and Harrison
- Served with Governors McCreary, Blackburn, Knott, and Buckner

US Congressman James B. Beck of Lexington was elected by the Kentucky legislature on January 18, 1876, to the US Senate seat held by incumbent Senator John W. Stevenson of Covington. Beck was elected on the eleventh joint ballot. The election results were Beck 106; Wadsworth (Republican) 15; William Preston, 4; and Proctor Knott, 1.[1]

James Burnie Beck was born in Dumfriesshire, Scotland. While in Scotland, he studied with the Reverend Henry Duncan, an economist and father of the Savings Bank Movement. Beck later immigrated with his parents to Wyoming County, New York, where his father farmed. In 1843, he came to Lexington, Kentucky, where he became an overseer on an estate in Fayette County. He studied law at Transylvania, from which he graduated with honors in 1846. He then began practicing law in Lexington. He eventually became the law partner with John C. Breckinridge in the firm of Breckinridge and Beck until Breckinridge joined the Confederacy.

Beck stayed in Lexington during the Civil War and remained neutral. However, it is said that Beck looked after Breckinridge's Lexington property interests during the Civil War and while Breckinridge was in exile after the Civil War.[2]

In 1866, he was elected to Congress from the Ashland District, based in Lexington, to the seat formerly held by Henry Clay. He served in the House for a total of eight years. Upon his election to Congress, a commission investigated his war record during the Civil War. Nothing was found in the investigation, so he was allowed to take his seat in March 1867. During his service in the House, he was known for his debates with members of the Ways and Means Committee about the "protective tariff." The purpose of the tariff was to protect manufacturing industries from foreign competition. As Kentucky's major industries concerned agriculture, Beck was a fierce opponent of the tariff from the beginning of his Congressional career.[3]

Upon entering Congress in 1867, he was assigned to the Committee on Reconstruction. It was his membership on this committee that gained him the position of the unofficial House minority leader due to his defense of the interests of the unrepresented southern states.

During his first term in the US Congress, Beck was described by *The New York Times* as follows:

> Mr. Beck was John C. Breckinridge's law partner and political backer before the war, and I understand, has ever since been his private and political correspondent, agent and home lieutenant. Mr. Beck is a politician of decided ability and force, and with such decided prejudices against 'those men at the North' as to make him an ever-reliable Democrat, who will scruple at nothing to gain his partisan ends.[4]

Beck had earned a positive national reputation when he served in the House, and that was reflected in the headlines of newspapers across the country upon his election to the US Senate.[5]

The article contained praise of his election from the *New York Times*, the *Springfield Republican*, the *Washington Republican*, the *New York World*, the *Philadelphia Times*, the *Columbus* (GA) *Enquirer*, the *Marion* (GA) *Telegraph*, the *Selma* (AL) *Times*, the *Washington Star*, the *Montevallo* (AL) *Guide Democrat*, the *Petersburg,* (VA) *Appeal and Index*, the *Little Rock Gazette*, the *Kansas City Times*, and the *Cincinnati Enquirer*. The *Kansas City Times* and *Little Rock Gazette* compared Beck to John Crittenden and Henry Clay.

Incumbent Democratic Senator Stevenson had disappointed many. The *Cincinnati Enquirer* noted:

Mr. Stevenson is an honorable man and a gentleman of excellent ability, but his intense desire to please the money aristocracy is the real cause of his late defeat. This wish to please the favored classes gave him a feeling of disregard for the Real Democracy of Kentucky, who would have never deserted him had he not taken the initiative. His vote in the Senate on the financial bill was the blow that struck his people.[6]

When Beck came to Lexington from Scotland via New York State in 1845, he came with the idea of studying law at Transylvania. However, in order to support himself, he worked as an overseer on a farm or plantation. It was said of Beck:

He could break more hemp in a day than any one on the place, and he could shear sheep better than anyone I ever knew. Why, after he became a Congressman, I met him in Lexington, and told him that I was about to have my sheep sheared and I would like him to come out and show the boys what to do. He agreed. I took him out, and the boys caught a sheep. Mr. Beck took the shears, and he had that sheep sheared in a jiffy, to the great amazement and delight of the boys. Not one of them could do the work as well. [According to Drummond Hunt of Fayette County][7]

In addition to being successful in politics, Beck and his family were successful in the social circles of the day. In April 1877, the marriage of Senator Beck's daughter Bettie Beck to Major Green Clay Goodloe of the US Marines made national news. The wedding took place at the Beck home on High Street in Lexington. Distinguished guests came from Louisville; Cincinnati; Washington, D.C.; and other cities. The Reverend Green Clay Smith, rector of Christ Church and the temperance candidate for the presidency, officiated. Reverend Smith was the nephew of General Green Clay Smith and the grandnephew of Cassius M. Clay. The romance was compared to that of Romeo and Juliet as the groom's family featured noted Republicans.[8]

As US Senator, Beck was beloved by all, including the staff. According to the article reporting Beck's death, the case of John Dudley, a black man, an old soldier and member of the Grand Army of the Republic, asked Beck for help in appealing his discharge from his position in the Senate. On the floor of the Senate, Beck made a plea for Mr. Dudley's reinstatement. At the time of Beck's death, Dudley was still part of the Capitol workforce. It was also noted that prior to that incident, Beck and Dudley had not been acquainted. It also noted that

Beck was a supporter of the botanical gardens situated west of the Capitol grounds. Beck used his influence to defeat attempts to abolish the Gardens.[9]

At the time of President Garfield's assassination, Senator Beck claimed to be within 600 yards of where the shots were fired. The following is according to the report published in the *New York Times*, courtesy of the *Courier-Journal*:

> I was about 600 yards from where the shots were fired. I was driving to the ticket office to buy my tickets home, and driving down Ninth street, just past the Patent Office, when a colored man who knew me ran out and said, 'The President has been shot.' 'I made some skeptical remark, when, looking down the street, I saw mounted men flying in every direction. I ordered the driver to go as fast as he could to the depot, and we arrived there while the President was yet lying on the floor. The crowd was already immense and increasing every moment and very much excited".[10]

In the year up to his reelection by the Kentucky Legislature, the *Courier-Journal* editorialized about Beck's reelection in July 1881. Within the editorial it said:

> We have favored the re-election of Mr. Beck on upon two sufficient grounds. In the first place, Kentucky can find no better man to succeed him as a working Senator; and in the second place, the Senate and the Democratic party of the nation, would sustain a real loss by his retirement from public life. Often wrong headed, he is always faithful to his convictions and open, fair and manly in action. Always genial and accessible, he is a prodigious worker, neglects nothing and is the best legislator in either house. A canny Scot he is a thoroughbred Kentuckian—as representative as though to the manner born—big—boned—big brained and big-hearted. Kentucky cannot afford to dispense with the services of such a man and has no notion of doing so.[11]

Republican Eugene Hale of Maine was a close friend of Beck's in both the House and the Senate. Beck recognized no barriers to friendship after working hours.[12]

Beck was personally popular not only among his colleagues in Washington but also with Kentuckians. This was reflected in the headlines concerning his first race for reelection, such as "John D. White Receives the Empty Honor of the Republican Senatorial Nomination."[13]

On December 6, 1881, a joint session of the Kentucky Legislature elected James B. Beck to a second term. It was for the term beginning on March 3, 1883. The vote was 101 for Beck; 28 for John D. White, Republican; and 4 for Charles W. Cook of the Greenback Party.[14]

In December 1881, after the death of President Garfield, Senator Beck addressed the Senate about the urgency for legislative action regarding presidential succession. He believed it was not clear about who should become president after the death of a president and vice president.[15] In January 1886, President Cleveland signed the Presidential Succession Act after the death of Vice President Thomas Hendricks in 1885. This law specified in the absence of a president and vice president, the heads of executive departments would succeed to the presidency in the order in which the departments were created, starting with the secretary of state. The Presidential Succession Act of 1886 remained in force until 1947.

In 1882, Cassius Clay was critical of remarks made by Senator Beck about another presidential race by Samuel Tilden. It seems that Beck wanted to know more about Tilden's views at the time.[16]

Even though Grover Cleveland was the first Democrat elected to the presidency in almost thirty years, Beck had some issues with the president. Beck was in favor of silver as legal tender, unlike Cleveland. It was noted in the *New York Times* that both Kentucky Senators Blackburn and Beck would fight President Cleveland on the silver question. In the same article, it was mentioned that one of the reasons Beck might be "pro-silver" was that he owned a lot of property in Montana. In addition to the silver question, Beck was angry over the Democratic president not giving him more federal patronage for Kentucky. This was of concern to Beck as he was facing reelection. Former Governor McCreary was thought to be interested in Beck's seat. Blackburn was upset due to the fact his brother was not made collector at Lexington.[17]

According to Gamm and Smith, Beck served as Democratic caucus chair from March 1885 until his death in May 1890.

The *New York Times* reported in 1888 noted that caucus chairs had subject matter expertise.

"Democratic caucus chairmen, two were numbered among the party's most influential senators. George Pendleton (D-Ohio), who chaired the Democratic caucus in the early and middle 1880s, helped lead the battle for civil [sic] service reform as a junior senator. The Pendleton Act, passed in 1883, was evidence of his success. Senator [James] Beck of Kentucky is the leading authority on the Democratic side on all subjects relating to the tariff and finance, and as he is the Chairman of the Democratic Caucus Committee his opinions have naturally great weight with his associates."[18]

Senator Beck's wife, Jane, died in Washington, D.C., in March 1887. They had five children. Three died in infancy. The survivors were "Mrs. Clay Goodloe wife of the Marine Quartermaster Major Goodloe and George Thornton Beck who was living in Wyoming Territory. She married Beck on February 3, 1848 in Louisville."[19]

Senator Beck, Senator Blackburn, and Congressman Breckinridge were in Richmond, Virginia, to look at Valentine's "heroic" statute of John B. Breckinridge, which was placed on the Fayette County Courthouse grounds in Lexington. (It was later moved.) Beck had practiced law with Breckinridge early in his career. He was on the committee to find an artist for the statute. At the same time, Beck was certain that Cleveland would be re-nominated by the Democrats in 1888. In speaking about President Cleveland's record, Beck said:

> Mr. Cleveland will be the Democratic nominee in 1888. Cleveland is a strong man. Indeed, he is the only man who that stands any chance. This is the only Administration the country has had since the war which has not tolerated corrupt rings, a fact that all honest thinking people appreciate. Then too, Mr. Cleveland's economic principles are right. The southern people ought certainly to be solid for Cleveland for he throws the rascals out and gave the offices to good Democrats.[20]

In the summer of 1887, Senator Beck was out campaigning for the statewide Democratic slate. That slate included General Simon Buckner for governor.[21]

Upon arriving from New York City with his daughter Bettie Goodloe on the afternoon of May 3, 1890, Senator James Beck dropped dead in Washington's Baltimore and Potomac Station. He had gotten off the train and, with his daughter, walked the entire length of the platform. After entering the station proper and meeting with his private secretary, the senator suddenly turned pale and said, "I feel dizzy," and ultimately fell to the floor, where he died.[22]

Senator Beck must have had some health issues just prior to his death. A blurb in the *Courier-Journal* on April 4, 1890, stated, "The report telegraphed from Washington that Senator Beck intended to resign his seat is denied. Mr. Beck's health is improving."[23]

The memorial ceremony afforded the memory of Senator James B. Beck was something of a state funeral. His chair and desk on the Senate floor were immediately draped in black. A joint committee from both the Senate and the House made arrangements for the funeral. The Committee of Arrangements of the two houses of Congress and the pallbearers were scheduled to meet at the Washington home of Congressman W.C.P. Breckinridge at 9:30 a.m. (May 6, 1890). There were twenty-six honorary pallbearers. They included Kentucky Governor Buckner and former Governor Beriah Magoffin. At 10:00 a.m., the body was taken to the Marble Room of the Senate for viewing by the public until 11:30 a.m. The doors of the Senate wing of the Capitol were to open to the public at 10:15 a.m. The funeral ceremonies were to begin at 1:00 p.m. upon the announcement of the presiding officer. Clergy would conduct the funeral ceremonies, including the Reverend Mr. Bullock, a former chaplain of the Senate and personal friend of Senator Beck. At the conclusion of the service, a funeral procession was scheduled to form and march to the Baltimore and Potomac Railroad Station in the following order: the clergy, Committee of Arrangements, the hearse, the family and relatives, the Senate and House of Representatives, and invited guests. The special train bearing the body, members of the family, and the committees of Congress was to leave Washington at 3:00 p.m. for Lexington over the Chesapeake and Ohio Railway. The train was to consist of three vestibuled Pullman coaches. It was scheduled to arrive at 9:00 a.m. Wednesday morning. The funeral in Lexington was scheduled to begin at noon on Thursday.[24]

Beck's funeral in Lexington was held at First Presbyterian Church. At noon that Thursday, there was not even standing room in the church as the service began. Outside, it was described as follows:

> thousands were unsuccessful in gaining an entrance into the church. So many carriages filled the street that all thoroughfare was blocked, and Mill Street, on which the church is located was a living mass of people from Main to Second Streets, two blocks. The crowd was so dense that many women fainted in the crush, and some little children were considerably bruised and crushed.[25]

It was estimated that the thousands of citizens that lined the streets from the church to the cemetery were similar in number to those who attended the route thirty-eight years previous for Henry Clay. Beck was buried in the shadow of Clay's monument in the Lexington Cemetery. It was said that Beck had chosen the plot for his family due to a remark made by his "little daughter on one occasion when he and his wife were walking through the cemetery. In her innocent way, as she approached the spot, she remarked that she would like to be buried there, because when the dead were raised from their graves, she would be the first to see the angels." A few weeks later, the Beck's youngest daughter was laid to rest in this beautiful spot.[26]

The ceremonies were not over in May 1890. The US Senate devoted most to the day of August 23, 1890, to eulogies for the late Senator Beck. Senator Blackburn began and Senator Carlisle closed the program.

While Beck was close to his daughter Bette, his son managed Beck property in Montana. Beck's son George Washington Thornton Beck was a state senator in the Wyoming territorial legislature and the Wyoming state legislature. In 1895, the younger Beck, an engineer with Buffalo Bill Cody, laid out the city of Cody, Wyoming.[27]

JOHN STUART WILLIAMS
(1818–1898)

- Class Three of Three
- Senate Service: 1879–1885
- Political affiliation: Democratic
- Residence at time of election: Clark and Montgomery Counties
- Served with Presidents Hayes, Garfield and Arthur
- Served with Governors McCreary, Blackburn, and Knott

John Stuart Williams was born near Mount Sterling, Montgomery County, Kentucky on July 10, 1818. His father was General Samuel Williams, a hero of the War of 1812. He attended the common schools of the area. He attended Oxford, which is now Miami University in Oxford, Ohio, where he was a classmate of President Benjamin Harrison. He studied law and was admitted to the bar in 1840. He practiced law in Paris the county seat of Bourbon County. He became famous due to his oratory in support of Henry Clay's candidacy as a Whig during the 1844 presidential election against Democrat James K. Polk.

The military achievements of the man who succeeded Thomas C. McCreery overshadowed his civic or political achievements, unless you count the role he played in the founding of the city of Naples, Florida. A hero of the Mexican War and the Confederacy, John Stuart "Cerro Gordo" Williams was elected senator on the eleventh ballot on January

16, 1878, by the legislature. He almost made it on the tenth ballot with Williams, forty-eight; Knott, twenty-six; Lindsay, twenty-five; and Governor McCreary, twenty-three. Governor McCreary dropped out on the eleventh ballot to give the election to Williams.[1]

Williams served in the Mexican War, first as a captain of an independent company attached to the Sixth US Infantry and afterward as a colonel of the Fourth Regiment of the Kentucky Volunteers. He received the nickname "Cerro Gordo Williams" for his gallantry at that battle in Mexico.

He was elected state representative from Clark County in 1851. Following his service in the legislature, he was selected to serve as an American observer of the Crimean War with Captain (and future General) George B. McClellan.[2]

He became known as a leading proponent of states' rights. He was initially an anti-secessionist but abhorred President Abraham Lincoln's policies against slavery and cast his lot with the Confederacy. With the outbreak of the Civil War, Williams traveled to Prestonsburg in early 1861 and was commissioned colonel of the Fifth Kentucky Infantry. He initially served in the Eastern Theater, under Humphrey Marshall in southwestern Virginia. He participated in Marshall's ill-fated invasion of Eastern Kentucky in 1862 against General (and future President) James Garfield. Williams was promoted to brigadier general in 1863 and assigned command of the Department of Southwestern Virginia.[3]

Williams returned home following the war and went on to engage in agricultural pursuits, with his residence in Clark County near Winchester, Kentucky.

He was an interesting politician as seen in this article published in the *Breckinridge News* (Cloverport, Kentucky) on October 10, 1883.

It is the constant habit of Williams when he visits a place, to have a friend point out to him the and tell the names of prominent people who may be in town. Then he will go up to them, call them by name, claim to have met them a dozen or more years ago, and pretend to be delighted at the chance meeting. He shakes their hand heartily enquires after the health of the wives and children with such perfect counterfeit of real interest that, in nine cases out of ten, he gets in his work on them in the most satisfactory style.[4]

He was elected to the State House for sessions in 1873 and 1875. He ran unsuccessfully for governor of Kentucky in 1875 and was a presidential elector (for Samuel Tilden) on the Democratic ticket in 1876.[5]

After his election in 1878 and prior to being sworn in, Senator Williams brought part of his tobacco crop to the Globe Tobacco Warehouse in Maysville, Kentucky. He brought fourteen hogsheads of tobacco. Hogsheads are a type of barrel that can hold over 1,000 pounds of tobacco. His tobacco brought an average price of 16.75¢ per pound. It was commented that the sale of tobacco should help him make it through one winter in Washington, D.C. His appearance at the warehouse caused some to ask him for a speech.[6]

As a senator, Williams was anti-tariff and anti-civil service reform. Below are summaries from articles written during his single term.

On March 12, 1880, Senator General Williams proposed a select committee on a canal, the Special Committee on an Interoceanic Canal (pre-cursor of the Panama Canal). He said in order to make a good decision, issues of foreign affairs, commercial affairs, and legal affairs need to be examined. There was also a need to examine the condition of the Army and Navy for this project.[7] Senator Williams's proposal for a Senate Special Committee on an Interoceanic Canal was defeated as the matter was sent to the Foreign Relations Committee over his strenuous objections.[8]

In 1882, there was significant tension between Williams and Congressman Blackburn. It seemed that the *Frankfort Yeoman* edited by Stoddard Johnston gave Blackburn credit for the $100,000 for a public building in Frankfort. Williams was upset that he was not given credit for passage of the appropriation in the Senate. Williams sent a letter to a Judge Lysander Hoard, an enemy of Blackburn. Williams claiming credit for the legislation. Williams made it known to Blackburn that he deserved credit for the legislation that provided the federal money for the building in Frankfort. Tension between Williams and Blackburn was so bad that Representative Carlisle and Senator Beck had to take the two men to a room and mediate a truce between the two federal legislators.[9]

He opposed the tariffs and made what were said to be wonderful speeches against it calling for reform.[10]

In January 1883, when the Pendleton Civil Service Act was before the Senate, Williams spoke in opposition to it. As seen by the headlines, Senator Williams opposed the Pendleton Civil Service Act: "CERRO GORDO'S BLAST: The Rough-and-Ready Old Senator Goes for the Office-holders," "Horse, Foot and Dragoons He Wants to Sweep Out Every Department of the Public Service With a New Broom And Believes That to the Victors Belong the Spoils," and "AN OLD-FASHIONED RATTLER."[11]

In covering the contest for the Williams' Senate seat in 1884, The *New York Times* was not kind to Senator Williams:

> Gen. Williams was elected six years ago through a particular state of political feeling. He had been a pestiferous office-seeker and made his campaigns and made his campaigns as the champion

of the people against the County-Courthouse and state rings of Kentucky. On the platform he was defeated by for the Gubernatorial nomination by ex-governor McCreary in 1876. Williams was really nominated but was tracked out of it by the party managers in the confusion attending the last ballot. Sore over this treatment, he announced himself for the Senate, and the Legislature elected him, though how to give him, the opportunity to expose the corrupt rings is not clear. At any rate, he has not performed the work, the indignation has subsided, and now there is a very large majority people in the State that he ought to be defeated.'[12]

On January 5, 1884, the Senate race became more complicated with the candidacy of the former congressman from Owensboro, W.N. Sweeney. At the same time, Colonel Thomas Jones of Newport was speculated to be a candidate.[13] They joined John G. Carlisle, Senator Williams, and Senator Blackburn as candidates for the Senate.

Throughout January 1884, the legislature took up the task of electing a new US senator. By January 15, 1884, ten ballots had been taken. Williams was at fifty-four votes; Blackburn, forty-four; and W.N. Sweeney of Owensboro twenty-three votes.[14] The following day, the vote was Williams, forty-six; Blackburn, forty; Sweeney, thirty-two; and Bennett, thirteen.[15]

Senator Williams was defeated after the legislature went through seventy-three ballots on February 4, 1884 on a rainy day. He was narrowly defeated by Congressman Joseph C.S. Blackburn of Woodford County 63–57.[16]

Williams took his defeat at the hands of the legislature hard as seen in this quote: "Senator Williams, of Kentucky, is evidently much affected by his defeat. He has no longer the smiles that made him something of an incarnate joy to the beholder. He broods at his desk and is a listless attendant upon the debates. He no longer spoke of himself as the 'farmer's friend.'"[17]

After leaving the Senate, Williams became involved in land development in Florida in the late 1880s. Along with a partner, Louisville businessman Walter N. Haldeman, the publisher of the *Louisville Courier-Journal*, they founded the town of Naples, Florida.[18][19]

Williams died two days short of his eightieth birthday in Mt. Sterling on July 17, 1898. He was described as an "orator, soldier and statesman." His funeral was held in St. John's Episcopal Church in Mt. Sterling. A delegation for Mexican War Veterans, as well as a Confederate Veterans honor guard, accompanied the body to the Winchester Cemetery in Winchester.[20]

He was survived by his second wife Henrietta Hamilton, whom he married in 1871. His first wife was Ann P. "Mary" Harrison, who died in February 1844, soon after the birth of their daughter. Their daughter Mary Elliott "Mollie" Williams Holloway had been born in July 1843.

JOSEPH CLAY STILES BLACKBURN
(1838–1918)

- Class Two of Three
- Senate Service: 1885–1897 (First Term)
- Class Three of Three
- Senate Service: 1901–1907 (Second Term)
- Political affiliation: Democratic
- Residence at time of election: Woodford County
- Served with Presidents Cleveland, Harrison, and McKinley (first term) and Presidents McKinley and T. Roosevelt (second term)
- Served with Governors Knott, Buckner, Brown, and Bradley (first term) and Governor Beckham (second term)

Joseph Blackburn was the younger brother of Governor Luke Blackburn. Joseph Blackburn was a US representative, and US senator born near Spring Station, Woodford County, Kentucky, on October 1, 1838. He attended Sayres Institute in Frankfort, Kentucky, and graduated from Centre College in Danville, Kentucky, in 1857. Blackburn studied law in Lexington, Kentucky, and he was admitted to the bar in 1858. He practiced in Chicago, Illinois, where his sister, Mary Blackburn Morris, lived with her husband, Judge Buckner Morris, who was a member of the Illinois Supreme Court and served as mayor of Chicago from 1838 to 1839.[1]

In 1860, Blackburn returned to Woodford County. He entered the Confederate Army as a private in 1861 and was promoted to lieutenant colonel before the close of the Civil War. He settled in Arkansas in 1865, where he was a lawyer and planter in Desha County until 1868. He then returned to Kentucky and opened law offices in Versailles.

Blackburn was a member of the State House of Representatives from 1871–1875. He was elected as a Democrat to the Forty-Fourth Congress and to the four succeeding Congresses (March 4, 1875–March 3, 1885). He served as chairman of the Committee on the District of Columbia (Forty-Fifth Congress) and on the Committee on Expenditures in the Department of War (Forty-Fifth and Forty-Sixth Congresses).

During his time in office, Blackburn was able to mentor political cartoonist Clifford Berryman (1868–1949), a Woodford County native. Berryman is famous for creating the "Teddy Bear" trademark. It was supposed to be a joke on the President "Teddy" Roosevelt, who refused to shoot a young bear while hunting in Mississippi in 1902. At age thirteen, Berryman played hooky to hear a speech given by Congressman Blackburn. After the speech, Berryman drew a picture of the congressman and mounted it on the lid of a cigar box. When Blackburn later saw the sketch, he urged the young artist to go to Washington, D.C. Four years later, Blackburn assisted Berryman in obtaining a thirty-dollar-a-month job as a draftsman at the US Patent Office. In his off hours, Berryman worked on his art. He sent some to the *Washington Post*, where they were published. The *Post* later hired Berryman as a full-time illustrator.[2]

Blackburn gained national attention in 1877 as a congressman when he took to the floor of the House to protest the result of the electoral commission in the disputed contest between Republican and eventual winner Rutherford Hayes and Democrat Samuel J. Tilden.[3]

In May 1882, an argument between then-Congressman Blackburn and incumbent US Senator John S. Williams almost ended in a duel. The argument began when Stoddard Johnson, the editor of the *Frankfort Yeoman* and a friend of Blackburn, gave the congressman credit for bringing a federal building to Frankfort valued at more than $100,000. Williams wrote a letter saying he sponsored the original legislation in the Senate, and then feelings got out of hand. Kentucky Senator James Beck and US Representative John G. Carlisle were given credit for assisting in resolving the hurt feelings and averting a duel.[4]

"Jo" Blackburn was known as a great orator of the era. After being elected to his first term in the Senate and prior to taking office, he was active throughout the state, speaking on behalf of the 1884 Democratic presidential candidate Grover Cleveland, who was facing Republican James Blaine. At a huge rally at Louisville's Liederkranz Hall on September 17, 1884, Blackburn was considered the "real orator" of the occasion.[5] He began his remarks by saying the "Republican record and party should be in the criminal docket."[6] He continued his criticism of the Republican Party during the Civil War and Reconstruction. He was particularly critical of the punishment dealt to Kentucky's congressmen elected during the 1866 election following the Civil War. Some of them were not seated when Congress opened in March 1867. To this, Blackburn said:

And the loyal State of Kentucky that had never seceded from the Union, but who, thank God, amid all her loyalty grew 47,000 of the finest disloyal sons upon whom the sun of God has ever fallen—the people of Kentucky sent their delegates [to Washington] composed of men of spotless character, admitted ability, unquestioned patriotism and loyalty. They, too, were exiled from the council of your country. For nearly one year the Kentucky delegation wandered as outcasts about the streets of the capital of your county, and this grand old Commonwealth was voiceless by reason of Republican Expatriation.[7]

"Jo" Blackburn was unanimously reelected by the Kentucky legislature on January 3, 1890. He was described as one of the most persistent, as well as most successful, ex-Confederate office seekers. He was a "bold, aggressive, and at times attractive fellow, a good 'mixer' and handshaker. He had made a name for himself through his eloquence.'"[8] Unlike his brother, he was very much a political person. His brother, Governor Luke Blackburn, had been active in the Confederate cause. However, once the war was over and he was governor, Luke Blackburn seemed more interested in "helping humanity."[9] "Jo Blackburn had "waved the bloody shirt" vigorously for more than a decade and had been a good Democrat." It was on his record as a partisan that Jo Blackburn believed that the Democrat-dominated legislature owed him another term. The legislature agreed.[10]

In seeking a third term, Blackburn faced a divided Democratic Party within Kentucky. Many Democrats believed that the "Bourbon" Democrats, like John G. Carlisle, had controlled the party for too long. Then there was the friction between Western Kentucky Democrats and Central Kentucky Democrats. There was also the issue of money and the changing economy. While the 1880s and '90s were part of the Gilded Age, the nation found itself in a depression during Cleveland's second administration. Economic prosperity had not reached farmers and small business owners. Democrats were split over the use of the gold standard. Blackburn supported the silver standard. Kentucky's Democratic governor in the early 1890s was John Young Brown, who turned out to be wildly unpopular. His unpopularity contributed in part to the election of Republican William O. Bradley in 1895.

Blackburn fought hard to retain his election for a consecutive third term. The "Free Silver" Democrats worked hard on behalf of Blackburn. At the beginning of the 1896 session of the legislature, things were unpredictable. The Senate elected Democrat William Goebel as president pro tempore, and the House elected Republican Charles Blanford as speaker. A committee was appointed to investigate "contested" legislative seats. By the end of January, twenty-nine votes had been taken with no candidates receiving a majority. In March 1896, by virtue of the contest committee, one Democrat was unseated in the House and two Republicans in the Senate. Armed Blackburn supporters guarded the doors to make sure the unseated Republicans would not get into the House Chambers to participate in the vote.

Both the Democrats and the Republicans in the legislature had difficulty supporting a single nominee due to the money issue. Republicans had originally supported Dr. Godfrey Hunter. However, on March 4, 1896, Hunter had withdrawn and endorsed Mr. St. John Boyle of Louisville as the Republican caucus candidate with State Senator W.J. De-Boe (the eventual winner) and Judge W.H. Holt withdrawing in favor of Hunter. St. John Boyle was said to be for sound money, though he had not taken much active interest in the issue. He believed in the coinage of both gold and silver and in gold being the standard of value.[11] At the same time, twenty-four "Sound Money" Democrats refused to endorse Blackburn, and only forty-three members of the legislature supported Blackburn. Forty-three was not enough to become the Democratic standard bearer. Blackburn refused to give up. He believed that some Republicans would eventually come to his side.[12]

The legislature adjourned in 1896 without electing a US Senator. It was not until April 28, 1897, that the legislature was able to elect a senator. On the sixtieth ballot, with seventy-one votes, DeBoe was able to defeat Blackburn, who had fifty votes.[13] As a result, Blackburn was defeated by Republican William DeBoe for a third term, which ran from March 1897 through March 1903.

Within a few years, Blackburn was reelected for the term from March 4, 1901, to March 4, 1907. Blackburn was elected to the seat held by Democrat William Lindsay. In 1896, Blackburn had campaigned throughout Kentucky for Democratic Presidential Candidate William Jennings Bryan.[14] In 1899, Blackburn had been an active campaigner for the election of William Goebel. Blackburn's work on behalf of the Democratic Party paid off. Blackburn was again elected to the Senate by the legislature and served from March 4, 1901, to March 3, 1907. At the time of Goebel's death on February 4, 1900, Blackburn was in the room with the certificate of Goebel's death was signed.[15]

Blackburn was recognized as a great speaker. In October 1903 at the Music Hall, the 2,000-plus crowd "yelled itself hoarse" prior to Blackburn and Louisville Mayor Grainger giving their speeches. Excerpts from Blackburn's speech indicate that he was racist and an elitist. In alleging that the Republican Party was not fit to govern, "He said the largest, if not the most respectable element of that party is the negro, while the remainder was composed of mountain feudalists in the Eleventh District." He further criticized the Republican Party for helping give "the Negro" the vote in order to make him master of the white man in the South.[16]

He was an unsuccessful candidate for reelection in 1907, even though he had been selected by fellow Senate Democrats as their leader as Democratic Caucus chairman 1906–1907.

Upon Blackburn's retirement from the Senate, President Theodore Roosevelt appointed him as a member of the reorganized Isthmian Canal Commission and civil governor of the Canal Zone on April 1, 1907. Roosevelt appointed Blackburn in part due to his involvement with Panama Canal issues beginning in 1901. This involvement or votes on issues on the Panama Canal did not always jibe with President Roosevelt's wishes. For example, he was in the minority in the 72–6 vote to ratify the Hay-Pauncefote Treaty, which nullified the Clayton-Bulwer Treaty of 1850 that pledged that both the British and Americans would never exercise exclusive control over an isthmian waterway or canal. On February 23, 1904, the Senate ratified the Hay-Bunau-Varilla Treaty between the US and Panama, 66–14. Blackburn was in the minority. While he was not active in the debate on the treaty, he had supported an amendment to compensate Colombia for the loss of Panama. When this amendment sponsored by Senator Augustus O. Bacon of Georgia was not added to the treaty, Blackburn voted against the treaty.[17] In the area of foreign affairs, Blackburn had expressed his disapproval of American support or sponsorship of the overthrow of foreign governments. He had opposed the overthrow of Queen Liliuokalani of Hawaii and supported legislation during his second term that would have compensated her.[18]

Within a month of completing his term in the Senate on March 1909, on April 1, President Roosevelt appointed Blackburn to the Isthmian Canal Commission and ultimately to territory governor of the Canal Zone. Speculation to why Roosevelt appointed Blackburn includes the fact Blackburn supported the Spooner Act, which created the commission, and the need for nonpartisanship in this foreign policy position. In this position, Blackburn oversaw the administration of the courts, schools, public works, and civil administration in the Canal Zone. He resigned in 1909 and returned home to Kentucky.

Blackburn died in Washington, D.C., on September 12, 1918, of a heart attack. At the time of his death, he was a resident commissioner of the Lincoln Memorial Commission. In a touch of irony, it should be noted that Blackburn, a former Confederate, was part of the commission that designed the monument and laid the cornerstone for the Lincoln Memorial.[19] Prior to his burial, at the invitation of Kentucky Governor Augustus Stanley, Blackburn was the first person to lie in state at Kentucky's present Capitol Rotunda. He is buried in the state cemetery in Frankfort. Senator Blackburn's public service has been recognized with many naming tributes. These include Mount Blackburn in Alaska, the fifth highest peak in the United States; the town of Blackburn, Oklahoma; the Joseph Blackburn Bridge in Lawrenceburg, Kentucky; and the Liberty Ship USS *Joe C.S. Blackburn*.

JOHN G. CARLISLE
(1834–1910)

- Class Two of Three
- Senate Service: 1890–1893
- Political affiliation: Democratic
- Residence at time of election: Covington
- Served with President Benjamin Harrison
- Served with Governors Simon Bolivar Buckner and John Young Brown

John G. Carlisle was elected as a Democrat to the US Senate to fill the vacancy caused by the sudden death of James B. Beck. Carlisle served from May 26, 1890, until February 4, 1893; he resigned to accept a position as secretary of the treasury in the cabinet of President Grover Cleveland from 1893–1897. Prior to his service as a US Senator, he served in the Kentucky General Assembly and as lieutenant governor of Kentucky and in the US House of Representatives.

Carlisle became a leader of the conservative "Bourbon Democrats" during the last two decades of the nineteenth Century. Bourbon Democrats were conservative Democrats who opposed Republican protectionism and fiscal conservatism, supported civil service reform, and opposed "big city" bosses. Because of his leadership role as a Bourbon Democrat, Carlisle was mentioned as a presidential candidate, but the Democrats passed him over at their conventions for Bourbon Democrats who were better known, such as Winfield S. Hancock in 1880 and Grover Cleveland in 1884. Discomfort with nominating a Southerner after the Civil War played a role in Carlisle's failure to win either nomination.

He was born in a part of Campbell County that was later taken to form Kenton County, on September 5, 1834. He was educated in the common schools in Covington. He taught school in Covington and studied law under John W. Stevenson of Covington, who later served as a Kentucky governor and US Senator. Upon Carlisle's admission to the bar in 1858, he formed a partnership with Judge Kinkaid of Kenton County.[1]

For a year during his service as lieutenant governor from 1871–1875, he was editor of the *Louisville Daily Ledger* in 1872. In November 1876, he was elected as a US Representative to the Forty-Fifth Congress and six succeeding Congresses. He served from March 4, 1877 to May 26, 1890. In the House, he served as chair of the Rules Committee during the Forty-Eighth, Forty-Ninth, and Fiftieth Congresses. He served as Speaker of the House for six years when the Democrats were the House majority during the Forty-Eighth, Forty-Ninth, and Fiftieth Congresses.

Carlisle was the fourth Kentuckian to serve as Speaker of the US House of Representatives—the first Kentuckian was Henry Clay. During his six years as Speaker, he was considered one of the best and most commanding Speakers. He had a full grasp of the rules of the House and was able to manage its membership. His service as Speaker was more notable than his service as a US Senator.

Carlisle's leadership was aided when he and his wife purchased a seventeen-room home at 1426 K Street, Northwest, which was a fashionable area of the capital. The home was a center for Kentucky politicians and natives in D.C. The Carlisles reserved Wednesday afternoons for wives of the members of the cabinet. As Speaker, the Carlisles would hold "teas" and would invite over 750 people, with music provided by the Marine band.[2] Carlisle lost the speakership with the opening of the Fifty-First Congress in 1889 and, with the election of President Benjamin Harrison in 1888, came a Republican majority in the House. Republican Thomas B. Reed was elected to the Speakership. Reed was elected by twelve votes over Carlisle.[3]

Carlisle's main interests while in both houses of Congress were economic. On the main issues of the day, Carlisle was in favor of coining silver but not for free coinage. He also favored lower tariffs. He became a leader of the low-tariff wing of the Democratic Party, and he was chosen by House Democrats to become Speaker in 1883 over Congressman Samuel J. Randall of Pennsylvania, a leader of the party's protectionist wing who served as Speaker from 1876 to 1881.[4] Carlisle's main goal as a federal legislator focused on opposition to tariffs. The only reason Carlisle would consider a tariff was to raise revenue, not protectionism. While the Democrats held the majority in the House of Representatives, this was the case. However, in 1890, that changed when Representative (and future President) William McKinley introduced tariff legislation. Carlisle led the charge in opposition to the legislation in both houses of Congress.

Carlisle was elected to the Senate by the Kentucky legislature on May 17, 1890. He did not take his seat in the Senate until May 26, 1890. During the interim, he led the charge against the McKinley Tariff in the House. On May 21, he began an effort to have Republican members of the House record their votes on individual items within the tariff bill. However, once the bill was passed in the House, he resigned his House seat and took his seat in the Senate.[5]

To the surprise of many, he received appointments to the Committees on Finance, Women's Suffrage, and Territories.[6] His service on the Committee on territories could explain his friendship with Kentucky native and Arizona Territorial Representative, Marcus Smith.

The McKinley Tariff was a tax placed on foreign manufactured goods by the federal government, which equaled about 50 percent of the value of the imported product. By placing taxes on foreign goods, these products became more expensive. As a result of the increased prices for foreign goods, the hope was for citizens of a nation to purchase items manufactured within their own country. The tariffs were placed on manufactured goods imported into the country, but staples such as sugar and coffee were on the "free" list and not taxed.[7]

The House passed the bill 164–142, and it slowly worked its way through the Senate.[8] President Benjamin Harrison convinced Senate allies to insert a provision permitting the president to raise duties matching foreign rate hikes and signing agreements to open foreign markets without congressional approval. McKinley unsuccessfully opposed the reciprocity provision on the grounds that it yielded closely held congressional powers.

Many voters, perceiving the McKinley Tariff as a boon to wealthy industrialists, registered their displeasure at the polls that fall. House Republicans lost ninety-three seats, and the Democrats swung comfortably into a commanding majority. The fight over the tariff question did not end after its passage and the 1890 midterm elections.

While Congressmen fought over the tariff question, the two parties prepared for the presidential campaign. The selection of a Democratic candidate was a perplexing problem. Grover Cleveland was the outstanding man of the organization, but he had already announced his unqualified condemnation of free coinage, and party success seemed to depend upon winning the vote of those Democrats who were locally allied with the Populists. John G. Carlisle, persistent advocate of tariff reform, had done little to offend the silverites, and his following was large—but he lived on the wrong side of the Ohio River.[9]

David B. Hill, William E. Russell, Horace Boies, Arthur P. Gorman, William R. Morrison, and Adlai E. Stevenson were possibilities for the Democratic candidate, but none possessed the popularity or the qualities of statesmanship that marked Cleveland and Carlisle. Carlisle's support in the Midwest and South was very strong. He was, perhaps, the nearest approach to a universally admired statesman that the South had produced since the Civil War. Many had "dreamed for years of putting him in the White House," and no one desired this more ardently than his old friend Henry Watterson, publisher of the *Louisville Courier-Journal*.[10]

In 1892, Carlisle was proposed as a candidate for president at the Democratic convention again, but this time Carlisle asked that he not be considered. It was reported at the time that Carlisle dropped out with the understanding that Cleveland, once nominated, would appoint him to his cabinet.[11]

The economy, under the Republicans and President Benjamin Harrison, was in bad shape. The Republicans, under President Benjamin Harrison, carried on an uninspiring campaign, and they were badly defeated. Democrats were ready to undertake tariff reform. Carlisle was selected as Treasury secretary early by President-elect Cleveland in January 1893 prior to his March 1893 inauguration.[12]

The financial situation under Harrison grew worse between November 1892 and March 1893. The Depression of 1893 began in January, two months before the newly elected President Cleveland was inaugurated. During this period, manufacturing had surged ahead of agriculture as measured by the gross national product, but beginning in 1893, manufacturing shrank, and unemployment tripled in 1893 to over 8 percent.[13]

Carlisle served as secretary of the treasury for the full four years of President Cleveland's second term. It was said by some that leaving the Senate to become Cleveland's treasury secretary, killed Carlisle's political career. One paper said:

> At the sacrifice of the principles of a lifetime. With a seat in the Senate which he might have held for life, and the possibility before him of achieving a place in history as one of the epochal leaders of the republic, he now sits in a cabinet where his influence is not

more than that of the office boy who shouts: 'I'm a comin' at the sound of his employer's bell.'[14]

Upon leaving the treasury, he went to New York City to practice law, though there are hints that in 1896 he was interested in seeking the presidency or being reelected to the US Senate from Kentucky. This is reflected in articles in the September 16 and October 14, 1899, editions of the *New York Times*. State Senator Goebel had been Carlisle's law partner. However, in 1896, Goebel, as a state senator and Senate president, had supported Kentucky Governor Luke Blackburn for the US Senate. It was further alleged that Goebel did not support "sound money" delegates to the Democratic Convention of 1896.

John G. Carlisle died in New York City on July 31, 1910, and was buried in Linden Grove Cemetery in Covington, Kentucky.

WILLIAM LINDSAY
(1835–1909)

- Class Two of Three
- Senate Service: 1893–1901
- Political affiliation: Democratic
- Residence at time of election: Hickman, Clinton County
- Served with Presidents Cleveland and McKinley
- Served with Governors Brown, Bradley, Taylor, Goebel, and Beckham

When Senator John G. Carlisle resigned to become treasury secretary in President Grover Cleveland's second term, the Kentucky General Assembly elected Judge William Lindsay to succeed him in January 1893. The legislature took over a week to deliberate over its choice to succeed Carlisle. Sitting Kentucky Governor John Brown was the first candidate to bow out of contention

The final vote of the legislature in the Senate was 18–6 in favor of Democrat William Lindsay (Democrat) over Republican Augustus E. Willson. The final vote in in the House was 63–13 for Lindsay. The Populists in the legislature voted for Lindsay.[1]

Lindsay was an elected member of the Kentucky Senate on two occasions prior to his election to the US Senate. He had previously been elected by the voters to the Kentucky Court of Appeals and had served as chief judge of the Court of Appeals from 1876 to 1877.

While in the Senate, he had a great interest in monetary policy regarding the gold and silver standard. However, he served as chairman of the Committee on Indian Depredations and on the Committee on Revolutionary Claims.

During his tenure in the Senate, he made a name for himself—or at least he made time for the media. He is described as "The Distinguished Kentuckian." The *New York Times* published a short article on August 14, 1896, entitled: "SENATOR LINDSAY PROSTRATED: The Distinguished Kentuckian Alarmingly Sick For One Night."[2] The article implies that he collapsed due to extreme heat at his home in Frankfort. He was out of danger in the morning.

In November 1896, Senator Lindsay, in an interview from Louisville, said that the US should provide aid to Cuba in order to protect its people from exterminations by Spain.[3] Other reports reflected his support of the Spanish-American War.

After the disputed gubernatorial election of November 1899, Senator Lindsay did not follow the Democratic Party line. He declared it a very delicate situation, saying, "If Goebel should receive the certificate of election, it would in my opinion, rest entirely with Gov. Bradley whether he took his seat or not."[4]

In the spring of 1900, Lindsay repeatedly told the press that "Anybody can beat Bryan." He continued and said, "The Democrats never had a better opportunity to elect a President than this year. But they must nominate someone the people are not afraid of. They are afraid of Bryan. Still, I do not see how his nomination can be prevented."[5]

He responded to the question, "What about the silver issue, Senator?" by saying,

"Oh, that amounts to nothing; silver as an issue, is dead for some time to come."[6]

In the same interview, the issue of campaign finance came up. The reporter asked, "What about the case of Senator Clark of Montana?" Lindsay replied, "I hope he will resign. I do not want to vote to put him out of the Senate, but in the face of the unanimous report of the committee I do not see what else I can do. When a man admits spending $135,000 to be elected in a State with only a population of 250,000, it certainly has a bad look."[7]

Lindsay's congressional biography notes that he did not seek re-election. The reason for not seeking re-election may be reflected in his actions during the 1900 elections. In 1900, Lindsay publicly opposed his party's nominees for president and governor. In February 1900, Democratic Governor William Goebel died from wound inflicted by an assassin's bullet. Lieutenant Governor J.C.W. Beckham assumed the governorship after the death of Goebel. There was a special election for governor on November 6, 1900, and Beckham won the balance of Goebel's term.

When his Senate term was over, Lindsay moved to New York City and resumed the practice of law. He was appointed US Commissioner to the Louisiana Purchase Exposition at St. Louis in 1901.

After leaving the Senate, he continued to show disdain for William Jennings Bryan. In an article published in the *New York Times* on August 10, 1902, when asked about the next presidential campaign— "How about Bryan?"—he responded:

> Not in it. Bryan is the biggest political fraud in history. He is in my recollection, the only man who made money after being twice defeated for the Presidency. In the olden days successful candidates went into bankruptcy, and the Government had to buy the libraries of Thomas Jefferson and James Madison to save them from starving. Bryan objects to being relegated to the rear and bobs up every now and again, but he will never be President.[8]

Senator William Lindsay died in Frankfort on October 15, 1909. He is buried in the Frankfort Cemetery. His wife, Eleanor, died in 1934 in their Frankfort home from burns caused by a fall on a bathroom heater.[9] They had married in December 1883. Eleanor was vice president of the Daughters of the American Revolution and a close friend of First Lady Cleveland. Lindsay had a daughter, Marion Semple Lindsay, by a former marriage to Hester Semple. Marion, Lindsay's daughter, married Frank O. Suire of Cincinnati in 1902. Marion and Frank had two children.

Part VIII

1896–1914

The Turn of a Century and the First Republicans Represent Kentucky in the Senate

The nation and parts of Kentucky became more industrialized. Railroads became a very important part of the Gilded Age. Kentucky's coalfields were used to fuel the Gilded Age through the nation's railroads. There were national concerns about the nation's money supply as seen in the arguments over the gold standard and "free silver," which continued as a dominant issue for the first decade of the 20th century.

Senator "Jo" Blackburn was a "free silver" Democrat. At the 1896, Democratic National Convention, he unsuccessfully faced the ultimate nominee for the Democratic Presidential nomination—William Jennings Bryan in four of five ballots. In April 1897, Blackburn was defeated by DeBoe after 112 ballots over two legislative sessions during one year. The final vote in the General Assembly was seventy-one for DeBoe, fifty for Blackburn, twelve for Martin, and one for Stone. Gold Democrats in the legislature voted for Martin. Protracted senate elections called for many popular elections of US senators.[1]

Blackburn returned to the Senate in 1900. His opposition to the taking of Panama from Columbia to build the Panama Canal brought him to the attention of the Republican President, Theodore Roosevelt. Roosevelt appointed him governor of the Canal Zone when Blackburn completed his last term as Senator in 1907.

During the ten-week Spanish American War in 1898, the US acquired Puerto Rico, Guam, and the Philippines and ended the last vestiges of the Spanish Empire in the Western Hemisphere.

Prohibition was becoming an issue in many parts of the nation, including Kentucky with its significant number of Baptists and Methodists who opposed the sale of alcoholic beverages.

In February 1908, Republican William McConnell Bradley defeated Democrat J.C.W. Beckham by thirty-nine ballots. While the legislature was majority Democratic, several Democratic legislators from Louisville could not bring themselves to vote for Beckham for some actions he had taken against Louisville during his term as governor.[2]

WILLIAM J. DEBOE, MD
(1849–1927)

- Class Three of Three
- Senate Service: 1897–1903
- Political affiliation: Republican
- Residence at time of election: Crittenden
- Served with President McKinley
- Served with Governors Bradley, Taylor, Goebel, and Beckham

William J. DeBoe, MD, was a Republican US Senator from Kentucky who served a single term at the turn of the nineteenth century into the twentieth century. He was born near Marion in Crittenden County, Kentucky, on June 30, 1849. He attended the public school in Crittenden County and went to Ewing College, a Baptist College in Ewing, Illinois, where he studied medicine and law—the college closed in the 1920s. De-Boe then went to Louisville, and he studied in the medical department at the University of Louisville. He practiced medicine for a few years but for health reasons returned to the study of law. Still, he continued to sign his name William J. DeBoe, MD. He was admitted to the bar in 1889 and practiced law in Marion and Crittenden County. He also served as superintendent of Crittenden County Schools.

DeBoe was an unsuccessful Republican candidate for Congress in 1892. The following year he was elected to the Kentucky State Senate, where he served from 1893 to 1897. While in the Kentucky Senate, he was elected as a Republican to the US Senate. From March 4, 1897 to March 3, 1903, he served as chairman on the Committee on Indian Depredations, Fifty-Sixth Congress, and on the Committee to Establish the University of the United States, Fifty-Seventh Congress. During DeBoe's tenure, he was part of an effort to have the Smithsonian become a degree-confirming university of the United States.

He began his initial campaign to become a US Senator with letters to his fellow state senators in November 1896. Some thought he was running at the behest of Republican Governor Bradley. He defeated incumbent US Senator J.C.S. Blackburn. He was elected after a heated campaign before the General Assembly, which included troops being called to the Capitol. The governor had wanted the distinction of being Kentucky's first Republican US Senator. However, Dr. W. Godfrey Hunter helped elect a significant number of Republican legislators for the sole purpose of electing himself senator.

When the legislature assembled, there were sixty-eight Democrats, sixty-eight Republicans, and two Populists. Fourteen Democrats who stood for the gold standard bolted when the Caucus made Blackburn the Democratic nominee in 1902.

When the McKinley administration took office in 1897, DeBoe seemed to have a significant role with other Republican leaders in parceling out federal patronage. The May 9, 1897, edition of the *Cincinnati Enquirer* was headlined: "Deboe Names the Winners. Johnnie Myers To Be Postmaster at Newport."[1]

In early 1898, DeBoe was active in the appointment of local postmasters in Kentucky, as seen in the February 1898 list of appointments to Maysville, Princeton, Williamsburg, Ludlow, and Owensboro.[2]

In 1899, the year before the 1900 Census, DeBoe claimed a right to name five out the eleven census supervisors for Kentucky. However, he was still negotiating that point with his colleague, Democratic US Senator Lindsay.[3]

DeBoe was a strong supporter of Sylvester Taylor during his candidacy against Goebel and during the contested general election of 1899. This is reflected in the December 4, 1899, *Courier-Journal* article, "DeBoe's men Go To Louisville to Help Taylor Pass Through Louisville."[4] The article noted that the Fifth Avenue Hotel had a full page of men from DeBoe's hometown of Marion registered. These were one of many groups making sure Taylor was going to take office, whether or not he received a certificate of election. Democrats referred to this group as "DeBoe's Blood Waders."[5]

In 1900, with the assistance of Senate President William Goebel, Blackburn succeeded incumbent Democratic US Senator William Lindsay.[6]

During the gubernatorial election crisis of 1899/1900, it was said that DeBoe played the role of "the brains" behind the crisis. He left Frankfort for Washington the night before Goebel was killed with Secretary of State Finley. The shot which eventually killed Goebel came from the window of Finley's office. Charles Finley was to serve until the first of the year—i.e., January 1900—when Caleb Powers would be inaugurated as secretary of state. The policy of retiring secretaries is that if they are not elected to successive terms, they remain in office until their successors take the oath of office. This policy still continues today. As a point of historical interest, Governor William S. Taylor included Charles Finley as well as Caleb Powers in his March 10, 1900, pardon of persons implicated in the assassination of Governor William Goebel. DeBoe was part of the Republican delegation that went to inform New York Governor Theodore Roosevelt at Oyster Bay, Long Island, of his nomination as vice president on the Republican ticket in 1900 on July 12 of that year.

He was not a candidate for re-nomination in 1902. This was due to the fact Democrats took control of the General Assembly of both houses.[7]

DeBoe was approached to be the Republican candidate for governor in 1903. In July 1902, he stated that he had no intention of running for governor. He was going to finish his term as US Senator, which ended on March 4, 1903, and resume the practice of law, as well as take care of his business interests. He took a jab at Democrats and the late Governor Goebel when he said, "I shall do whatever I can to aid my party in re-establishing civil liberty in Kentucky and reclaiming the State from the Goebel freebooters, who are now enjoying the fruits of their dishonesty and perfidy."[8]

His pre-occupation with patronage is reflected in the headlines of the *Courier Journal* during his term. Some of these headlines include:

- "Unbroken: Is the Prepared Patronage Slate of Deboe Senator Sees the President Settled That Sapp's Name Will Go To the Senate,"[9]
- "Sam Roberts: Comes To the Defense of Senator Deboe in the Matter of Patronage Says His Critics Have Been Too Severe On the New Statesman What Kentucky Will Get,"[10]
- "Deboe: And Lindsay Consult Over Census Patronage the Result Not Known Senator and Governor meet on and speak on Street an Amusing Incident,"[11]
- "Hot Words: Deboe and Dye Nearly Come To Blows Trouble over Patronage Laure County Man Says Senator Broke His Pledge Postmaster at Hodgenville Legislator Declares

Deboe Will Lose Nomination For United States Senator Will Work for His Defeat,"[12]

- "War at the White House: Between Two Kentuckians Narrowly Averted Lively Little Scene Between John D. White and Senator Deboe Over Patronage,"[13]

- "Uphill Job: Senator Deboe Has Had All Along He Addresses the people "No Senator has had such Environments," "Has favored his Friends He and the President Decided Upon the Republican Policy In Kentucky his Philippine Ideas,"[14]

- "New Slate: For Eastern Kentucky Judicial Offices the President's Request Pugh's Candidacy Never Seriously Considered Bradley's Chances Good Indications That Senator Deboe Will Indorse[sic] Him For the Judgeship in the Interest of Harmony,"[15] and

- "The Machine Senator."[16]

Once his Senate term ended, DeBoe served as chairman of the Kentucky Republican Party.[17]

DeBoe was a delegate from Kentucky to the 1912 Republican National Convention. Ten years later he served as the postmaster of Marion, Kentucky, from 1923 to 1927. He died in Marion and was buried in Mapleview Cemetery.

JAMES B. McCREARY
(1838–1918)

- Class Three of Three
- Senate Service: 1903–1909
- Political affiliation: Democratic
- Residence at time of election: Richmond
- Served with President T. Roosevelt
- Served with Governor Beckham

In addition to serving as a one-term US senator, James B. McCreary has the distinction of being both one of Kentucky's youngest governors (he was thirty-seven when he began his first term) and one of Kentucky's oldest governors (he was seventy-three when he began his second term). In his youth, he served in the Confederate Army, a lieutenant colonel at the time he surrendered with his regiment at Appomattox. Following his service in the Senate, he served as president of the American Peace and Arbitration League.

McCreary was elected to the US Senate on January 14, 1902, by the Kentucky General Assembly. The vote in the House was 74–24 for McCreary over DeBoe. In the Senate, McCreary won 23–11.[1] McCreary had been nominated on January 9, 1902, by the legislature's Democratic Caucus for the US Senate nomination for the seat held by Senator DeBoe. He was nominated by a 62–37 vote over Judge James E. Cantrill, which was tantamount to election by the General Assembly. McCreary had come to notice in 1862 when he raised troops for the Confederates' Eleventh Kentucky Calvary. He served with distinction in the Army of the Tennessee under Morgan and Bragg and with Breckinridge in Virginia.[2]

James B. McCreary was the son of Dr. E.R. and Sabrina Bennett McCreary of Madison County. He was educated in the common or public schools prior to attending Centre College, where he earned a bachelor's degree. In 1859, he earned a law degree from Cumberland University of Tennessee. He then practiced law until his military service in the Civil War.

In 1867, McCreary married Kate Lee Hughes, who grew up near Lexington. She graduated from a young ladies' seminary in Norristown, Pennsylvania, in 1865. They had one son, Robert H. McCreary, who was an attorney in Chicago.[3]

In 1869, he was elected to his first elective office. He served in the Kentucky House of Representatives until his election as governor in 1875. He served as Speaker during his last two terms in the Kentucky House. To become governor, he defeated Republican John Marshall Harlan, who later became an associate justice of the Supreme Court.

During his first term as governor, McCreary saw little legislative success, with the exception of the state board of health. Much of his time was devoted to suppressing violence. He ordered the use of force to suppress violence in Breathitt County in 1878 and 1879.

Following his first term as governor, he returned home to Richmond, where he practiced law. In 1885, he was elected to the US House of Representatives, where he served until 1897.

McCreary sponsored legislation that resulted in the convening of an international world monetary conference. In 1892, President Harrison appointed McCreary as one of five commissioners sent to the World Monetary Conference in Brussels.[4] In Brussels, McCreary spoke in favor of bimetallism, or the use of both gold and silver for monetary standards. Simply stated, bimetallism was a policy that linked the value of a nation's currency to certain quantities of the two metals, gold and silver. Linking currency to gold ended in the 1970s. McCreary also sponsored legislation for the free coinage of silver. When the Democrats were in the majority, McCreary served as chair of the House Foreign Relations Committee.

During his service in the House, he was opposed to the annexation of the Hawaiian Islands by the United States. He opposed the subsidy of submarine cables from San Francisco to Hawaii. The reason for his opposition to subsidy for such cables was that there were already fourteen in operation that had been built with private capital.[5]

As a member of the US House of Representatives, he authored legislation that influenced international relations. This included a bill that would establish a court that would adjudicate land claims growing out of the Gadsden Purchase and Guadalupe Hidalgo treaties with Mexico. He was also the author of the bill that created the Pan-American Congress. During this time, he advocated for the creation of a US Department of Agriculture.[6] While in the House, he sponsored the McCreary Amendment to the Geary Act, which required all Chinese residents of the US to carry an internal passport. The McCreary Amendment gave these residents an additional six months to register and required them to have a photo on the permit.

While the General Assembly elected US senators, the Democrats had a primary election to determine which Democratic candidate the legislature would consider. The Democratic primary for the US Senate was in November 1901. The candidates seeking the nomination for the US Senate included McCreary, Judge James E. Cantrill, Congressman David H. Smith, and Congressman Charles K. Wheeler. There were seven joint debates for the four candidates. The first one was at Maysville on September 23, 1901, and the seventh was at Paducah on November 4, 1901.[7]

Prior to his election by the legislature to the Senate in 1902, McCreary had been an unsuccessful candidate in 1878, while he was governor. The legislature elected John S. Williams over him that year. He attempted to succeed James Beck in 1887 but was defeated by John G. Carlisle. In 1902, McCreary had the support of incumbent Governor Beckham, who had succeeded the martyred Governor Goebel.

The election of McCreary was well received beyond the borders of Kentucky. A local paper cited a Tennessee paper: "It is Senator McCreary, of Kentucky. A very good selection; a vast improvement over DeBoe, who is about the smallest man Kentucky ever permitted to go to the Senate".[8]

Due in part to his foreign policy experience in the House, McCreary was appointed to the Senate Foreign Relations Committee, where he served as a member from 1903 until 1909.

In 1904, McCreary campaigned for the Democratic candidate for president, Alton Parker.

McCreary criticized the Republicans for refusing to admit Arizona, New Mexico, and Oklahoma as states as pledged in their 1900 platform. He also criticized the increase in spending (up from $318,000,000 the first year of Cleveland's administration to $782,000,000 the last year of Roosevelt's administration).[9]

In an interview in December 1905, McCreary indicated that the most important issues that would be coming up in Congress were the tariff and railroad rates. McCreary was in favor of federal regulation of railroad rates and revisions to the tariff. However, he was not specific.[10]

It was the custom to annually read President Washington's Farewell Address in the Senate. On February 22, 1906, by appointment of Vice

President Charles Fairbanks, Senator James McCreary read Washington's Farewell Address.[11] During the twentieth century, only two other Kentucky senators had that honor: John Sherman Cooper in 1953 and Walter D. Huddleston in 1978.

Before the 1906 Senate election for Blackburn's seat, McCreary announced his intention to seek reelection in two years even if Governor Beckham were to seek to oppose him. He was quoted as saying, "It has been the rule of Kentucky Democrats to give a United States Senator two terms, and I do not expect be made an exception to the rule. It looks now as though I will have an easy time in my campaign in 1907. More than two thirds of the State Senators who were elected this fall, and will hold over until then, are ready for me."[12]

During his time as a senator, McCreary was the only senator to speak against the tobacco trusts. McCreary was ruled out of order when speaking in defense of the tobacco farmer against the trust.[13]

McCreary was recognized as an "Irish American" in the endorsement he received from the *Kentucky Irish American* newspaper in his reelection campaign in November 1906 for the Democratic nomination. The endorsement was found on the paper's front page. Within the paper, McCreary was noted as a "Model Governor" and as a "clean Christian gentleman."[14]

Unfortunately for McCreary, Governor Beckham had his eyes on McCreary's seat. In order to secure the Democratic nomination, Beckham moved the Democratic senatorial primary to 1906, a year prior to the end of his gubernatorial term. Using the resources of an incumbent governor, Beckham defeated McCreary in the 1906 Democratic primary. However, even with a Democratic majority in the legislature, Beckham was defeated by former Republican Governor Bradley in several weeks of balloting.[15]

Senator McCreary was part of the peace movement and served as president of the Peace Society in 1910.[16] The American Peace and Arbitration League announced that twenty-four treaties of arbitration in the previous two years were entered into between the US and other nations. Incumbent President William Howard Taft was honored at the League's banquet.

> In addition to the President and foreign dignitaries:
> Republicans and Democrats, Union and Confederate veterans, soldiers and civilians, men and women, will all unite in launching at this banquet the society that recognizes and acts upon all the elements in our country's foreign relations, preparing our armed forces, as present conditions require and peaceable agencies as

excellent and useful as international public and official opinion will unite upon.[17]

McCreary's interest in resolving international disputes ran to his early days in Congress. In 1888, he unsuccessfully sponsored legislation that would authorize the president to call a conference of all the nations of the Western Hemisphere to establish a mechanism for resolving international disputes by arbitration.

In 1911, McCreary successfully won his second term as governor of Kentucky at age seventy-three. At this time, he was considered a progressive.

McCreary County, Kentucky, was named in honor of Senator James B. McCreary.

THOMAS H. PAYNTER
(1851–1921)

- Class Two of Three
- Senate Service: 1907–1913
- Political affiliation: Democratic
- Residence at time of election: Greenup County
- Served with Presidents T. Roosevelt and Taft
- Served with Governors Beckham and McCreary

Kentucky Court of Appeals Judge and former US Representative Thomas H. Paynter defeated incumbent Senator J.C.S. Blackburn and other candidates in a vote by the legislature in January 1906. Headlines read: "PAYNTER NAMED ON FIRST BALLOT; ALSO M'CUTCH-EN AND BROWN: Decisive Victory In Democratic Caucus Paynter 59, Blackburn 34, Haldeman 10 Two Votes For D.H. Smith, of Fourth District Nominee Accepts Honor In a Graceful Speech Defeated Candidates Address the Caucus McCutchen Gets 78, Brown 74, Fennell 44."[1]

Thomas Paynter made his formal announcement to challenge incumbent Senator Blackburn on March 17, 1905. The article in the *Cincinnati Enquirer* states: "The announcement has been expected for several months. It is conceded that he will have the united backing of the state administration" [Governor Beckham's administration].[2]

189

Thomas Paynter was born on a farm near Vanceburg, Lewis County, on December 9, 1851. He attended the common schools and Rand's Academy in Lewis County. From there, he attended Centre College in Danville, where he studied law. He was admitted to the bar in 1872 and commenced practice in Greenup, Kentucky. He served as prosecuting attorney of Greenup County from 1876 to 1882. He was elected as a Democrat to the Fifty-First, Fifty-Second, and Fifty-Third Congresses and served from March 4, 1889, until his resignation, effective January 5, 1895, upon his election to the Kentucky Court of Appeals. At the time of his election to the Senate, he was serving on the Court of Appeals.

At that time, even though the General Assembly elected US Senators, candidates often campaigned to garner support from the party "rank and file." Incumbent Senator Blackburn challenged Paynter as early as April 1905 to resign from his seat on the Court of Appeals and join him in a canvas of the state, beginning in Williamstown. This is seen in the headline: "Paynter: Makes Public His Letter to Blackburn His Services on the Bench Needed Because of Illness of Judge Cantrill Issues Between Aspirants He Says Are Not So Great As To Require a Joint Discussion Which Might Hurt the Party in the Close Districts."[3]

In 1907, Paynter was among the elected officials attempting to have Louisville secure the 1908 Democratic Convention. A headline read: "Old Fashioned: Will Be Louisville's Welcome To Democratic Convention Kentucky Congressman Join in City's Invitation Advantages Offered by Armory Cannot be Overcome Committeemen Confident."[4]

Paynter was an ally of Governor Beckham, as seen in Beckham's support of Paynter in 1906. In 1909, Paynter attempted to repay the favor. It was reported in the *Courier Journal* on January 24, 1908 that Senator Paynter spent time in Frankfort working the legislature to help elect former Governor Beckham to the Senate. However, Paynter's efforts were unsuccessful. Due to the legislative deadlock, some Democrats voted for former Republican Governor Bradley, and thus, he was elected.[5]

Soon after the 1909 legislative elections, it was obvious that First District Congressman Ollie James was going to seek the Senate seat held by Paynter. In November, State Senator R.M. Salmon of Hopkinsville announced that he was going to vote for James in 1912.

As a senator, Paynter went after the Tobacco Trust. The *Cincinnati Enquirer* of May 13, 1909, contained the headline: "Paynter Asks Justice For Kentucky Farmers And Arraigns the Tactics of Tobacco Combine." Within the article Paynter is described: "If there ever was any milk of human kindness in the breast of one, the vials of his wrath toward the

Tobacco Trust have surely converted to limburger cheese, for he certainly has soured upon that 'infant industry.'"[6]

Senator Paynter was selected as a member of the Senate committee formed to investigate the disputed election of Illinois Senator William Lorimer by the Illinois legislature. William Lorimer, a Republican from Chicago, known as the "Blond Boss," defeated incumbent Senator Albert J. Hopkins, and there was election deadlock in the legislature for about four months. Hopkins had been endorsed by the popular vote, but he was opposed by a majority of legislators. In April 1910, allegations surfaced in the *Chicago Tribune* that State Representative Charles White of O'Fallon claimed he and others received money for voting for Lorimer. Rather than be tried by a court in Illinois, Lorimer requested that the US Senate investigate the charges. On June 20, 1910, the matter was taken up by the Senate Committee on Privileges and Elections with a subcommittee named to conduct the investigation.

The subcommittee was comprised of four Republicans and three Democrats. Senator Thomas Paynter was one of the Democrats on the subcommittee.[7]

The subcommittee met in Chicago and began taking testimony on September 26, 1910.

> Response of the Senate—First Investigation:
> When the committee reported on December 21, 1910, a majority report exonerated Lorimer. In previous bribery cases, the report noted, the Senate had held that an election would only be invalidated if the senator involved had participated in or sanctioned an act of bribery or if bribery committed without his knowledge or sanction affected enough votes to change the outcome of the election. In this case, a subcommittee had held hearings in Chicago and received no testimony that implicated Lorimer himself in any acts of bribery, although four legislators claimed to have received bribes to vote for him. Several of these, however, had later changed their stories and denied receiving any bribes, and the three legislators accused of giving the bribes also denied any involvement. The committee therefore found no reason to believe that the Democrats who voted for Lorimer had been bribed to do so.
> One committee member, Albert J. Beveridge (R-IN), despite his party affiliation with Lorimer, refused to sign the majority report and submitted his own minority report.[8]

Around February 1, 1913, the Senate voted 47–23 for an amendment to the Constitution that would limit the president to one six-year term.

Paynter voted for the proposed amendment, and his colleague Senator W.O. Bradley voted against the proposed amendment.[9]

One of the last votes Paynter cast was to sustain President Taft's veto of the Webb-Kenyon bill. This bill would have prohibited the transportation of intoxicating liquors into dry territories.[10]

Unfortunately, Paynter's career was tarnished after he left office. In June 1914, Paynter owed the bank owned by Illinois Senator Lorimer over $29,150 from November 1, 1911, to October 1, 1912. On July 14, 1912, Lorimer was ousted from the Senate by a 55–28 vote after a Senate investigation. Paynter voted with the minority.[11] A year later, C.B. Munday, a former vice president of the La Salle Street Trust and Savings Bank testified that Paynter was loaned $40,000 without having to put up collateral.[12]

In his defense, Paynter released a statement stating that Lorimer had no knowledge of the loan as Munday was dealing with him.[13] Paynter said that he gave Munday four demand notes for $10,000 each and deposited them in banks in Illinois: "Senator Lorimer knew nothing about this transaction whatsoever. My deal was postponed and became temporarily embarrassed in taking care of the demand notes. It seems that Mr. Munday had to take care of them through the La Salle Street bank and that was how I became indebted to the bank."[14] At the time of the statement, Paynter said he had repaid everything but $2,676.45. The La Salle Street Bank was being investigated because it failed.

Following his Senate career, Paynter moved to Frankfort, Kentucky, in 1913 and continued the practice of law as well as farming. He had at least one child, a daughter named Winifred Yont, who was the wife of Morton K. Yont. He had three grandchildren named Elizabeth, Mary, and Thomas. He died in Frankfort on March 8, 1921, and was buried in the State Cemetery there.

WILLIAM O. BRADLEY
(1847–1914)

- Class Three of Three
- Senate Service: March 4, 1909–May 23, 1914
- Political affiliation: Republican
- Residence at time of election: Garrard County
- Served with Presidents Taft and Wilson
- Served with Governors Willson and McCreary

Former Kentucky Governor William O. "Billy O." Bradley was unexpectedly elected by the Democratic legislature in 1908 after almost six weeks of balloting. He was elected on February 28, 1908. The legislature began balloting for the Senate seat to choose a successor for US Senator James McCreary on Tuesday, January 14, 1908. It was on the thirty-ninth ballot that the legislature elected Bradley when he accumulated the necessary sixty-four votes.[1] While Democrats were in the majority, the Democratic nominee, former Governor Beckham, was opposed by the publisher of the *Courier Journal*, Henry Watterson.

William O'Connell Bradley was born in south central Kentucky near Lancaster in Garrard County. His father, R.M. Bradley, was a distinguished lawyer of the region. The family moved to Somerset soon after his birth.

In Somerset, he was educated by private tutors as well as at a private school. As a teenager, Bradley ran away from his family home to join the

Union Army. Being only fourteen, he was returned home. As a teenager, Bradley served as a page for the Kentucky legislature and began the self-study of law with the assistance of his father. At age eighteen, the General Assembly passed a special law allowing Bradley to take the bar exam. After passing the bar, he practiced law with his father.

In 1867, Bradley married Margaret Robertson Duncan. They had two children, Robert and Christine. They were Presbyterians.

In 1870, Bradley was elected Garrard County attorney. During the 1880s and 1890s, he ran unsuccessfully as a Republican for various positions, including US representative for Kentucky's Eighth District, governor, and US senator. Bradley was an early advocate of former President U.S. Grant serving a third term as President.[2] In fact the "magnetic young Kentucky Republican" seconded the nomination of Grant at the 1880 Republican National Convention.

In 1889, he declined an appointment from President Benjamin Harrison as ambassador to Korea. Bradley was active within the national and state Republican Party organizations. In 1890, he became a member of the Republican National Committee.

In 1895, Democrats were split in a three-way race for governor. The Democrats nominated attorney general P. Wat Hardin, and the Populists nominated Thomas S. Petitt. This split assisted in the election of "Billy O" as the thirtieth person to serve as Kentucky's governor.

A year after Bradley left the Governor's Mansion, it was speculated that he would be appointed by newly re-elected President McKinley as a federal judge upon the recommendation of Kentucky Republican Senator William DeBoe.[3]

In 1908, Senator-elect Bradley was blocked from going to the Republican National Convention as a delegate to the convention that nominated William Howard Taft for President. According to the *Courier Journal* report, Richard Ernst, Kentucky Republican Chair and future US Senator, and W. Marshall Bullitt attempted to block Bradley's control of the Republican Party apparatus in Kentucky.[4] Prior to the Republican National Convention, Bradley had supported Vice President Fairbanks. Ernst and Bullitt had been for Taft originally and were furious with Bradley. They blocked Bradley from being elected as an at-large delegate to the Republican National Convention. However, due to Bradley's unexpected election to the Senate, he was much sought out at the Convention. The Taft forces recognized Bradley's popularity and the antagonism shown by Ernst resulting in Ernst's defeat as national committeeman. It was Taft that personally reached out to Bradley in September 1906 in order to find out about the situation in Kentucky. One meeting was in Cincinnati's Hotel Sinton and later at Taft's home.[5]

After being sworn in, Bradley seemed to have significant influence with the Taft administration. This was seen in the administration's approval of eight of eleven of his choices for census supervisors.[6]

During his tenure in the US Senate, Bradley served as chair on the Committee on Expenditures in the Department of Justice, on the Committee to Investigate Trespassers upon Indian Land, and on the Committee on Revolutionary Claims.

Senator Bradley was a featured speaker of the dedication of Kentucky's new capitol building on June 2, 1910.[7]

In 1912, Bradley with Senator Borah of Idaho supported the purchase of the Lincoln Farm for a national park. It was actively supported in the House by future US Senator and then-Congressman A.O. Stanley. At the same time, Bradley and Borah supported the creation of Mammoth Cave National Park, alongside a local booster of that idea and another future US Senator, Marvel Mills Logan.[8]

In 1912, Senator Bradley was chair of the Kentucky Republican Delegation to the Republican National Convention in Chicago. Vice Chair was former US Senator DeBoe. In respect to the Presidential nomination, twenty-four were for President Taft, and two were for Theodore Roosevelt.[9]

On May 23, 1914 at 9:45 p.m., Senator Bradley died after suffering complications from a fall on May 14, 1914, while boarding a streetcar in Washington, D.C. The senator had just announced that he would not be seeking re-election to the Senate for the term beginning in March 1915.

At the moment of death, present at his bedside was his daughter, Mrs. John G. South of Frankfort, and Miss Rella Lane, characterized as "faithful friend and employee of many years," and others, including his Democratic Senate colleague, Senator Ollie James.[10] In a tribute to his departed colleague, Kentucky Democratic Senator Ollie James was quoted saying:

> Senator Bradley was the only Republican that served as both Governor and Senator from Kentucky. He was the most distinguished Republican in the South and undoubted leader of the party in the state. He was a platform orator of surpassing ability, a lawyer of great ability and an old school Republican—a real partisan of the most pronounced type. Senator Bradley was idolized by the rank and file of his party as no other Republican has ever been. He was held in high esteem by his colleagues of the Senate and his death will be regretted by them all.[11]

Senator William O. Bradley was buried in the Frankfort Cemetery.

Part IX
1914–1920
World War I

In 1914, a new era in Senate politics came into being with the enactment of the Seventeenth Amendment to the US Constitution, which provided for the popular election of US senators. Senators were no longer to be elected by state legislatures. In Kentucky, former Democratic Governor J.C.W. Beckham defeated former Republican Governor Augustus Willson to become Kentucky's first popularly elected US senator. However, it can be argued that Johnson Camden Jr., who had been appointed by Governor James McCreary in June 1914 to complete the term of Senator Bradley who died, was first. Camden was elected in November 1914 to complete Bradley's term when it ended in March 1915. Beckham was elected in November 1914 for the six-year term beginning in March 1915.

In August 1914, World War I started in Europe. The United States entered the War in February 1917. The face of Kentucky was impacted with the building of Camp Zachary Taylor in Louisville and Fort Knox was established as a permanent training camp in 1918.

Kentucky's Senator Ollie James was an early supporter of Woodrow Wilson. James and Kentucky's senators throughout this period supported the policies of the Wilson administration, including the League of Nations.

Prior to America's entry into World War I, Kentucky's National Guard was nationalized by President Wilson. Mexican rebels under Pancho Villa made raids into Texas and New Mexico.[1,2]

During this period Prohibition and Women's Suffrage were two overarching issues. Prohibition divided not only the nation but also the Commonwealth. Kentucky was divided by religion and economics. Baptists, Methodists, and evangelical Protestants supported Prohibition, which resulted in the passage of the Eighteenth Amendment to the Constitution. Kentucky's bourbon whiskey and related industries opposed Prohibition. The women's suffrage movement resulted in the passage of the Nineteenth Amendment, enabling American women to vote in elections beginning in the fall of November 1920.

OLLIE M. JAMES
(1871–1918)

- Class Two of Three
- Senate Service: 1913–1918
- Political affiliation: Democratic
- Residence at time of election: Crittenden County
- Served with President Wilson
- Served with Governors Willson and Stanley

Senator James, who died at the age of forty-seven during the last year of his first term in the US Senate, was compared to Clay and Lincoln for his oratorical and leadership skills. It was said that he was "with the exception of Mr. Bryan and the late President Roosevelt, the most popular campaign orator of his day."[1] Ollie James was the last Kentucky US Senator elected by both houses of the Kentucky General Assembly in January 1911. He succeeded Thomas H. Paynter.[2]

Although Senator James's life and career was cut short, there are three things that make him memorable. Of these, his service as the chair of the Democratic National Convention in both 1912 and 1916 shows the beginning of a long and influential career. Another reason is the fact he was caught carrying a concealed pistol during a filibuster.

Ollie M. James was born July 27, 1871, in a double-log cabin, two miles or so southeast of the village of Sheridan in Crittenden County. He was the son of Judge Lemuel H. and Elizabeth Braley James. His father, L.H. James, was a noted lawyer in Marion. Ollie received a thorough and excellent education to the standards of his day in the common schools of Crittenden County and the Marion Academy. He became a page in the Kentucky legislature in 1887 at age fourteen and was clerk of the cloakroom for the Kentucky Senate of 1889. His naturally deep and re-sounding voice, which he could bend to catch the desired emotion at the proper time, plus the mastery of parliamentary procedure and legislative action made the legal profession and its usual subsequent entrance into the field of politics a logical next step for young Ollie.

He studied law with his father and admitted to the bar in 1891 at age of twenty. Ollie then went into partnership with his father, and the firm of James and James was soon one of the best-known and most-respected law firms in Kentucky.

Ollie James first received statewide attention when he was one of the successful attorneys in Goebel's bid to become Kentucky's governor. At the same time, Ollie James soon gained high esteem within the Kentucky Democratic Party. He was selected to go to the national convention at Chicago in 1896 and at Denver in 1908; he was elected chairman of the Kentucky delegation both times. Ollie gained the recognition of the national Democratic Party by his brilliant seconding speech to William Jennings Bryan's nomination in 1896. He was elected chairman of the Kentucky Democratic Party's Convention in 1900.

Ollie James was elected to the US House of Representative to serve as a Democrat to the Fifty-Eighth Congress in 1902 and to the four suc-ceeding Congresses from March 4, 1903 to March 3, 1913. He was con-sidered a hard worker, but he seemed to like to play pool, as referenced in these 1904 headlines from the *New York Times*:

> Fled From Raid; Ollie James Jumped Out of Poolroom Window and Ran Through Field. —Rep. James jumped out of the 'high window' of the Turf Exchange Poolroom in South Louisville. He landed in a cornfield leaving his broad rim hat behind. He broke all sprinting records getting to the street car track, and when he ar-rived minus two buttons from his trousers and with his suspenders around his neck, he learned to his disgust that the officers were only after the proprietors and employes [sic].[3]

James began his campaign to succeed Senator Paynter in September 1910, prior to his last election to the US House of Representatives in 1910. The headline in the *Courier-Journal* of September 23, 1910, re-ported: "James Candidate for U.S. Senator: First District Congressman

198

Makes Announcement Would Succeed Paynter in United States Senate Not After Speakership."[4]

In January 1912, James was elected by the legislature to the US Senate for a six-year term beginning March 4, 1913. He was nominated by State Representative Charlton B. Thompson of Covington. The Republican opposing him in the legislature was Edwin T. Morrow, future governor. According to an article in the *Courier Journal* titled "James Campaign Expenses—Costs Kentucky's New Senator $2,832 To Land New Toga," James spent $2,832 for his election campaign.[5]

As Kentucky's senator-elect, Congressman Ollie James attained national prominence in 1912 when he was elected permanent chair of the Democratic Convention held in Baltimore. In 1896, 1900, 1904, and 1908, James had been chairman of the Kentucky delegation to the Democratic National Convention. He was defeated for that position at the Kentucky State Convention in Louisville in 1912.[6] However, he was a delegate to the national convention. He was originally a staunch supporter of "Champ" Clark for the Democratic presidential nomination in 1912. Champ Clark had been Speaker of the US House of Representatives during James's service there. Additionally, Clark had Kentucky roots. He was a native of Anderson County and had attended the University of Kentucky until his expulsion his senior year for shooting a classmate.[7] However, the convention went on to nominate New Jersey Governor Woodrow Wilson. James became a champion for Wilson. It was later said by many that Senator Ollie James was President Wilson's "mouthpiece" in the Senate. Ollie James was given control over federal patronage in the Commonwealth over original Wilson supporters.

In respect to the issues of the day, James opposed to Prohibition but supported most measures espoused by the Wilson administration concerning tariffs, taxation and Wilson's position of keeping the US out of World War I prior to 1917.

With the death of Senator William O. Bradley, James became the Commonwealth's senior senator. In May he was assigned the three-office suite formerly assigned to Kentucky Senator Bradley.[8]

Senator James made a significant mark in Democratic politics during his short time in the Senate. He was also the chair of the Democratic Conventions in 1916. In September 1916, James went to Long Branch, New Jersey, to inform President Wilson of his nomination. The *New York Times* gave Senator James more than a page's coverage of his remarks, which was titled "Senator James Eulogistic.; Tells President He Is Called Again to Serve Nation and Mankind."[9]

Soon after President Wilson's re-election in 1916, speculation focused on the possibility that James would seek the 1920 Democratic nomination.[10]

Prior to his championing of the policies of the Wilson administration, he was considered something of a "pacifist."[11] His defense of the Wilson administration could be seen as somewhat strident, as illustrated by his reaction to Wisconsin Senator Robert La Follette's remarks.

Senator James opposed Senator La Follette's filibuster in March 1917 to prevent the arming of American merchant ships. James, one of six senators wishing to speak in opposition to La Follette, was seen to have a concealed pistol:

> With only 26 hours remaining in the life of the 64th Congress on March 3, 1917, Progressive Republican Senator Robert La Follette of Wisconsin launched a filibuster. At issue was whether the Senate would pass House-approved legislation to arm merchant ships against a renewed campaign of German submarine attacks. Seeing passage of this measure as taking the nation closer to intervening in World War I, La Follette sought a national referendum to demonstrate his belief that most Americans opposed that course.
>
> A dozen senators who agreed with La Follette's tactic spoke around the clock until 9:30 on the morning of March 4. When La Follette rose to deliver the concluding remarks, the presiding officer recognized only those who opposed the filibuster. The Wisconsin insurgent erupted with white-hot rage and screamed for recognition. While Democrats swarmed around the furious senator to prevent him from hurling a brass spittoon at the presiding officer, Oregon Senator Harry Lane spotted a pistol under the coat of Kentucky Senator Ollie James. Lane quickly decided that if James reached for the weapon, he would remove from his pocket a heavy steel file and plunge its sharp point into James' neck. While La Follette dared anyone to carry him off the floor, the Senate ordered him to take his seat. He then blocked a series of unanimous consent agreements to take up the bill, which died at noon with the 64th Congress.[12]

James was often referred to as "the biggest man in the Senate," and if his size were the most notable thing about him, nobody ever knew it. The implication was undeserved, but Senator James was "the most good natured of men, and took what came to him just as whole-heartedly as he gave others what he thought they deserved."[13]

Senator James was reported going to the hospital as early as April 16, 1918, in Baltimore. He was examined by Dr. Llewellyn Barker. He was accompanied by President Wilson's physician, Admiral Cary T. Grayson.

Admiral Grayson had been attending to Senator James for some time. Friends of the senator said they expected him to have an operation.[14]

In May 1918, Senator James filed his papers with the Office of the Kentucky Secretary of State to run for re-election.[15]

On June 1, 1918, James was reported to have undergone an operation for removal of his tonsils and adenoids. It was said the senator's condition was much improved.[16]

As the filing deadline for the August primary came, Senator James received last-minute opposition for the Democratic primary from Lexington resident William Presly Kimball. James had been ill at Johns Hopkins and had been unopposed until that time.[17]

During the last year of his life and Senate term, he was considered the voice of the Wilson administration in the US Senate.

He died from kidney disease in 1918 at the Johns Hopkins Hospital in Baltimore, where he was taken after collapsing at his post in the US Senate. He was accompanied to the hospital by his wife, Ruth, and his brother, E.H. James. At the time of his death, it was noted that he was the tenth US Senator to die in office since America's entry into World War I.[18]

Among the fifteen US senators appointed to "superintend" the funeral of Senator Ollie James in Marion, Kentucky, were Senator and future President Warren G. Harding and Senator Fall, who would become Harding's disgraced secretary of the interior.[19]

On February 2, 1919, there were memorial addresses in Senator James's honor in the US Senate. Six of his colleagues eulogized Ollie for over three-and-a-half hours.[20] It is interesting to note in the address by his colleague, Senator J.C.W. Beckham, it was cited that of the ninety-six members of the Senate in 1915, fifteen had died. As a reason for this high mortality rate, Beckham said, "I have no doubt that this unusual and excessive mortality is in a large measure due to the extraordinary and tremendous amount of work that has fallen upon the Members of Congress in these troublous and eventful years of sorrow [World War I] and death."[21]

On February 23, 1919, thirteen members of the US House of Representatives, where James had served for nearly ten years prior to his election to the Senate, eulogized him.

Nearly three years after James' death, Joseph P. Tumulty, secretary to President Wilson from 1913 to 1921, wrote an article about Ollie James that focused on his humor and love of practical jokes. Tumulty wrote:

> I like to think of Ollie's sympathy and humanity, but I would rather tell of the other side of him. He had more humor, more joy of life, than anyone in the Washington procession.

One of my earliest experiences with him was a lesson in politics. The country was in a period of financial depression, or rather threatened depression, for the situation was not yet acute. Everyone had heard talk of the approaching panic. In a luncheon group while he consumed large quantities of food, Ollie was dilating upon the Republican Party's responsibility for all ills past present and those to come. Republican ideas were responsible said he, for the troubles of American business. That was all there was to it.

'But this panic is not ours alone; it is worldwide.'

'My boy,' he replied, 'don't you ever dare say that in public.' 'Why if you were making a campaign speech against me and got off such a thing as that, I would annihilate you, I would simply eradicate you, I would put you out of the running, I would stampede the audience.'

'And how?'

'All I would have to say to them would be this: You have heard my honorable opponent declare this Republican panic not only paralyzes the business of our own land but destroys the trade of the whole world. Ladies and Gentlemen, do you understand what this means? It means fellow citizens that the devastating hand of the Republican Party lays its deadly touch upon the universe. Its malignity is not content with the ruin of its own country. It spreads ruin to the ends of the earth.'[22]

He is buried in the Mapleview Cemetery in Marion, Kentucky. His monument is the tallest one in the cemetery. His wife, Ruth, died in September 1961.[23]

JOHN N. CAMDEN
(1865–1942)

- Class Three of Three
- Senate Service: June 16, 1914–March 4, 1915
- Political affiliation: Democratic
- Residence at time of election: Versailles
- Served with President Wilson
- Served with Governor McCreary

On May 30, 1914, Kentucky Governor McCreary announced the appointment of Johnson N. Camden to the Senate seat held by W.O. Bradley at the time of Bradley's death. Camden was chair of the Kentucky's Democratic State Central Committee. Press reports noted that former Governor Beckham was considering being a candidate for the full term, which began in March 1915. General Bennett H. Young, head of the United Confederate Veterans located in Louisville and former Congressman David H. Smith were also thought to be running.[1] Camden was a November 1914 candidate for election for the balance of Bradley's term from November 1914 through March 4, 1915.

As early as November 1912, he had been speculated as a candidate for the Democratic nomination for the Senate for Republican Bradley's seat. At that time, Camden stated that he would not be a candidate for the US Senate.[2]

At noon on June 16, 1914, Camden was escorted to take his oath by Kentucky's senior Senator, Ollie James. Kentucky's US Representatives Fields (later a Kentucky governor) and Barkley (later a US senator from Kentucky and vice president) as well as Kentucky Representative Rouse observed the Senate pro tempore administer the oath to Camden. He was given the late Senator Bradley's desk.

In his first remarks after being sworn in, Camden spoke in favor of a bill for establishing an armor plate plant in Ashland or Paducah, Kentucky. He also spoke in favor of President Wilson's policy on Mexico.[3]

During the summer of 1914, both Camden's wife and his colleague Senator Ollie James's wife were in Europe at the time of the beginning of World War I. There was a headline in the *Courier Journal* on August 5, 1914 that read: "Neither Mrs. James nor Mrs. Camden Heard From: Wives of Both Kentucky Senators Are Abroad In War Stricken Europe."[4]

Camden was the son of the Johnson Newlon Camden, a US Senator from West Virginia from 1881 to 1887 and 1893 to 1895. Camden Sr. was considered the richest man in West Virginia.[5] Camden Jr. was born in Parkersburg, Wood County, West Virginia on January 5, 1865. He attended a series of boarding schools, including the Episcopal High School in Alexandria, Virginia; Phillips Academy in Andover, Massachusetts; and Virginia Military Institute.

He attended Columbia Law School in New York City and the law school of the University of Virginia at Charlottesville. He was admitted to the bar in 1888, but he never practiced law. Following graduation from law school, he went to work for the Ohio River Railroad as treasurer and paymaster. His father had built the Ohio River Railroad. Camden encountered health problems and had to temporarily retire.

In 1890, he moved to Spring Hill Farm near Versailles in Woodford County, his wife Susanna Preston Hart's 1600-acre estate. It was here he began one of the leading Thoroughbred-breeding establishments of the American turf from 1890 to 1930:

> Among the noted stallions were Spendthrift, Esher, Albert, Ben Brush, winner of the 1896 Kentucky Derby; Peter Quince and Light Brigade. The progeny of Light Brigade won 1,123 races and $1,630,709 by 1930.
>
> Senator Camden serves as chairman of the American Turf Association and the Kentucky Jockey Club and had been a member of the New York Jockey Club.[6]

In 1920, Camden served as Kentucky chair for James Cox's run for president.

According to his *New York Times* obituary, "He was a sponsor of progressive agriculture and served as Director of the National Hereford Association. Mr. Camden was one of the advocates of the bill establishing the Kentucky State Racing Commission and served many years as a member of the commission, three times as its chairman."[7]

He was buried next to his wife, Susan, in the Frankfort Cemetery in Frankfort, Kentucky.

In what is considered a mystery to many, the university library at Morehead State Teachers College (now Morehead State University) in Morehead, Kentucky, was named after him in 1929. Johnson Camden had no ties to the school nor had he ever visited.

JOHN C.W. BECKHAM
(1869–1940)

- Class Three of Three
- Senate Service: 1915–1921
- Political affiliation: Democratic
- Residence at time of election: Bardstown/Frankfort
- Served with Presidents Wilson and Harding
- Served with Governors McCreary, Stanley, Black, and Morrow

John C.W. Beckham has a unique place in Kentucky senatorial history. He was a candidate prior to the Seventeenth Amendment when the legislature elected US senators, and he was a candidate after 1913 when the electorate elected US senators.

Assuming the office of Kentucky governor at the age of thirty-one, John C.W. Beckham could be described as a "golden boy" of Kentucky Democratic politics at the beginning of the twentieth century. Beckham first came to the nation's attention as Governor Goebel's lieutenant governor. Beckham assumed the office of Kentucky governor on February 3, 1900, one hour after the death of Mr. Goebel due to wounds suffered from an assassination the previous month.[1] Beckham was the first US senator from Kentucky elected by popular vote after the enactment of the Seventeenth Amendment.

John C.W. Beckham was born into a politically connected Central Kentucky family. He was the grandson of former Governor and US Postmaster General Charles Anderson Wickliffe. He was born on the family estate of Wickland in Bardstown, Kentucky. He attended the Roseland Academy at Bardstown and later Central University, now known as Eastern Kentucky University, in Richmond.

Following his time in Richmond, he served as a high school principal while studying law. He was admitted to the bar in 1889 and began to practice law in Bardstown in 1893. In the same year, he was elected as a state representative and served in the Kentucky House from 1894 through 1898. During his last term in the Kentucky House, he was elected by his colleagues as Speaker. In 1899, he ran as the Democratic candidate for lieutenant governor, with Goebel running for governor.

After assuming the office of Kentucky governor (Senator-elect Joseph Blackburn observed Beckham's swearing-in ceremony, which occurred within one hour of Goebel's death), one of Beckham's first actions as governor was to sign Blackburn's certificate of election.[2] He was subsequently elected for the balance of Goebel's term and elected to a full term in 1903. His term ended in December 1907.

Beckham sought election to the US Senate on four occasions. The first time was a month after leaving the office of Kentucky governor. Beckham made his plans known for seeking election to the US Senate in 1908, as early as the spring of 1906. As governor, Beckham had scheduled a special Democratic primary for the 1908 Senate race nomination to coincide with the general election of November 1906. In that special primary, Beckham won 91 of 119 counties and 6,000 votes over incumbent US Senator James B. McCreary for the Democratic nomination for the US Senate seat.[3]

In January and February 1908, the Kentucky General Assembly met to elect the US Senator. However, even with a Democratic majority in the legislature, a Democratic Senate primary win would not guarantee Beckham's election.

In 1907, Governor Beckham became involved in a public dispute with Henry Watterson, the editor of the *Louisville Courier-Journal*. Beckham supported Prohibition, and Watterson opposed it. Beckham's dispute with Watterson over Prohibition may have cost the Democrats the Governor's Mansion in 1907. This was when Republican Augustus Willson defeated Democrat Samuel W. Hager.

Additionally, in May 1907, the Kentucky Court of Appeals invalidated municipal elections in Louisville due to fraud by the "whiskey ring." As governor, Beckham appointed a Robert W. Bingham, future owner of the *Courier Journal*, as mayor to head a reform group that abolished graft in the police department, closed gambling houses, and enforced Sunday closing laws for saloons.[4]

The 1908 session of legislature took almost two months to elect a US Senator. As the Democratic presidential candidate, William Jennings Bryan was popular in Kentucky, so he was brought to Frankfort to campaign for Beckham but to no avail.[5] After thirty-nine ballots and four Democratic votes, the majority Democratic Kentucky General Assembly elected former Republican Governor William O. Bradley on February 28, 1908.

Sample headlines of the time:

- "Beckham Is Still Three Votes Short of Election as Senator"
- "Ex-Gov Beckham is still 3 votes short of election and Bradley lacks 5 votes while 6 Democrats, who are opposed to Beckham, hold the balance of power"
- "Beckham Loses Another Vote"
- "Balloting Beckham 52, Bradley 51, McCreary 2, Baird 1, Blackburn 1 and John R. Allen 3"
- "Beckham Defeated in Legislative Vote by Former Republican Governor William O. Bradley 64 to 15 on the 39th Ballot".

He would seek the same seat in 1914. By the time of the 1914 elections, the Seventeenth Amendment to the US Constitution mandated the direct or popular election of US senators rather than by the legislatures of the states. There was one roadblock to Beckham's election. Augustus O. Stanley, the popular US congressman from Henderson, decided to seek the Democratic nomination to the Senate as well. Stanley had helped settle the "Black Patch," or "Tobacco Wars," which plagued Western Kentucky, with his work on antitrust legislation. Congressman Stanley was a hard-drinking man who opposed Prohibition. Beckham supported Prohibition. "The rift between factions occurred in part because Stanley's defense of the Kentucky's famous bourbon whiskey industry may have cost him the 1914 U.S. Senate race won by Beckham, who had clung to a platform composed of one issue—prohibition."[6]

His support of Prohibition helped Beckham earn the honor of being Kentucky's first popularly elected US Senator following the enactment of the Seventeenth Amendment. Prohibition would later be one of the factors that cost him the same seat in 1920. His support of Prohibition is rather strange considering his hometown of Bardstown calls itself the "Bourbon Capital of the World."

It should be noted that Senator Bradley died in May 1914. Governor James McCreary appointed Democratic Party Chair Johnson M. Camden to fill Bradley's term until the election. It was agreed that Camden would seek the balance of Bradley's term between November 1914 and March 1915. Beckham would then seek the full term from 1915 to 1921.

The headlines just prior to the November 1914 election showed the excitement and the power of the Kentucky Democratic Party at that time. From the *Courier Journal* of November 3, 1914, the headlines of the activities from November 2 read:

"Beckham Speaks At Final Rally Held in Frankfort," "Crowd Too Great To Use Capital Theater," "Many Country People Among The Audience," "The campaign in Franklin county closed this afternoon with a monster rally in the Old Capitol yard, at which former Gov. J.C.W. Beckham and Lieut. Gov. E.J. McDermott spoke," and "The meeting was to be held in the Capital Theater, but when the crowd gathered it was apparent that the theater was not large enough to hold it, and, the weather being find, it was decided to hold the rally outdoors."

Beckham is quoted as saying:

This is my home, but I do not ask any citizen of Franklin county to vote for me for that reason. . . .. The triumph of any one party or the success of any one man or set of men is of no importance to the people. Vote for me if you believe in the policies of Woodrow Wilson and want a representative in the Senate who will support his policies. That is the only ground on which I solicit your support.[7]

Once in the Senate, he served as chairman of the Committee on Expenditures in the Department of Labor; was a strong supporter of the Wilson administration, particularly after the end of World War I; and supported the League of Nations.

Among his duties was taking care of federal patronage.[8] Kentucky's senior US senator, Ollie James, was designated by the Wilson administration as the point person for federal patronage in the Commonwealth. Individual Democratic congressmen controlled the appointments of postmasters in their respective districts. The Tenth and Eleventh Congressional Districts had Republican congressmen. Therefore, Senators Beckham and James selected the postmasters for the cities in those districts. For example, James selected postmasters for Pikeville, Whitesburg, and Williamsburg. Beckham selected postmasters for Barbourville, Harlan, and Prestonsburg.

In 1916, Senator Beckham traveled throughout Kentucky campaigning for the reelection of President Woodrow Wilson. In his speeches, he noted that Republican Henry Ford supported President Wilson over Charles Evans Hughes.[9]

Once the United States entered World War I, Beckham's attention turned to legislation relating to the war. One included the taxing of profits for those who sold to the government at a 73 percent rate. Both

Beckham and his Kentucky colleague, Senator James, voted with the majority in opposing the tax proposed by the progressive members of the Senate.[10]

With the end of the war, Beckham was an outspoken advocate of the League of Nations.

A headline from an article in the *Courier Journal* of March 20, 1919, read, "Beckham Favors Indorsement[sic] of Nation's League, Says American Isolation is a Vain Dream of Statesman." At an interview at the Seelbach Hotel, he said the following:

> I am heartily in favor of the adoption by the Peace Conference and of the ratification of the nations of the earth of a plan for a League of Nations. The constitution for such a league, which was published some time ago, had defects. It was evidently submitted for the purpose of sounding the sentiment and obtaining the ideas on the subject of the peoples of the various countries. It has accomplished that purpose. It has brought forth the widest and most exhaustive discussions. Its objectionable points have been subjected to the searchlight of the world's best thought and out of it all I believe the Peace Conference, in the light of such thorough criticism will be able to formulate a constitution that will obviate all reasonable objections. That will meet the sanction of the American people and be ratified by the Congress.[11]

His support of the League is reflected in these excerpts from the *New York Times* in July 1919: "Senator McNary, Republican of Oregon; Beckham, Democrat, of Kentucky and Johnson, Democrat of North Dakota, supported the League of Nations covenant in the treaty debate in the Senate today, while Moses, Republican of New Hampshire, opposed it with other provisions of the treaty."[12]

The article continues regarding the debate in the Senate:

> "No advocate of this document,' Senator Beckham said, 'can proclaim it perfect. No idealist can safely promise that it beyond all doubt removes the possibility of war in the future. But it at least comes to us with a promise that, if given a fair trial, if improved where improvements may be found necessary later on, and if supported by the civilized governments of the earth, it will certainly be a tremendous advance over all previous plans, and one that may in reality fulfill the dream of its most enthusiastic advocates, a worldwide and enduring peace."[13]

Additionally, "Senator Beckham warned Republican leaders against making the League of Nations a partisan question, declaring it to be one which 'transcends all partisan or political issues.'"[14]

Senator Beckham was a member of the Democratic National Convention of 1920's Resolution Committee, which met in San Francisco. The Resolution Committee rejected a resolution in support of independence for Armenia; however, it accepted a substitute resolution offered by Senator Beckham "expressing sympathy for the Armenian people and promising assistance so far as it would be considered possible and proper."[15]

Beckham was up for reelection in 1920. It was a year that showed difficulties for Democrats. Beckham's Republican opponent was Richard Ernst of Covington—a former city councilman and longtime chair of the Republican Party in Kentucky. The Democratic presidential candidate, James Cox of Ohio, carried Kentucky. In the Senate race, Senator Beckham had a 35,685 vote over Ernst prior to the counting of the votes in the Eleventh Congressional District. Beckham was defeated due to the large Republican turnout in the Eleventh Congressional District (situated in southeastern Kentucky). Richard Ernst received 63,788 votes to Beckham's 20,524. Thus, Ernst came out of the Eleventh Congressional District with about a 7,000-vote lead and the election.[16]

Beckham's defeat could be attributed to three things. First, Beckham supported Prohibition. With the enactment of Prohibition in Kentucky, thousands became unemployed in the bourbon industry, including not only distillers but also teamsters and barrel makers. The second thing was that Beckham was not a supporter of women's suffrage. With women voting for the first time, most of them probably did not vote for the senator who did not support their right to vote. Lastly, the nation wanted a change from Wilson and the Democrats.

Beckham did not completely "flee" Washington after his defeat. In February, he and his wife were Kentucky guests at a large dinner party that Judge Ansberry and his wife gave for the former governor of Ohio and his wife Mrs. James Cox.[17]

After his senatorial term was over in March 1921, Beckham resumed the practice of law in Louisville, Kentucky.

In 1927, Beckham attempted to revive his political fortunes, by seeking another term as governor. However, the incumbent Democratic governor, William J. Fields, supported Robert T. Crowe of Oldham County, who had been elected to the Kentucky House in 1916 and 1918 and served as Speaker in his last session. In addition, the Jockey Club supported Crowe. Beckham had signaled his opposition to pari-mutuel gambling and horse racing. When Beckham won the Democratic primary over Crowe, the Jockey Club threw its support to Republican Judge

Flem D. Sampson. Judge Sampson won the governorship over Beckham by 32,131 votes. It was estimated that the Jockey Club spent half a million dollars to defeat him. It should be noted that while Beckham was defeated, the rest of the Democratic ticket was elected, including both houses of the General Assembly.[18]

Beckham was an unsuccessful candidate for nomination to the US Senate in 1936 against incumbent Democrat US Senator Marvel Mills Logan. Jim Brown's financial empire had collapsed. Brown had previously financed the Jockey Club's political candidates. Beckham had allies in Ambassador Bingham and Governor Happy Chandler and the United Mine Workers. However, John Y. Brown Sr. entered the Democratic primary. Brown had been elected congressman-at-large at age thirty-two. He agreed, in 1935, to stay out of the governor's race and support Chandler. In return, Chandler would support Brown for the Senate the following year. However, Chandler failed to support Brown as promised. Chandler supported former Governor and Senator Beckham over incumbent Senator Logan and John Y. Brown Sr. Brown ran in the primary anyway, which is said to have assisted Logan in his primary win.

In the Democratic primary of 1936, Senator Logan won over Beckham and Brown by 2,385 votes out of 454,000 cast.[19] Thus Senator Beckham's hopes for a political comeback ended.

Senator Beckham died in Louisville on January 9, 1940. He was buried in the Frankfort Cemetery in Frankfort, Kentucky. Beckham County, Oklahoma, was named in his honor.

GEORGE BROWN MARTIN
(1876–1945)

- Class Two of Three
- Senate Service: 1918–1919
- Political affiliation: Democratic
- Residence at time of election: Boyd County
- Served with President Wilson
- Served with Governor Stanley

George Brown Martin was appointed by Democratic Governor A.O. Stanley to fill the unexpired term of Kentucky's late US Senator Ollie James. Martin was an unexpected choice by some, including the *Courier Journal*. In an editorial titled "A Public Duty," the *Courier Journal* stated:

> The State will be disappointed and mystified, Mr. Martin is not known to the citizens of Kentucky, and his public services have been obscure. For these reasons it is impossible as of yet to place an estimate upon his capabilities for the great place he has called upon to fill. It is, as most, us the bud, not the flower of expectancy that Senator Martin enters the history of the world, and the *Courier Journal* tenders him its sincere good wishes and earnest hope that he will ably and honorably administer the great trust which the Governor has consigned to him.[1]

The *Courier Journal* received one letter, published on September 18, 1918, complaining about the article written on September 7. In an article with the title, "The Old Lady's Letterbox: Old Woman to Old Lady," the writer states, "Your statements, reasoning and conclusions in your first paper were shockingly surprising and to an unsympathetic reader appeared weak and unsupportable as the knees of a stripling soldier must be when he is suddenly drenched with his first noxious gas blast."[2]

At the time of the appointment, Governor Stanley was the Democratic candidate in the November 1918 election for the full six-year term.

Senator George Brown Martin was born in Prestonsburg, Kentucky, on August 18, 1876. In 1877, he moved with his parents to Catlettsburg in Boyd County. He attended the public or common schools in the Catlettsburg area. He attended Central Kentucky University in Richmond, and he graduated in 1895. He then studied law and was admitted to the bar in 1900.

He practiced law in Boyd County, and he was associated with numerous local businesses. His associations included service as general counsel and director of the Big Sandy & Kentucky River Railway, vice president of the Ohio Valley Electric Railway, and director of Kentucky-Farmers Bank in Catlettsburg. In 1904, he was appointed Boyd County judge by Governor Beckham due to a vacancy.

He was a member of the Council of National Defense for Kentucky in 1917. Prior to his appointment as US Senator, he was about to enter as a major in the Judge Advocate General's Department of the US Army, but he did not serve due to his Senate service.

After his appointment by Governor Stanley, he took the oath of office in the Senate Chambers on September 17, 1918.[3] At the time of his appointment, Congressman and future Governor W.J. Fields, who represented Catlettsburg, said, "he is one of the finest lawyers in the South and a fine gentleman."[4]

Prior to being sworn in, he was unsure as to his position on woman's suffrage. However, he was determined to support President Wilson's position on the war. This is indicated in the *Courier Journal* article of September 10, 1918, titled "Senator Martin Does Not Regard Woman's Suffrage As War Measure: Reiterates Intentions To Support President's War Policies." However, the October 1918 meeting of the Executive Committee of the Kentucky Equal Rights Association adopted a resolution thanking Senator Martin for his vote on the federal suffrage amendment. It sent another resolution protesting Senator Beckham's vote against the federal suffrage amendment.[5]

He was made a committee chair less than a month into his term. He was made chair of the Senate Committee on Expenditures, succeeding

Senator Kirby of Arkansas, who was made chairman of the Committee on Patents and, filling the vacancy caused by the death of Senator Ollie James.[6]

Senator George Martin was looked upon favorably by those with whom he worked in Washington, as seen in this December 1918 headline: "Kentucky's Junior Senator has made a good impression at the Capital; Quiet Mountain Bachelor Does Not Take Himself Too Seriously." The article said he lived at the "New Willard Hotel."[7]

In January 1918, he publicly opposed the reorganizing of the IRS offices in Kentucky, which would result in the closure of some. He stated that he would like to see an office in Ashland.[8]

In February 1919, Democrats in Ashland wanted Senator Martin to announce for governor. Lieutenant Governor Black, who succeeded Governor Stanley, was not acceptable to all factions of the Democratic Party.[9]

Less than a month before the expiration of his term, Martin indicated he wanted to visit a World War I battlefield.[10]

With a couple of exceptions, there is little immediate record of Martin's public life after he left the Senate other than the fact that he returned to Boyd County to practice law. The exceptions are set forth below.

Senator Martin's public service continued as one of Kentucky's commissioners to the Conference on Uniform State Laws in 1920. Prohibition must have been an important issue with Martin. In June 1932, he filed papers to oppose incumbent US Senator Alben Barkley in the Democratic Primary. He said he thought that repeal of the Eighteenth Amendment (Prohibition) unwise. Barkley was a supporter of the repeal of Prohibition, even though he had supported Prohibition as a congressman.[11]

Martin was soundly defeated in his attempt to return to the Senate in 1932. Incumbent Senator Alben Barkley received over twice as many votes as Martin. The returns showed 96,259 votes for Barkley and 42,719 for Martin in 3,045 precincts out of 4,195 precincts.[12]

Senator George Brown Martin died in Catlettsburg, Kentucky, on November 12, 1945. He was buried in Catlettsburg Cemetery.

Part X

1920–1930

Republican Ascendency, Prohibition, and the Great Depression

In 1919, Edwin Morrow, a Republican, was elected governor after being defeated in 1915 by fewer than 500 votes by A.O. Stanley. The 1920 presidential election saw Democrat James Cox receive Kentucky's electoral votes over the national winner Warren G. Harding. However, Republican Calvin Coolidge carried Kentucky in 1924 and Herbert Hoover won Kentucky in 1928.

While the Democrat William J. Fields took the Governor's Mansion in 1923, Republican Flem Sampson won the 1927 general election to become governor.

During this period, two Republicans were elected by popular vote, defeating senators who had previously served as Kentucky governor. In 1920, Covington resident Richard P. Ernst defeated incumbent US Senator John C.W. Beckham. In 1924, Louisville business executive Fred Sackett defeated US Senator A.O. Stanley.

However, in 1926 the Democratic congressman from the First District in Western Kentucky, Alben Barkley, defeated Senator Ernst.

The overriding issue during most of the decade of the 1920s was Prohibition and the enforcement of Prohibition. This seems to be one of the forerunners of "single issue" politics of the late twentieth and early twenty-first centuries. For the record, Republicans in Kentucky tended to be for Prohibition and pro-enforcement.

Democrats like Senator A.O. Stanley was against Prohibition most of his career and even gave speeches on the Senate floor talking about the hypocrisy of pro-Prohibition senators. Alben Barkley was for Prohibition until after he became a senator. Kentucky's Democratic Governor Field was for Prohibition and did not allow alcoholic beverages at the Capitol or the Mansion.

Congressman John M. Robsion was Hoover's Kentucky campaign chair in 1928. He was threatening to primary incumbent Republican Fred Sackett in 1930, when President Hoover appointed Sackett US ambassador to Germany. Republican Governor Sampson appointed Robsion to the vacancy caused by Sackett's becoming ambassador to Germany. However, the onset of the Depression hurt Robsion's election in 1930 when a little-known Democrat, Judge M.M. Mills, defeated Robsion.

AUGUSTUS OWSLEY STANLEY
(1867–1958)

- Class Two of Three
- Senate Service:1919–1925
- Political affiliation: Democratic
- Residence at time of election: Henderson
- Served with Presidents Wilson, Harding, and Coolidge
- Served with Governors Black, Morrow, and Fields

Augustus Owsley Stanley is probably best known for his work as Kentucky's Second District congressman and as governor. His record as an US Senator is overshadowed by his record as governor and the fact the Democrats were in the minority during his single term. He is given little credit for his often-overlooked attempts to bring forward the discussion of the constitutionality of various practices during the Prohibition Era, including "warrantless searches."

Senator A.O. Stanley was the son of the Reverend William Stanley and Amanda Owsley Stanley. Reverend Stanley had served in the Confederate Army during the Civil War. He became a Disciples of Christ Minister. Amanda Stanley, a native of Shelby County, Kentucky, was the daughter of Eudigate Owsley, who served in the Kentucky legislature for Shelby County. Eudigate's brother was Kentucky Governor William Owsley.

Stanley was born in Shelbyville, Kentucky. He was given the name "Nudicut Owsley Stanley". At age ten, he convinced his parents to change his first name to "Augustus" in honor of his grandmother, Augusta Owsley, so that no one could call him "NO Stanley."

He briefly attended the state college in Lexington before attending Centre College in Danville, where he graduated in 1889. While studying for the bar, he briefly taught school before practicing law in Flemingsburg, where his parents lived. After he was defeated in a race for county attorney and his law practice floundered, he moved from Flemingsburg to Henderson, Kentucky.

Stanley was first elected to public office in Henderson, Kentucky, in 1902. In November of that year, A.O. Stanley was elected to the first of six terms in the US House of Representatives from Western Kentucky's Second District. The American Tobacco Company, with its monopoly on the tobacco markets in Western Kentucky and Tennessee, made it impossible for most tobacco farmers to make a living. As a result, farmers were literally in a war with American Tobacco and those who still did business with it. This included the burning of American Tobacco's cigarette factory in Princeton, Kentucky.

He served in that position for twelve years. His most notable work during his twelve years in the House was going after US Steel and other "trusts." As a congressman, Stanley championed the interests of tobacco growers and opposed trusts. Due to the antitrust practices of Duke's American Tobacco Company in Western Kentucky, Stanley introduced legislation in the Congress to go after the tobacco trust and used his position to convince the Theodore Roosevelt administration and the Taft administration to pursue antitrust suits against the American Tobacco Company.

He led a congressional investigation of US Steel. US Steel was a billion-dollar corporation or trust assembled by J.P. Morgan during the 1890s. J.P. Morgan's trust controlled over 60 percent of the nation's production of steel and owned over 1,000 miles of railroads and a significant portion of the nation's coal and iron ore reserves, as well as 112 ships that shipped iron ore. In 1907, Morgan purchased Tennessee Coal, Iron, and Railroad. In 1911, Congressman Stanley began hearings and investigations concerning US Steel and legislation that resulted in the Clayton Antitrust Act.

In 1914, the first direct elections for the US Senate were held in Kentucky. Foregoing a seventh term in the House, A.O. Stanley challenged former Governor J.W. Beckham for the Democratic nomination for the US Senate in which he was defeated by Beckham, who became Kentucky's first popularly elected US senator.

The following year, A.O. Stanley was nominated for governor. Stanley's Republican opponent was Edwin P. Morrow of Somerset (who was elected governor in 1919). Stanley and Morrow often traveled together during the 1915 gubernatorial campaign, even staying at the same hotel while they verbally blasted each other. One example of the antics of the campaign is cited in Thomas Ramage's "Augustus Owsley Stanley—Early 20th Century Democrat" found in *Kentucky Profiles Biographical Essays in Honor of Holman Hamilton*. It reads:

> Morrow and Stanley shared the same platform. Speaking first, Morrow thrilled the crowd with his brilliant oratory. Stanley, who had drunk too much bourbon prior to the engagement, managed to sit quietly during Morrow's address, but when he rose to make his own speech 'his head swam, and his knees buckled.' Nauseated, he staggered to the back of the platform where he vomited. Then, embarrassed but not at a loss for words, he returned to the speaker's stand where he said: 'Gentlemen, I beg you to excuse me. Every time I hear Ed Morrow speak; it makes me sick of my stomach.'[1]

Issues during the campaign included Prohibition, which Stanley opposed. Another issue was the $1.00 tax on dogs. When speaking about the tax on dogs, Stanley would often howl like a dog.

A.O. Stanley defeated Morrow by only 487 votes.

As governor, A.O. Stanley enjoyed a Democratic majority in both houses of the General Assembly.

Stanley was successful in having his legislative programs enacted into law. These programs included the first workers' compensation law and antitrust legislation. Stanley successfully pushed progressive legislation through the General Assembly, including a corrupt practice act and an anti-lobbying act. During a 1917 special session, the General Assembly enacted a tax reform package that would help Kentucky's farmers. After the start of World War I, Stanley vetoed legislation that would have banned the teaching of German in Kentucky.

Stanley was also quite the orator. He stopped a lynchings of a black prisoner, a judge, and a commonwealth attorney in Murray by the sheer force of his personality. He made national news in January 1917 when he took a night train from Louisville to Murray as he said, "I shall give the mob a chance to lynch the governor of Kentucky first."[2] Upon arriving in Murray, he personally went to where the circuit judge and the commonwealth attorney were being held hostage and dared the mob to kill him.

With the death of Kentucky Senator Ollie James, Governor Stanley made it evident that he would be seeking the full term to fill Senator

James's seat. In the interim, Governor Stanley appointed George Martin of Boyd County to serve the remainder of James's term. During the fall 1918 campaign for a full term, Stanley had the support of President Woodrow Wilson and Kentucky's other US senator, John C.W. Beckham, who had been Stanley's opponent in the 1914 Democratic senatorial primary.[3]

Stanley delayed taking his seat in the Senate until after the 1919 session of the Kentucky General Assembly. On Wednesday, May 19, 1919, Augustus O. Stanley was sworn in as a US senator. He was escorted by his colleague Kentucky US Senator J.C.W. Beckham to the desk of Vice President Marshall, who administered the oath. His new offices were filled with flowers, "sheaves of roses having been sent to him by the Kentucky State Senate."[4] He initially stayed at the Occidental Hotel in Washington as he arrived in the nation's capital the same day he took the oath.

The same day, Senator Stanley went to the Shipping Board at the request of Louisville Mayor George Weissinger Smith. He requested that the Board provide adequate ships at New Orleans and other Southern ports in order for Louisville to benefit of increased export trade.[5]

In 1922, Senator Stanley proposed an amendment to the legislation known as the Willis-Campbell "Anti-Beer" Act. The Willis-Campbell Act prohibited physicians from prescribing beer or liquor as a "drug." Stanley opposed the Willis-Campbell Act. His colleague Senator Ernst supported it. Stanley's legislation would have required warrants for acts of enforcement of Prohibition. The failure to use warrants would result in fines and prison time. The Stanley Amendment was originally passed unanimously by the Senate on August 8, 1922. However, the House Conference Committee would not accept the amendment. There was an attempt at a compromise that would permit searches of baggage, cars, and buildings other than dwelling places.[6] Stanley's amendment for a warrant provision threatened to deadlock Congress and delay a congressional recess. The Senate stood firm on the requirement for inclusion of Stanley's amendment requiring a warrant. This included Senator Borah, who was a strong supporter of Prohibition. In the House, Representative Volstead believed that enforcement of Prohibition could not be done with a warrant requirement.[7] The conference committee eventually compromised. The legislation passed contained a warrant requirement for searches of dwelling places or homes.

Stanley was becoming a nationally known orator and advocate of individual rights, as well as an opponent of Prohibition. Before the annual convention of the New Jersey Bar Association, in a speech titled "Outgrowing Our Independence," he equated Prohibition with "Paternalism and interference by the Government in the liberty of the citizen".[8]

In May 1921, Senator Stanley gave the principal address before the state convention of the North Carolina Banker's Association in Greensboro. Senator Stanley's address was described as powerful. He did not propose a panacea to be introduced by Congress. In his remarks, he said; "I hope for the return of prosperity, I believe it is coming, if the Federal government will let it come, not by enacting legislation, but by preventing foolish legislations." He also gave tributes to the South and noted his father's participation in the Confederate Army.[9]

During the 1922 midterm elections, Stanley opened the Democratic campaign in Missouri. In an appearance at Mexico, Missouri, with Arkansas Senator Joseph Robinson, both criticized the Harding-Coolidge administration for its "incompetency and inefficiency." "Senator Stanley stressed that freedom and liberty are being trampled upon and that bureaucratic government is being established in this country." On behalf of Democratic Senator James A. Reed, who was seeking reelection, Stanley characterized him as a "Fearless Defender of Human Rights."[10]

In April 1923, Senator Stanley spoke at Temple Emanu-El in New York City. Stanley spoke about the need for good will between nations during a service at the Temple. In his speech, he said; "Above all the imperative need of the hour for the world for every nation, every commonwealth, every community and every individual, at this tragic hour is tolerance."[11]

While serving as a US Senator, Stanley's widowed mother lived with him and his wife. Senator Stanley's mother, Amanda Owsley Stanley, died at age eighty-six of pneumonia at his home in Washington, D.C.[12]

In the Democratic primary of 1924, Stanley faced John J. Howe of Carrollton.[13] The American Federation supported Stanley's reelection. The AFL claimed that "Stanley's labor record is 100 per cent good."[14]

In his campaign for reelection to the Senate, Senator Stanley would often open by giving tribute to the administration of Woodrow Wilson. Then he would discuss the corruption of the Harding administration with the "Teapot Dome" and related scandals and contrast it with the scandal-free Wilson administration. He was critical of the Fordney McCumber Tariff, which he said brought in $500,000 and put $6 billion in the pockets of special interests. He would point out that the wealth of the US was about $300 billion at the end of the Wilson administration and was now reduced to $224 billion.[15]

In November 1924, Stanley was defeated by Frederic Sackett. The defeat was blamed in part on Stanley's active stands against Prohibition, which resulted in opposition from the Anti-Saloon League. Due to his stand against lynching, he was opposed by the Ku Klux Klan. This, coupled with a divided state Democratic Party and a popular national Republican Party with

President Coolidge running against a lackluster Democratic presidential candidate, combined to help defeat his reelection to the Senate.

Less than a month before leaving office, Senator Stanley was struck by a hit-and-run motorist. The car hit him and placed him directly in the path of an approaching streetcar. Stanley said after the accident: "I was able to save myself from being run over by the street car. I saw it coming; tried to get to my feet, sagged at the knees and dropped down. Then I thought of rolling myself off the tracks and succeeded in doing so just in time."

Physicians at the emergency hospital found the senator had suffered from a badly lacerated nose, a bruised shoulder, and a couple of fractured ribs. The accident occurred a little after midnight. The column mentioned that this was one of a rash of hit-and-run automobile accidents in Washington, D.C.[16]

Perhaps the longest position of public trust held by Augustus Stanley was that of member of the International Joint Commission on the Boundary with Canada. Stanley served the majority of his time on that commission as the chair for the US. He was originally appointed to the commission in 1930 by Republican President Herbert Hoover. The purpose of the commission was to resolve not only boundary disputes but also water rights and resource issues along the US and Canadian border. By the time he was eighty-five and had served on the commission twenty-three years, an article described Stanley as "Kentucky's candidate for the title 'indestructible public servant.'" In 1939, FDR, in an economic move, attempted to remove Stanley from the commission. In 1953, the Republican Eisenhower administration attempted to get Stanley off the commission and ultimately succeeded in 1955.[17]

A.O. Stanley died at age ninety-one on August 12, 1958, at his home in Washington, D.C. There were services in Washington and Frankfort. Announcements of his death were made to the US House of Representatives by Second District Congressman William Natcher and to the Senate by Kentucky Senator John Sherman Cooper.[18]

As a result of the efforts of Governor Happy Chandler, Augustus Stanley laid in state at the Kentucky Capitol for twenty-five hours before his funeral with an honor guard from the Kentucky National Guard. He was the second Kentuckian given the honor to have lain in state in the rotunda. The first was US Senator J.S.C. Blackburn in September 1918 when Stanley was governor.[19] All living Kentucky governors were present for the service. Rev. Dwight E. Stevenson remarked that Stanley's ninety-one years of life equaled half of the age of the nation at that time (182 years). The year of Stanley's birth was the year Alaska was purchased by the US, and the year of his death was the year Alaska became a state. He was buried in Frankfort in a plot he chose near his friend and rival Republican Governor Edwin Morrow.

In a letter to the editor soon after the death of Senator Stanley, a reader wrote about a speech Stanley once made at the University of Kentucky during the presidency of Dr. H.L. Donovan. The reader quoted from Stanley's speech in a tribute to him: "Only those of great heart, strong mind and noble soul have the humility to serve others. Service is the basis of all religions and I have never thought on the last great Day of Judgment, we will be asked what we believed but rather what we did".[20]

Senator Stanley was survived by his wife and two sons, Naval Commander A.O. Stanley Jr. and William Stanley. He was also survived by several grandchildren.[21] His grandson, Augustus Owsley Stanley III (1935–2011), was the Grateful Dead's first live sound engineer and a manufacturer of LSD.

RICHARD P. ERNST
(1858-1934)

- Class Three of Three
- Senate Service: 1921–1927
- Political affiliation: Republican
- Residence at time of election: Covington/Kenton County
- Served with Presidents Harding and Coolidge
- Served with Governors Morrow and Fields

Richard Ernst made his formal announcement for the Republican nomination for the US Senate in May 1920. Ernst had been active in Kentucky Republican politics for several decades, including chairing the Kentucky Republican Party and being an unsuccessful candidate for Congress. In an article concerning his candidacy, it notes his interest in education. He had served as a trustee at his alma mater, Centre College, as well as at Pikeville College and the University of Kentucky. He was active in the First Presbyterian Church of Covington, serving as its Sunday school superintendent and delegate to the Presbyterian General Assembly. He was active in the YMCA of Covington. It was his activity in the YMCA for which he is most noted today. He and his family were responsible for helping found the YMCA's Camp Ernst in Boone County.

Ernst was born in Covington, Kentucky, on February 28, 1858. His father was a prominent banker in the area. He attended the public schools

225

until high school. For high school, he attended Chickerings Academy in Cincinnati, Ohio. He graduated in 1874. He attended Centre College in Danville, Kentucky, from which he graduated in 1878. Following Centre, he attended the law school of the University of Cincinnati. He graduated from law school and was admitted to the bar in 1880.[1] It is interesting to note that future President William Howard Taft attended the law school at the University of Cincinnati at about the same time and was admitted to the bar in 1880 as well. There is no record that he and Taft were acquainted at that time. However, in 1908, Ernst was a Taft delegate to the Republican National Convention.

Ernst practiced in Covington and Cincinnati. He had an office in Cincinnati and was well thought of in that city. Accord to an article in the *Cincinnati Enquirer* entitled "MEN WE MEET":

> "Although he resides in Covington, Richard P. Ernst, the attorney, is virtually a Cincinnatian. He has an office here and knows everyone worth knowing here. 'Dick' Ernst has widespread popularity. He is leader of the Republicans in Kenton County and has run for Congress in that strong Democratic District. He is one of the old Chickering Boys."[2]

Richard Ernst was very active in Kentucky's Republican politics since the 1890s. He was the Republican candidate in 1896 against Democratic Congressman Albert Berry of Newport. In addition to his activity in the Republican Party, Ernst served on the Covington City Council from 1888 to 1892. Prior to his candidacy for the Senate, he was known as an advocate for higher pay for public school teachers and college professors.[3]

Ernst had attempted to secure the Republican nomination for the US Senate in 1914. In that race, he was supported by the US Attorney Edwin Morrow, who was to become governor in 1919.[4,5] Ernst was defeated in his efforts to secure the Republican Senate nomination by former Governor Augustus Willson, who was defeated by J.C.W. Beckham in the 1914 general election. It was Senator Beckham who was defeated by Ernst in 1920.

The year 1920 was a presidential election year. The Democratic presidential ticket of Cox-Roosevelt narrowly won Kentucky by 3,858 votes over the Republican Harding-Coolidge ticket on November 5, 1920. At the same time, Ernst was elected over incumbent Senator J.C.W. Beckham by 7,288 votes.[6]

During his first years in the Senate, Ernst was not as talkative as many of his Kentucky predecessors. Within a political column, it was noted that at over two years into his term, Senator Ernst had yet to make a speech on the floor of the Senate. The column had a subheading: "du Pont Sphinx Like Ernst." Within a blurb about an election in Delaware, it is said:

> Senator du Pont's silence on the floor is no less marked than that of Senator Richard P. Ernst of Kentucky. Each has respected the somewhat worn tradition that a senator must be seen not heard much too much during his first year or so of tenure. Beyond answering roll calls and announcing votes neither has seen fit to clutter up the Congressional Record, and both are esteemed for that.[7]

As many Kentucky Republicans, Ernst was a strong supporter of Prohibition. In 1922, Ernst sponsored legislation to make the Prohibition Bureau separate from the Department of the Treasury and the Bureau of Internal Revenue. This legislation was supported by the Anti-Saloon League. It did not pass.[8]

In 1922, there was some question as to Ernst's support for Prohibition. To reassure the public, the senator wrote a letter to the *New York Times* stating he opposed any modification of Prohibition.[9]

In September 1922, President Warren G. Harding vetoed the World War I veterans' bonus. With his veto, President Harding said that he did not approve of the bill "to provide Adjusted Compensation for the veterans of World War I and other purposes" as there was not enough money in the budget.[10] When Congress voted to override President Harding's veto, it failed by four votes in the Senate. Senator Ernst voted against overriding the president's veto.[11]

During his term in the Senate, Ernst continued to keep his hand in Kentucky Republican organizational politics. In 1923, Ernst sought the chairmanship of the Republican State Convention against then-Louisville-Mayor Huston, which was held on June 23.[12]

Ernst must have won that fight as he served as chair of the Kentucky Republican Party Convention held in Lexington. This was an important convention as Republicans held the Kentucky Governor's Mansion and most statewide offices with term-limited Governor Ed Morrow. Kentucky Republicans used the convention system to nominate their statewide candidates. The article noted that Ernst's friend from Covington, Maurice Galvin, was pulling the strings at the convention.[13]

In addition to Ernst's failure to vote for the World War I veterans' bonus, there seemed to be a lack of interest by the senator in the issue itself. In 1924, during the First Session of the Sixty-Eighth Congress, Senator Ernst served on the Senate Finance Committee. The committee held hearings on H.R. 7959, "An Act to Provide Adjusted Compensation for Veterans of the World War (WWI) and for Other Purposes" from March 25– through29, 1924. The report on the hearings indicates that Senator Ernst often was not present. This would later be used against him in his reelection campaign in 1926 by Congressman Alben Barkley.[14]

Senator Ernst assisted with federal funds for the expansion of the Dixie Highway from Cincinnati through Northern Kentucky to Lexington. Kentucky's Democratic Governor W.J. Fields praised Ernst for his efforts in obtaining federal funding for that road known as US 25.[15]

As chair of a Senate judiciary subcommittee, Senator Ernst drew the ire of women. As chair of the subcommittee, Ernst was holding hearings on a proposed "Equal Rights Amendment." Members of the National Woman's Party, an organization founded by Alice Paul, wanted to testify on behalf of the proposed Equal Rights Amendment. The National Woman's Party accused the senator of allowing opponents of the amendment to testify against it but not giving supporters the same opportunity. Because of this slight, the National Woman's Party, through its secretary, Miss Mabel Vernon, called newspaper offices throughout Kentucky, painting the dashing "Kentuckian as an arbitrary ogre who was trying to take unto himself the prerogatives of the whole sovereign Congress of the United States." It was pointed out that Senator Ernst had provided an opportunity for representatives of the party to testify in February 1924. However, that was the date of former President Woodrow Wilson's funeral. Members of the party and at least two members of Ernst's committee would not be at the committee meeting due to attendance at President Wilson's funeral. It was said that Ernst would not reschedule the opportunity to testify.[16]

Ernst was re-nominated by the Republican State Convention, where his colleague Senator Fred Sackett presided as chair.[17] Following his re-nomination by the Kentucky State Republican Convention in March 1926, First District US Congressman Alben Barkley announced his candidacy to oppose Ernst in the November 1926 general election in Paducah.

During the 1926 campaign, Ernst was criticized for his support of the Fordney-McCumber Tariff. It was Ernst's position that the tariff protected American farm products from foreign competition while imported agricultural implements were on the "free list." Ernst was also criticized for his opposition to the veterans' bonus bill of 1924.[18]

In 1926, Ernst was probably one of the first Kentucky senators to use the medium of radio. Louisville's WHAS Radio had him scheduled for a half-hour address on Thursday, October 26, 1926 at 7:30 p.m.[19] During that broadcast, Ernst defended his record, including his votes on veterans' issues.

Barkley and his surrogates, who included former Senator A.O. Stanley, assailed Ernst's lack of support for veterans' bills.[20]

The morning after the election of November 2, 1926, Ernst was 24,000 votes behind First District Congressman Alben Barkley, with only 650 precincts outstanding out of a total of 4,063 precincts. In the 1925 midterm elections, Republicans lost seven Senate seats, including Kentucky.[21]

After his defeat, Richard Ernst resumed the practice of law in Cincinnati, Ohio. He was also engaged in banking in Covington. In 1930, former Senator Ernst took exception with Republican Kentucky Governor Flem Sampson's attempt to have a hydroelectric generator built below Cumberland Falls. Ernst was president of the Cumberland Falls Preservation Association. Ernst and the association were ultimately successful in having the du Pont Family purchase the land around the Falls for a state park.[22]

Ernst died at Johns Hopkins Hospital, Baltimore, Maryland, on April 13, 1934, after returning from a trip to Panama. He is buried in Highland Cemetery in Fort Mitchell, Kentucky.

FREDERIC M. SACKETT
(1868–1941)

- Class Two of Three
- Senate Service: 1925–1930
- Republican
- Louisville
- Served with Presidents Coolidge and Hoover
- Served with Governors Fields and Sampson

Frederic Sackett became Kentucky's US senator after defeating incumbent Senator A.O. Stanley in the 1924 general election. Sackett's career as the US ambassador to Germany following his service in the US Senate was probably as important as his Senate career.

Sackett was Kentucky's Ivy-League senator. He was born in Providence, Rhode Island, where he attended the public schools before going to Brown University, from which he graduated in 1890. He then attended law school at Harvard and graduated in 1893. Prior to arriving in Kentucky, he practiced law in Columbus, Ohio, and, later, in Cincinnati. He moved to Louisville in 1898. It was in 1898 that Sackett married Olive Speed, the daughter of James Breckenridge Speed, a Louisville businessman and philanthropist. As a philanthropist, Speed donated the statute of Abraham Lincoln that stands in the Kentucky State Capitol.[1]

After his marriage to Olive on April 12, 1898, he gradually abandoned the practice of law in favor of his in-laws' many business interests, which included coal and cement businesses. The coal business included mines in Eastern Kentucky and Northern Tennessee.

Prior to his election to the Senate, he was an active civic leader in Louisville. He served as president of the Louisville Board of Trade in 1917, 1922, and 1923. He is known for three Louisville civic projects. These projects are a bridge across the Ohio to Indiana, construction of Memorial Auditorium, and the establishment of Camp Zachary Taylor during World War I.

His first important appointment was Federal Food Administrator for Kentucky during World War I. This gave him responsibility for controlling, distributing, and rationing food in Kentucky. In this position, Sackett worked with Herbert Hoover, who had been appointed administrator of the United States Food Administration. Sackett's work for the Food Administration led to his appointment by Governor Edwin Morrow to the Kentucky State Board of Charities and Corrections.

Kentucky Republicans believed that Sackett could take Kentucky's other US Senate seat after the election of Republican US Senator Richard P. Ernst in 1920 over the incumbent Senator Beckham. Since the 1890s, the incumbent Kentucky senator had not won re-election. There was a divided Kentucky Democratic Party, and Senator Stanley was against Prohibition.

Sackett ran on a platform of continued prosperity for the nation under policies such as the national tariff and gave full support to Prohibition. The Anti-Saloon League endorsed Sackett even though he had his own private stock of liquor.[2] Sackett reinforced his support of Prohibition on at least two occasions in the month before the election. He supported "strict enforcement of the 18th Amendment,"[3] and in a Louisville speech, "he supported the dry cause."[4]

Incumbent Stanley did not help himself with the voters when he read into the *Congressional Record* on September 23, 1921 the following poem or parody of "My Country Tis of Thee" he calls "The Song of the Moonshiners." Here are the second of three verses entered by Stanley during a discussion of an anti-beer legislation.

My country tis of thee
Land of home breweries
Thy brew I love
I love thy booze and thrills
and thy illicit still,
the moonshine runs in rills
from high above.[5]

Sackett believed that the place for America was in "economic, not political affairs," though he was in favor of a world court.[6] He was ahead of his time when he came out in support of constructing highways with federal appropriations.[7]

Sackett had the support of many who ordinarily supported Democrats, including *Louisville Courier-Journal* editor Robert W. Bingham. Additionally, Democratic Governor Fields provided tepid support for incumbent Democratic Senator Stanley. On Election Day 1924, Sackett won with 406,141 to Stanley's 381,623. That was a margin of 24,518 votes. Additionally, Democratic apathy had lowered participation from 71.2 percent in 1920 to 60.5 percent in 1924. When Sackett was sworn into office in March 1925, Kentucky had two serving Republican US Senators for the first time in history.[8]

Sackett's social life is probably as memorable as his legislative achievements. Because he and his wife's personal wealth, they were able to maintain two large homes fully staffed with servants in both Washington, D.C., and Louisville. In Washington, they had the mansion that once belonged to Charles Evans Hughes, where much of the work on the Washington Conference had occurred while Hughes was secretary of state. In Louisville, they had Edgecomb in the Cherokee Park section of Louisville. They also belonged and were active in clubs in Louisville, New York, and Washington.

As a legislator, Sackett preferred to work behind the scenes within the inner circles of Republican leadership. He eventually became chair of the Republican steering committee, which guided legislation through Congress.[9] He chaired the Senate Committee on Expenditure in the Executive Department.

Throughout his Senate career, he supported the "drys" on all issues relating to Prohibition. One example could be his introduction in 1928 of a resolution that asked for the recall of any diplomat who was guilty of drunken driving and the freezing the pay of federal employees convicted of drunk driving.[10] He supported and spoke for the World Court. The Republican administrations of Harding, Coolidge, and Hoover all supported American membership in the Court of International Justice even though membership continued to be opposed by Congress. Sackett tried to find ways to foster American membership.[11]

The most controversial stand that Sackett made during his Senate tenure was for government ownership of the nitrate-producing facility at Muscle Shoals, Alabama. He was part of a joint committee assembled to consider disposition of the facility, which began operations during World War I. He came to the conclusion that it was in the best interests of the federal government to continue operating this facility. He came to this conclusion due to the rising cost of fertilizer. With government owner-ship, fertilizer would be cheaper for farmers.

In 1927, Eastern Kentucky Republican Flem Sampson was elected governor of Kentucky. Sackett had supported his opponent in the 1927 Republican primary. Governor Sampson had close ties with Congress-man Robsion, who was from Barbourville, as was the governor. In 1928, Robsion was state campaign manager for President Herbert Hoover. Hoover carried Kentucky in the 1928 election. Now, Robsion wanted to run for the US Senate in 1930, even if it meant opposing incumbent Republican Sackett. Sackett turned to the president for assistance in deal-ing with this opposition from Robsion in a 1930 Republican primary.[12]

Unbeknownst to Sackett, Hoover needed a new ambassador in Berlin to replace the seventy-five-year-old Jacob Shurmann, a former president of Cornell University who had been a Coolidge appointee in 1925. At the same time, the Hoover administration was looking for a man with business experience and proper Republican Party credentials to serve as the American ambassador to Germany. Sackett's name was already on Hoover's desk when the Republican issue in Kentucky came to his at-tention.[13]

Prior to his resignation to become ambassador to Germany, Sackett indicated that he planned to seek reelection to the Senate. He sent a letter to the Republican State Central Committee urging a convention to select the Senate nominee in February 1930.[14] He had also contacted his friend President Hoover for assistance in dealing with this issue.

Claudius Huston, Chairman of the Republican National Commit-tee, took credit as the architect of the plan to send Sackett to Germany in order to avoid a GOP bloodbath in Kentucky between Sackett and the Sampson-Robsion faction of the Republican Party.[15] He (Sackett) was also considered for secretary of war, which went instead to Patrick J. Hurley.

Bernard Burke, in his book *Ambassador Frederic Sackett and the Col-lapse of the Weimar Republic, 1930–1933*, explains how Kentucky Repub-lican Party politics looked at a national level.

> The midterm election in 1930 was pivotal for Hoover. The Re-publicans held a paper-thin majority in the Senate, which meant control of the Congress a matter of first priority. Among the sen-ators in harm's way was Sackett, who had been elected in 1924 with the largest majority given to a Republican candidate up to that time. It was an axiom in Kentucky politics that no one from Louisville could be elected to the United States Senate. Sackett's election had broken a ninety-year precedent only because it was

part of a national Republican trend. Sackett had won by riding the wave of Republicanism that swept the nation and carried Calvin Coolidge to victory in Kentucky and back to the White House. Six years later, in the midterm election, without a popular president to head the Republican ticket, the Kentucky senate seat appeared to be in jeopardy.

Congressman Robsion, an astute politician and skilled organizer, had been the Kentucky campaign manager for Hoover when he carried the state in 1928. Robsion certainly could count on Hoover's favor, but he now saw another Hoover favorite, Sackett, as almost certain to go down to defeat. Robsion already was wary of Sackett as a spokesman for urban Louisville. Sackett was allied to a group of Republican leaders characterized as 'outstanding Louisville men comprising the so-called "best minds" who lend dignity to the party' and who stood in opposition to rural leadership for control of the Kentucky GOP.[16]

As American ambassador to Germany, he was received with enthusiasm. He spent much of his time working to support the government of Chancellor Heinrich Brüning. Sackett was one of the first Western diplomats to realize the threat that Adolf Hitler and the Nazi Party posed. One of the biggest issues was the German payment of reparations.

In December 1930, Sackett and Brüning planned a World Economic Conference for heads of state, which would eliminate reparations and address issues caused by the worldwide depression. This eventually emerged as the London Economic Conference of 1933.

At the end of his tenure as US ambassador to Germany, he was deeply saddened by the assumption of power by Hitler in January 1933 as chancellor.

Sackett submitted his letter of resignation to President Franklin Roosevelt on Inauguration Day on March 4, 1933. His resignation was not accepted for two weeks and was effective only upon his (Sackett's) departure from Berlin.

After leaving his position as ambassador, he resumed his former business activities, which then included his horse farm near Lexington.

Frederic Sackett died while on a trip on May 18, 1941, in Baltimore, Maryland. He is buried in Cave Hill Cemetery, Louisville, Kentucky.

ALBEN W. BARKLEY
(1877–1956)

- Class Three of Three
- Senate Service: 1927–1949 (First Four Terms)
- Political affiliation: Democratic
- Residence at time of election: McCracken County
- Served with Presidents Coolidge, Hoover, F.D. Roosevelt, and Truman
- Served with Governors Fields, Sampson, Laffoon, Chandler, Johnson, Willis, Clements, and Wetherby

Alben W. Barkley was Kentucky's most popular elected official for most of the twentieth century. He served in the US Congress from 1913–1949 (or 1953 if you count his time as vice president presiding over the Senate) and from 1955 until 1956.

Barkley was a noted orator even prior to his election to the Senate.[1] His own father noted his oratorical ability. When Barkley graduated from Marvin College, his father said that Alben probably could never improve on the speech he gave on the day of his graduation.[2]

Due to his speaking ability and the impact he had upon a crowd, he played a significant role in the national Democratic conventions. In 1940, in addition to serving as majority leader, Barkley served as chairman of the National Democratic Convention that nominated FDR

235

for a third term.[3] It was the third Democratic National Convention in which Barkley played a major role. Barkley gave the keynote address at the 1932[4] and 1936 Democratic Conventions.[5] In 1928, he gave one of the speeches seconding the Democratic nomination of Governor Al Smith for President.[6] In 1924, he presided over the Democratic National Convention in New York when the permanent chair, Montana Senator Thomas Walsh, needed a break. The 1924 Democratic Convention was the longest political convention in American history, lasting from June 24 through July 9, 1924. On the 108th ballot, the Democrats nominated John W. Davis to challenge Calvin Coolidge. Due to the unusual length of the convention, First District Congressman Barkley ended up presiding over the convention several days.[7]

Soon after his election as an US Senator but prior to being seated, Barkley gave the Jackson Day Dinner Address for Democrats in Springfield, Missouri. In his speech he talked about the corruption under Harding.[8] In September 1927, he spoke at the Piatt County (Illinois) Farm Bureau Picnic. He spoke about the need for the federal government to control surplus agricultural products.[9] When his wife Dorothy became ill in the 1940s, he took on speaking engagements when Congress was not in session to pay for her around-the-clock care.

Barkley was born in a two-room log cabin[10] in rural Graves County, Kentucky, in the Jackson Purchase in far Western Kentucky. His parents were tenant farmers whose primary crop was tobacco. He was the first-born of John and Electra Barkley, who later gave him four brothers and three sisters.

He worked as a janitor while he attended the Methodist-sponsored Marvin College in Clinton, Kentucky. After graduating from Marvin, he briefly attended Emory College (now Emory University) in Georgia. Running out of money while at Emory, he returned to Kentucky to teach at Marvin College. He left Marvin College and Clinton to go to Paducah, where he read law with Charles K. Wheeler until Wheeler was elected to Congress. While reading law, Barkley worked as the official court reporter for McCracken Circuit Court. Then in 1902, he left to attend law school at the University of Virginia. Later, he returned to Paducah and started practicing law.

Early in his career, he married Dorothy Brower of Paducah. By the time he ran for the Senate, they had three children. Their names were David Murell Barkley, Marian Frances Barkley, and Laura Louise Barkley.[11]

In 1905, he ran for McCracken County Attorney. During his 1905 campaign, he sometimes rode a gray mule to rural parts of the county to contact potential voters. His efforts paid off, and he was elected county attorney. In 1910, he was elected McCracken County Judge (an executive position that included misdemeanor and juvenile court responsibilities). As county judge, his primary emphasis was on road building. McCracken County, under Barkley's leadership, soon had the best roads in the First Congressional District.[12]

Alben Barkley announced his intention to run to succeed Ollie James as congressman from Kentucky's First Congressional District on Friday, December 15, 1911. The first sentence in the article in his hometown Paducah newspaper began, "Alben W. Barkley, M.C. First district Kentucky. How does that sound? Well, you may read it someday. For, formal announcement of his candidacy for congress from the First district to succeed Congressman Ollie James was made by County Judge Alben Barkley."[13]

After serving as Kentucky's First District Congressman for over a decade, on January 15, 1923, Barkley announced his candidacy for the Democratic nomination for Kentucky governor. This campaign boasted a twelve-point plan that included building good roads and promoting good government. Following the congressional recess, Barkley drove a Model-T Ford around Kentucky delivering five or more speeches a day.[14]

Barkley lost the August 1923 Democratic primary for governor. However, he carried every rural county west of Louisville and Lexington.[15] Barkley's energy and support for the Democratic Party and its candidates impressed Congressman Cantrill's organization and other Democrats. In September after the Democratic primary, Congressman Campbell Cantrill, the Democratic candidate for governor, died of a ruptured appendix. The decision of who would replace Cantrill was adjudicated by the Democratic Party's State Central Committee. This committee was dominated by members with ties to those who opposed Barkley; they instead nominated Congressman William J. Fields ("Honest Bill from Olive Hill") to run against Republican Charles Dawson. Barkley was undeterred and campaigned energetically for Fields and, as a result, neutralized special interests who opposed him. Because of his groundwork, the 1926 Democratic Senate primary field was cleared, and he easily won the nomination to oppose incumbent Senator Richard Ernst.

His 1926 campaign manager was Congressman Fred Vinson (future Chief Justice of the United States Supreme Court) from Kentucky's old Fourth District situated in northeastern Kentucky. Barkley was supported by farmers due to his work on their behalf during his fourteen years in the US House of Representatives. He gained support from railroad workers because of his support of the Railway Labor Act signed into law on May 20, 1926, one of the few pieces of progressive legislation passed during the 1920s.[16] He also gained support from veterans due to Senator Ernst's opposition to the veterans' bonus bill of 1924.[17]

Alben Barkley's first twenty-two years as a US senator covered two critical periods in American history: The Great Depression and World War II. While President Franklin Roosevelt (FDR) may have been the primary author of the New Deal, Barkley was FDR's counterpart in the Senate, providing the leadership needed to pass New Deal legislation and policies. During World War II, Barkley provided leadership that passed legislation ensuring American forces had the money and equipment needed to win World War II.

Barkley defeated Ernst in the general election for the US Senate in November 1926. He was not sworn in until December 5, 1927. Until that time, Barkley continued to serve as Congressman from Kentucky's First Congressional District.

When he was sworn in, he was one of forty-seven Democrats with forty-eight Republicans. His fourteen years of service in the House were recognized with appointments to important committees unusual for the average Senate freshman. He was appointed to the Banking and Currency Committee and the Finance Committee. Two years later, he was appointed to the Interstate Commerce Committee. These committees would later prove crucial when FDR assumed office in 1933 and New Deal legislation was coming before the Senate.[18]

In 1929, Barkley spoke in favor of the Kellogg-Briand Pact, whose national signatories pledged to give up war and seek peaceful means to settle disputes. It was one of the first times Barkley showed interest in foreign affairs. It was popular with Americans due to the impact of World War I in the previous decade. It should be noted that after passage of the Kellogg-Briand Pact, Barkley supported the legislation to construct fifteen new cruisers for the Navy after the collapse of the Naval Disarmament Conference in Geneva in 1927.[19]

In 1932, Senator Barkley was called to be the keynote speaker at the Democratic National Convention that nominated Franklin D. Roosevelt. It was in this speech that he reversed his position on Prohibition. Until this time, he had favored Prohibition. In it, he excoriated Republicans and President Hoover's administration. Barkley made national news in an Associated Press (AP) article titled in some papers "Keynoter of Democrats Favors Vote By People On Prohibition Repeal. Senator Alben W. Barkley Denounce Republicans and President Hoover for 'Exorbitant And Indefensible Rate' of Tariff Act." The article takes some interesting phrases from the speech as seen in the opening paragraphs of the article:

"Describing the Republican plank on prohibition as a *promiscuous agglomeration of scrap-lumber*, The Kentuckian said the Democrats should recommend passage of a congressional resolution repealing the Eighteenth Amendment to be voted on by state conventions, chosen solely for that purpose."

Barkley denounced the Republicans and President Hoover for the "exorbitant and indefensible rates of the Smoot-Hawley tariff act and promised to lift tariff-making above the sordid processes of log rollers and back-scratchers."[20]

In 1932, Barkley was the first Kentucky senator to win a second consecutive six-year term since Joseph Blackburn in 1890.

When the new Senate organized in March 1933, Democrats were in a majority for the first time in more than a decade. Senator Joseph T. Robinson of Arkansas was elected majority leader. Senator Joseph B. Kendrick of Wyoming was the assistant majority leader until he died in late 1933. With Kendrick's death, the job of assistant majority leader went to Barkley.[21]

After being inaugurated on March 4, 1933, FDR called a special session of Congress to begin on March 9, 1933. On that day, Congress passed the emergency banking relief legislation in seven hours. Barkley endorsed and voted for that legislation, which was to prevent further meltdown of America's banking system.[22]

During the first 100 days of FDR's administration, Congress passed legislation creating the Tennessee Valley Authority (TVA) to build dams and recreation areas and provide cheap electricity for states such as Kentucky, Tennessee, Alabama, Virginia, North Carolina, and Georgia. This was important as most people living in these states, particularly in rural areas and on farms, were without access to electricity.

Barkley was also directly responsible for legislation removing the United States from the gold standard. The legislation canceled the gold clause in all federal and private debts and allowed all debts be payable in legal tender. This was signed into law on June 5, 1933.

In a speech to the Lions Club in Paducah in December 1933, Barkley talked about the positive impact of those policies on the American dollar with the abolishment of the gold standard. In an article entitled "Barkley Says Dollar Sound," Barkley praised Roosevelt's economic recovery programs:

'We have a no baloney dollar' Senator Barkley said. 'We have as a firm a dollar as ever, and it is well managed as ever'

Speaking of inflation, the senator said inflation is just a mere step beyond expansion. The only effort of the President is to put our dollar today on the same basis with the dollar of 1926.

And did anyone in 1926 call that dollar unsound? Barkley asked.

The United States, legally speaking, is not off the gold standard,

'She is merely not paying off in gold.' Senator Barkley declared in closing his address.'[23]

Barkley participated in the Banking and Currency subcommittee that conducted an investigation into the stock exchanges. That investigation resulted in the Federal Securities Act, which required that newly issued securities (stocks) be registered with the Federal Trade Commission (FTC). Additionally, the Glass-Steagall Banking Act was another result of the subcommittee's work. It separated deposit banking from investment banking and created the Federal Deposit Insurance Corporation (FDIC), which protects money in personal checking and savings accounts from bank failure.[24]

In July 1937, Barkley succeeded the late Majority Leader Joseph Robinson as Democratic leader in the Senate. He was selected by the Democratic Caucus over Mississippi Senator Harrison, who was considered more conservative. FDR's administration assisted Barkley's election as majority leader due to Barkley's unrelenting support for New Deal Programs.[25]

During a difficult five-week November to December 1937 special session, Barkley allowed an anti-lynching bill to go to the floor. Unfortunately, it was filibustered. The following year, the fair labor standards act was passed, which established the minimum wage and a forty-four-hour work week, which was reduced to forty hours in 1939.[26]

In 1938, Barkley received his strongest challenge for the Democratic nomination for reelection to the Senate. Kentucky's young governor, A.B. "Happy" Chandler filed to oppose Barkley in the Democratic primary, which was scheduled for August 6, 1938. Chandler ran an aggressive campaign against Barkley. One example of this can be seen in the famous photo of Chandler "crashing" a Barkley rally in Covington. FDR had come to Kentucky to campaign for Barkley in Covington, Louisville, and Bowling Green. Chandler, as governor of Kentucky, went to Covington to welcome the president to the Commonwealth. That day is memorialized with the three of them in the backseat of an automobile together. Ultimately, Barkley won the Democratic primary on August 6, 1938, by more than 70,000 votes over Chandler.[27]

In the years prior to American entry into the World War II, Barkley led the Army Air Corps expansion in the Senate to a 77–8 victory.[28]

Following FDR's State of the Union Address on January 6, 1941, Barkley and his House counterpart, John McCormick, co-sponsored the "Bill to Promote the Defense of the United States." The legislation allowed the US to provide more military aid to Great Britain.[29]

After the attack by the Japanese on the American naval base at Pearl Harbor, Hawaii, on December 7, 1941, Congress passed the declaration of war and brought it to the White House with other Congressional leaders.[30] On December 26, 1941, British Prime Minister Winston Churchill addressed a joint session of Congress arranged by Senator Barkley.[31]

On many pieces of legislation concerning support of the war, Barkley had little problem finding support. Between January 6 and December 16, 1942, most legislation in the Senate were passed with less than an hour's debate. During that period, the Selective Service Act, the War Powers Act, the Emergency Price Control Act, and many funding bills were passed.[32]

In addition to war issues, during 1942–1944, Barkley faced down southern segregationists on the issue of the poll tax. An anti-poll tax measure that was approved by the Senate Judiciary Committee on November 13, 1942. This measure would prohibit payment of a poll tax to vote in federal elections. Barkley opposed the use of the poll tax and wanted a federal law to outlaw the poll tax.[33] Barkley had the Senate Sergeant At Arms arrest Tennessee Senator Kenneth McKellar when Barkley tried to procure a quorum to defeat a filibuster against legislation to repeal the poll tax.[34] The filibuster lasted at least six days.[35]

When Congress was in session, Barkley regularly met with FDR on Mondays.[36] That continued when Truman became president. With Truman, the meetings were in the executive offices rather than the president's bedroom.

One of the defining moments of Barkley's leadership was in February 1944. FDR, in his State of the Union address, had requested that Congress increase taxes by $10.5 billion for domestic expenses and the war. This was at a time when Congress had already taken steps to increase revenue by expanding the taxpayer base and withholding taxes. The House and Senate had different funding bills, resulting in a conference committee report reconciling the amount to $2.3 billion, less than one-fourth of what FDR wanted. This passed on February 7, 1944. Barkley and his House counterparts met with FDR on the Mondays of February 14 and 21. The meeting turned into a dialogue between Barkley and FDR. Vice President Wallace was silent.

Speaker Rayburn and House Majority Leader McCormick let Barkley do most of the talking in part due to his financial expertise from almost twenty years' service on the Senate Finance Committee. FDR vetoed the budget.

In his veto of the budget bill, FDR criticized Congress. One phrase he used to which Barkley took great offense — "It is not a tax bill but a tax-relief bill providing relief not for the needy but for the greedy."[37]

On Wednesday, February 23, Barkley announced a meeting for the Democratic Caucus for Thursday where his resignation as Majority leader will be tendered.

On Friday, February 25, 1944, votes were taken in the Senate (72–14) and the House (292–95) and FDR's veto was overridden, and the congressional version of the budget passed.[38] Afterwards, the Senate Democratic Caucus reelected Barkley as its leader. Barkley's actions reinforced the principle of separation of powers between the branches of government.

After Barkley was chosen by President Harry S. Truman to be his running mate in the 1948 general election, columnist Drew Pearson wrote that, "If you took a poll of senators as to the best loved man in the United States senate, the winner—among both Democrats and Republicans would probably be Alben Barkley of Kentucky."[39]

Pearson goes on to write that though Barkley has a good sense of humor, he can be made to anger as he was in 1944 when FDR vetoed the budget bill.

Then there was that occasion in 1944 when the Kentucky mountaineer that lurks within Alben Barkley's soul flared to the surface with a vitriolic denunciation of FDR for his veto of the tax bill.

That speech—that flare-up of temper—probably affected the history of the United States more than any senate speech in a half a decade. For had Barkley not lashed out at Roosevelt, FDR would undoubtedly would have picked him for vice-president at the Chicago convention three months later. In that case Alben Barkley, not Harry Truman would be president of the United States today.[40]

During his inauguration as vice president, which resulted in his resignation from the Senate, Barkley was sworn in by Associate Supreme Court Justice Stanley F. Reed, originally from Maysville, Kentucky. President Truman was sworn in by Chief Justice Frederick Vinson, formerly of Lawrence County, Kentucky.[41]

Unfortunately, Barkley's wife did not live to see him become Vice President of the United States. Dorothy Barkley suffered a severe heart attack in 1942. Due to the lack of advanced medical treatment available at the time, Dorothy would be an invalid for the rest of her life. She died on March 9, 1947, after suffering a stroke the previous month.[42]

In a profile such as this, it is difficult to cover the accomplishments and personality of a complex personality like Alben Barkley. Prior to covering some of the highlights of Barkley's first Senate career, the *New York Times* summarized some of his accomplishments after his death:

> History will remember Alben Barkley for his sponsorship of, and leadership of, in putting through much of the important and beneficial social legislation of the Thirties. It will remember him for his leadership in such grave matters as Lend Lease and ratification of the United Nations Charter. It will remember him and the high offices he had held, for the good work he has done in those high offices and for the powerful influence he bore in getting opposing factions to compromise their differences in times of emergency.
>
> But now we think of him for his warm, human colorful qualities, for the respect and affection he evoked in others, not least the of whom were the voters of Kentucky who elected him time and time again, to office. A vital man, he had much still to give back to his country, even at the age of 78. He will be sorely missed and long remembered.[43]

JOHN MARSHALL ROBSION
(1873–1948)

- Class Two of Three
- Senate Service: January 9, 1930–November 30, 1930
- Political affiliation: Republican
- Residence at time of election: Barbourville
- Served with President Hoover
- Served with Governor Sampson

John Robsion's eleven months as a US senator does not reflect his ambition. Elected to Congress in 1918 to represent Kentucky's old Eleventh Congressional District, Robsion became an influential Republican organizer. In 1928, he had served as Herbert Hoover's campaign manager for Kentucky.[1] That year, Hoover carried Kentucky by over 177,000 votes in the election.[2] The previous year, Republican Governor Flem Sampson from Robsion's hometown of Barbourville was elected governor of Kentucky.

Robsion was born in rural Northern Kentucky near Berlin in Bracken County, Kentucky, on January 2, 1873. He attended the public schools of Bracken County. He then attended the Ohio Northern University in Ada, Ohio, and Holbrook College in Knoxville, Tennessee. He graduated from the National Normal University in Lebanon, Ohio and from the law department of Centre College in Danville in 1900.

He taught in public schools for several years, as well as at Union College in Barbourville, Kentucky. He was admitted to the bar and practiced law in Knox County and Barbourville. Simultaneously, he was president of the First National Bank of Barbourville.[3] In 1918, he was elected from Kentucky's Eleventh District as a Republican to the Sixty-Sixth Congress and to the five succeeding Congresses, serving from March 4, 1919 until January 10, 1930, when he assumed his seat in the US Senate. Kentucky's Eleventh District was centered in the mountains of southeast Kentucky.

After the 1928 general election, Robsion set his sights on the seat of incumbent Republican US Senator Fred Sackett of Louisville via Rhode Island and Columbus. During the Republican gubernatorial primary, Senator Sackett supported Robert H. Lucas of Louisville, who had been US collector of revenue since 1921. Unfortunately for Sackett, Judge Flem Sampson won the Republican primary and became Kentucky governor in 1927.[4]

In order to prevent a divisive Republican primary in 1930, President Hoover appointed Senator Sackett ambassador to Germany; this is where he served from 1930 until 1933.[5]

Robsion was appointed by Governor Sampson to fill the vacancy caused by Sackett's resignation to become ambassador to Germany. Robsion was nominated by the State Republican Convention on March 4, 1930, to run for the balance of Sackett's term and for the full six-year term, which began on March 4, 1931.[6]

Unfortunately for Robsion, Governor Sampson's popularity was declining along with President Hoover's, partially due to the Great Depression. Robsion carried Louisville with the help of organized labor. However, he did not get the margin he needed in his Eleventh Congressional District. He carried it by only 2,100 votes. The smaller margin in the mountains is thought to be due to the Democratic Party's control of the Highway Commission and its related patronage.[7]

Senator Robsion was defeated by Democrat Marvel Mills Logan of Bowling Green for the six-year term and by Democrat Ben Williamson of Ashland for the three remaining months on Sackett's term.

In addition to the attacks of patronage used by the Democrats, Robsion used the politics of religion. On January 31, 1931, the *Courier-Journal* reported that the former senator, in an effort to advance his election, had purchased over 135,000 copies of a special edition of the Klan's *The Fellowship Forum* to circulate in the anti-Catholic areas of the state. However, Republican headquarters staff burned over 70,000 copies of the publication without the senator's knowledge. Republican State Chairman Thomas S. Yates would not allow them to be distributed unless requested by a county chair. However, it is thought that the Democrats obtained some copies and distributed them in the more Catholic areas of the state, resulting in Robsion's loss.[8]

After Robsion's defeat in 1930, he returned to practice law in Barbourville and briefly practiced with Governor Sampson. He was re-elected to Congress in 1934. He served in Congress from 1935 until his death on February 17, 1948. He was survived by at least one son, John Marshall Robsion Jr., who was a circuit judge and later a congressman from Louisville, as well as an unsuccessful Republican candidate for governor in 1959 against Bert Combs.

Senator John Marshall Robsion was buried in Barbourville Cemetery.

BEN M. WILLIAMSON
(1864–1941)

- Class Two of Three
- Senate Service: December 1, 1930–March 3, 1931
- Political affiliation: Democratic
- Residence at time of election: Boyd County
- Served with President Hoover
- Served with Governor Sampson

During the 1930 general election, Kentucky Democrats nominated not only a candidate for the full term beginning on March 3, 1931, but also a separate candidate to oppose incumbent Senator Robsion This was for the balance of Sackett's term, which ended March 3, 1930. Judge M.M. Logan was the Democratic candidate facing Republican Robsion for the full term, beginning March 3, 1931. While it was not explicitly said, the fielding of two candidates against the incumbent Republican was a strategic move. Democrats fielded Ben Williamson from Northeastern Kentucky and Logan from Western Kentucky against Republican Senator Robsion, who was from Barbourville in Southeastern Kentucky.

Williamson was born in Pike County. His parents, Wallace J. and America Slater Williamson, were from neighboring West Virginia and were said to be one of the founding families of Williamson, West Virginia. Ben attended the public schools in Pike County and graduated from

Bethany College in Bethany, West Virginia. It was said that he started college at age thirteen.[1]

He was active in many civic and business endeavors. His primary business endeavor was the Ben Williamson Company, a wholesale hardware supplier in Boyd County, Kentucky. He also engaged in banking and in coal mining. He was one of the founders of the Kentucky Crippled Children's Commission, serving as president from 1924 to 1941. He was also a member of the board of charities and correction for the Commonwealth of Kentucky from 1929 to 1930 and the director of the International Society for Crippled Children. The commission later partnered with the Shriner's Hospitals in Louisville and Lexington.

Soon after entering the US Senate in December 1930, Senator Williamson's name was considered as a possible candidate for the Democratic nomination for governor in 1931. It was noted that Williamson and Congressman Fred Vinson were close political allies and that Williamson was reluctant to run for the short term for the Senate, due to being sixty-six years old.[2]

Williamson was described as the only senator to take his oath of office in a "morning coat." He is further described as "a wholesale hardware merchant and banker of Ashland. In appearance, he is tall and slender, with sandy hair and light complexion. His friends say he is very substantial citizen, well read, and widely traveled."[3]

On leaving the Senate after his short tenure, Williamson recommended service in the US Senate to other businessmen: "There's a place in the halls of the national congress for businessmen. Lawyers have their place there but a good leaven is a few capable business men. Some of the big-fellows in the country ought to stop making money and try it."[4] He is also described "as one who said little but observed much."

One of Williamson's colleagues, Republican W.P. Pine of Oklahoma, who was leaving the Senate at the same time, is quoted as saying, "It will be quite a relief to get back into private business where I have control. Here no one has control, not even the President of the United States".[5]

In 1935, Williamson actively supported the Democratic statewide ticket, headed by then Lieutenant Governor "Happy" Chandler in his first election as governor.

In 1936, Williamson became finance director for the Democratic National Committee and chair of Kentucky's electors for Roosevelt.[6]

Senator Williamson died on June 23, 1941, at Holmes Hospital in Cincinnati, Ohio. He had been a patient there since February 14, 1941. He was survived by his wife, Ceres Wellman Williamson; a son, Ben; and a daughter, Mrs. David Geiger. Another son, Wallace J. Williamson, died in 1933.[7]

In August 1941, the Ohio River Bridge connecting Ashland, Kentucky, and Coal Grove, Ohio, was dedicated and named in his honor.[8]

MARVEL MILLS LOGAN
(1874–1939)

- Class Two of Three
- Senate Service: 1931–1939
- Political affiliation: Democratic
- Residence at time of election: Warren County
- Served with Presidents Hoover and F. Roosevelt
- Served with Governors Sampson, Laffoon, and Chandler

One of the most overlooked Kentucky senators of the twentieth century was Marvel Mills Logan. A diligent public servant, Senator Logan served during a period dominated by Alben Barkley and Happy Chandler. Logan's Senate career was cut short due to his sudden death in 1939. After his death, he was remembered most for being the person who held the Senate seat filled by Happy Chandler.

By the time M.M. Logan sought election to the US Senate in 1930, he had served in many state offices and civic offices for almost twenty years. He was active in the Independent Order of Odd Fellows,[1] where he had served as international grand sire and was an active member of the Baptist Church. At the time of his election in 1930, he was chief justice of the Kentucky Court of Appeals.

A week prior to the fall 1930 general election, Judge M.M. Logan was endorsed by the *Louisville Courier-Journal* and its evening edition, the *Louisville Times.*[2] The article points out that Judge Logan is charging that the Republican Party is responsible for high unemployment and the Depression. Logan was rough in his characterization of his opponent, Senator Robsion. Logan charged that "Senator Robsion is ignorant and illiterate and in denying it Senator Robsion alleges that Judge Logan is poorly informed on public questions." During the campaign, former Navy Secretary (under President Wilson) Josephus Daniels campaigned on behalf of Logan. Daniels was a nationally prominent Democrat who owned the *News & Observer* (a newspaper in Raleigh, North Carolina) and would be a prominent supporter of Franklin Roosevelt in 1932.

As a result of the general election of November 9, 1930, Logan was one of fourteen new Democratic senators and five Republicans, including Huey Long of Louisiana, James F. Byrnes of South Carolina, and Cordell Hull of Tennessee.[3]

Marvel Mills Logan was born on a farm near Brownsville, Kentucky, in Edmondson County on January 7, 1874. He was the son of Franklin Gillis and Georgie Ann Logan. He was educated in the public and private schools at Leitchfield and Brownsville. He began the practice of law in his hometown of Brownsville in 1896. He served on the town council and was elected Edmonson county attorney. In 1911, he became an assistant attorney general before his election as Kentucky's attorney general on a ticket with A.O. Stanley. He also served as a member of the state tax commission. One of the most important issues decided by the Kentucky Tax Commission was inheritance tax received by the Commonwealth from the estate of the late Mrs. Robert Worth Bingham, formerly Mrs. Henry Flagler. The estate paid $345,402.01 on $7,500,000. Her husband Robert Bingham received an inheritance of $1 million and paid taxes of $146,000. Bingham used the inheritance to buy the *Courier-Journal*.[4]

In 1933, Senator Logan made national headlines when he chaired a Senate committee investigating the 1932 Senate election in Louisiana of Senator John H. Overton, an ally of Huey Long. While presiding over a hearing in Louisiana in November 1933, Logan called federal marshals to cite several spectators with contempt after a disturbance in the hearing room.[5]

During the summer of 1934, Senator Logan made waves about the way federal relief was being distributed in Kentucky. After visiting fifty counties:

> Senator Logan demanded a house cleaning in the Kentucky relief administration today. Logan's demand follows an announcement from Washington federal relief headquarters that Harry L. Hopkins, Relief Administrator, intends to withdraw all federal relief from

Kentucky October 1 unless Governor Ruby Laffoon pays over $600,000 funds to the Kentucky Emergency Relief Association. The $600,000 represents state payments of $200,000 per month toward relief in Kentucky for June, July and August.[6]

Senator Logan was extremely critical of the way in which relief was administered under Thornton Wilcox. He described Thornton's work as "a stench in the nostrils of all decent people."[7] Logan was critical of political favoritism being practiced and tremendous overhead. He cited the example of an investigator being sent out to meet with a man who had a family with six children. The cost of the investigator was $6. The investigator gave the man and his family a certificate for one pound of lard a month (worth about six cents).

It was Logan's suggestion that the local county governments take over the administration of the relief programs as county judges would know the local situations.[8]

At the 111th Convention of the Independent Order of Odd Fellows held in Atlantic City, Senator Logan made the principal address. Logan's subject was "world peace." He said that the prevention of war is the chief duty of all nations. Without specifically mentioning the non-membership of the U.S. in the League of Nations or the World Court, he said: "The United States has not done its part to assure international peace and thus has contributed to the weakness of the anti-war structure." He further stated: "International controversies could be settled through tribunals set up by cooperation between nations. They should and could, on the facts and under the rules of international law, enter judgment which could be effective and conclusive".[9]

In 1935, Senator Logan had originally supported Thomas Rhea over the eventual Democratic nominee for governor, Happy Chandler. However, in the fall, Logan campaigned throughout Kentucky for Lieutenant Governor Chandler and the Democratic ticket. Logan noted the appeal of Chandler to the people and the importance of Kentucky Democrats in supporting the policies of President Franklin Roosevelt by electing Chandler.[10]

Senator Logan and Congressman Brent Spence of Fort Thomas were instrumental in creating a position for a third US District Court judge for Kentucky. By June 1936, a bill creating a third judicial position to cover both the Eastern and Western Districts was before President Franklin Roosevelt. Logan sponsored the legislation creating the position in the Senate, and Congressman Spence was instrumental in getting it through the House Judiciary Committee and passed by the House.[11]

In his efforts to seek reelection in 1936, Logan was opposed by former Governor and US Senator J.C.W. Beckham who was supported by

Governor A.B. "Happy" Chandler and his administration. in the August primary. Logan's second major competitor was former US Representative John Y. Brown, Sr (whose son would later become governor in 1979). All three candidates pledged support for President Franklin Roosevelt. Early returns had Beckham carrying five of the (then) nine Congressional Districts — First, Third (Jefferson County), Fourth, Seventh, and Ninth (Eastern Kentucky, where he had the support of the UMW). Logan led in the Second, Sixth, and Eighth. Brown lead in the Fifth (Northern Kentucky).

Weather for the August primary was "cool and the skies cloudless.... No shootings at the polls, such as marked Kentucky elections in the past, were reported. A heckler was shot in the leg at Bedford, Ky., in a pre-election disturbance."[12] As Beckham was supported by Governor Chandler, both Logan and Brown attacked him on the issue of recently passed taxes on tobacco, ice cream, and cosmetics.

This was one of the first elections under Kentucky's "Honest Election Law." Ballots were counted in the courthouses instead of at the precinct voting places. "Ballot boxes in each county are secured with three locks and the keys held by the Sheriff and one representative each of the Republican and Democratic parties."[13] Logan went on to win reelection in the fall of 1936 over Republican Robert Lucas 58.8–39.8 percent. President Roosevelt won Kentucky's eleven electoral votes by receiving 58.51–39.92 percent of the popular vote over Alf Landon.

In 1937, Logan was one of the Senate point persons for the Roosevelt administration's legislation to reorganize the US Supreme Court. Roosevelt's legislation to increase the size of the court, as well as implement mandatory judicial retirement, divided Senate Democrats. Logan made it an issue. He contended that rejection would be humiliating to the President.[14] Logan was one of the first members of the Senate Judiciary Committee to back Roosevelt's court-packing plan. However, Logan suggested a compromise of adding only two new members for the court.[15]

Supreme Court Justice George Sutherland had submitted his resignation. At the urging of Kentucky Governor "Happy" Chandler, the Kentucky General Assembly passed a joint resolution supporting Senator Logan's appointment as Justice Sutherland's replacement on the Supreme Court.[16]

In 1938, Kentucky Governor Chandler made allegations that Senator Logan had "begged" for a federal judgeship earlier in the year. Chandler made the allegations in a speech he made over the telephone from his bedroom in the executive mansion and relayed it by telephone and loudspeaker to a crowd in Paintsville. Chandler was ill, allegedly from "poisoned drinking water." He was conducting his primary campaign against incumbent Senator Barkley from his bed via telephone.[17]

Logan replied that night that Chandler's allegation that he "begged" for a federal judgeship was "a damned lie."[18]

Senator Logan died suddenly on Tuesday, October 3, 1939, of a heart attack. He had had another heart attack on the previous Saturday, but it was not seen as a life-threatening.

After the senator's death, radio station WCKY (then in Covington) broadcast a thirty-minute memorial program in honor of the memory of Senator Marvel Mills Logan. It was a program of organ music by John Quincy Bass.[19]

In one obituary, it was noted that he was one of the few senators who remained in Washington during the summer recess. Due to his accessibility, he received more Kentucky visitors than any other member of the Kentucky Delegation. For those close to him, he was known as "the Old Indian" for his ability to remember names and faces.

At the time of his death, Senator Logan was a member of First Baptist Church of Bowling Green, Kentucky. He had taught Sunday school for thirty-three years at churches in Brownsville, Bowling Green, Frankfort, and Washington, D.C.

He was survived by his wife, Mrs. Susan Della Logan, and four children. His sons were Victor H. Logan of Covington, Leland H. Logan of Bowling Green (an attorney), and Ralph H. Logan of Louisville (also an attorney). His daughter was Mrs. George Horschel of Louisville. His brother David Logan was state auditor from 1940 to 1943.[20] Among the eight senators designated to represent that body at Logan's funeral were Alben Barkley, Harry Truman of Missouri (future President), and Senator Sherman Minton of Indiana (future associate justice of the Supreme Court).

M.M. Logan was buried in the Logan Family Cemetery near Brownsville, Kentucky.

Part XI

1941–1948

World War II and the
Beginning of the Cold War

The 1940s were a transformative period for the US. At the end of 1941, the United States entered World War II on the side of the Allies after giving Lend-Lease aid to Great Britain. The U.S. went through its largest military mobilization from a military of less than a half million (458,365) in 1941 to over twelve million (12,209,238) at the end of hostilities in 1945.[1] Congress, including the Senate, made that possible. Throughout this period, Alben Barkley was the Senate majority leader crafting together votes on financing of the mobilization as well as the drawdown and the post-war peace.

As you will read, though Barkley and President Franklin Roosevelt were both Democrats, there were disagreements, including over the size of the 1944 budget.

Senator Happy Chandler spent a significant portion of his time "investigating the war" as seen by his travels. His travel to Alaska was instrumental in convincing Congress to help finance and build the ALCAN Highway from the Lower 48 states to Alaska.

In an effort to avoid the mistakes following World War I, FDR — with the help of the leadership of Majority Leader Barkley — passed the "Serviceman's Readjustment Act of 1944" or "GI Bill." After World War I, most military service members only received $60 and a train ticket home when the war ended (The World War Adjusted Compensation Act was not enacted until 1924.)

The "GI Bill" as signed into law by FDR on June 22, 1944, provided for education and training benefits, which resulted in the expansion in size of most state universities, including the University of Kentucky. It also provided for low-cost home loans for veterans and their families. Additionally, there was funding for more VA medical facilities.[2]

It was during this period in 1948 that Congress passed the "Marshall Plan" or European Recovery Plan. The purpose of this was to help rebuild war-devastated Europe and avoid the mistakes of the post-war peace after World War I, which had led to totalitarian dictators. Barkley and especially John Sherman Cooper, an army veteran of World War II, took particular leadership in international affairs. It was Cooper's interest and legislative expertise in international affairs as a senator that led Democratic President Harry S. Truman to appoint Cooper, a Republican, to a position as a delegate to the United Nations after his defeat for reelection in 1948.

In 1948, Alben Barkley was elected vice president of the U.S. alongside Harry Truman as president. Barkley resigned as senator in January 1949 to become Vice President and presiding officer of the Senate until January 1953.

ALBERT BENJAMIN "HAPPY" CHANDLER
(1898–1991)

- Class Two of Three
- Senate Service: 1939–1945
- Political affiliation: Democratic
- Residence at time of election: Versailles
- Served with Presidents F. Roosevelt and Truman
- Served with Governors Johnson and Willis

The year following his 1938 primary challenge of Senator Alben Barkley, A.B. Chandler took advantage of the opportunity provided by the unexpected death of Senator Marvel Mills Logan. Chandler resigned as a governor, and Keen Johnson, Chandler's lieutenant governor, appointed him to the vacancy for the period from 1938 through the 1940 general election. Even after getting to the Senate, Chandler continued his dislike for Barkley, who was the Senate majority leader. In his autobiography, Chandler said: "In the Senate I was the freshman, seated in the last row. They made me see right away that I was Number 96." (Until 1958, there were only ninety-six senators.) "Barkley tried to keep me off committees that I wanted. Senator Byrd helped me. He did not like Barkley, he thought he was too liberal. I thought the same thing. Old Alben wanted to give the country away."[1]

Happy Chandler is probably one of the best-known former Kentucky senators in recent history due to his stint as commissioner of Major

League Baseball when Jackie Robinson, the first African American player, entered Major League Baseball and his two terms as Kentucky's governor.

His achievements as governor significantly overshadow his work during his six years in the US Senate.

Albert Benjamin "Happy" Chandler was born in the Henderson County town of Corydon in 1898. He was the oldest child of Joseph and Callie Chandler. He had a younger brother, Robert, who died from a fall from a tree at age thirteen. Chandler's mother had abandoned the family before he was five years old, leaving his father to raise two boys.

Chandler graduated from Corydon High School. He was captain of the high school's baseball and football teams. He then enrolled at Transylvania University in Lexington, where he was captain of both the basketball and baseball teams and was quarterback of the football team. (Transy no longer has a football team.) It was at Transy that Chandler received his nickname "Happy." Chandler attended college during World War I, and he was part of the US Army's Student Officers' Training Corps. However, World War I ended prior to his being called to active service. (Because of his participation in the Student Officers' Training Corps, he claimed to be a World War I veteran.)

Happy Chandler received a BA from Transylvania University in 1921 and then entered Harvard Law School. He was unable to afford Harvard after a year and transferred to the University of Kentucky, where he completed law school in 1924.

After admission to the bar, he moved to Woodford County, where he practiced law from an office in Versailles and coached high school football. In 1925, Chandler married Mildred Watkins (Mama), a teacher at the Margaret Hall School for Girls. They had four children: Marcella, Mildred, Albert Jr., and Dan.

Chandler's entry into politics began with his selection as chairman of the Woodford County Democratic Party, and in 1929 he was elected to the Kentucky Senate. He was part of the group that stripped Republican Governor Flem Sampson of some of the governor's statuary powers during the 1930 session. In 1931, he was selected at the Kentucky Democratic State Convention as the Democratic nominee for lieutenant governor with Ruby Laffoon for governor. Laffoon and Chandler easily won their respective elections during this Depression Era election.

Upon becoming lieutenant governor, Chandler set up an office in the Capitol. This was unusual as most Kentucky lieutenant governors up until that time were only in Frankfort for special occasions and during legislative sessions to preside over the State Senate.

Lieutenant Governor Chandler and Governor Ruby Laffoon's relationship became strained when Laffoon, over the vocal opposition of

Chandler, had the General Assembly pass a 3 percent sales tax. Due to Chandler's opposition to Laffoon's policies, Laffoon had his allies in the legislature strip the office of lieutenant governor of what power it had. However, on one occasion, Governor Laffoon left the state to attend meetings in Washington, D.C. As a result, Chandler became acting governor in Laffoon's absence. Partially out of retaliation for Laffoon's actions and partially because Chandler wanted to succeed the term-limited governor, Chandler called a special session of the General Assembly in early 1935 that required candidates for governor to be chosen by party primary rather than convention.

There was four-person primary contest in the Democratic primary for governor in 1935. Laffoon's choice, Thomas Rhea, won the initial primary race with Chandler coming in second. Since Rhea did not receive a majority, there was a runoff, which was won by Chandler. Chandler then faced Republican King Swope in the general election. Chandler won the 1935 general election over Swope by 35,000 votes to become one of the youngest governors in the nation at age thirty-seven.

Chandler's first act as governor was to repeal the sales tax passed during the Laffoon administration. He replaced it with excise taxes on alcohol, including whiskey, which became available with the repeal of Prohibition. The General Assembly, under Chandler's direction, enacted Kentucky's first income tax.

One of Chandler's achievements was the Governmental Reorganization Act, which reduced the size of the executive branch of state government. He is also responsible for the establishment of the Kentucky Teachers' Retirement System.

Chandler was praised for his handling of the 1937 Ohio River Flood in January and February of that year. It was a natural disaster in Kentucky that stretched the full length of Kentucky's northern border from east of Ashland to west of Paducah.

In 1938, Governor Chandler decided to challenge Kentucky's senior US Senator Alben Barkley, who was also the Democratic majority leader. During the bitter primary campaign, President Franklin D. Roosevelt openly supported Barkley over Chandler. FDR came to Kentucky to campaign on Barkley's behalf. During one such visit by President Roosevelt at a Barkley Rally at Covington's old Latonia Race Track in Covington, Chandler showed up to greet FDR. Barkley won the primary election over Chandler by a significant margin and won in the 1938 general election.

In 1939, Kentucky's junior US Senator Marvel Logan unexpectedly died. As the governor has the power to fill a Senate vacancy, Chandler resigned, and Lieutenant Governor Keen Johnson became governor and appointed Chandler to the US Senate.

Chandler was elected to serve the balance of Logan's term in 1940. During the 1940 campaign, Chandler promised during a debate over the extension of the Selective Service Act that he would join the Army if he voted for a declaration of war. "Immediately after he voted for the declaration of war against Japan, he telephoned the White House and offered to 'put on a uniform and go out and fight.' He made the same offer to the Army's chief of staff, General George C. Marshall. Neither the White House nor General Marshall replied."[2]

In July 1941 (five months before Pearl Harbor), as a member of the military affairs subcommittee, Chandler had voted to approve a resolution authorizing to indefinitely extend the enlistments of all "selectees, members of the National Guard and members of the regular and reserve components of the Army." This had been done at the request of President Roosevelt.[3]

As a US Senator, Chandler is best known for his travels as a member of the Senate Military Affairs Committee. This included membership in the subcommittee to investigate Alaskan defenses.[4] Chandler, as usual, was very outspoken and perhaps a bit defensive in his comments. He received a front-page headline preceding the trip to Alaska in the *Anchorage Daily Times*: "Senator Urges Aleutian Drive At Any Cost." At that time, the Japanese were occupying several islands in the Aleutian chain. Chandler was quoted as saying, "Japanese occupation of the outer Aleutian Islands is a direct threat to this country." Chandler went on to say: "This is no junket or lark. We're not sure what our itinerary will be, but we're going up there to find out what's going on. We want to find out how the inland highway is progressing, all about the morale of the civilians and troops. The people all over the country are more alarmed over the Aleutian situation than about any other phase of the war."[5]

In 1942, Chandler was elected to a full six-year term of his own in the 1942 August Democratic primary. For the Democratic nomination, he beat John Y. Brown Sr. in August 1942. Chandler said: "an important secret military mission might force him to be absent from Kentucky on primary day."[6] The biggest issue of the primary campaign was Brown's charge that Chandler accepted the gift of a swimming pool from Louisville war contractor Ben Collings.[7]

He served on the Committee on Military Affairs during World War II. He traveled on behalf of the committee, inspecting bases around the world, including those in Alaska. He held hearings throughout Alaska during the early months of the war, which were influential in Congress authorizing the construction of the ALCAN Highway.

In early 1943, Chandler was appointed to chair the Senate Military Affairs Subcommittee to Investigate the War Relocation Authority (WRA). The WRA was the government agency that oversaw the internment of Japanese Americans. Due to unrest at least two of the camps—Poston and Manzanar—Senator Monrad C. Wallgren of Washington and Senator Rufus Holman of Oregon introduced legislation for the Army to take control of the internment camps. The matter was referred to the subcommittee headed by Chandler, which held hearings at various camps. Chandler himself held hearings at Phoenix, Arizona, and McGehee, Arkansas. The subcommittee's final report recommended that the army not run the camps.[8]

As a senator, Chandler had his own strategy to win World War II. He stated that the United States should concentrate on Japan first and Germany second. His reasoning for that was to attack Japan prior to it getting too deeply situated in its conquered lands of the Pacific. Chandler believed after the US had ended the war with Japan, Britain and Russia would withdraw from the war, leaving the US to finish the war in the West. Churchill responded to Chandler in a joint address to Congress. In that reply, Churchill assured Congress that the British would fight side by side with Americans against Japan. Churchill noted that a "Grand Strategy" was needed. The fall of Japan would not mean the fall of Germany, and the fall of Germany would not mean the fall of Japan.[9]

Additional duties on the Senate Military Affairs Committee for Chandler included being part of a delegation of five senators on a round-the-world warfront inspection, which began at Washington, D.C., on July 25, 1943, with Senators Richard Russell of Georgia, Henry Cabot Lodge of Massachusetts, James M. Mead of New York, and Ralph O. Brewster of Maine. During the inspection of the Eighth Air Force in England, the group visited Prime Minister Churchill at 10 Downing Street. It was during that visit that Chandler arranged to have Bob Hope meet Churchill by adding him to the senatorial party going to 10 Downing Street.[10]

During the 1943 elections for Kentucky governor and other statewide offices, Democrats saw Senator Chandler as mixed blessing. Though he attracted large crowds, he was more critical of the British and the conduct of the war than other Kentucky Democrats were.[11]

Chandler served seven years in the Senate with Harry Truman of Missouri. In his autobiography, he was not very complimentary of the future president. Chandler said, "One I didn't care for was Harry Truman. I was in the Senate with him for seven years. All he did was drink whiskey and play cards. He wasn't even the best senator from Missouri—Champ Clark, Jr., was. And he drank too much whiskey too."

Chandler goes on to say that FDR chose Truman because he would stay out of the limelight. "And he picked old Truman because Truman had a passion for anonymity. Nobody knew Truman. Nobody gave a damn about Truman and they gave him that investigating committee to get him acquainted."[12]

In February 1945, Chandler was outspoken in his opposition to legislation titled "May-Baily," which was intended to prevent workforce shortages by jailing workers who refused to work.[13]

In the spring of 1945, Chandler accepted the job of commissioner of Major League Baseball. He was selected on the first ballot by the team owners who voted on the position. Others considered included Ohio Governor Frank J. Lausche and former Postmaster General James A. Farley.[14] For a few months, Chandler attempted to serve both as a US Senator from Kentucky and commissioner of Major League Baseball. He did not want to leave the Senate until after the end of the war. In September 1945, the Townsend Organization of Northern Kentucky sent a resolution requesting that Chandler resign from the Senate. "He cannot maintain his Senate position with dignity and at the same time 'lobby' for any type of business, the organization asserted."[15]

Senator Chandler's resignation from the US Senate was formally accepted by Kentucky Governor Simeon Willis on November 1, 1945.[16]

Commissioner of Major League Baseball was a post Chandler held until 1951. During this period, he was instrumental in establishing a players' pension fund and the integrating Major League Baseball, with Jackie Robinson becoming the first African American to become a major league player.

Chandler later returned to the practice of law and farming in Versailles. In 1955, Chandler won the Democratic primary for governor over Bert Combs and the general election over Republican Edwin Denny.

Chandler's second term as governor saw the issuance of a bond that helped fund highways throughout Kentucky. One of the most important legacies of Chandler's second term is the establishment of a medical school and medical center at the University of Kentucky. The medical center is known as the "A.B. Chandler Medical Center."

Chandler unsuccessfully ran for governor in 1963, 1967, and 1971. His endorsement of Republican Louie Nunn in 1967 might have made the difference in Nunn's win over Democrat Henry Ward.

In his later years, Chandler became a beloved figure at University of Kentucky athletic events. Chandler became the oldest living person inducted in the Baseball Hall of Fame in 1982.

Prior to his death on June 15, 1991, Chandler was able to savor his grandson Ben Chandler's victory for nomination as Kentucky state auditor during the May 1991 Democratic primary. Chandler is buried in the churchyard of Pisgah Presbyterian Church near Versailles.

WILLIAM A. STANFILL
(1892–1971)

- Class Two of Three
- Senate Service: November 19, 1945–November 5, 1946
- Political affiliation: Republican
- Residence at time of election: Hazard
- Served with President Truman
- Served with Governor Simeon Willis

William Stanfill, an attorney from Hazard, Kentucky, and chair of the Republican State Central Committee, was appointed by Governor Simeon Willis on November 19, 1945, to succeed Senator A.B. "Happy" Chandler, who resigned on November 1, 1945, to become commissioner of Major League Baseball. At the time of his selection, Stanfill indicated that he would seek election to the balance of the term ending in January 1949.[1]

Stanfill was sworn in on November 23, 1945, by Senator Carl Hayden of Arizona, acting presiding officer of the Senate.[2] He was accompanied by Senate Majority Leader and Kentucky's senior Senator Democrat Alben Barkley.

William Abner Stanfill was born in Barbourville, Knox County, Kentucky, on January 16, 1892. He was the son of Joshua and Lura Faulkner Stanfill. He attended the public schools and Union College in Barbourville. He graduated from the law department of the University of Kentucky in Lexington; he was awarded a Bachelor of Law degree here in 1912. He began his legal career in Barbourville. He later moved to Hyden in Leslie County in 1915 and to Hazard in Perry County in 1916. On July 17, 1917, he married May Begley of Hazard.

He was an attorney in Hazard for decades as a member of the law firm of Faulkner, Stanfill, and Faulkner from 1916 until 1925 and Craft and Stanfill from 1925 until 1950. He was member of the Board of Regents of Morehead State Teachers College from 1927 to 1931. He served as a member of the Board of Governors of the Kentucky Children's Home at Lyndon from 1933 to 1936. In 1945, he became chairman of the Kentucky Republican Party.

Due to his brief tenure, there is not much to distinguish Senator Stanfill. However, there are at least two instances that were noteworthy.

In February 1946, Republican Senator Stanfill supported his Democratic colleagues regarding the creation of the Fair Employment Practice Commission. The headlines were: "RULING BALKS MOVE FOR FEPC CLOSURE; Filing of Petition by Barkley Brings Senate Filibuster Within a Filibuster; WASHINGTON, Feb. 4—Senator Barkley, leader of the majority, attempted today to invoke closure to break the three-week filibuster in the Senate against the bill to create a permanent Fair Employment Practice Commission"[3]

Senator Stanfill made national news around April 18, 1946, in a New York Times article concerning a loan to the British: "—STANFILL SUPPORTS LOAN FOR BRITISH; Senator Argues Both Sides and Says He Will Back it as 'Investment in Peace.'"

Another article that made national news was "WASHINGTON, April 18—Senator William A. Stanfill of Kentucky, gave the Senate a picture today of the 'mental torture' through which he had to go to reach a decision to support the $3,750,000,000 British credit legislation."

Within the article, Stanfill's observations were explained as follows:

> While he said this was the only argument which impressed him, he also mentioned that it would reap profits for our business men and farmers, and lighten the burden upon future taxpayers if it is repaid.
>
> He observed that science had truly made this 'one world' and added that 'we can no more survive another economic war than we can survive another atomic war.'[4]

Contrary to Stanfill's original intention to seek election to the seat, he stepped aside for Judge John Sherman Cooper, who was elected in November 1946. After his brief tenure, Senator Stanfill returned to Kentucky to practice law. After retirement, he resided in Lexington, where he died on June 12, 1971. He is buried in Hillcrest Memorial Park in Lexington.

JOHN SHERMAN COOPER
(1901–1991)
First Term

- Class Two of Three
- Senate Service: 1946–1949 (First Term)
- Political affiliation: Republican
- Residence at time of election: Somerset
- Served with President Truman
- Served with Governors Willis and Clements

On November 1, 1945, Senator A.B. "Happy" Chandler resigned from the US Senate after deciding he could not serve as both the commissioner of Major League Baseball and US Senator from Kentucky. Upon Chandler's resignation, Kentucky's Republican Governor Simeon Willis appointed William Stanfill to fill the seat until the November 1946 general election.

On May 6, 1946, the *Courier-Journal* reported that Stanfill may not run and "J.S. Cooper Mentioned As Candidate." The article, complete with a photo of Cooper, said, "Circuit Judge John Sherman Cooper would run for the two-year unexpired Senate term and that his candidacy would not be opposed by any seriously regarded contender within the Republican party."[1]

Cooper had run for the Republican nomination for governor in 1939 but lost in the primary. Cooper made a good impression during 1939, and Republican leadership tried to convince Cooper to return from

Army service during World War II to run as a Republican candidate for attorney general in 1943.

The Democratic nominee for the Senate seat was John Y. Brown Sr., who had been a former US Congressman and Speaker of the Kentucky House. The election between Cooper and Brown was contentious. An article in the *Courier-Journal* in October 1946 stated:

> John Young Brown facetiously put forward two new planks for his senatorial campaign. They are, he said, the type of planks which his Republican opponent, John Sherman Cooper, had been offering from time to time 'whenever he finds that local conditions compel him to his position in order to gain votes.' The two new Brown planks are: 1. 'A thick juicy steak for every man and child,' 2. 'Make Ermal Allen [football player] eligible for the University of Kentucky:"
>
> "In trying to follow the example of my opponent,' Brown said, 'I don't know which plank to put first. So, I asked the advice of an audience at Greenup, and they said: "Never mind about the steaks; we need a football player right away."
>
> Brown said the reason he has been seeking two such plans is that 'my opponent has carefully been saying the things people want to hear.' In one town, Brown said, his opponent was in favor of an all-out unrestricted production.
>
> But when he got into the Bluegrass, Brown said, his opponent found the tobacco farmers there are against unlimited production, so he came out in favor of crop quotas. He has been against federal subsidies, but he found out the teachers are in favor of federal assistance, so now he is in favor of Government subsidies to the schools.
>
> He says to the old people, 'I think the Government ought to balance the budget, but also ought to increase the amount of old age pensions.' In other words, my opponent believes in feeding his audiences what they want to hear.[2]

Cooper defeated Democrat John Y. Brown Sr. by a margin of 53.3 to 46.5 percent. Republicans in the 1946 midterms took the US Senate majority. When Cooper entered the Senate, the majority leader was Republican Wallace White of Maine. The minority leader was Kentucky Democrat Alben Barkley.

An excerpt from Robert Schulman's *John Sherman Cooper—The Global Kentuckian* reads:

> Cooper remembers with pride that one of his first actions upon taking his Senate seat in 1947 was to co-sponsor legislation to allow emergency admittance to the United States each year for four

years 100,000 persons displaced by Hitler. A Texas Senator spoke of 'subversives, revolutionists and crackpots,' but Cooper said simply, 'These are people who resisted and will not return to a totalitarian state.' [Most of these displaced persons were from the nations that had been conquered by Hitler and later taken over by Stalin and the communists after the war.]

His maiden speech in the Senate was on January 22, 1947. It was in support of his vote against the transfer of the investigation of World War II graft and profiteering from the regular Senate committee on executive expenditures to a special committee. This, Cooper felt, would turn the investigation into political hay-making. So, his vote went against the wishes of his party's leadership. He was only able to get his say in the floor debate by a grant of time from the Democrats.

Just before Cooper spoke, Wisconsin Senator Joseph McCarthy played to the gallery. He suggested that failure to shift the war investigation to a special committee would be a message to 'the wives and mothers of the 250,000 men who died during the war...the legless and sightless that wartime delinquencies would be left unproved."

Cooper's position was a forecast of many similar positions he would take in that body. The freshman senator saw no reason why the procedural rules needed to be changed. Not himself a member of the committee being challenged; his approach was on principle. He said that continuation of the probe by the regular committee would provide a needed expertise for future decisions in the area. He concluded with a statement which could now be repeated when illegalities by the CIA and other executive agencies came to light in the wake of the Watergate cover-up.

In his first speech on the Senate floor, he said, "It may be of no importance to anyone except the present speaker, but it seems to me, speaking from the viewpoint of one coming recently from the outside, that one of the most disturbing factors we have seen during the past thirteen years has been ignoring of rules of law, and sometimes an actual contempt of those rules, by some of those who were part of the Government itself. For myself, I should like to uphold in this body, when I can, rules of law."

A quiet, stubborn force for decency consistent with the law and rules had come to the Senate. When John Sherman Cooper again voted against the Republican Party leadership, urging that the proceeds from the sale of surplus war material should be paid on war debts, it brought the late Senator Robert Taft of Ohio up the aisle to ask the newcomer angrily, 'Are you a Democrat or Republican? When are you going to start voting with us?' In reply Cooper replied, 'I was sent here to represent my constituents and I intend to vote as I think best.'

Later acting Majority Leader Kenneth Wherry, Republican of Nebraska called Cooper to try to bend him in line on another upcoming vote, with an appeal to party loyalty. As Cooper told a magazine interviewer, his quiet but firm rebuttal to Wherry was, 'You remind me of a basketball coach I had up at Yale. He used to talk just like you do before a big game Maybe you're in the wrong business. We're not playing a game here.'[3]

It was America's role in the world that Cooper's 1947–1948 Senate debut permitted him to make his mark. "It was a special opportunity to be on hand during the great debates that set the patterns for the defense and the economic rebuilding of Europe, so absolutely essential to our national security and economic well-being," Cooper said.[4]

Some Republicans opposed the Marshall Plan, which was an unprecedented, massive, and long-term program for the reconstruction of war-ravished Europe, but not Cooper. He caught the eye and earned the respect of Michigan's Republican Senator Arthur Vandenberg, the one-time isolationist who was participating with the Truman White House in the formulation of a bipartisan foreign policy. As a freshman, Cooper's immediate involvement with foreign policy was not very visible. Even so, Massachusetts Senator Henry Cabot Lodge, a vigorous supporter of the Marshall Plan, remarked on Cooper's "vigorous and independent mind."

At the 1948 Republican National Convention, Cooper supported Arthur Vandenberg. Cooper chaired the Kentucky Delegation to the convention. Vying for the Republican presidential nomination in addition to Vandenberg were Thomas Dewey, Harold Stassen, and Robert Taft. In the end, Thomas Dewey won the Republican nomination for president in 1948.[5]

During the 1948 general election for a full six-year term, Cooper was opposed by Congressman Virgil Chapman of Paris. Chapman was a longtime congressman from Central Kentucky. While President Truman might have been considered a liability for some Democratic candidates in 1948, he had chosen Cooper's Senate colleague, Alben Barkley of Paducah, as his running mate for vice president. Governor Dewey came to Kentucky to campaign for himself and Cooper. Senator Wayne Morse of Oregon came to Kentucky to campaign for Cooper, as well.

In the end, Chapman, with the assistance of Alben Barkley as Truman's vice president, defeated Cooper and Dewey in Kentucky.

After his defeat, President Truman appointed Cooper to represent the United States in the fall of 1949 to replace John Foster Dulles as a delegate to the United Nations General Assembly.

Part XII

1948–1956
Cold War, Civil Rights, and Korea

This was a period of historical and political transition following World War II.

Alben Barkley's election as Vice President in 1948 and, to a lesser extent, Happy Chandler's resignation in 1945 to become Commissioner of Major League Baseball set off a chain reaction that resulted in seven individuals serving as Kentucky's two US senators during an eight-year period.

Virgil Chapman's Senate career was cut short by an auto accident. Earle Clements had the longest career during this period—seven years. He was defeated in a year when Republican President Eisenhower was on the ballot. He was opposed by the medical establishment for voting for the enactment of social security disability coverage and was narrowly defeated by Thurston Morton. Robert Humphreys had the shortest tenure—four months.

The election of 1954 saw the battle of two political giants—Cooper and Barkley. Barkley won that battle only to be brought down by death two years later. Cooper during his two years out of the Senate was appointed ambassador to India. As ambassador to India during the Cold War, Cooper was seen as a more-than-able diplomat. With Barkley's death, Cooper was able to reclaim by election the Senate seat he lost two years previously. Cooper was to hold this seat until retirement in 1973.

For Kentucky, these senators were advocates of the tobacco industry as well as flood control on Kentucky's rivers.

VIRGIL MUNDAY CHAPMAN
(1895–1951)

- Class Two of Three
- Senate Service: 1949–1951
- Political affiliation: Democratic
- Residence at time of election: Bourbon County
- Served with President Truman
- Served with Governors Clements and Wetherby

Due to his untimely death, Senator Chapman's contributions as a US Senator are overshadowed by serving more than twenty years in the US House of Representatives. In the election of 1948, Chapman reclaimed the Senate seat held by Vice President Alben Barkley for Kentucky Democrats.

Virgil Munday Chapman was born in Simpson County, which is located between Bowling Green and the Tennessee line, on March 15, 1895. He was educated in local schools and graduated from Franklin High School in 1913. Chapman attended the University of Kentucky in Lexington, and he graduated with a Bachelor of Law degree in 1918. Chapman's college career included serving as senior class president, participating as staff on the student newspaper, and serving as editor-in-chief of the *Kentucky Law Journal*. He was admitted to the Kentucky Bar in 1917, a year before he finished college.

Following graduation, Chapman established a law practice in Estill County and served as attorney for the city of Irvine. When he married Mary Adams Talbott in 1920, he moved to Paris in Bourbon County, Kentucky. While his practice was centered in Paris and Bourbon County, he also practiced law in neighboring Lexington and Fayette County.

In 1924, Virgil Chapman ran unopposed as the Democratic candidate from the old Seventh Congressional District. He succeeded Democratic Congressman Joseph Morris of Henry County, who had been secretary for Congressman J. Campbell Cantrill. Cantrill died while running for governor in 1923. Chapman served two terms but was defeated by Republican Robert E.L. Blackburn in the "Hoover landslide of 1928." The election of 1928 was when Republicans took charge of Congress. Chapman defeated Blackburn in 1930 to reclaim his seat and then served for eight consecutive terms. Due to redistricting, Chapman represented the Sixth Congressional District centered in Central Kentucky until taking his seat in the Senate in 1949.

During his time out of office, Chapman assisted in organizing the tobacco growers of Kentucky and nearby states' tobacco marketing cooperatives. His work with tobacco and the fact that he was from a tobacco-growing region was reflected in Chapman's championing of Kentucky's tobacco growers and various farm aid bills. He also helped draft and pass the Food, Drug, and Cosmetic Act of 1938, which was a landmark legislation. According to the FDA website:

> More consumer-oriented than its predecessor, the 1938 Food, Drug, and Cosmetic Act was a watershed in US food policy. In contrast to the limited health-based standards that the Ministry of Health proposed in Britain during the Depression, the US, largely through the efforts of women's groups, pioneered policies designed to protect the pocketbooks of consumers, and food standards were enacted to ensure the 'value expected' by consumers. The 1938 Act eliminated the 'distinctive name proviso' and required instead that the label of a food 'bear its common or usual name.' The food would be misbranded if it represented itself as a standardized food unless it conformed to that standard. The law provided for three kinds of food standards: 1) standards (definitions) of identity, 2) standards of quality, and 3) standards regulating the fill of container. Regulators had the discretionary authority to set standards 'whenever in the judgment of the Secretary such action will promote honesty and fair dealing in the interests of consumers.'[1]

Chapman took a political step forward when he was elected to the US Senate in 1948, defeating the Republican candidate, John Sherman Cooper. During the 1948 campaign, President Truman came to Kentucky campaigning for Chapman on his campaign train. On September 30, 1948, President Truman campaigned for himself and Chapman at a train stop by 3:55 p.m. in Henderson and at 4:50 p.m. the same day in Owensboro.[1]

While Truman's visit to Kentucky was significant, the most notable event of Chapman's political career came on Election Day in his home county of Bourbon. Chapman's election, particularly the part in Bourbon County, is described in the biography of Ed Prichard Jr., *Short of the Glory: The Fall and Redemption of Edward F. Prichard Jr.*:

> Chapman's rival for the Democratic nomination was John Y. Brown of Lexington. Bourbon Countians wanted to support their favorite son, whose local campaign committee was headed by Billy Baldwin and Ed Prichard, Sr. Chapman headquarters in Louisville asked Baldwin and Prichard 'to aid in rounding up every possible Democratic vote.' Chapman won the primary election, certainly helped along by his 2,012 to 148 vote margins in Bourbon County. For the general election, the *Paris Kentuckian-Citizen* predicted that 'the Democrats in Bourbon County undoubtedly will give Paris's Virgil Chapman on of the greatest margins any Democrat ever achieved.' On the eve of the election, the paper's columnist wrote that 'Bourbon Countians will rally to the voting places Tuesday, that is, every single Democratic voter, and help Virgil in the most important race of his career.'[2]

Then Election Day is described in Bourbon County:

> Early on the morning of election day, Tuesday, November 2, 1948, a Republican precinct officer carried to the polls a ballot box he obtained at the county courthouse. When he heard a rattling sound at the bottom of the box, he asked Bourbon County Deputy Sheriff John Neal to what was at the bottom of the box that was supposedly empty. The deputy used a penknife to extract the source of the noise, a ballot that had already been scratched in favor of the Democratic slate. Further extractions revealed that seventeen ballots were lying at the bottom of the box, all but one marked Democratic. The fraudulent ballots were brought to Sheriff J.M. Leer, who placed them in the county vault. The box in question was Clintonville #3, whose precinct officer was listed as Edward F. Prichard, Jr.

When Sheriff Leer went out to the Clintonville precinct to check the ballot book, the ballots in question were missing. Reports of missing ballots from six other precincts were soon verified. County Republicans were furious to discover the fraud, and local Democrats implied it was a Republican setup. As statement released by the Bourbon County Democratic Committee, led by Frank Kiser, Dan Peed, William Blanton and Billy Baldwin declared, 'We hope that whoever is guilty of this despicable trick will be detected and prosecuted.'

At 10:00 pm an overconfident Dewey, wired Republican Cooper JS Cooper—saying 'Am overjoyed at your re-election. Heartiest congratulations and best wishes, Thomas E. Dewey.'[3]

When the votes were counted, Chapman beat Cooper by 21,000 votes. Ed Prichard Jr. was eventually convicted of voter fraud in this matter and served some time in federal prison.

In respect to his brief time in the Senate, "In the words of journalist Mark Etheridge, Chapman was a 'most rabid conservative' who opposed the party's recent stands on civil rights and labor."[4] His friends in the Senate described him of having "independent thought." He supported the Truman administration for the most part during his time in the Senate, particularly in the area of foreign policy and military affairs.[5]

This was also the beginning of the Cold War. Chapman's cold warrior stance is reflected in his words at a speech to veterans in Louisville. He was a supporter of compulsory uniform military service. Virgil Chapman was not one to be called a progressive. In an address to the Kentucky Farm Bureau in Louisville on November 1950, Chapman equated fair employment practices and mandatory health insurance to the "isms" of socialism and communism. He said he supported the League of Nations and the United Nations as well as compulsory military service. He believed that if we would have had compulsory military service prior to World War I, we would not have had that war.[6]

In many of his speeches, Chapman ripped on the Soviet Union. In a speech to the Twelfth Armored Association at Louisville's Seelbach Hotel in September of 1949, he said, "Preparedness is the answer to the narrow, selfish ambitious Soviet Union. . .. Russia is now making a dire threat to the efficacy of the United Nations as an instrument of peace."[7] Chapman was a member of the Senate Armed Services Committee.

He cited Switzerland as an example of preparedness, saying,

The little country, model land of liberty and democracy, adopted George Washington's recommendation that was unheeded by his own country, and provided military training for every abled body citizen. When the flames of war swept over Europe in 1914, little Switzerland placed in the field in four days a trained equipped citizens army of 300,000 men. . .. Through four years of devastating war Switzerland maintained her neutrality without the firing of a gun or the tread of a hostile footstep on her land.[8]

At the time of his death on March 8, 1951, the Democratic leadership in the Senate had assigned him the task of leading the debate against an amendment to take away a provision to set up universal military training at an indefinite future date from a pending "draft bill." The Senate had tentatively agreed to lower the draft-induction age from nineteen to eighteen. In his remarks that day, he said, "overwhelming preponderance was in favor of placing the 18-year old boys in their country's uniform for military training and service."[9]

Chapman was working on legislation related to lowering the draft age from age nineteen to eighteen when he left his Capitol offices at a little after 11:00 p.m. on March 7, 1951, to get something to eat in nearby Maryland before going to his room at the Army and Navy Club. At about 3:30 a.m. on March 8, Chapman made a left-hand turn and collided head-on with a grocery truck. When police reached Chapman, he was conscious. He said he had only been traveling about twenty-five miles per hour at the time of the accident. The life squad from Chevy Chase, Maryland, took about twenty minutes to get Chapman out of the car. He was taken first to Emergency Hospital (now part of MedStar Washington Hospital Center) and then to Bethesda Naval Hospital. It was ascertained that he had suffered from internal injuries. Soon after being taken to the operating room, Senator Chapman died.

He was buried in the Paris Cemetery in Paris, Kentucky. His wife, Mary, and a daughter, Mrs. Francis J. Danforth Jr. of New Canaan, Connecticut, were his survivors.[10]

GARRETT LEE WITHERS
(1884–1953)

- Class Three of Three
- Senate Service: 1949–1950
- Political affiliation: Democratic
- Residence at time of election: Webster County
- Served with President Truman
- Served with Governor Clements

Garrett Lee Withers was appointed to the US Senate on January 20, 1949, by Governor Earle Clements upon Alben Barkley's resignation to become vice president of the US under President Harry S. Truman. Withers served as Clements' highway commissioner from 1947 until he entered the Senate in 1949.

Senator Withers was born on a farm in Webster County, Kentucky, near Clay on June 21, 1884. He studied at M.&F. Academy in Providence, Kentucky. According to a postcard of the era, M.&F. Academy provided "COURSES Leading to Common School Diploma, County Certificate, State Certificate and State Diploma." It further states, "Excellent General Discipline and Thorough Work... Refined Association... Courteous Treatment."[1] After attending the academy, Withers attended Southern Normal School in Bowling Green, Kentucky. Southern Normal School was later absorbed by Western Kentucky University.

Withers taught school and became an attorney. He practiced in Webster County beginning in 1911. He served as circuit court clerk from 1910 to 1912 and as master commissioner from 1913 to 1917. He was a member of the Kentucky Highway Commission from 1932 to 1936. He served a referee in the Federal Bankruptcy Court from 1941 to 1945.

He was proud of being an attorney and practicing law, as was reflected in him saying, "I would rather be known as a fairly good lawyer than anything else in the world. The stability of the government the world over is due to the profession of law."[2] (Page 52 Memorial Addresses Delivered in Congress; Garrett Lee Withers – Late A Representative And A Former Senator From Kentucky; Eighty-Third Congress-First Session (Stennis) U.S. Government Printing Office : Washington (1953)

Garrett Withers served less than two years in the Senate. However, he was able to garner national headlines in the *New York Times* by defending the Truman administration's threat to seize private property during an emergency. An article dated June 9, 1949, and published on June 10, 1949, said:

TRUMAN'S POWERS ARGUED IN SENATE
Withers Says He Has "Inherent" Rights as Taft Insists on Need for Labor Injunction Law
By Louis Stark

Sharp debate on the President's 'inherent powers' to seize property during an emergency enlivened debate in the Senate today on labor legislation.

In his maiden speech, Senator Garrett L. Withers, Democrat, of Kentucky, said he inclined to the opinion of those lawyers who maintained that the Chief Executive had 'implied powers' to act in an emergency and seize property.

This view was challenged by Senator Robert Taft of Ohio and Senator Wayne L. Morse of Oregon, both Republicans. They contended that there was nothing that could be read into the Constitution that would permit such an action by the president.

The views of Senators Taft and Withers on 'national emergency' strikes were diametrically opposed, so much so that each held that the other's ideas would actually lead to a change in our present form of government.

The junior Senator from Kentucky asserted that Senator Taft's proposal calling for an injunction to end national emergency strikes meant 'the beginning of the abridgement of our liberties.'[3]

Senator Withers gained front-page attention by accident in July 1949. He had gone home for dinner and was called back to the Senate for a vote. While at home, Withers took off his tie. He returned to the Senate Chamber without a tie. A Senate aide gave the senator his tie.[4] Later that year, he made national news when it was found that he worked in office with his shoes off when he thought there were no visitors.[5] During Withers' first year in the Senate, he served on the Labor Committee. In January 1950, he moved to the Senate Judiciary Committee.[6] In February 1950, Withers declared that he would not be a candidate for election in November 1950.[7]

It should be noted that during his short tenure, Withers defended Secretary of State Dean Acheson and the State Department against Senator Joseph McCarthy. McCarthy had said that the State Department had been harboring communists. Withers believed that McCarthy should name names. By failing to do so, Withers said, "His case fails for lack of proof."[8]

As a member of the Rules Committee, Withers voted with the 10–3 majority on cloture procedure with the idea of eventually eliminating the filibuster. The reason for doing this was to help move President Truman's civil rights program.[9]

Withers' last day as a senator was on November 26, 1950. On November 27, 1950, Governor Earle Clements was sworn in to succeed Withers after the results of the November 1950 election.[10]

In 1951, Withers was a successful candidate for the Kentucky House of Representatives. He was elected in a special election on August 2, 1952, as a Democrat to the Eighty-Second Congress to fill the vacancy caused by the death of Kentucky's Second District Congressman, John A. Whitaker. Withers was re-elected to the Eighty-Third Congress and served from August 2, 1952, until his death caused by a cerebral hemorrhage on April 30, 1953.

Garrett Withers is one of the few members of the House in the twentieth century who had previously served in the US Senate. The other notable fact is that he was succeeded in the House by legendary Kentucky Congressman William H. Natcher, who cast 18,401 consecutive roll-call votes between 1953 and 1994. Withers and Natcher both died at Bethesda Naval Hospital.

Garrett Withers was buried in the IOOF Cemetery in Clay, Kentucky. He was survived by his widow, two sons (Thomas L. and Dr. John C.) and a daughter, Mrs. R.B. Griffin.

EARLE C. CLEMENTS
(1896–1985)

- Class Three of Three
- Senate Service: 1950–1957
- Political affiliation: Democratic
- Residence at time of election: Morganfield
- Served with Presidents Truman and Eisenhower
- Served with Governors Wetherby and Chandler

Earle Clements is considered Kentucky's first modern governor. This is due to several factors. He was the first governor after World War II. It was also due to his programs of building of roads and schools and expanding the state colleges to accommodate returning veterans. In respect to the operation of government, he helped create the Legislative Research Commission (LRC), which assists the legislature in researching and drafting legislation, etc. When Senator Alben Barkley was elected vice president in 1948, Kentucky Governor Earle Clements had eyes on filling Barkley's seat in the US Senate. In January 1949, when Barkley resigned from the Senate to become vice president, Clements appointed Garrett Withers to fill the seat in the interim until the 1950 general election, when he would seek the full six-year term. Clements defeated Republican Charles I. Dawson in November 1950 to become a US senator from Kentucky for the six weeks remaining on Barkley's term, in addition to a six-year term. Clements served from November 27, 1950, to January 3, 1957.[1]

Clements was born in Morganfield, Union County, Kentucky, on October 22, 1896. He was the youngest of six children born to Aaron Waller and Sallie Anna Clements. He was from a politically active family as his father was elected county judge and sheriff of Union County. Clements was a football star at Morganfield High School, from which he graduated in 1915 before entering the University of Kentucky.

At the University of Kentucky, Earle Clements played center on the UK football team in 1915 and 1916. In 1916, he was recognized for his efforts on the gridiron when he was named to the All Southern Team.

Clements' career at UK was interrupted by World War I. During the summer of 1917, he enlisted in the Kentucky National Guard and served at Camp Taylor, near Louisville. When the National Guard was federalized, he was selected for Officers Training School (OTS) at Fort Benjamin Harrison at Indianapolis. He was commissioned as a first lieutenant. As a first lieutenant, Clements served as a professor of military science at OTS. He attained the rank of captain prior to his discharge in September 1919.

Following the war, Earle Clements went to Texas, where he worked in the oil fields. In 1921, Clements returned home to assist his father, whose health was failing. In doing so, Clements worked the family farm and served as a deputy sheriff for his father. He also coached football at Morganfield High School. After the death of his father in 1922, he was appointed to serve the remainder of his father's term and was subsequently elected to a full term as sheriff. At that time, county sheriffs were unable to seek a consecutive term, so he ran for and was elected as Union County clerk.

A year into his term as county clerk, Clements married his high school sweetheart, Sara M. Blue, on January 18, 1927. They had one child, a daughter, Elizabeth. Elizabeth later became the social secretary for First Lady Claudia "Lady Bird" Johnson.

In 1934, Clements was elected county judge of Union County. In 1935, he was asked by Thomas Rhea, a prominent Democratic power broker, to serve as campaign chair for his run for governor. Rhea hoped to succeed Governor Ruby Laffoon. Clements agreed to serve, resulting in his refusal to support his old friend Lieutenant Governor "Happy" Chandler in the Democratic primary. Clements's support of Rhea over Chandler began a thirty-year rift in the Democratic Party of Kentucky.

In 1941, Earle Clements was elected to the Kentucky Senate. By 1944, Clements was the majority leader of that body. During the 1944 session, he successfully opposed many of Republican Governor Simeon Willis' conservative programs and also wrote the state's budget during that session. At the same time, Earle Clements successfully sought election in November 1944 as the US Representative from Kentucky's Second District to Congress.

As a member of the US House of Representatives, Clements was a strong supporter of the New Deal. He supported the National School Lunch Act, which became the permanent basis for the national school lunch program. In his two terms of in Congress, Clements supported bills that banned lynching and poll taxes.

In 1947, Earle Clements decided to run for governor of Kentucky. He defeated House Speaker Harry Lee Waterfield in the Democratic primary. In the general election, Clements defeated Republican Attorney General Eldon S. Dummit.

One Kentucky landmark that came into being during the Clements administration was the purchase of over 400 acres in Louisville for the State Fair and Exposition Center. Another was the building of the State Capitol Annex behind the Capitol in Frankfort.

During his term as governor, the non-partisan LRC was created to assist the General Assembly. For the first time, there was a full-time professional staff to assist with governmental research.

In his 1950 campaign for the Senate, Clements campaigned on the New and Fair Deal(s). Soon after his arrival in the Senate, he became part of the inner circle of Democrats. Lyndon Baines Johnson became one of his closest friends. At the beginning of 1953, the Senate Democratic Caucus elected Clements to the role of whip, with Senator Lyndon Johnson of Texas serving as the Senate minority leader. Clements's nomination was made by New Mexico's Senator Clinton B. Anderson, a longtime friend, and was seconded by Senators Lehman and Humphrey.[2]

Clements must have stuck close to the Capitol. In a survey by *Congressional Quarterly* for attendance during the Eighty-Second Congress during 1951 and 1952, Kentucky Senator Clements and his colleague Senator Tom Underwood had a 10 percent better record than the average senator. Out of 331 votes in 1951 and 1952, Clements was present 293 times, or 89 percent of the time. As Underwood was sworn in on March 19, 1951, he had the opportunity to be present for only 311 roll call votes. He was, in fact, present 280 times, or 90 percent of the time.[3]

On one of the hot-button issues of the day, Clements expressed an opinion that was unusual for a Southern Democrat. In respect to *Brown v. Board of Education*, Clements, in an Omaha, Nebraska, interview, called the decision "a fine thing," a directive that the state and the nation should obey. Additionally, he believed that the Democrats, rather than the Republican administration of President Eisenhower, should claim credit for it since Democratic presidents had appointed eight of the nine justices on the Supreme Court.[4]

During the 1955 Kentucky Democratic primary for Governor, Happy Chandler was seeking a second term against Judge Bert Combs. Combs was supported by both incumbent Governor Wetherby and Clements. The primary was bitter. Happy Chandler, in so many words, indicated, "a prime purpose of his campaign was to win control of the party machinery and fight to see that Clements does not return to Washington in 1956."[5]

In July 1955, Clements became the acting Senate majority leader due to Senator Johnson's near-fatal heart attack. Clements was described as more of a vocal critic of the Eisenhower administration than Johnson, particularly in the area of foreign affairs.

A *Courier-Journal* editorial on Friday, July 8, 1955, said the following about Clements:

> Yet his noisiest detractors cannot change the fact that his effect on the state has been good. He has been the primary power in Kentucky politics since 1944 when as Senate Leader under Republican Governor Simeon Willis, he actually ran the state. And in those 11 years (1944–1955) Kentucky has made progress. The Clements administration was a model for efficient administration, and through it and the succeeding WETHERBY Administration Kentucky has achieved many long-sought laws in education, mental-treatment resource development, economic improvement and increased public service despite crippling inflation.
>
> His effect on the nation, we felt, will be equally good, if only for the reason of his oft-demonstrated ability to think.[6]

Unfortunately for Clements, it was the year before his next Senate election year. As acting majority leader, Clements was unable to get back to Kentucky often enough to prepare for his reelection in 1956.

In order to make life difficult for Clements, Governor Chandler found a candidate to oppose him in the 1956 Democratic primary. Kentucky Governor Chandler supported former US Representative Joe Bates from Greenup. However, Clements was able to defeat him by about 78,000 votes. His race in November 1956 against Republican Thurston Morton was going to be difficult due to Morton's support from the Eisenhower administration.

In 1956, the AFL-CIO supported legislation to expand Social Security to include disabled workers. Lyndon Johnson was pushing legislation hard for disabled workers. When the issue came up for a vote during the summer of 1956, Johnson's vote total was forty-six for and forty-six against. At the time, Clements had told Kentucky doctors he was not going to vote for this legislation. An excerpt from Robert Caro's *The Years of Lyndon Johnson: Master of the Senate* speaks of Senator Clements's dilemma:

Malone's vote made the count on Social Security 46 to 46. The proposal would fail on a tie; Johnson needed one more vote. That vote belonged to Earle Clements. Of all the senators 'loyal' to Lyndon Johnson in the way Lyndon Johnson wanted men 'loyal,' none was more loyal—'dog loyal'—than the Kentucky Senator, who was willing to 'do anything for the Leader.' Clements was well aware by now that his re-election campaign against Thruston Morton, Assistant Secretary of State, was in George Smathers' words, 'in serious trouble.' He had not dared oppose the doctors; whose opinions carried great weight with the unsophisticated voters in the rural Kentucky counties that were his stronghold and had flatly promised the AMA that he would vote against the disability amendment. 'Bob, I'm not with you on this bill,' he told the UAWs Oliver, labor's chief representative on the issue. 'I gave a commitment back home that I would vote against this bill.' When Oliver started to protest, Clements cut him off. 'I can't do it. I made a commitment.' But the doctors' support was not all Clements needed against the well financed Morton. He needed cash—campaign financing on a scale far beyond what Kentucky would provide. Johnson had already provided some from Texas, and had promised Clements there would be more. Now, some weeks before the vote on the disability amendment, he told Clements he could have as much as he needed—but he might need something too: Clements' vote in favor of the disability amendment. He didn't think he would need his vote, Lyndon Johnson said; the amendment was probably going to be defeated overwhelmingly, he said. But if it turned out that he did need Clements' vote, Johnson said, he wanted to know that he had it. Clements could vote against the amendment at first, Johnson said, but if the decision came down to one vote, Clements would have to change his vote on the amendment from 'nay' to 'aye.' Clements told Johnson that breaking his word to the doctors might cost him the election, and Johnson was aware of that; 'Johnson fully recognized that this would subject Clements to the full wrath of the doctors' lobby,' Evans and Novak were to write.[7]

With 74 percent of 4,052 precincts reported, Thurston B. Morton defeated Clements by 6,004 votes. Eisenhower defeated Adlai Stevenson by more than 95,000 votes in 1956. In 1952, Stevenson defeated Eisenhower by 700 votes in Kentucky.[8]

Incumbent Governor Chandler's opposition to Clements in the primary, the well-funded Morton, and the opposition of the AMA helped defeat Clements's bid for reelection in 1956. Clements's defeat in 1956 ended his unbroken thirty-five-year streak of service in elected office.

"I never ran for anything with the idea that it was a steppingstone to a higher job," Mr. Clements once said. "I always got accused of that, but those folks were wrong. You run for office because you want to represent all your people. And when you get that office, you devote all your time to it."[9]

At the end of his Senate career, at the direction of Lyndon Johnson, Clements served as executive director of the Senate Democratic Reelection Committee. In this position, he helped Democrats elect a fourteen-seat majority in the Senate after the 1958 elections

He returned to Kentucky as highway commissioner under Governor Bert Combs. He resigned in September 1960 to work for Johnson's campaign for the Democratic presidential nomination.

Clements served in various roles as a lobbyist. He was a consultant for the American Merchant Marine Institute from 1961 until 1963. From 1964 until 1976, Clements worked as a lobbyist for Philip Morris Inc., the tobacco company. While he was at Philip Morris, he was president of the Tobacco Institute, a trade organization, from 1966 until 1970.[10]

Clements died on March 12, 1985, in Morganfield, Kentucky. He was buried in Morganfield Independent Order of Odd Fellows Cemetery. The Earle C. Clements Jobs Corps Center in Morganfield was named in his honor. The Kentucky Department of Education has an annual Earle C. Clements Innovation in Education Award for Civics and History Teachers sponsored by the National Archives and the University of Kentucky Libraries and Wendell H. Ford Public Policy Research Center.[11]

THOMAS R. UNDERWOOD
(1898–1956)

- Class Two of Three
- Senate Service March 19, 1951–November 4, 1952
- Political affiliation: Democratic
- Residence at time of election: Lexington
- Served with President Truman
- Served with Governor Wetherby

The unexpected death of Senator Virgil Chapman resulted in Kentucky Governor Wetherby appointing Sixth District US Congressman Thomas R. Underwood of Lexington in March 1951 to replace Chapman. Prior to his service in Congress, Underwood had been secretary of the State Racing Commission. His most recent stint in that position was when Governor Earle Clements appointed him in March 1948.[1] Congressman Underwood was a logical choice at the time. In his most recent election to Congress in 1950, he had been unopposed.[2] He was also the managing editor of one of Kentucky's largest newspapers—the *Lexington Herald*.

The headlines in the *Louisville Courier-Journal* from the March 18, 1951, read: "Fayette County Sends Seventh Man to Senate—Thomas R. Underwood is the seventh resident of Fayette County to serve in the United States Senate."

This same article went on to say:

> The first was John Breckinridge. The others were Henry Clay, who was in the Senate for four separate terms; John Pope; William T. Berry; John Cabell Breckinridge and James B. Beck.
>
> Underwood, as congressman from the Sixth Kentucky District will be the first Lexington resident in the Senate in 61 years.[3]

Thomas R. Underwood was born in Hopkinsville, Kentucky. He graduated from the University of Kentucky. During World War I, he served in the student Army Training Corps at the University of Kentucky. It was reported: "On June 20, 1925, Underwood—then managing editor of the *Lexington Herald* married Miss Eliza Pigott, the State Editor of the *Lexington Herald* at Tynebrae the home of Dr. W.B. McClure on the Harrodsburg Pike in Lexington."[4]

With Happy Chandler's return to private life after serving as baseball commissioner, there were some who thought of Chandler being appointed to the vacancy. There was also the sitting Governor, Lawrence Wetherby. Many believed that Lawrence Wetherby would be the best person for the appointment. However, Wetherby had only become governor after Clements had won election to the Senate. According to the *Courier-Journal*, "Governor Wetherby was thought to be the only 'real' contender for the appointment. Though—Happy Chandler was thought to be interested and the Governor Wetherby called and told 'Happy' of his intention to appoint of Underwood to the vacancy."[5]

The Governor and Chandler talked on the day of Chapman's death. "Like Chapman, Underwood is a specialist in tobacco legislation, the first requirement in this burley-conscious district. Like Chapman, he is addicted to pleasant oratory in the old Kentucky manner. And like Chapman, he is rooted in culture and traditions of the Bluegrass country."[6]

It was a contentious campaign between Underwood and Cooper. New Deal-related farm issues seemed to dominate the race. In October, Underwood was quoted below:

> Cooper accused Underwood of being a handpicked nominee of U.S. Senator Earle C. Clements. Underwood accused Cooper of favoring cuts to the school lunch program, as Cooper was a member of the Republican-controlled 80th Congress, which reduced the penny school lunch program by $15 million.[7]

Though not mentioning his Republican opponent—former Senator John Sherman Cooper—by name, Underwood said:

He has minimized my record. He has called me an errand boy.
He has criticized my grammer. He has even butchered up my jokes
and tried to tell them back and misconstrue them and answer them
seriously.[8]

Underwood then cited a signed statement by 356 of Kentucky's most
active farmers in which they stated that he, Underwood:

Aided in the fight to obtain funds for research into black shank;
helped continue the price support program for tobacco and other
farm products; helped to keep tobacco in the foreign aid program;
assisted the R.E.A. programs; opposed ceiling prices on tobacco;
helped prevent tobacco tax increases of a harmful nature; helped
defeat a proposal to cut appropriations for the soil-conservation
program; made the motion to set aside the plan to federalize and
socialize the Department of Agriculture; helped obtain drought aid
for Kentucky, and helped obtain a support price for Kentucky 31
fescue (a forage grass)."[9]

During the last month of the campaign, Governor Wetherby campaigned for the Democratic ticket in Kentucky. This was headed by Adlai
Stevenson and Senator Thomas R. Underwood.[10]

The day after the election (November 5, 1952), there were 2,654 out
of 4,135 precincts reporting; Cooper had 334,30 votes to Underwood's
324,103, and Stevenson was winning 346,056 to 333,700 over Eisenhower.[11]

Senator Underwood died in Lexington and was buried in the Lexington Cemetery. He had one son, Thomas R. Underwood Jr., an attorney
who served several terms as a Lexington city commissioner in the late
1960s and early 1970s before the formation of the Urban County Government.

Underwood was also the editor of two books dealing with horse racing—*Thoroughbred Racing & Breeding: The Story of the Sport and Background of the Horse Industry* and *Call Me Horse: Interesting, Humorous,
and Informative Notes About Horse Racing and Breeding.*

JOHN SHERMAN COOPER
(1901–1991)
Second Term

- Class Two of Three
- Senate Service: 1952–1955 (Second Term)
- Political affiliation: Republican
- Residence at time of election: Somerset
- Served with President Eisenhower
- Served with Governor Wetherby

The announcement that John Sherman Cooper was seeking another term was made by State Senator Thomas W. Hines after Cooper's address at the annual dinner of the Second District Lincoln Club.[1] In his speech to the Lincoln Club, he "denounced the high spending of the present Administration and warned that present practices threaten to wreck the stability of America's government."[2]

The *Courier-Journal*, in its editorial from February 29, 1952, was titled "Good Choice for U.S. Senator, But There's a Lot to Consider." The editorial characterized both gentlemen as "two popular and able public servants."[3]

The same editorial also criticized Senator Underwood for voting against admitting Alaska to the Union. It also noted that Senator Clements voted the same way in the 45–44 vote against admission. The rationale was that Alaskan statehood would eliminate one Kentucky seat in the US House of Representatives.

Cooper announced his intention to run for his old seat in the Senate in the 1952 election early that year. One of Cooper's first appearances was in March before the Jefferson County Young Republican Club at the Plantation Room of the Seelbach Hotel in Louisville.[4]

One of the issues during the campaign was "The Big Sandy Canal: An Issue 62 Years."[5] In the editorial, it is stated, "He is right when he points to the Big Sandy Canal proposal as unrealized opportunity for developing and improving the economy of the mountains."

The following is from the editorial:

> Mr. Cooper is on less solid ground when he charges, as he did before a recent Paintsville audience, that the Democrats have neglected the development of the Eastern Kentucky. Dewey Dam and Wolf Creek Dam are both located in Eastern Kentucky. Wolf Creek Dam and the resulting development of Cumberland Lake have brought untold benefit to Mr. Cooper's home county of Pulaski. Both these projects were proposed, approved and built under Democratic administrations, and largely through the efforts of Kentucky Democrats.[6]

Democrat Adlai Stevenson of Illinois barely carried Kentucky in the 1952 general election for Kentucky's ten electoral votes. Two days after the election, the *Courier-Journal* reported that Stevenson had a "majority of 1,047 votes."[7] The unofficial total in Kentucky's 4,135 precincts gave Stevenson 494,109 votes to 493,063 for Eisenhower.

In the Senate race between Underwood and Cooper, it was not close. Cooper received 491,532 to Underwood's 463,731 votes. Cooper was able to finish the balance of the term he had previously sought in 1948.[8]

Once his election was over, he noted that dealing with the Soviets was frustrating. This is why he believed that ties with Germany and Japan must be strengthened and that "maintaining and building the United Nations is important because that group has weight, even with Russia."[9]

Upon his return to the Senate, Cooper got a position on the Armed Services Committee. It came as a result of Oregon Senator Wayne Morse being taken off the Committee. Morse was a Republican who supported Stevenson over Eisenhower in the 1952 presidential election.[10]

One of the issues in Kentucky facing Cooper was the plan to enlarge Fort Knox. Officials in Bullitt and Hardin Counties were assured by Cooper in February 1953 of having complete hearings before Congress decided to enlarge Fort Knox by 29,000 acres. Farmers were concerned about losing grazing land. Officials were concerned about the loss of property taxes in Bullitt and Hardin Counties. There were concerns about Army rocket-firing plans. Their firing into the Rolling Fork of the Salt River had killed all the marine life, polluted the stream, and caused serious erosion. This erosion had silted up the river and caused more frequent flooding around Boston and other communities.[11]

US Senators and Representatives of the president's political party had significant authority over federal jobs and patronage in their respective states prior to the modern era. Following the 1952 general election, Dwight Eisenhower was the first Republican president in twenty years. Following the 1952 general election, Kentucky had six Democratic US Representatives and one Republican US senator. With a new Republican administration in the White House, Cooper was the most influential Republican office holder in Kentucky. He had responsibility for patronage, such as the appointments of postmasters. In 1953, Kentucky ranked second of the forty-eight states for the highest number of post offices—there were 2,303 post offices. Pennsylvania ranked first with 2,472. Postmaster positions are usually the purview of the local congressmen. In 1953, there were only two Republican congressmen; therefore, in the six districts represented by Democrats, the sole Republican US senator, Senator Cooper, was responsible for overseeing the appointments in those districts. There was also the issue of civil service requirements, which needed to be considered when replacing a postmaster.[12]

A year prior to the 1954 elections, Allen Trout of the *Courier-Journal* wrote of Cooper:

Bedrock of Service

Cooper's strength of course, rests upon the bedrock of public service that began in the House of Representatives at Frankfort when he was 26. Since then, this sixth-generation scion of a mountain Republican family has been Judge, Circuit Judge and United States Senator in 1946–48.

He has been U.S. Delegate to the United Nations, special adviser to Secretary of State Dean Acheson at the London and Brussels conferences of the North Atlantic Treaty Organization. Currently, he is in the Senate for the last two years of the unexpired Term of the late Senator Virgil M. Chapman.

Beyond this record, however, Cooper has attained a priceless asset in politics. He has become legendized. The unfathomable alchemy of his reaction upon the voters has made him a legend of earnestness, a legend of invincibility, a legend of selfless service.

Cooper's superstructure of legend, I believe, springs primarily from the look on his face. His is a sort of pleading countenance. When he looks at an audience, his face seems to say: If you can't vote for me, at least feel sorry for me.[13]

As a Republican officeholder in a state dominated by Democrats, Cooper was aware as early as September 1953 that former Vice President Barkley might consider running for the Senate in 1954.[14]

It was also noted that Senator Cooper was one of the growing numbers of Republican senators who had distanced himself from Wisconsin Senator Joseph McCarthy.[15]

In December 1953, Cooper felt sure that the Bureau of the Budget would recommend that Congress appropriate funds for two new flood-protection projects in Kentucky. Additionally, he believed that the Bureau would approve funds to continue three Ohio River projects in Covington, Louisville, and Maysville, as well as to one Cumberland River project underway.

Cooper and Senator Earle Clements asked the Army Corps of Engineers and the Bureau of the Budget for appropriation of funds to begin improvements on the Green River in Western Kentucky.[16]

In running for reelection in 1954, he said he "based his campaign for re-election on his record and the accomplishments of the Eisenhower Administration."[17]

Robert Schulman summarizes some of the achievements of Cooper's, which will be further summarized here.[18]

While Cooper did not flaunt it, the Americans for Democratic Action rated Cooper the Senate's "most liberal Republican" at the end of 1953.[19]

He won an extension of 90 percent parity price supports for tobacco, which he had initiated in 1948. As a member of the Labor Committee, he helped amend the Taft-Hartley Act, which was recognized as desirable by both labor and management.

He was vocal in his opposition to Ohio Republican Senator John Bricker's resolution for a constitutional amendment to limit the president's treaty-making powers. On all six key roll call votes on the resolution, Cooper was the only Republican senator who voted "no."

Cooper fought the Eisenhower administration's attempt to destroy the TVA under the "dubious Dixon-Yates contract."[20] As an alternative, he proposed successful legislation that allowed the TVA to authorize its own bonds for capital outlays, such as construction.[21] He opposed the administration's appointment of Albert Cole as Federal Housing Administrator as Cole was an opponent of public housing.

"This is the first administration in 20 years that has faced the facts," Cooper said.[22]

President Eisenhower flew to Louisville to campaign for Cooper and the Republican ticket on October 29, 1954.[23] Vice President Nixon and other prominent US senators, including Everett Dirksen, had come to Kentucky to campaign on behalf of Senator Cooper in 1954.

Cooper was defeated by a former Vice President Alben Barkley by about 70,000 votes. The *Courier-Journal* pointed out three possible reasons for Cooper's defeat in addition to the popularity of his opponent, the former Vice President, also known as the "Veep": "The Democrats got out their votes in great numbers; Republicans, generally apathetic, failed to get out their vote; and the Republicans who did vote showed little enthusiasm for Cooper, presumably because of his unorthodoxy."[24]

Despite his opposition to many of the Eisenhower policies, the president appointed Senator Cooper as ambassador to India and Nepal.

Within three years, Cooper would finally be elected to a full term of his own and serve three uninterrupted six-year terms.

ALBEN BARKLEY
(1877–1956)
Fifth Term

- Class Two of Three
- Senate Service: 1955–1956 (Fifth Term)
- Political affilition: Democratic
- Residence at time of election: Paducah
- Served with President Eisenhower
- Served with Governors Wetherby and Chandler

Alben Barkley decided to return to the Senate after his term as vice president ended in 1953. For twenty-six weeks in 1953, Barkley had a television show on NBC for fifteen minutes each week called *Meet the Veep*. On the show, he discussed national issues and talked about his time in politics. After his show was canceled in September 1953, he worked with freelance writer Sidney Shalett on his autobiography. Shalett helped publish sections of the autobiography in the *Saturday Evening Post* prior to the release of the full autobiography in October 1954.[1]

Barkley ran in 1954 for two reasons. First, he missed the limelight that campaigns and public office brought. Secondly, Governor Wetherby and the Kentucky Democrats believed he was the only strong Democrat that could beat the incumbent Senator, John Sherman Cooper.

Barkley resumed his Iron Man campaign style, campaigning for up to sixteen hours a day, countering the "too old" charge that cost him the presidential nomination in 1952. He campaigned on the achievements of past Democratic administrations. In a speech at Harrodsburg on October 22, 1954, he said that "under Democratic administrations, electricity was brought to 4,500,000 rural homes through the Rural Electrification Administration. And if you elect a Democratic Congress this fall; we will see to it that electricity is in every farm home in the United States of America." Barkley said the prices of farm products dropped 20 percent in those past twenty months and that the Eisenhower administration had violated its promises to the American farmer.[2]

During the campaign, incumbent Senator Cooper brought Republican stars to Kentucky to campaign on his behalf. On the day the Republicans brought President Eisenhower to Louisville, Alben Barkley said, "If this campaign went on another week, I think they'd bring Herbert Hoover down." Barkley went on to say, "When the campaign began, I thought John Sherman Cooper was my only opponent." Then he found Congressman Joseph Martin, Senator Everett Dirksen, and Vice President Richard Nixon campaigning in Kentucky and said, "And now even Eisenhower is running."[3]

He won the general election by a vote of 434,109 to 362,948, giving Democrats a one-vote advantage in the Senate. Barkley's win over Cooper gave him a then-unprecedented fifth term as US Senator from Kentucky. Barkley's margin of victory of 70,000-plus votes was his second smallest margin in his five races for the Senate. In his first election, he had defeated incumbent Richard Ernst by 20,340 votes in 1926.[4]

On January 3, 1955, Alben Barkley, accompanied by Kentucky's senior senator, Earle Clements, was given the oath of office by Vice President Richard M. Nixon.

West Virginia Senator Harley Kilgore offered to exchange seats with Barkley, putting Barkley on the front row with the Chamber's senior members and himself on the back row with the freshman senators. In recognition of helping the Democrats becoming the majority in the US Senate and enabling Senator Lyndon Johnson to become Senate majority leader, Johnson appointed Barkley to the Foreign Relations and Finance Committees.

As a member of the Foreign Relations Committee, Barkley endorsed President Eisenhower's appointment of John Sherman Cooper as the US ambassador to India and Nepal.

Unfortunately, during this term, Barkley was not the political force he once was. He was going blind and was unable to read legislation. Therefore, he was unable to speak with authority on the legislation.

On April 30, 1956, Alben Barkley gave the keynote address at Washington and Lee University's Mock Convention. In his remarks, he spoke of his willingness to sit on the back row with other freshman senators. He ended his remarks with an allusion to Psalm 84:10, saying, "I'm glad to sit on the back row, for I would rather be a servant in the House of the Lord than sit in the seats of the mighty."[5] He then collapsed. His wife, Jane, was the first reach him. He was thought to have died instantaneously of a heart attack.

Services were held for Alben Barkley at Foundry United Methodist Church in Washington, D.C., where President Eisenhower, Vice President Nixon, and the entire Senate attended. Services were also held in his hometown of Paducah. On the funeral train from Washington to Paducah, there were more than a dozen senators, including future Vice President Hubert Humphrey, William Fulbright, and Earle Clements. Three candidates for the Democratic presidential nomination in 1956 also attended—Illinois Governor Adlai Stevenson, New York Governor Averell Harriman, and Tennessee Senator Estes Kefauver. Kentucky local officials included Governor Happy Chandler.[6]

Associated Press Reporter Paul R. Jordan found President Harry Truman in Paducah's Irvin Cobb Hotel. When introducing himself prior to an interview with Truman, Jordan said, "It is good to see you, Mr. President." Truman, who was personally close to Barkley from their time together in both the Senate and the White House, replied, "Yes, but not on this occasion," thus indicating Truman's grief at the passing of his friend and colleague.[7]

Barkley was buried in Mount Kenton Cemetery, near Paducah. Lake Barkley and Barkley Dam in Western Kentucky were named in honor of Senator Barkley.

ROBERT HUMPHREYS
(1893–1977)

- Class Two of Three
- Senate Service: June 21, 1956–November 6, 1956
- Political affiliation: Democratic
- Residence at time of election: Mayfield
- Served with President Eisenhower
- Served with Governor Chandler

Robert Humphreys was appointed by Governor A.B. "Happy" Chandler on June 21, 1956, to fill the vacancy caused by the sudden death of Senator Alben Barkley.

Humphreys was born in Fulgham, Hickman County, Kentucky, on August 20, 1893. He was educated in public schools and graduated from Marvin College in Clinton, Kentucky. His predecessor, Alben Barkley, also attended the now-defunct Marvin College in far Western Kentucky. Humphreys attended the University of Wisconsin for his pharmacy education.

During World War I, he served overseas from 1917 to 1919 and was discharged as a first sergeant. He was a registered pharmacist in the retail drug business in Mayfield, Kentucky.

He became a member of the Kentucky House of Representatives in 1920. He served in the Kentucky Senate from 1932 to 1936. He was elected by his colleagues as president pro tempore of State Senate in

1934. He left the Kentucky Senate and served as clerk of three Senate sessions from 1936 to 1942. He also served as Kentucky highway commissioner from 1936 to 1940 under Governors Chandler and Johnson.

He enlisted in the Army during World War II. Using his background as a pharmacist, he served as a captain from 1943 to 1945 in the Medical Corps during World War II. With Chandler's re-election as governor, Humphreys was appointed State Highway Commissioner from 1955 to 1956.

As a state senator in 1935, Humphreys served as president pro tempore of the Kentucky Senate. At that time, Happy Chandler was lieutenant governor under Governor Ruby Laffoon. Chandler, a candidate for governor, wanted to change the method for nominating candidates for statewide offices from conventions to primaries. The convention method favored Laffoon's choice to succeed him, Thomas Rhea. When Laffoon left the state for Washington, D.C., Lt. Governor Chandler was "acting governor." As "acting governor," Chandler called a special session of the General Assembly that mandated candidates for the Democratic nomination for governor would be selected by a primary election. Senator Humphreys sided with Chandler in this dispute.[1]

Chandler originally appointed his adviser Frankfort Joseph J. Leary. After the Democratic State Central Committee nominated former Governor Lawrence Wetherby to run in November 1956, Leary turned the appointment down. Chandler then turned to his highway commissioner, Humphreys.[2] He resigned that position to accept the appointment to the Senate.

Humphreys was sworn in on June 25, 1956.[3] On July 5, he appointed Ben Chandler, the son of Governor Chandler, as his administrative assistant.

Humphreys' time in the Senate was not long enough to leave a legacy. However, the atmosphere in the Congress was tense due to the legacy of Wisconsin's Joseph McCarthy. This can be seen in the following events:

- June 21, 1956: Playwright Arthur Miller appears before the House Un-American Activities Committee.
- July 30, 1956: A joint resolution of Congress is signed by President Dwight D. Eisenhower, authorizing "In God We Trust" as the national motto.

Humphreys was not a candidate for election to the seat in November 1956. Barkley had died after the May primary, and the Democratic Party's State Central Committee nominated former Governor Lawrence Wetherby for election to the vacancy. However, Wetherby was defeated by former US Senator John Sherman Cooper.

Humphreys resumed the practice of pharmacy and worked in the retail drug business in Frankfort. He died in Frankfort on December 31, 1977. He was buried in Highland Park Cemetery in Mayfield, Kentucky.[4]

Part XIII

1956–1973

Republicans, the Cold War, Civil Rights, and Vietnam

For thirty years after World War II, politics in the world, the nation and the state reflected changes resulting from the Allied victory and conflict with the former Soviet Union. The fifteen years from 1956-1973 two Republicans for the first time in Kentucky history represented the Commonwealth for an uninterrupted fifteen-year period in the US Senate. All three of these Republican senators, John Sherman Cooper, Thurston Morton and Marlow Cook were veterans of World War II. In addition to military service, Cooper had served in a diplomatic post at the UN and as ambassador to India. Morton served as an Assistant Secretary of State in the first Eisenhower Administration. Cook was the County Judge or administrator of the largest urban county in Kentucky.

Due in part to their previous positions as presidential appointees, both Cooper and Morton were given deference by their colleagues on both sides of the aisle. Their backgrounds were an asset in understanding conflict during the Cold War. The US was growing its role as leader of the "free world." Additionally, the Soviets began the "Space Race" with the launch of Sputnik in 1957 in an effort to strengthen their position against the US and its allies

The Cold War escalated as seen in the building of the Berlin Wall in Germany and by wars in Vietnam and Cuba.

At the same time, the fourth American president to be assassinated was killed on November 22, 1963. Senator Cooper was a member of the Warren Commission that investigated the assassination of President John F. Kennedy.

Since the Supreme Court's decision in *Brown v. Board of Education*, the Civil Rights Movement began to gain support. In 1964, Congress passed the Civil Rights Act of 1964. It was not until 1968 that the Kentucky General Assembly passed the "Open Housing Law" that prohibited hotels, motels, and places that offered accommodations from discriminating based upon a person's race.

In 1968, the assassinations of Martin Luther King Jr. and Senator Robert F. Kennedy shook the conscious of the nation.

In 1968, there were three candidates who won electoral votes: Democratic candidate Vice President Hubert Humphrey, Republican former Vice President Richard Nixon, and American Party candidate Alabama Governor George Wallace. With the election of Richard Nixon, the nation saw the Vietnamization of the Vietnam War and the beginning of the end of American involvement.

JOHN SHERMAN COOPER
(1901–1991)
Third through Fifth Terms

- Class Two of Three
- Senate Service: 1956–1973 (Third through Fifth Terms)
- Political affiliation: Republican
- Residence at time of election: Somerset
- Served with Presidents Eisenhower, Kennedy, Johnson, and Nixon
- Served with Governors Chandler, Combs, Breathitt, Nunn, and Ford

After his defeat by Alben Barkley in 1954 during Barkley's second stint in the US Senate, John Sherman Cooper was appointed ambassador to India and Nepal by President Dwight D. Eisenhower. As ambassador, he helped improve relations with India through his friendship with Prime Minister Nehru. Before moving to India, he married Lorraine Shelvin.

In 1956, with the blessing of President Eisenhower, Cooper accepted the Republican nomination to run for the US Senate against former Kentucky Governor Lawrence Wetherby.[1] Barkley had died suddenly, and the seat formerly held by Cooper in 1954 was open for someone to fill the balance of the term ending in 1960.

The campaign was underway in earnest by mid-September. On September 18, 1956, the Democrats opened their campaign against Cooper and Thurston Ballard Morton (Morton was seeking the Senate seat held by Earle Clements) in Shelbyville to a rally that was thought to number 8,000 to 10,000 people. At the same time, Cooper and Morton toured the Purchase region of Kentucky. In Shelbyville, Governor Chandler was noticeably absent (because he had to be in Chicago). Cooper and Morton hammered Democratic presidential candidate Adlai Stevenson's inconsistency on labor and agriculture issues.[2]

Before the election, all four senatorial candidates spoke at the Kentucky Federation of Labor (KFL) Convention in Paducah. In his appearance before the KFL, Cooper cited four years of progress under Eisenhower. "More people are working than ever before, the country's nearly 67 million workers are earning higher wages than ever before, inflation has been held in check, social security had been extended, strike losses reduced and union membership is larger than ever before."[3]

Cooper defeated former Kentucky Governor Wetherby by 63,365 votes in November 1956. It was better than his Republican colleague Thurston Morton, who defeated incumbent Clements by 6,981 votes. President Eisenhower defeated Adlai Stevenson by 90,580 votes in Kentucky.[4]

In 1957, members of Congress had some influence over patronage in the US Postal Service. According to an AP article in the *Paducah Sun* from February 17, 1957 titled "Senator Gets Many Requests for Positions," postmaster and rural mail carrier appointments were made through patronage. However, the applicants had to be one of the three highest-scoring applicants on the civil service examination to receive a recommendation from the Republican Party. If there were no Republicans who made the top three, then a Republican would not receive an appointment.[5]

In late 1958 to early 1959, Cooper challenged Senator Everett Dirksen of Illinois for the position of Republican leader of the Senate after the retirement of Senator William Knowland of California. Cooper was considered part of the liberal wing of the Republican Party.[6]

After Cooper's three years (1957–60) in the US Senate, the *Louisville Courier-Journal* summed up his work in its endorsement:

> In the race for United States Senator, Kentuckians have a choice between two men of dignity, integrity and solid accomplishment. Either would represent the state with honor and credit.
>
> In such a case, it seems to this paper that the scales should come on the side of the incumbent in office. Keen Johnson, the Democrat might be expected on his record to become a distinguished Senator. Republican John Sherman Cooper already is one.
>
> Cooper's qualifications are unusually broad. He served with notable success as Ambassador to India and Ambassador to the United

Nations. Without ever having had the advantage of a full six-year term in the Senate, Cooper had been able to make a remarkable impression on that body. He is an acknowledged leader in foreign policy. On domestic issues, he has departed at times with from the leadership of his own party on matters of deep concern to his Kentucky constituents, such as agriculture, the T.V.A. and rural electrification.[7]

Cooper was respected by all who knew him in the Senate. He and Massachusetts Senator John F. Kennedy were close friends. During Kennedy's last years in the Senate, Cooper and his wife, Lorraine, often had Kennedy and his wife, Jacqueline, to their Georgetown home for dinner. Soon after Kennedy's election to the presidency, Kennedy quietly sent Cooper to the Soviet Union on a fact-finding mission for him.[8]

For his first election to a full six-year Senate term in November 1960, Cooper set a Kentucky record with an 187,867-vote margin over his opponent, former Governor Keen Johnson. With 95 percent of the vote tabulated, Cooper had 617,194 votes to 429,327 for Johnson. For the presidential election Nixon received 577,391 votes to 513,243 votes for Kennedy, a winning margin of 64,148.[9]

Cooper's achievements as a senator were acknowledged on New Year's Day 1961, when WHAS presented him with one of its "Man of the Year" awards. Barry Bingham—president of WHAS Inc., the *Courier-Journal*, and the *Louisville Times*—made the presentation to Cooper's brothers Don and Richard, as the senator was unavailable. Senator Cooper was recognized for his fight for "enlightened legislation" in many fields, including labor, education, civil rights, and aid to underdeveloped areas.[10]

Later in April 1961, Senator Cooper was honored at the groundbreaking of the John Sherman Cooper Power Station, owned by East Kentucky Rural Electric Cooperative Corporation at Burnside, Kentucky. Initially, the plant served seventy-five counties with over 135,000 consumers.[11]

Cooper was interested in restoring the land in Eastern Kentucky that had been mined for coal. This was seen in his request for funds for Berea College's partnership with the US Forest Service to research conservation and measures to restore the natural mountain beauty to Eastern Kentucky and other areas that had been mined. Cooper was successful in bringing $180,000 to Berea for this effort.[12]

In 1964, after the death of President Kennedy, President Lyndon Johnson appointed Cooper to the Warren Commission, which investigated the circumstances surrounding the assassination. Cooper and the commission agreed that Lee Harvey Oswald was the only perpetrator.

When the Warren Commission's report was released, it was praised by the press as being the model of objectivity.[13] Within twenty-four hours of the report's release, the Senate approved a constitutional amendment that would allow the president to appoint a new vice president if the office become vacant. This would eventually become the Twenty-Fifth Amendment to the US Constitution.

In 1979, the House Assassinations Committee concluded that a second gunmen probably fired at Kennedy from an area known as the grassy knoll. Cooper was critical of the House Committee's report. Cooper said, "I know of no finding that would change the conclusion of the Warren Commission — that there was no conspiracy."[14]

In 1966, Cooper won his second full term to the Senate. When he announced that he was running for reelection, he noted his work in the areas of water resources, education, tobacco, and civil rights. He won easily over Democrat John Y. Brown Sr., whom he had defeated in 1946.[15] Many Democrats of the time crossed over to vote for Cooper. The *Paducah Sun* was a Democratic newspaper at the time. It endorsed Republican Cooper because of his support of federal programs important to Kentuckians, including the Tennessee Valley Authority (TVA), tobacco support programs, and the REA, which helped establish the Jackson Purchase Rural Electric cooperative.[16]

In the 1967 Republican gubernatorial primary, Senator Cooper endorsed Jefferson County Judge Marlow Cook just before the primary. Cooper had originally intended to stay neutral.[17] Cooper believed that Governor Louie Nunn was "stirring religious and racial prejudice," as Cook was Catholic. Nunn won the primary and was elected Kentucky governor in November 1967.

By 1967, both of Kentucky's US senators wanted the nation to de-escalate its involvement in Vietnam. Cooper had been against the nation's involvement since 1965. Morton's opposition was recent and was more politically based compared to Cooper, whose opposition was rooted in policy.[18] Cooper became vocally opposed to stockpiling nuclear weapons and the president waging war without congressional approval.

In January 1968, Cooper told President Johnson to halt the bombing of North Vietnam. In an article, columnist Drew Pearson characterized Cooper as part of a bipartisan group that included Democratic Senator Mike Mansfield and former Kansas Governor Alf Landon, who believed it was time for intensive peace efforts in Vietnam.[19]

During the summer of 1969, Cooper led an effort with Democratic Senator Philip Hart of Michigan against President Nixon's Safeguard antiballistic missile (ABM) system. The Cooper-Hart amendment limited ABM funding to research and development and barred deployment of any of the components for at least a year.[20]

Cooper and Hart continued their fight against the ABM system in the summer of 1970. However, their legislation was defeated twice when they tried to block construction of two ABM sites.[21]

At the same time, Cooper worked with Democratic US Senator Frank Church of Idaho in 1969 to curtail presidential use of ground troops for expanding the war in Vietnam. In December of that year they were successful in amending a Defense Appropriations Act prohibiting the use of funds for sending American ground troops into Laos or Thailand. In May 1970, a Cooper-Church Amendment was made to a military material-sales measure to prohibit sending ground troops into Cambodia.[22]

With President Nixon's SALT talks in 1971, Cooper indicated that he would take no action to further reduce the Safeguard ABM program. Part of the rationale was that US negotiators could use the ABM as a bargaining chip with the Soviets.[23]

As he left office, Cooper was recognized as an effective congressional leader even amid an institution that was obstructive rather than constructive in dealing with the president. It was said: "There are thoughtful men like the retiring Senator John Sherman Cooper (Rep.-KY) who are deeply concerned over the erosion of the checks and balances written into the Constitution. 'I don't believe Congress will be able to uphold its authority unless it reorganizes,' he told an interviewer. 'Congress can't cope with the Executive Branch if it was not willing to find a way to reform.'"[24] In his article journalist Ralph de Toledano emphasized the information gap between the president and Congress, in addition to lack of good congressional leadership.

Cooper retired from the Senate at age seventy-one and was succeed by Walter "Dee" Huddleston. Cooper was appointed ambassador to East Germany by President Gerald Ford in 1974.

He was honored in 1987 when his bust was placed in the Capitol in Frankfort. He had previously been honored by Governor John Y. Brown Jr. with the Governor's Distinguished Service Medallion in 1983.[25]

Cooper died about 4:30 p.m. on Thursday, February 21, 1991, while taking a nap at a retirement home in Washington, D.C., at age eighty-nine. He was eulogized by Democrats as well as Republicans. Senator Wendell Ford said of Cooper: "Kentucky lost one of its greatest sons in John Sherman Cooper. Rare, indeed, are the likes of this man. He sprang from the soil in Pulaski County and never really left it, traveling the world as he did." Senator Edward "Ted" Kennedy said: "John Sherman Cooper was one of the authentic Senate giants of our time. Kentucky gave us Henry Clay in the 19th Century and John Sherman Cooper in the 20th century, and they rank together among the greatest senators to ever to serve the nation."[26]

Cooper was buried in Arlington National Cemetery.

THURSTON B. MORTON
(1907–1982)

- Class Three of Three
- Senate Service: 1957–1968
- Political affiliatin: Republican
- Louisville
- Served with Presidents Eisenhower, Kennedy, and Johnson
- Served with Governors Chandler, Combs, Breathitt, and Nunn

Thurston Morton was a World War II veteran, like many other politicians, such as Presidents Kennedy, Nixon, and Ford, who were elected to Congress after serving in the Navy, Due in part to an admitted lack of interest in the family grain and milling business, Morton ran for the US House of Representatives and was elected in the Republican landslide of 1946. Morton said, "And anybody that had run on the Republican Ticket without a jail record would have been elected—."[1] During the Republican Primary for the Louisville-based House seat, Morton was criticized by one of his five opponents, John M. Robsion Jr., as not qualified, as Robsion said the law required the nominee to have actively supported the party's nominee in the previous election. Morton had registered after coming home from active duty during the war. Morton's voter registration had been canceled in 1943.[2]

Morton served as a lieutenant commander in the US Naval Reserve from 1941 to 1946. He had commanded at least three ships during the war. He began on a minesweeper and finished on the *Doyle*; a destroyer commissioned in 1943.[3]

Thurston B. Morton was born in Louisville, Jefferson County, Kentucky, on August 19, 1907. He attended public schools in Louisville and Woodberry Forest School in Orange, Virginia. Following high school, he attended Yale University, where he graduated in 1929. After graduating from Yale, he returned to Louisville, where he engaged in the family grain and milling business. They were later sold to Pillsbury.

Prior to politics, Morton was also involved in the Louisville Board of Trade, Louisville Goodwill Industries, Frontier Nursing Service, and Lincoln Institute.

He was elected as a Republican to the Eightieth, Eighty-First, and Eighty-Second Congresses (January 3, 1947–January 3, 1953). Morton represented Louisville and Jefferson County in the US House of Representatives from 1947 to 1953. In 1953, he was appointed assistant secretary of state for congressional relations by President Eisenhower, a post he held until 1956 when he ran for the US Senate.[4]

Thurston B. Morton was elected a US senator from Kentucky during the Eisenhower sweep of Kentucky in 1956. Morton defeated Senator and former Kentucky Governor Earle C. Clements, who was acting Senate majority leader during Lyndon Johnson's extended absence due to a heart attack in late 1955. With such a close race, many said that Clements had to spend too much time in Washington rather than campaigning. Morton won 50.4–49.7 percent. He beat Clements by about 7,500 votes.[5]

As a senator, Morton saw American involvement in Vietnam, the assassination of President Kennedy, the Civil Rights Act, and the Great Society.

Even though he was a Republican and opposed many of Lyndon Johnson's policies, Morton was close to LBJ. He was an early friend of Lyndon Johnson's. Though Johnson was a Democrat, he took an interest in Morton's legislation to allow private industry to take over synthetic rubber plants in Louisville.[6]

Morton served with LBJ in the Senate from 1957 until Johnson's election as vice president. In an interview that Morton made for the LBJ Presidential Library when commenting about the working conditions under Johnson, he said, "In the first place, he was a tough leader, and I think you have to be tough to run that place. I can remember time after time when then Senator Johnson would say, 'All right, I don't care how late we stay here tonight, we're going to finish this bill.' Well, we generally finished by about eight or nine o'clock."[7]

Morton was a partisan Republican, as seen by his leadership of the Republican National Committee from 1959 through 1961. In 1960, there was speculation that he might be Richard Nixon's running mate on the Republican ticket.[8] He was chair during the 1960 presidential election in which John Kennedy defeated Richard Nixon. During this period, it should be noted that Morton must have had a sense of humor and took advantage of popular television. Morton appeared on television's *What's My Line* as a mystery guest on October 2, 1960. On that show, both Morton, the Chair of the Republican National Committee, and Senator Henry Jackson, Chair of the Democratic National Committee, appeared as guests.[9]

Morton voted against the Great Society and the confirmation of Abe Fortas. He voted against the initial Medicare legislation in 1962 when the vote was 52–48 against; this was one of the few times all 100 senators were there. Kentucky Lieutenant Wilson Wyatt used Morton's 1962 vote against Medicare against Morton in his 1962 reelection campaign. Morton voted against Medicare again, when it passed in July 1965. His Republican colleague, Cooper, voted with the 68–21 Senate majority when Medicare finally passed.[10] Morton voted with John Sherman Cooper in favor of the 1964 Civil Rights Act.

One of the defining issues during the 1960s was Vietnam. Morton's interview for the LBJ Library revealed Senator Morton's changing views on the subject of Vietnam: "I went along on Viet Nam as the thing grew and grew like Topsy, and we got more and more involved."[11]

The interviewer, Joe Frantz, asked: "Did this begin before you left the State Department? [in 1956]"

He responds:

> I always regretted the fact that the Chinese went Communist, and I didn't want to see this Southeast Asia (nation) become Communist. Then I realized that I thought we were on a very bad wicket. We had gotten ourselves in an absolutely hopeless situation. Two wars—North Vietnam versus South Vietnam, and then a civil war within South Vietnam; and there's no front there.

By the end of his second term, Morton spoke out about the need for the US to get out of Vietnam.[12]

Even though Morton opposed LBJ's policies concerning Vietnam, LBJ called Morton come to the White House when he (Morton) announced he was not seeking re-election. LBJ wanted to reminisce about their time in the House and the Senate together. While he was there, LBJ arranged to have one of Morton's staffers Brooke Bush appointed to a Republican vacancy on the Federal Power Commission after Morton ended his time in the Senate.[13]

Morton thought there was a leadership vacuum among the Democrats (and in the Senate) because Senator William Fulbright, the chair of the Foreign Relations Committee, had broken with the President (Mansfield was not tough like LBJ). Morton liked Mansfield, but he did not enforce discipline or become the wheeler-dealer that LBJ had been as majority leader.[14]

In February 1968, Morton announced that he would not seek a third term "To use an old Kentucky expression, I suppose I am just plain 'track sore,'" said the senator.[15]

He was succeeded by Jefferson County Judge/Executive Marlow Cook. In order to give Cook a jump in seniority, Morton resigned on December 16, 1968.

Senator Morton was considered for a position with the Nixon administration; however, Morton's brother, Maryland Congressman Rogers C.B. Morton, was appointed as Nixon's secretary of the interior, succeeding Walter Hickel. Rogers Morton served as secretary of the interior under both Nixon and Ford. He also served as Ford's commerce secretary.

Senator Thurston Morton returned to Louisville after leaving the Senate. He served as vice chairman of the board and director of Liberty National Bank in Louisville, Kentucky. He also served as chairman of the board and director of Churchill Downs in Louisville, Kentucky, as well as the president of the American Horse Council. He was also on the boards of the Texas Gas Transmission Corporation and Pillsbury.

The motor vessel MV *Thurston B. Morton* was named in his honor. The vessel joined the fleet of American Commercial Lines, Inc., a division of Texas Gas Transmission Corporation, moving tows on the inland waterways system, which included the Ohio River.[16]

Morton died on August 14, 1982. He was buried in the family plot at Cave Hill Cemetery in Louisville, Kentucky. He was survived by his wife, Belle Clay Lyons, and their two sons, Clay Lyons Morton and Thurston Ballard Morton Jr., as well as five grandchildren.[17]

MARLOW W. COOK
(1926–2016)

- Class Three of Three
- Senate Service: 1968-1974
- Political affiliation: Republican
- Served with Presidents Johnson, Nixon, and Ford
- Served with Governors Nunn and Ford

Marlow Cook was Kentucky's last one-term US Senator of the twentieth century. He was also the last "liberal to moderate Republican" elected to the US Senate from Kentucky. During his single term he gave two long-serving Kentucky members of Congress their start. Future Senator Mitch McConnell was Cook's statewide youth chairman and later his chief legislative assistant. Future US Representative John Yarmuth served as Cook's legislative assistant and legislative director from 1971 to 1974.

Cook, a World War II Navy veteran, came to Louisville after his service on submarines in the Atlantic and Pacific. He attended the University of Louisville Law School, graduating in 1950. Cook was born in Akron (Erie County), New York, on July 27, 1926, to Mary Lee and Floyd Cook. He married Nancy Remmers of Louisville on November 22, 1947. They had five children.

While practicing law in Louisville, Cook was elected to the Kentucky House of Representatives in 1957. In 1961, Cook was elected county judge of Jefferson County (the county that includes Louisville). He was re-elected county judge in 1965. From the position of county judge, Cook positioned himself to run for statewide office. In 1967, Cook entered the Republican primary for Kentucky governor. He faced Louie B. Nunn of Barren County, who had run against incumbent Democratic Governor Edward "Ned" Breathitt in 1963. Nunn had also been a classmate in Cook's University of Louisville College of Law graduating class of 1950. After a campaign in which Nunn was critical of Cook being from New York and tried to characterize him as a liberal New Yorker, Nunn won over Cook by a small margin.

One of Cook's most enduring legacies from his service as county judge would be the purchase of the decrepit steamboat Avalon at an auction in Cincinnati. The Avalon would be re-built and re-christened the "Belle of Louisville." The Belle of Louisville continues to be a landmark on the Ohio River to this day [2020].

With incumbent Republican US Senator Thurston Morton's announcement that he would not seek a third term, Cook announced that he would seek the Republican nomination. This time the Republican establishment in Kentucky under the leadership of Governor Louie B. Nunn backed Marlow Cook. Cook was elected to the Senate over Kentucky Commerce Commissioner (former Kerner Commission member) Katherine Peden 52–48 percent.

In his single term in the US Senate, Senator Marlow Cook's most notable contribution was his service on the Senate Judiciary Committee. President Nixon during the 1968 presidential campaign said he would appoint conservatives to the US Supreme Court if possible. Nixon was unsuccessful in obtaining confirmation with his first two Supreme Court appointees—Judge Clement Haynsworth, followed by Judge Harrold Carswell. Senator Cook played a significant role in the confirmation hearings of both men.

Senator Cook was one of the Nixon administration's managers of the Supreme Court nomination of Judge Clement E. Haynsworth Jr. In that position, he valiantly defended Judge Haynsworth. He accused opponents of Haynsworth of "character assassination" and the Nixon White House and Republican leadership of not doing enough to help him with the nomination to the Supreme Court. In fact, "sloppy work" was how he (Cook) characterized Senator Birch Bayh of Indiana's Bill of Particulars concerning Haynsworth. Cook noted that there were at least nine errors in Bayh's accusations against Judge Haynsworth.[1]

With the Haynsworth nomination, Cook, as a member of the Senate Judiciary Committee, voted with the 10–7 majority to send the nomination to the floor of the Senate for a vote.[2] Although Cook voted with the

Yeas, Haynsworth's nomination was voted down by the full Senate by a vote of 45–55.[3]

As a member of the Judiciary Committee member, Cook voted with the majority of the committee to send the nomination of Judge Carswell to the Senate floor. During the floor vote on the Carswell Supreme Court nomination, Cook was one of seven senators who changed their minds about Carswell when his vote came to the floor—

> The seven Senators who switched sides today were Mrs. Smith and Senators Cook, Mark O. Hatfield of Oregon, Charles H. Percy of Illinois, Hiram L. Fong of Hawaii and Robert W. Packwood of Oregon, all Republicans, and Quentin N. Burdick, Democrat of North Dakota.
>
> Administration forces were reported to have made an effort to restore their position this morning by passing the word among vulnerable Senators that Mrs. Smith had decided to vote for Judge Carswell and that only one more vote was needed to accomplish a tie vote. One Senator said he was told that Senator Cook had advised Mrs. Smith to vote for confirmation, if she wished, because he would cast the deciding vote to defeat the nomination.
>
> Asked about the reports of this maneuver, Senator Jacob K. Javits, New York Republican, said 'there were a lot of gyrations by the White House around Maggie Smith.'[4]

When Cook was interviewed by C-SPAN in 1987, he reminisced about his experience on the Senate Judiciary Committee. In the interview he said, "Who is a federal judge? A person who knows a senator. Who is a Supreme Court Justice? A person who knows a President."[5]

In 1970, Senator Cook showed his continuing interest in old Ohio River steamboats. He was a sponsor or co-sponsor of several pieces of legislation to help save Cincinnati's Delta Queen.

Cook was a co-sponsor of the Equal Rights Amendment to the US Constitution, as well as a co-sponsor with Indiana Senator Birch Bayh of SJ 1 –93rd Congress (1973-1974) a joint resolution that proposed an amendment to the Constitution for the direct popular election to the president and vice president of the US. He sponsored S. 4107 93rd Congress "Red River Gorge National Park Act."

At the end of his term, Cook was the subject of at least two articles by Washington, D.C., columnist Jack Anderson that accused Senator Cook of accepting free apartments and cars. The articles and his association with a Republican administration reeling from the aftershock of Watergate handicapped Senator Cook's reelection prospects.

In 1974, Senator Cook faced a popular Democratic governor, Wendell Ford. Ford outspent Cook $746,000 to about $341,000. It was a feisty campaign as Ford refused to debate Senator Cook. Ford called Cook "Marvelous Marlow, the Wonderful Wobbler," alleging that that he had changed his stance on issues. He also accused Cook of losing touch with the state while he was in Washington.

Senator Cook, taking a more aggressive tack, accused Governor Ford of giving state contracts to friends and political supporters and angered Mr. Ford with a television commercial carrying the voices of Nelson Eddy and Jeanette MacDonald singing 'Sweethearts' and declaring that Mr. Ford was 'an expert on sweetheart contracts.'

Mr. Cook's campaign literature contained a quotation from Senator Barry Goldwater, the Arizona Republican, telling Senator Cook: 'There's one thing—that sticks out more than your gray hair—that's your integrity.'

The Senator also stirred up an environmerital [sic] issue by actively campaigning against construction of a dam; across, the Redd River in central Kentucky. According, to a Cook Campaign flyer, 'Some of his [Mr. Ford's] political cronies stand to get rich if the dam is built.'

Mr. Cook repeatedly emphasized his support for the Federal revenue-sharing program, which he co-sponsored and which, he reminded his audiences, has brought $231 million to Kentucky since 1972.[6]

Senator Cook was defeated by Governor Wendell Ford in the November 1974 election. In order to give Kentucky more seniority, he resigned his seat in December and returned to private life. Most of his post-political career he spent as a lobbyist. To the disappointment of his former protégé Mitch McConnell, Cook supported incumbent Senator Walter Huddleston over McConnell in 1984. In 2004, Cook wrote an op-ed piece supporting Democrat John Kerry over incumbent President George W. Bush.

Cook retired to Florida where he died in February 2016, just short of his ninetieth birthday. Following his death, US Senate Majority Leader Mitch McConnell announced Cook's death on the floor of the Senate. The Senate further honored Cook by unanimously passing a resolution honoring his life. The resolution was sponsored by Senators McConnell and Rand Paul. The Kentucky House of Representatives in which Cook served in the late 1950s sponsored a similar resolution, which passed and was presented to Cook's family.

Part XIV
1974–1985
Huddleston and Ford

This is an unusual eleven-year period in which Kentucky had two Senators that were personally, as well as politically, close. Dee Huddleston and Wendell Ford began their careers with their respective elections to the Kentucky Senate in 1967. During Ford's 1971 successful campaign for governor, Huddleston was his campaign manager. With Senator John Sherman Cooper's retirement, Ford (as governor) supported Huddleston's election to the US Senate in 1972.

This was an era that transitioned from Watergate to Ford and Carter to Reagan.

Huddleston was in the Senate when it voted to investigate the Watergate Scandal and passed SR 60—Ninety-Third Congress (1973–1974), which established the Senate Select Committee to conduct an investigation on the Watergate break-in. The bill passed the Senate 770. Huddleston would later serve on the Senate's Select Committee to conduct an investigation and study of governmental operations with respect to intelligence activities established by the Senate in 1975 with S.Res.21—Ninety-Fourth Congress (1975–1976).

The two senators were moderate Democrats who supported Kentucky's primary industries of the time: tobacco, coal, bourbon, and horses. However, Huddleston could be seen as slightly more liberal with his votes on the vote to return the Panama Canal to Panama. Huddleston voted to return it, and Ford voted against returning it.[1]

Ford and Huddleston were the last veterans of World War II to represent Kentucky in the Senate.

WALTER D. HUDDLESTON
(1926–2018)

- Class Two of Three
- Senate Service: 1973–1985
- Political affiliation: Democratic
- Residence at time of election: Hardin County
- Served with Presidents Nixon, Ford, Carter, and Reagan
- Served with Governors Ford, Carroll, Brown, and Collins

Walter Darlington Huddleston was elected in 1972 and assumed office during the last years of the Nixon presidency. He is known to his friends and supporters as "Dee." At the time of his election, Huddleston was the first Democrat elected to the US Senate from Kentucky in eighteen years.

Huddleston was born in Burkesville, Cumberland County, Kentucky, on April 25, 1926. He was educated in the public schools and served in the US Army from 1944 to 1946, serving in the Army as a tank gunner in the Ninth Armored Division in Europe.

Upon his discharge from the army, he married Jean Pierce and attended the University of Kentucky. He attempted to become a walk-on basketball player under Coach Adolf Rupp.

Upon graduation from the University of Kentucky, he became involved in broadcasting. He worked in Bowling Green, Kentucky, at the station WKCT as program and sports director from 1949 to 1952. He moved to Elizabethtown, Kentucky, where he became general manager of radio station WIEL. In 1957, he also became partner and director of a radio station in nearby Lebanon WLBN. He was involved with both radio stations until his election to the US Senate in 1972.

In 1965, he was elected to the Kentucky State Senate. During his two terms as a state senator, he rose to the position of majority leader. In 2005, he was recognized for his work as a state senator with induction into the Kentucky Human Rights Commission Hall of Fame.[1] As a state senator, he championed the rights of minorities, women of all races, and the disabled during the 1960s. He co-sponsored an open housing law as a state senator with Georgia Powers, the first African-American woman to serve in the Kentucky Senate. He led efforts in Kentucky to pass the Equal Rights Amendment.

Huddleston met Wendell Ford of Owensboro in the Kentucky Senate. Ford was elected to the Senate the same year as Huddleston. In 1967, Ford was elected lieutenant governor and became presiding officer of the Senate while Huddleston was majority leader. When Ford ran for governor in 1971, Huddleston was his campaign manager.

With Ford's election as governor of Kentucky and Republican US Senator John Sherman Cooper's decision not to seek re-election, Dee Huddleston ran against former Republican Kentucky Governor Louie B. Nunn in November 1972.

Despite Republican President Richard Nixon carrying Kentucky by 64 percent, Huddleston defeated former Kentucky Governor Louie B. Nunn by a vote of 510,535–471,641 for the Senate seat vacated by John Sherman Cooper. In the campaign, Nunn tried to link Huddleston to Democratic presidential candidate Senator George McGovern. Huddleston primarily campaigned on the removal of the sales tax on food. Huddleston, as the leader of the Kentucky State Senate, led the effort in the General Assembly to remove the 5 percent tax imposed under Governor Nunn's leadership.[2]

When Huddleston and his wife initially moved to Washington, they briefly lived in the Hotel Washington, near the White House. When the time came for Nixon's inauguration, because the apartment/hotel had a "superb view of the parade route" 'they were told to leave for security reasons." Jean and Dee Huddleston were shocked at Washington, D.C., area real estate prices. They purchased a home similar to what they had in Elizabethtown for twice the price.[3]

He made national headlines with a sponsorship of a joint resolution for a Vietnam Monument in Washington, D.C.[4]

Early in his Senate career, Huddleston opined on the mistakes of the Vietnam War. He was one of fifty-seven Senate co-sponsors of the "so-called war powers bill" in 1973. That legislation would limit the president's power to commit American troops to battle. It would restrict the president's ability to send troops into harm's way for no more than thirty days without Congressional approval.

In remarks made to the Kentucky National Guard Association, Huddleston said, from the lesson of Vietnam, "to never again get involved in an undeclared war."[5]

In September 1974, Huddleston headed a delegation to Fort Knox, Kentucky, to inspect the gold depositary. US Representative Philip Crane (R-Ill) had questioned Secretary of the Treasury William Simon about charges or rumors that gold depository was empty in July 1974. In response, it was suggested that a congressional delegation visit the vaults at Fort Knox. In addition to Huddleston, Director of the Mints Mary Brooks accompanied the delegation and cut the seal that had been in place since 1968. In addition to Huddleston, Crane, and Ms. Brooks, Representative Gene Snyder (R-KY), Representative John Conlan (R-AZ), and 100 photographers and journalists were present. It was the first-time journalists were allowed to take photographs inside the two-story depository. According to Director Brooks, an estimated $6.2 billion worth of gold was in the depository in September 1974.[6]

One of the most significant contributions of Huddleston's Senate career was his participation in the work of the "Church Committee." It was officially titled the United States Senate Select Committee to Study Governmental Operations with Respect to Intelligence Activities. It was chaired by Idaho Senator Frank Church. Members, in addition to Church and Huddleston, included Senators Barry Goldwater, Walter Mondale, John Tower, Howard Baker, Philip Hart, Richard Schweiker, Charles Mathias, Gary Hart, and Robert Morgan. The committee investigated abuse by the CIA, FBI, IRS, and National Security Agency (NSA). The committee was established as a part of a series of investigations into intelligence abuses, which included the Watergate Hearings, the Rockefeller Commission, and the Pike Committee.

After holding 126 full committee meetings and forty subcommittee hearings, interviewing some 800 witnesses in public and closed sessions, and combing through 110,000 documents, the committee published its final report on April 29, 1976. Investigators determined that, beginning with President Franklin Roosevelt's administration and continuing through the early 1970s, "intelligence excesses, at home and abroad," were not the "product of any single party, administration, or man," but had developed as America rose to a become a superpower during a global Cold War. The final report included ninety-six recommendations, legislative and regulatory, designed "to place intelligence activities within the constitutional scheme for controlling government power."[7] One of the results of the committee's work was the establishment of the permanent Senate Select Committee on Intelligence.

Thirty years after the work of the Church Committee, Huddleston and former Vice President Walter Mondale participated in a forum concerning American intelligence after 9/11.

While Huddleston was recognized beyond his two terms in the Senate for his work on the Senate Select Intelligence Committee, he was involved with many things that were important to Kentuckians. Huddleston was initially assigned to two committee posts—government operations and agriculture—and chaired one agriculture subcommittee.

Senator Huddleston was set to win his third term in the Senate in 1984. However, the tenacity of his opponent, Judge Mitch McConnell of Louisville, was underestimated by most. McConnell's ads against Huddleston have become a classic in the lore of political advertising. As stated in this quote from the *Christian Science Monitor* newspaper in September 1984, things looked like they were going Huddleston's way:

> The ads Republican Mitchell McConnell is running in his well-financed quest for a US Senate seat are admittedly colorful. In one, a good old country boy and his hound dogs try to track down elusive Sen. Walter D. Huddleston (D) everywhere from the US Capitol to a beach in Puerto Rico. Mr. McConnell, a county executive officer, argues that Senator Huddleston has often missed key Senate votes to give paid speeches to various groups and is a tool of liberal Democratic Party leaders.
>
> Despite the energy of his opposition and the fact that Reagan is favored to win in Kentucky, Huddleston, seeking a third Senate term, continues to enjoy a comfortable lead in the polls. He has spent more than $1 million in his campaign to date. Kentucky has had two Democratic US senators for the last decade and the pattern is not expected to change in 1984.[8]

On election night, Tuesday November 6, 1984, Mitch McConnell defeated Senator Walter Dee Huddleston in an upset by 3,437 votes out of about 1.2 million cast.[9]

Following his Senate service, Huddleston was recognized with a Distinguished Service Medal by then-CIA Director William Casey in 1985 for his work on several Senate Intelligence subcommittees. He also served on the agriculture and appropriations committees.[10]

In addition to his recognition for his service to civil rights by the Kentucky Human Rights Commission and in the intelligence community, Senator Huddleston has been recognized for sponsoring Senate Joint Resolution 298 of the Ninety-Eighth Congress for "National Ice Cream Day" on July 15 and July as National Ice Cream Month.[11]

WENDELL H. FORD
(1924–2015)

- Class Three of Three
- Senate Service: 1974–1999
- Political affiliation: Democratic
- Residence at time of election: Daviess County
- Served with Presidents Ford, Carter, Reagan, G.H.W. Bush, and Clinton
- Served with Governors Carroll, Brown, Collins, Wilkinson, Jones, and Patton

The only US. senator from Kentucky who served without a break in elected office from the state senate, lieutenant governor, governor to service in the US Senate. At the time of this writing, Wendell Ford is second only to Mitch McConnell in his tenure in the US Senate from Kentucky at twenty-four years.

Ford grew up on a farm in Yellow Creek near Owensboro, Kentucky. He attended the University of Kentucky in 1943, prior to serving in the Army from 1944 to 1946. Upon his return from military service, he entered the family insurance business, E.M. Ford & Company. He attended the Maryland School of Insurance.

He entered the Senate after serving as Kentucky's governor for three years. During that time, he reorganized state government and replaced the sales tax on groceries, prescription drugs, and farm machinery with the four-cent-a-ton severance tax on coal mined in Kentucky.[1]

When Ford ran in 1974, he was supported by all of Kentucky's living former Democratic governors and lieutenant governors, including Happy Chandler. This was a first for Kentucky Democrats.[2]

He defeated incumbent Marlow Cook and joined Dee Huddleston to represent Kentucky in the US Senate. From 1974 to 1985, when Huddleston was defeated for re-election, the close bond between Ford and Huddleston was like no other, though Huddleston introduced Ford at Ford's inauguration as governor in 1971 and called him "William" rather than "Wendell."[3]

Ford was defender/advocate of Kentucky's largest industries from his first day in the Senate. This is reflected in a statement he made 1978. "I have been in the senate four years and half the time I am defending tobacco. The other half, I am defending coal, bourbon and Billy Beer."[4,5] Ford was also proud of his part in airline deregulation, which resulted in more flights and lower airfares.

During his first year as a US senator, Ford suggested that the Appalachian Regional Commission, the Federal Development agency for the Appalachian regions in thirteen states (from New York to Alabama), should be moved from Washington, D.C., to Appalachia to be closer to its mission. One location suggested was Huntington, West Virginia.[6]

During the energy crisis of the 1970s, Ford advocated coal and coal derivatives as short-term answers to energy shortages. Ford had a three-point plan for making the nation competitive in energy resources. It was conservation, existing resources, and a massive synthetic fuel program. The synthetic fuel program of course included coal and coal-based derivatives. He also spoke of tar sands, shale, and alcohol fuels from agricultural crops, residues as well as food and wood processing wastes for these new synthetic fuel program.[7]

One of the few times Ford differed with his colleague Huddleston was on the Panama Canal Treaty. Ford was one of thirty-two senators who voted in opposition to ratifying the first of two treaties (guaranteeing the neutrality of the canal after 1999). Huddleston was one of the sixty-eight who supported the Carter Administration in ratifying the Panama Canal Treaty. When asked about the difference, Huddleston said "he and Ford just disagreed." This was echoed by a Ford staff member.[8]

In 1979, on some of the key votes before the Senate, Ford voted for the $3.5 billion rescue package for automaker Chrysler; he voted for a tougher tax on windfall profits caused by deregulation of oil and voted for a six-month moratorium on issuance of licenses for nuclear power plants until a thorough study could be made after Three Mile Island.[9]

Soon into his Senate career, he became chair of the Democratic Senatorial Campaign Committee (1977–1983). He was chair during the 1980 elections when the Democrats lost control of the Senate. Ford's explanation for that setback was due in part to the fact the Committee had borrowed money in 1978 and had to spend time raising money to pay back those loans. Additionally, with a popular presidential candidate at the head of the ticket in 1980 in Ronald Reagan, the Republicans were able to outraise the Democrats.[10]

In the spring of 1984, Ford supported his colleague Dee Huddleston's opposition to the CIA's mining harbors in Nicaragua. He joined Huddleston in voting against funding for sabotage or terrorism in Nicaragua and Central America.[11]

Ford's membership on the Inaugural Committees from 1985 through 1996 raised his national profile. The was the committee that set up the inaugural ceremony and related festivities for the inauguration of the president and vice president. Ford was chair of the committee during the 1989 inauguration of President George H.W. Bush and the 1993 inauguration of President Bill Clinton. Ford also served as a member of the committee during President Reagan's 1985 inauguration and President Clinton's 1997 inaugurations.[12]

During his 1986 campaign for election to a third term, Ford used a variation of the famous hound dog commercial that Mitch McConnell had used against Dee Huddleston. The commercial has Ford in his Capitol office working late. The announcer says: "Nobody works harder than our senator, Wendell Ford." Then Ford is shown taking off his glasses and sighing wearily and patting a hound dog next to his desk. "Let's call it a day, pal." When asked why he used the hound dog, Ford said: "We just wanted to make sure the hound dog was ours this year." Prior to using the hound dog, Ford ran it by his friend Huddleston to make sure he was not offended. Huddleston said that he supported "any kind of message" to help Ford.[13] That fall, Ford defeated his Republican opponent Jackson Andrews with 74 percent of the vote, carrying all 120 counties.

Ford was a consistent supporter of public education. In 1992, the American Federation of Teachers ranked the Senator at 100 percent for supporting education and labor issues.[14] His colleague McConnell was given a 10 percent.

The Americans for Democratic Action gave Ford a rating of voting liberal 56 percent of the time during his twenty-four years in the Senate.

Following his retirement from the Senate, he established the Wendell H. Ford Government Education Center at the Owensboro Museum of Science and History in his hometown of Owensboro.[15]

He was a staunch defender of and advocate for his rural constituents. As a member of the conference committee that produced the Telecommunications Act of 1996, he helped shape the compromises that require companies to provide the same basic services to all Americans, regardless of geography or income.

He also won an amendment to the 1996 farm bill for the Fund for Rural America program to help pay for rural development projects, such as water and sewage grants.[16]

In 1998, Congress was considering ending the sixty-eight-year subsidy programs that supported tobacco and its growers. One proposal was from Indiana Senator Richard Lugar, a Republican from Indiana. It would end the subsidy by 2002 and buy out persons who held "quotas" or "licenses" to grow tobacco. It would pay farmers who hold quotas $8 per pound over three years. Those who did not hold quotas would receive $4.[17]

In respect to working with Senator McConnell after McConnell's defeat of Dee Huddleston, the biggest disagreements between the two were over tobacco legislation. In 1998, Ford penned an op-ed piece concerning the "Leaf" Program.[18]

One of the longest lasting imprints of Wendell Ford's legacy is his imprint on aviation legislation. The Wendell H. Ford Aviation Investment and Reform Act for the twenty-first century provided legislation concerning noise levels at airports, passenger rights, and other laws concerning air travel.[19]

At the end of his time in the Senate, the biography in his tribute stated:

> Over the years, FORD has become known as a staunch supporter of the economic interests of Kentucky and as a national leader on energy, aviation, Federal-election reform and other issues. He has shaped such legislation as the National Voter Registration Act, the Federal Aviation Administration Authorization Act of 1994, the Family and Medical Leave Act, the National Energy Security Act of 1992, the Aviation Safety and Capacity Act of 1990, the Airport and Airways Capacity Expansion Act of 1987, the Age Discrimination in Employment Act Amendments of 1986, the Tobacco Reform Act of 1985, the Energy Security Act of 1977 and the Surface Mining and Reclamation Act of the same year. He has taken the lead in many other legislative initiatives, including a long and persistent drive to adopt a 2-year budget as a tool to improve the Federal Government's trouble plagued budget-making process. FORD is the ranking member of the Senate Committee on Rules and Administration, where he has pressed for campaign-finance reform, improved voter registration procedures.[20]

In recognition of his leadership regarding National Guard issues, the Kentucky National Guard's Wendell H. Ford Regional Training Center, near Greenville, Kentucky, was named in his honor. Hazard's Wendell H. Ford Airport and Western Kentucky Parkway was also named in his honor.

Part XV
1999–Present

Since Wendell Ford left the Senate in January 1999, Republicans have occupied both of Kentucky's Senate seats for an unprecedented twenty years. Senator McConnell has been in the Senate since 1985. In addition to providing leadership to the Republican Party in the Senate, McConnell has made the Republican Party of Kentucky an electoral machine.

Like the national Republican Party, the Republican Party in Kentucky has become more conservative than the Republican Party of John Sherman Cooper and Marlow Cook or even Louie Nunn.

ADDISON MITCHELL
"MITCH" MCCONNELL
(1942–)

- Class Two of Three
- Senate Service: 1985–present
- Political affiliation: Republican
- Residence at time of election: Jefferson County
- Served with Presidents Reagan, G.H.W. Bush, Clinton, G.W. Bush, Obama, Trump, and Biden
- Served with Governors Collins, Wilkinson, Jones, Patton, Fletcher, Beshear, Bevin, and A. Beshear

Kentucky's longest-serving US Senator, Addison Mitchell "Mitch" Mc-Connell, was born in Tuscumbia, Alabama, on February 20, 1942. He was the only son of A.M. and Odene Shockley McConnell. Both parents were natives of Alabama. His father was a civilian employee at the Army's Huntsville Arsenal. As the United States was engaged in World War II, McConnell's father joined the Army and served in Europe. At the same time, it was discovered that the future senator, as a two-year-old, had polio. With the help of his mother and time at Warm Springs, Georgia, McConnell was able to beat polio and walk normally. Following World War II, McConnell and his family lived in Athens, Alabama, before moving to Augusta,

Georgia, before moving to Louisville, Kentucky, while McConnell was in the eighth grade.

McConnell graduated from Louisville's duPont Manual High School, where he was elected student body president. Upon graduation, he went to the University of Louisville, where he was involved in student government and elected student body president for the College of Arts and Sciences. While a student at U of L, he interned for Fourth District US Representative Gene Snyder. He went to law school at the University of Kentucky in Lexington. After law school, he briefly practiced law before signing on for a paid position with Marlow Cook's campaign for the US Senate in 1968. While he was Cook's youth chairman, he also wrote speeches and position papers for the campaign. Once Cook was elected, McConnell became part of Cook's Washington staff as a legislative assistant.[1] In 1971, he joined the campaign of Republican gubernatorial candidate Tom Emberton. Emberton lost the election to Democrat Wendell Ford.

For several years, McConnell was eyeing the 1977 race for Jefferson County judge (now judge-executive). In that race, McConnell faced incumbent Judge Todd Hollenbach Sr. Hollenbach had wounded himself in 1975 when he took on Kentucky Governor Julian Carroll in the Democratic primary. McConnell won the election against Hollenbach 53–47 percent. It had been one of the most expensive campaigns for Jefferson County judge, with McConnell's campaign spending a record $355,000.

In 1981, McConnell was reelected. His Democratic opponent was Commissioner Jim "Pop" Malone. That year, McConnell ran with a slate of three Republican candidates for Jefferson County commissioner openings. One of those who ran was John Yarmuth, who later changed parties and was elected to Congress as a Democrat. The election results were closer than expected. McConnell won by only 1.5 percent after raising almost $600,000, which is thought to be more than four times the amount raised by Malone.[2]

As is his practice to prepare early, McConnell filed with the Federal Election Commission in April 1982 so that he could begin fundraising for the 1984 race for the US Senate against incumbent Walter "Dee" Huddleston.[3] During 1982 and 1983, McConnell visited every one of Kentucky's 120 counties in anticipation of 1984.[4]

Due to McConnell's prolific fundraising, he was able to run radio and television advertisements without stop from Labor Day through Election Day during the 1984 election season. The most famous was McConnell's use of hound dogs searching for Senator Huddleston and alleging that he was missing from his job as senator and was actually on a private speaking tour.[5] It is thought that the "Hound Dog" ads were the ads that helped McConnell come from behind Huddleston at 64–24 percent June 1984 to win 49.8–49.5 percent in November.[6]

One of the groups that claimed to help McConnell in his surprise win over Huddleston was the Moral Majority. The Reverend LaVerne Butler, the state chair, wrote: "We feel the Moral Majority of Kentucky was instrumental in sending a conservative senator to Washington as Mitch McConnell narrowly defeated incumbent Walter Huddleston by only 5,000 votes. Since we hand-distributed 15,000 issues-oriented flyers just prior to the election, I believed we played a part."[7] Lawrence's article noted that the Reverend Jerry Falwell had cut an ad for McConnell.

During his first term, McConnell went to great lengths to put on a bipartisan face in public. He announced to his Republican brethren in Kentucky that defeating Wendell Ford was not a priority. He broke with the Reagan administration to support trade sanctions against the apartheid regime in South Africa. However, he supported Reagan's policy of aiding the Nicaraguan contras against the Sandinistas.[8] It was in his first term he was noticed by conservative writer James K. Kilpatrick for championing "tort reform."[9]

In October 1987, McConnell was one of forty-two senators who voted in favor of confirming Reagan's controversial Supreme Court nominee Robert Bork.[10]

In 1988, he was an early supporter of George H.W. Bush for president. He was a national co-chairman for Bush and led the thirty-eight-member Kentucky delegation to the Republican Convention in 1988.[11]

Two years after his first reelection, McConnell had raised more than $1 million in anticipation of 1990.[12]

Tobacco was a big issue early in McConnell's tenure. In addition to having a disagreement with his colleague Senator Wendell Ford on the amounts paid to tobacco farmers for ending price supports, in 1988 he was at odds with Lexington GOP Congressman Larry Hopkins. Hopkins sought to have the US Department of Agriculture rescind a tobacco policy McConnell worked to get. Under McConnell's policy, export aid would be extended to tobacco shipments with up to 25 percent foreign leaf. Hopkins wanted to change it back to requiring tobacco exports to be 100 percent American leaf.[13]

In his first campaign for reelection in 1990, McConnell faced Dr. Harvey Slone, a former Jefferson County judge and Louisville mayor. He defeated Slone 52.2–47.5 percent.

During his second term, McConnell began to reshape Kentucky's political landscape. In 1993, he turned his efforts to fill Kentucky's Second District Congressional seat by helping elect Ron Lewis to succeed the late longtime Democrat William Natcher. In 1994, McConnell helped secure the election of Ed Whitfield as a Republican to the First Congressional District in far Western Kentucky.[14]

In December 1995 McConnell voted against the Flag Resolution, SJ Res. 31, which would make it a crime to desecrate the US flag.[15]

During his third re-election campaign, he faced former Lieutenant Governor and Attorney General (and future Governor) Steve Beshear. Much to McConnell's surprise, McConnell was endorsed by former Democratic Governor Wallace Wilkinson. McConnell had a war chest of $5 million. He defeated Beshear 55–43 percent, even though Republican presidential candidate Bob Dole was defeated by President Bill Clinton in Kentucky. Republicans carried five of Kentucky's six US House seats.[16]

In 1997, McConnell was often in the news as an opponent of campaign finance reform. McConnell wants unlimited campaign spending but full public disclosure of contributions. In an article appearing in the *Paducah Sun* (March 16, 1997), the headline was "Mitch McConnell proud to be 'the abominable no-man'."[17] In a news conference in March 1997, he brought diverse groups of "special interests" that opposed campaign finance reform. They ranged from anti-abortion supporters and the NRA on the right to the National Education Association and American Civil Liberties Union on the left. McConnell cited the First Amendment as the basis for this opposition.

On the other side of the campaign finance reform debate were Senators John McCain (R-Ariz.) and Russell Feingold (D-Wisc.). One thing everyone agreed upon was that "behind McConnell's staid, low-key persona is a tenacious, disciplined man who keeps his eyes focused on his goal." McConnell is quoted as saying: "In the last [election cycle (1996)] we spent a little less than what was spent advertising cosmetics in this country, and a little more than what we spent on yogurt."[18]

Campaign finance bills failed in the Senate in 1999 due in part to the leadership of McConnell. McConnell led a filibuster to defeat a measure whose sponsors were again McCain and Feingold. The bill would have reduced the influence of special interest money in politics. McConnell saw things differently: "The measure would have quieted the voices of American citizens and destroyed the effectiveness of our national parties."[19]

During the 2000 election cycle, McConnell was chair of the Republican Senatorial Committee. In addition to raising money, he was making the necessary contacts to become the Republican leader of the Senate. Fred Barnes, executive editor of The Weekly Standard, a conservative news magazine, noted that McConnell was the point man for unpopular causes, such as tobacco and the current campaign finance system: "Him being out front on those issues protects a lot of other Republicans."[20]

In 2001, both McConnell and his colleague Jim Bunning were criticized for recommending for federal judgeships people with whom they had close personal relationships — in Bunning's case, his son David; in

McConnell's case, a former girlfriend, Karen Caldwell. It should be noted that almost twenty years after the controversial appointments, both judges are well respected for their judicial integrity.[21]

In 2002, McConnell sought reelection for the fourth time. He faced the daughter of former Kentucky Governor Bert T. Combs, Lois Combs Weinberg, an educational activist from Knott County. Following that election, McConnell became the Republican majority whip in 2003.

Following the November 2006 general election, McConnell was elected the Republican leader of the Senate, succeeding departing Tennessee Senator Bill Frist. His Republican colleagues elected him without opposition, and he became minority leader. The majority Democrats were led by Harry Reid of Nevada.

In 2008, McConnell faced Louisville businessman Bruce Lunsford in what would be one of his closest reelection campaigns. That year was a tough one for Republican senators seeking reelection because of the economic downturn, the unpopularity of outgoing President George W. Bush, and the popularity of Democratic presidential candidate Senator Barack Obama. McConnell won 53–47 percent. In 2002, McConnell had defeated Weinberg by about twenty-nine percentage points.

During the spring 2010 Republican primary, Kentucky had a competitive contest for the nomination for the Senate seat being vacated by Jim Bunning. In that contest, McConnell's choice was Kentucky Secretary of State Trey Grayson. Grayson's opponent was Tea Party favorite Rand Paul of Bowling Green. Grayson lost to Paul by a significant margin. After the primary, McConnell made a special point of quickly indicating his support for Rand Paul, despite the issues over Paul's support of civil rights when there was some indication of Paul supported the right of business' to refuse service to any person it choses choose.[22]

After the November 2010 general election, McConnell made clear his opposition to President Obama and his policies. In a speech to the Heritage Foundation, a conservative think tank, McConnell is quoted as saying that "the only way to achieve key party legislative goals such as ending government bailouts, cutting spending and repealing the health care law 'is to put someone in the White House who won't veto' them."[23]

During the summer of 2013, two challengers to McConnell's 2014 reelection surfaced—Democratic Secretary of State Alison Lundergan Grimes and Louisville businessman and Tea Party favorite Matt Bevin on the Republican side. All three spoke at the 2013 Fancy Farm Picnic, the state's traditional kickoff of the campaign season. At that time, McConnell was thought to have had close to $15 million in his 2014 campaign coffers.[24] The big issues of that campaign included McConnell's opposition to the Affordable Care Act (Obamacare) and President Obama himself.

The 2014 election proved competitive. As late as July, polls suggested that McConnell and Grimes were neck and neck.[25] But ultimately, it was another romp for McConnell, as he defeated Grimes by over 15 percentage points, 56.2–40.7 percent. McConnell's campaign spent $22.5 million to Grimes' $15.1 million.[26]

During that election, the Republicans took control of the Senate and McConnell realized his dream of becoming the Senate majority leader.

In 2015, obvious strain was evident following the May gubernatorial primary, which Matt Bevin captured. During the 2014 senate primary campaign, McConnell ran ads against Bevin that said, "How can you believe [Bevin] on anything?" Bevin canceled an appearance at the Elizabethtown Rotary Club where McConnell was the featured speaker. Then McConnell said he would not attend the state Republican Party's Lincoln Day dinner. McConnell said his absence was due to a rare Sunday session of the Senate to avert the expiration of the Patriot Act.[27]

As the Republican leader of the Senate, McConnell takes credit for blocking the US Supreme Court nomination of Judge Merrick Garland to fill the vacancy caused by the death of Justice Antonin Scalia in February 2016. President Obama nominated Garland in March 2016. The Senate, which has to approve Supreme Court nominations, was controlled by Republicans and their leader, McConnell. McConnell declared that any appointment by the sitting president in 2016 would not be considered. He said that the Supreme Court justice should be chosen by the president elected in November 2016. As a result, President Donald Trump was able to appoint Neil Gorsuch to the seat formerly occupied by Scalia.[28]

Among the legislation particular to Kentucky sponsored by Mitch McConnell, enacted into law includes Mill Springs National Monument Act, Camp Nelson Heritage National Monument Act and Hemp Farming Act of 2018.

Regarding international issues, McConnell sponsored a series of bills relating to import restrictions on items from Burma under the Burmese Freedom and Democracy Act of 2003. Prior to her release, McConnell was a prominent supporter of Burmese dissident Aung San Suu Kyi. He was the sponsor of the S. 625: Iran Nuclear Agreement Review Act of 2015 in the 114th Congress, which provided for congressional oversight on the nuclear agreement with Iran. The most controversial legislation sponsored by McConnell enacted into law is S.1927 (110th) Protect America Act of 2007. It is an amendment of the Foreign Intelligence Surveillance Act (FISA), which removed the warrant requirement for government surveillance of foreign intelligence targets "reasonably believed" to be outside the country.[29]

As majority leader with President Trump, McConnell helped confirm the appointments of 50 judges on the US Circuit Courts of Appeal and

120 District Court judges by December 2019[30]. In 2020, McConnell's motto for the judiciary was "leave no vacancy behind."

After the death of Supreme Court Justice Ruth Bader Ginsberg on September 18, 2020, McConnell was instrumental in the confirmation of her successor, US Court of Appeals for the 7th Circuit Judge, Amy Coney Barrett. President Trump nominated Barrett on September 26, 2020 and McConnell as Majority Leader held the confirmation vote on October 27, 2020.

In March 2020, McConnell worked with House Speaker Pelosi to pass the $2 trillion CARES (Coronavirus Aid Relief Economic Security Act) during the coronavirus pandemic. In a summary, it provided Public Health about $153.5 B (billion), State and Local Government $399.8 B, Education $43.7 B, Individual $566 B (in payments of up to $1,200), Big Corporations $500 B, Small Business $377 B and Safety Net $26 B[31].

In November 2020, Kentucky voters returned McConnell to the Senate for an unprecedented 7th Term. He defeated retired Marine Pilot and Lt. Col. Amy McGrath, 1,233,315 votes to 816,257. McConnell received over 60% of the votes cast. It is interesting to note that McGrath was the first McConnell opponent to raise and spend more money than McConnell. According to Senate records, when Mitch McConnell is sworn in for his 7th term, he will be tied with five others for being the 19th longest serving US Senator. When he completes his 7th term in January 2026, he will be tied with former Utah Senator Orrin Hatch in 5th place at 42 years.

McConnell is married to Elaine Chao, whom he wed on February 6, 1993. He was previously married to Sherrill Redmon, with whom he shares three daughters. They divorced in 1980. Chao, who is twelve years younger than McConnell, was born in Taiwan and immigrated to the US with her parents at age eight. She has served in a number of government roles, including Secretary of Labor in the George W. Bush administration and Secretary of Transportation in the Trump administration.

McConnell established the McConnell Center at the University of Louisville. The Center has four programs: McConnell Scholars Program, the Public Lecture Series, Civic Education Program, and the US Senator Mitch McConnell and Secretary Elaine L. Chao Archives. The archives had not been opened for research as of early 2020. Over the years, the Public Lecture Series has brought many congressional leaders to the Center, including the late Senator Edward "Ted" Kennedy.[32]

Projects named in McConnell's honor include Mitch McConnell Park in Bowling Green, the Mitch McConnell Plaza and Walkway in Owensboro, the Mitch McConnell Integrated Applications Laboratory at Western Kentucky University, and the Mitch McConnell Center for Distance Learning at the University of Kentucky.[33]

JAMES "JIM" BUNNING
(1931–2017)

- Class Three of Three
- Senate Service: 1999–2011
- Political affiliation: Republican
- Residence at time of election: Campbell County
- Served With Presidents Clinton, Bush, and Obama
- Served With Governors Patton, Fletcher, and Beshear

The only member of Congress to be a member of the Baseball Hall of Fame in Cooperstown, New York, is Jim Bunning. Senator Bunning was born in the city of Southgate in Campbell County in 1931 to Gladys and Louis Bunning. He had two brothers, Robert and Louis. He attended parochial school in Southgate and St. Xavier High School in Cincinnati where he graduated in 1949. He attended Xavier University in Cincinnati, where he graduated in 1953.

As a freshman at Xavier, he played baseball for the Musketeers. Following his freshman year, he signed a minor league contract with the Detroit Tigers. He continued to attend classes at Xavier and played in the minor leagues during the summer. On July 20, 1955, Jim Bunning played his first major league game for the Detroit Tigers. He pitched for Detroit until 1963. In 1963, he was traded to Philadelphia. He retired from Major League Baseball in 1971.

In addition to being an outstanding pitcher, he was an active member and leader of the Major League Baseball Players' Union. Under Bunning's leadership, the Players' Union became the force it is today.

Upon his retirement from baseball he entered politics. He served two terms on the Fort Thomas City Council (1977–79), one term in the Kentucky State Senate (1979–1983) and was elected to the US House of Representatives from Kentucky's Fourth Congressional District in 1986. With the retirement of Kentucky's senior US Senator Wendell Ford in 1998, he ran for Ford's seat, narrowly defeating Sixth District US Representative Scotty Baesler of Lexington.

Throughout his political career, Bunning was considered a social and fiscal conservative. His conservativism was unlike predecessor Republican senators.

Some of the highlights of Bunning's time in the House include voting in favor of the four articles of impeachment against President Bill Clinton. (Only two passed the House.) Bunning originally stated that he would not vote on the impeachment in the event he was elected to the Senate and would be a juror.[1]

This conservative legacy continued in the Senate; he was known as one of the most conservative members of that body. He voted "yes" to use force in Iraq, ban late term abortions, pass a constitutional amendment to ban flag burning, eliminate funding for the National Endowment for the Arts, and to confirm John Ashcroft. He voted "No" to campaign finance reform and a ten-year, $180-billion farm subsidy bill. He received perfect scores from special interest groups like the Christian Coalition, American Conservative Union, and the National Federation of Independent Business. He received a score of zero from League of Conservation Voters, Human Rights Watch, and Americans for Democratic Action.[2]

While he was a senator, Bunning attended baseball card shows. In his 2001 financial disclosure filed with the Senate, he indicated that in addition to his $141,300 Senate salary, he earned raised $30,000 for his foundation—The Jim Bunning Foundation. He earned a $15,000 salary from the foundation. Unlike other members of Congress, an exception was made to allow him to sell his autographs due to his career in Major League Baseball.[3]

In the spring of 2001, his son David, a thirty-two-year-old assistant US attorney, was nominated for a federal judgeship for the Eastern District of Covington. There was some controversy considering the younger Bunning's youth and experience. After over a decade of service, David Bunning is a respected member of the bench.

Bunning had a role in another significant piece of legislation concerning the release of presidential papers. In 2001, the National Archives was about to release 68,000 pages of Reagan's presidential papers. President George W. Bush issued an Executive Order #13,233, which would give ownership of presidential papers to the President and his/her heirs. Bush's executive order was contrary to Presidential Records Act of 1978 (PRA), which required former presidents to release their records no later than twelve years after they leave office. Under the PRA, as amended, the US government asserts complete "ownership, possession, and control" of all presidential and vice-presidential records. Upon conclusion of the president's term in office, the national archivist is required to assume custody of the records and to make them available to the public when permissible under the PRA. Access to the records may be denied after the end of the twelve-year embargo only if a former or incumbent president claims an exemption based on a "constitutionally based" executive privilege or continuing national security concern. President Bush stalled the release of Reagan's papers and then issued the executive order. Congress objected to the president's action with H.R. 1255, passed by the US House of Representatives on March 14, 2007, by a vote of 333–93. The White House threatened to veto the bill if it is passed in the Senate. H.R. 1255 was stalled in the Senate by a "hold" placed on the bill by Bunning.[4] Because of Bunning's hold on the legislation, the issue concerning release and ownership of presidential papers was not resolved until Bunning left the Senate.

In respect to legislation with his name on it, the Bunning-Bereuter-Blumenauer Flood Insurance Reform Act of 2014 reforming the National Flood Insurance Program is Bunning's Senate achievement. The Act sponsored by Bunning, Representative Doug Bereuter (R-Nebraska), and Representative Earl Blumenauer (D-Oregon) was designed to "reduce losses to properties for which repetitive flood insurance claim payment have been made."[5]

As a senator, Bunning continued his interested in the operations of Major League Baseball with his sponsorship of legislation. In 2005, Bunning, with Senator John McCain, co-sponsored legislation that would standardize drug testing and penalties for professional sports leagues. It was based on the Olympic model. It would provide for a two-year suspension for an athlete who failed the first time and a lifetime suspension for failing a drug test a second time. In addition to Major League Baseball, it would apply to the NFL, NBA, and NHL.[6]

It was during the last year of his second term, Bunning was again recognized as "practiced wielder of the hold." During the spring of 2010, Bunning used the "hold" to delay extensions of unemployment and health insurance benefits for millions of recipients. A year later, after Bunning had retired the Senate voted 94–4 to abolish the "hold."[7]

While Bunning did not seek reelection in 2010, Bunning's actions during the Republican primary reflected his sometimes-strained relationship with his Republican colleague Senator Mitch McConnell. McConnell's choice for the nomination to replace Bunning was Kentucky's Secretary of State Trey Grayson of Northern Kentucky. Also, in the race was Bowling Green ophthalmologist and son of Representative Ron Paul, Rand Paul. Bunning announced his support of Rand Paul in the Republican primary. Paul went on to win Bunning's seat.

Bunning during his retirement lived in Southgate, Kentucky. He delighted in the achievements of his children and grandchildren, including grandson Patrick Towles, who played quarterback for the University of Kentucky and Boston College.

Bunning died at age eighty-five and was buried in St. Stephen Cemetery in Fort Thomas, Kentucky.[8]

RANDAL "RAND" HOWARD PAUL
(1963–)

- Class Three of Three
- Senate Service: 2011–Present
- Political affiliation: Republican
- Residence at time of election: Warren County
- Served with Presidents Obama, Trump, and Biden
- Served with Governors Beshear, Bevin and A. Beshear

Rand Paul was the middle of five children born to Dr. Ron Paul and Mrs. Carol Paul in Pittsburgh, Pennsylvania, on January 7, 1963. The family moved to Lake Jackson, Texas, where his father practiced medicine. As a child, his family called him Randy.

While he was in high school and college, his father ran for US representative in 1974, finally winning a seat in 1976. Rand was active in his father Ron Paul's congressional campaigns.

In 1981, Paul entered Baylor University in Waco, where he studied biology and contributed to the college newspaper. His writings in the paper were influenced by Ayn Rand. He was on the Baylor swim team and was a member of the Young Conservatives of Texas.

In 1984, Rand Paul took a semester off from college to work on his father's campaign for the Republican nomination for the US Senate. His father Ron Paul was defeated by Phil Gramm.

In the fall of 1984, Paul scored high enough on his MCATs that he was accepted at the Duke Medical School in Durham, North Carolina, without having to graduate from Baylor. At Duke, he studied ophthalmology. After graduating from Duke, he moved to Atlanta for an internship in ophthalmology. It was in Atlanta he met his wife, Kelley Ashby, from Russellville, Kentucky. It was his wife Kelley who told him that he should be "Rand" rather than "Randy," and the name has stuck. After serving a residency in ophthalmology in North Carolina, he and Kelley moved to Bowling Green.

While a practicing ophthalmologist in Bowling Green, he was not politically active, except as creator of the anti-tax organization Kentucky Taxpayers United. Unlike his libertarian free-market father Ron, Rand Paul accepted Medicare and Medicaid as payment from patients for his services.

Prior to 2010, Rand Paul's political presence in Kentucky was as a newspaper letter writer, an occasional columnist, and a frequent guest on Kentucky Educational Television (KET)'s *Kentucky Tonight*. His contribution was primarily tax policy. In 2008, his father, Ron Paul, decided to run for the Republican nomination for president. Rand, with Jesse Benton, managed the Ron Paul Presidential Campaign in 2008. While Ron Paul failed to win the Republican nomination, it had raised over $35 million from a small donor base.

When Senator Jim Bunning decided not to seek a third term in 2010, Paul decided to seek the Republican nomination for the US Senate. Using the base from his father's unsuccessful presidential run, he opposed Senator Mitch McConnell's choice, Kentucky Secretary of State Trey Grayson. Using Tea Party support, Paul defeated Grayson in the primary and Democratic Attorney General Jack Conway in the general election.

When Paul was sworn in as a US senator on January 5, 2011, his father, Ron, was simultaneously being sworn in as a US representative. He became the first senator from Kentucky to have his father serving in Congress at the same time. Additionally, he became the second physician to serve as a US senator from Kentucky. The first was William Joseph DeBoe, who served from 1897 to 1903.

As an US Senator from Kentucky, Paul is very active in seeking and receiving media coverage. Almost every week since before his election in 2010, Senator Paul has been a guest or featured on all national cable news networks including both FOX and MSNBC, radio in and out of Kentucky as well as the print media. (The exception being November 3, 2017, after Paul was attacked by a Bowling Green neighbor who broke several of his ribs.[1]) In many respects, he has received more media coverage than his colleague, Kentucky's senior Senator and the Republican Majority Leader Mitch McConnell, since 2010.

In 2015 and 2016, Senator Paul sought the 2016 Republican presidential nomination. On April 10, 2015, the *Des Moines Register* published an article, "Top 10 list of Rand Paul accomplishments." These were the top ten actions during his Senate career ranked by his staff. It was noted that Senator Paul elevated the issues of federal surveillance and criminal justice reform to national attention. Number one was his thirteen-hour filibuster against the nomination of John Brennan as director of the Central Intelligence Agency on March 6–7, 2015. The second was the lawsuit he filed against President Obama and the National Security Agency in February 2014 to stop a program collecting metadata from "vast swaths of Americans," arguing it was an invasion of privacy. His number eight action was his February 2014 appearance before a Kentucky legislative committee, arguing for the restoration of voting rights for non-violent felons. In February 2015, he filed federal legislation that would restore voting rights to individuals who had completed their sentences for non-violent federal felonies.[2]

Senator Paul's filibuster of the confirmation of John Brennan as CIA Director ranked number nine on a list of the longest Senate speeches kept by the Senate Historian's Office at 12 hours, 52 minutes. Paul's filibuster fell eleven hours short of the record set by Senator Strom Thurmond when Thurmond protested the 1957 Civil Rights Act for 24 hours, 18 minutes. Paul joked that he had wanted to eclipse Thurmond's record, but he needed a bathroom break.[3]

In January 2018, Senator Paul had a mini filibuster when he read 600 pages of the 2,232-page budget bill. In doing so, he held up the already-late FY 2018 budget bill.[4]

During the evening of February 8–9, 2018, Senator Paul, through a filibuster and procedural maneuvers, shut the federal government down for about 8 hours, 45 minutes, while most of America slept. Senator Paul was concerned about the cost of the legislation. Prior to this legislation, Republicans had passed a tax bill that was estimated to add $1.5 trillion to the national debt over the next ten years. This bill Paul protested was estimated to raise spending by an additional $400 million. Paul wanted a vote on his amendment that essentially makes senators say they broke a pledge to rein in spending. Leaders refuse to give it to him, concerned that could create an all-night marathon of amendment votes from other senators.[5]

During his Senate career, he has blocked amendments to international tax treaties. It was Senator Paul's position that such treaties invaded American rights to privacy. The US Treasury in 2012 began signing new tax pacts with countries as part of implementation of the US Foreign Account Tax Compliance Act, a 2010 anti-tax-evasion law. The law, known as FATCA, which took effect in January 2014, requires foreign financial institutions to disclose to the US information about Americans' accounts worth more than $50,000.[6] Due to Paul's hold, hearings on tax treaties were not held until March 2014. However, he continued to be a thorn in the side of those who favored tax treaties until the end of his first term.

According to the senator's web page, there over 300 pieces of legislation that he has sponsored or co-sponsored since 2011. Some of the legislation has been introduced during more than one session of the Congresses in which he has served.[7]

In 2011, he introduced S.RES.82, "Resolution to provide sufficient time for legislation to be read." The same year he filed S.162, "Cut Federal Spending Act."

Since 2013, Senator Paul has been interested in the release of Dr. Shakeel Afridi, who was arrested and imprisoned by Pakistan. Dr. Afridi is thought to have aided American forces with locating Osama bin Laden at Abbottabad. Paul filed legislation on behalf of Dr. Afridi in 2012 and 2013 (S.3269, S.3259). Senator Paul's bills relating to Dr. Afridi provide that no assistance from the US to Pakistan be provided until Afridi is released (S.3269, S.3260). In 2018, he again sponsored legislation to deny assistance to Pakistan (S.2333).

In 2015, he sponsored a national "Right to Work Law" in respect to labor unions (S.391). In 2013, he sponsored SB 785, which would limit or eliminate administrative leave for government employees who were involved in labor negotiations or related business.

He has sponsored legislation for the audit of the Federal Reserve in 2013, S.209. That same year he sponsored a SJ Res. 3, a constitutional amendment for term limits for members of Congress.

As late as 2018, he sponsored legislation to remove the excise taxes on indoor tanning with S.2600.

In 2015 and 2018 he sponsored legislation to repeal the Gun-Free School Zones Act of 1990 and amendments to that act.

In 2015 (S.1441) and 2017 (S.1856), he sponsored legislation to prevent the "militarization" of federal, state, and local law enforcement by federal excess property transfers and grant programs.

After his re-election in 2016, he voted for all but three of President Trump's cabinet members. Senator Paul voted against confirmation of Gina Haspel as director of the CIA. However, in respect to the confirmation of President Trump's cabinet, Paul was one of three Republican senators who voted "no" for only two of fifteen cabinet secretaries and eight other positions that require Senate confirmation.[8] Paul voted against confirmation of Mike Pompeo as director of the CIA but voted for him for secretary of state. He voted against Daniel Coats to serve as director of national intelligence.[9]

In voting for President Obama's cabinet nominees specific philosophical reasons for his votes are not obvious. In June 2013, Paul was one of ninety-four senators who voted for the confirmation of John Kerry as secretary of state. The same year he voted for the confirmation of Jacob "Jack" Lew as secretary of the treasury, while McConnell voted "nay" on the Lew confirmation. On the April 23, 2015, vote on the nomination of Loretta Lynch to be attorney general, Paul voted with the forty-three "nays" and McConnell voted with the fifty-six "yeas."

During the 2020 coronavirus pandemic, Senator Paul was the first US Senator to test positive for the virus. He had a mild case and quarantined for 14-days. There was some concern about how the virus would affect his health due to a partial removal of a lung due to being assaulted by a neighbor in 2017.[10]

The election of Rand Paul to the US Senate reflected the strength of the Tea Party movement in Kentucky. Senator Paul moved Senator McConnell and traditional Republicans (Eisenhower-Nixon-Ford) farther to the political "right" or a mix of libertarianism and conservatism. This description combined with single issue politics of the late twentieth century and early decades of the twenty-first century including abortion, guns and nationalism. With this philosophy, there is a question whether Republicans of the twenty-first century would accept former senators Cooper and Cook.

APPENDIX I
U.S. Senators from Other States Born in Kentucky

Senator	State Represented	Dates of Service	Place of Birth
Allan Bowie Magruder	Louisiana	1812–1813	Near Lexington
William Allen Trimble	Ohio	1819–1821	Woodford County
Thomas Buck Reed	Mississippi	1826–1827, 1829	Lexington
George McCracken Robinson	Illinois	1830–1841	Georgetown
Alexander Buckner	Missouri	1831–1833	Jefferson County
John Pendleton King	Georgia	1833–1837	Glasgow
Lewis Fields Linn	Missouri	1833–1843	
William Lee D. Ewing	Illinois	1835–1837	Paris
Richard M. Young	Illinois	1837–1843	Lexington
John Norvell	Michigan	1837–1841	Danville
Ephraim H. Foster	Tennessee	1838–39, 1843–45	Bardstown
James Semple	Illinois	1843–1847	Green County
David Rice Atchison	Missouri	1844–1855	Frogtown near Lexington
Thomas Corwin	Ohio	1845–1850	Bourbon County
Jefferson Davis	Mississippi	1847–1851, 1857–1861	Christian County
Orville Hickman Browning	Illinois	1861–1863	Cynthiana

James Lane	Kansas	1861–1866	Boone County
Henry Smith Lane	Indiana	1861–1867	Sharpsburg
William Alexandria Richardson	Illinois	1863–1865	Lexington
Benjamin Gratz Brown	Missouri	1863–1867	Lexington
Richard Yates	Illinois	1865–1871	Warsaw
Francis Preston Blair Jr.	Missouri	1871–1873	Lexington
Richard James Oglesby	Illinois	1873–1879	Floydsburg, Oldham County
Samuel B. Maxey	Texas	1875–1887	Tompkinsville
George Graham Vest	Missouri	1879–1903	Frankfort
Shelby Moore Cullom	Illinois	1883–1913	Monticello
Randall L. Gibson	Louisiana	1883–1892	Versailles
John M. Palmer	Illinois	1891–1897	(Eagle Creek) Scott County
Roger Q. Mills	Texas	1892–1899	Todd County
William J. Stone	Missouri	1903–1918	Richmond
Samuel H. Piles	Washington	1905–1911	Smithland
Joseph L. Bristow	Kansas	1909–1915	Hazel Green
Albert B. Fall	New Mexico	1912–1921	Frankfort
Marcus A. Smith	Arizona	1912–1921	Cynthiana
Oscar Wilder Underwood	Alabama	1915–1927	Louisville
John W. Harreld	Oklahoma	1919–1927	Morgantown
Harry B. Hawes	Missouri	1921–1926	Covington
Walter Walker	Colorado	1932	Marion
James G. Scrugham	Nevada	1942–1945	Lexington
Paul Fannin	Arizona	1965–1977	Ashland

APPENDIX II
The Seventeenth Amendment to the U.S. Constitution

Amendment XVII

The Senate of the United States shall be composed of two Senators from each state, elected by the people thereof, for six years; and each Senator shall have one vote. The electors in each state shall have the qualifications requisite for electors of the most numerous branch of the state legislatures.

When vacancies happen in the representation of any state in the Senate, the executive authority of such state shall issue writs of election to fill such vacancies: Provided, that the legislature of any state may empower the executive thereof to make temporary appointments until the people fill the vacancies by election as the legislature may direct.

This amendment shall not be so construed as to affect the election or term of any Senator chosen before it becomes valid as part of the Constitution.

APPENDIX III
Senate Salaries since 1789

Date	Senator's Salary
1789-1815	$6.00 per diem (per day)
1815-1817	$1,500 per annum (per year)
1817-1855	$8.00 per diem
1855-1865	$3,000 per annum
1865-1871	$5,000 per annum
1871-1873	$7,500 per annum
1873-1907	$5,000 per annum
1907-1925	$7,500 per annum
1925-1932	$10,000 per annum
1932-1933	$9,000 per annum
1933-1935	$8,500 per annum
1935-1947	$10,000 per annum
1947-1955	$12,500 per annum
1955-1965	$22,500 per annum
1965-1969	$30,000 per annum
1969-1975	$42,500 per annum
1975-1977	$44,600 per annum
1977-1978	$57,500 per annum
1979-1983	$60,662.50 per annum
1983-1984	$69,800 per annum
1984-1985	$72,600 per annum
1985-1986	$75,100 per annum
January 1, 1987-February 3, 1987	$77,400 per annum
February 4, 1987-February 2, 1990	$89,500 per annum
February 3, 1990-August 14, 1991	$98,400 per annum
January 1, 1991-August 14, 1991	$101,900 per annum
August 15, 1991	$125,100 per annum

1992	$129,500 per annum
1993-1997	$133,600 per annum
1998-1999	$136,700 per annum
2000	$141,300 per annum
2001	$145,100 per annum
2002	$150,000 per annum
2003	$154,700 per annum
2004	$158,100 per annum
2005	$162,100 per annum
2006-2007	$165,200 per annum
2008	$169,300 per annum
2009—2020	$174,000 per annum

Information from the Senate Historical Office:

http://www.senate.gov/artandhistory/history/common/briefing/senate_salaries.htm

Since the 1980s, Senate leaders—majority and minority leaders and the president pro tempore—have received higher salaries than other members. Currently, members in leadership positions, earn $193,400 per year.

BIBLIOGRAPHY

BOOKS

Baker, Richard A., *200 Notable Days: Senate Stories, 1787 to 2002*, Washington, DC: U.S. Government Printing Office, 2006.

Barnes, James A. *John G. Carlisle—Financial Statesman*, Dodd, Mead and Company, (1931) Reprinted 1967.

Burke, Bernard B. *Ambassador Frederic Sackett and the Collapse of the Weimar Republic, 1930–1933*, Cambridge University Press.

Bussey, Charles J. James Guthrie: *Kentucky Politician and Entrepreneur; Kentucky Profiles: Biographical Essays in Honor of Holman Hamilton. Edited by James C. Klotter and Peter J. Sehlinger*, Frankfort: The Kentucky Historical Society, 1982.

Campbell, Tracy, *Short of the Glory: The Fall and Redemption of Edward F. Prichard Jr.*, Kentucky: University of Kentucky Press, 2004.

Caro, Robert. *The Years of Lyndon Johnson: Master of the Senate*, New York: Alfred A. Knopf, a division of Random House, Inc., 2002.

Chandler, Albert B., Trimble Vince H., *Heroes, Plain Folk and Skunks: The Life and Times of Happy Chandler*, Chicago: Bonus Books, 1989.

Collins, Lewis, J.A. James, and U.P. James, *History of Kentucky*, Lexington: Henry Clay Press, 1968.

Crittenden, John J. *The Life of John J. Crittenden, With Selections from His Correspondence and Speeches. Edited by his daughter, Mrs. Chapman Coleman, Vol. II*, Philadelphia: J.P. Lippincott, 1871.

Dyche, John David, *Republican Leader: A Political Biography of Senator Mitch McConnell*, Wilmington, Delaware: Intercollegiate Studies Institute, 2009.

Fielder, Elizabeth Rouse, *Kentucky's Joseph C.S. Blackburn*, Sikeston, MO: Acclaim Press, 2018.

Hardin, John A. *Fifty Years of Segregation: Black Higher Education in Kentucky, 1904–1954*. Lexington: University of Kentucky Press, 1997.

Heidler, David S. and Jeanne T. Heidler. *Henry Clay—The Essential American*, Random House: 2010.

Heller, J. Roderick, *Democracy's Lawyer: Felix Grundy of the Old Southwest*, Louisiana State University Press, 2010.

Hernon, Joseph M., *Profiles in Character: Hubris and Heroism in the U.S. Senate, 1789–1990*, New York: M.E. Sharper, 1997.

Jackman, William James and Jacob Harris, *History of the American Nation: A History of the American People*, 1911.

Jordan, Paul R. "Journey from Beavercreek," Xlibris (2004).

Kentucky Profiles—Biographical Essays in Honor of Holman Hamilton, Edited by James C. Klotter and Peter J. Sehlinger, Frankfort: The Kentucky Historical Society, 1982.

Kirwan, Albert D. *John J. Crittenden Struggle for the Union*, Lexington: University of Kentucky Press, 1962.

Kleber, John E. editor in chief. *Kentucky Encyclopedia*. Thomas D. Clark, Lowell H. Harrison, James C. Klotter, associate editors. Lexington: University Press of Kentucky, 1992.

Klein, Philip S., *President James Buchanan, A Biography*, Sixth Printing of the First Edition, Newtown, CT: American Political Biography Press, 2015.

Klotter, James C. *Henry Clay: The Man Who Would Be President*, New York: Oxford University Press, 2018.

Klotter, James, C. *Kentucky: Portrait in Paradox, 1900—1950 Politics the Damnedest—In Kentucky: 1900—1950*, Frankfort: The Kentucky Historical Society, 1996.

Libbey, James K. *Alben Barkley—A Life In Politics*, Lexington: University Press of Kentucky, 2016.

MacGillis, Alec. *The Cynic—The Political Education of Mitch McConnell*, New York: Simon & Schuster Paperbacks, 2014.

Mathias, Frank F. *Kentucky's Governors*, ed. Lowell H. Harrison, Lexington: University of Kentucky Press, 2004.

McNeil, Neil and Baker, Richard A., T*he American Senate—An Insider's History*, New York: Oxford University Press, 2013.

Ollie M. James (Late a Senator from Kentucky) Memorial Addresses; Delivered in the Senate and the House of Representatives of the United States; Sixty-Fifth Congress Third Session; Proceedings in the House, February 2, 1919 Washington: Joint Committee on Printing, 1920.

Patler, Nicholas, "Chapter 12: The Startling Career of P.B.S. Pinchback: A Whirlwind Crusade to Bring Equality to Reconstructed Louisiana" Matthew Lynch, editor. *Before Obama: A Reappraisal of Black Reconstruction Era Politicians, Volume 1: Legacies Lost: The Life and Times of John R. Lynch and His Political Contemporaries*. Praeger, an Imprint of ABC-CLIO, LLC, Santa Barbara: 2012.

Perrin, William Henry, Battle, J.H., Kniffin, G.C. *Kentucky: A History of the State, Embracing a Concise Account of the Origin and Development of the Virginia Colony; Its Expansion Westward and the Frontier Beyond the Alleghanies; The Erection of Kentucky as an Independent State and Its Subsequent Development*. 7th Edition, Louisville & Chicago: F.A. Battey, 1887.

Remini, Robert V. *Henry Clay: Statesman for the Union*, W.W. Norton: November 17, 1993.

Schulman, Robert, *John Sherman Cooper—The Global Kentuckian*, Lexington: University of Kentucky Press, 1976.

Tapp, Hambleton, and Klotter, James C. *Kentucky: Decades of Discord, 1865–1900*. Kentucky Historical Society, University Press of Kentucky, 1977.

Watson, Harry L., *Liberty and Power: The Politics of Jacksonian America*. Hill & Wang. New York, NY: 2006.

GOVERNMENT DOCUMENTS AND WEBSITES

American State Papers

Appendix to the Congressional Globe, The

Biographical Directory of the United States Congress, 1774 to Present. Directions for use—Input the name of any senator or congressman in history and retrieve a biography or biographical information. Retrieved from http://bioguide.congress.gov/biosearch/biosearch.asp (Accessed 11/05/2019).

Brief History of Naples, Florida

Bunning-Bereuter-Blumenauer Flood Insurance Reform Act of 2004

Densho Encyclopedia

Economic History Association

Encyclopedia Britannica
Explore Kentucky History
Gov Info
GovTrack
History of Congress (Annals of Congress)
History, Art & Archives, "U.S. House of Representatives, Individuals Who Have Lain in
    State or Honor"
Journal of the Senate of the United States of America
Kentucky Department of Education Website
LBJ Presidential Library
Letters from Filson Historical Society
McConnell Center, The
National Security Archive
National World War II Museum, The
Senate Executive Journal
Senator Rand Paul's Senate Office Web page
Truman, Harry, *Public Papers of the Presidents of the United States: Harry S. Truman, 1948*
    (1963): 132–133.
US Capitol Visitor's Center
US Congressional Record
U.S. Election Atlas, The
US Food and Drug Administration
US Senate Historical Office
US Senate Website
UVA Miller Center
VA Benefits and Healthcare

JOURNAL ARTICLES

Finch, Glen. "The Election of United States Senators in Kentucky: The Beckham Period,"
    Filson Club History Quarterly, Jan., 1970, 39.
Gamm, Gerald and Smith, Steven S. "The Rise of Floor Leaders in the United States
    Senate, 1890–1915." A paper presented for the Conference on the U.S. Senate,
    Rothermere American Institute, Oxford University: April 2–3, 2005.
Harris, William C. "His Loyal Opposition: Lincoln's Border State Critics," *Journal of the
    Abraham Lincoln Association*, Vol. 31, 1, 2011, 1–7 (Accessed Dec. 24, 2016). Re-
    trieved from http://quod.lib.umich.edu/j/jala/2629860.0032.103/--his-loyal-op-
    position-lincolns-border-states-critics?rgn=main;view=fulltext.
Mason, Matthew E. "Slavery Overshadowed: Congress Debates Prohibiting the Atlantic
    Slave Trade to the United States, 1806–1807," *Journal of the Early Republic*, no. 20
    (Spring 2000): 59–62
Schlup, Leonard. "Joseph Blackburn of Kentucky and the Panama Question." *Filson Club
    Quarterly* 51, October 1977, 353–354.
Warren, Elizabeth, "John Brown and His Influence on Kentucky Politics: 1784–1805"
    Ph.D. diss., Northwestern University: 1937, 90.

NEWSPAPERS

The *Advocate-Messenger* (Danville, Kentucky)
Anchorage Daily Times
The *Argus of Western America* (Frankfort, Kentucky)

The *Baltimore Sun*

Beatrice Express (Beatrice, Nebraska)

The *Big Sandy News* (Louisa, Kentucky)

The *Boston Globe*

Breckinridge News (Cloverport, Kentucky)

Burlington Weekly Free Press (Burlington, Vermont)

Chattanooga Daily Times

Cincinnati Enquirer

Cincinnati Times Star

The *Clarksburg Telegram* (Clarksburg, West Virginia)

Commercial Advertiser and Journal (Buffalo, New York)

The *Courier-Journal* (Louisville, Kentucky)

The *Daily Times* (Davenport, Iowa)

Democrat and Chronicle (Rochester, New York)

The *Des Moines Register*

The *Dispatch* (Moline, Illinois)

The *Escanaba Daily Press* (Escanaba, Michigan)

Fort Lauderdale News

The *Frankfort*

The *Gastonia Gazette* (Gastonia, North Carolina)

The *Gazette and Daily* (York, Pennsylvania)

Honolulu Star-Bulletin

The *Indiana Herald*

The *Indianapolis News*

The *Indianapolis Star*

The *Inter Ocean* (Chicago, Illinois)

Interior Journal (Stanford, Kentucky)

The *Ithaca Journal* (Ithaca, New York)

The *Jackson Sun* (Jackson, Tennessee)

Jefferson City Post Tribune

Kentucky Advocate

Kentucky Irish American (Louisville)

Kentucky Reporter

The *Kentucky Tribune*

Kingfisher Daily Star (Kingfisher, Oklahoma)

The *Kokomo Tribune* (Kokomo, Indiana)

Lancaster Gazette Eagle (Lancaster, Ohio)

Lexington Herald-Leader

Liberty Advocate (Liberty, Mississippi)

Long Beach Independent (Long Beach, California)

Los Angeles Times

The *Louisville Daily Courier*

The *Louisville Daily Journal*

Louisville Journal (predecessor of The *Courier-Journal*)

Louisville Morning Courier

The *Messenger* (Madisonville, Kentucky)

Messenger-Inquirer (Owensboro, Kentucky)

Nashville American

The *Nashville Banner*

The *Neosho Times* (Neosho, Missouri)
The *New York Times*
News and Observer (Raleigh, North Carolina)
News-Democrat (Paducah, Kentucky)
Niles Weekly Register (Baltimore, Maryland) (early nineteenth century news magazine)
Oakland Tribune (California)
The *Owensboro Messenger*
The *Paducah News-Democrat*
The *Paducah Sun*
The *Paducah Sun Democrat*
Pallidum-Item (Richmond, Indiana)
The *Pantagraph* (Bloomington, Illinois)
The *Petaluma Argus-Courier* (Sonoma County, California)
The *Philadelphia Inquirer*
The *Pittsburgh Press*
The *Portsmouth Herald* (Portsmouth, New Hampshire)
Press and Sun Bulletin (Binghamton, New York)
Reno-Gazette Journal
The *Saint Paul Globe*
The *Santa Fe New Mexican*
Spirit of the Age (Raleigh, North Carolina)
The *Springfield News-Leader*
St. Louis Post-Dispatch
Star-Tribune (Minneapolis, Minnesota)
The *Summit County Beacon*
The *Sun* (New York)
The *Susquehanna Democrat* (Wilkes-Barre, Pennsylvania)
Taos News (Taos, New Mexico)
The *Tennessean*
The *Tribune* (Scranton, Pennsylvania)
USA Today
Washington Post
The *Weekly Standard* (Raleigh, North Carolina)
Weekly Town Talk (Alexandria, Louisiana)
Wilmington Morning News (Wilmington, Delaware)

VIDEOS
C-SPAN
TV.com

WEBSITES
G Captain
Ice Cream Geek
NPR
Politico
Rare
Reuters
Roll Call

REFERENCES AND ENDNOTES

PART I:
1   Baker, Richard A., 200 Notable Days: Senate Stories, 1787 to 2002, (Washington, DC: U.S. Government Printing Office): 2006.

John Brown
1   Warren, Elizabeth, "John Brown and His Influence on Kentucky Politics: 1784–1805" Ph.D. diss., Northwestern University (1937): 90.
2   Ibid, 114.
3   Ibid, 126.
4   Ibid. 148.
5   *Louisville Morning Courier*, "Kentucky U.S. Senator," June 26, 1848.
6   Mathias, Frank F. *Kentucky's Governors*, ed. Lowell H. Harrison, (University of Kentucky Press, Kentucky, 2004): 36.
7   *Journal of the Senate of the United States of America*, 1789–1873, Dec. 11, 1848, 50. https://memory.loc.gov/cgi-bin/ampage?collId=llsj&fileName=040/llsj040.db&recNum=49&itemLink=D?hlaw:3:./temp/~ammem_RpC1::%230400139&linkText=1 (Accessed April 9, 2019).
8   *Journal of the Senate of the United States of America*, Monday, January 22, (1849): 140. https://memory.loc.gov/cgi-bin/ampage?collId=llsj&fileName=040/llsj040.db&recNum=139&itemLink=D?hlaw:3:./temp/~ammem_RpC1::%230400139&linkText=1(Accessed April 9, 2019).

John Edwards
1   *History of Congress*, (March 1793): 677–688.
2   Mathias, Frank F. Ed. Lowell Harrison. *Kentucky's Governors*. (Lexington: University of Kentucky Press, 2004): 8–9.

Humphrey Marshall
1   *History of Congress (Senate) Proceeding*, 855–866.
2   Heidler, David S. and Jeanne T. Heidler. *Henry Clay—The Essential American*, (Random House, 2010): 56–57.
3   Heidler and Heidler, *Henry Clay*, 71–73.

John Breckinridge
1   "A Century of Lawmaking for a New Nation: U.S. Congressional Documents and Debates, 1774–1875; Annals of Congress, 7th Congress, 1st Session", 1 & 11. Retrieved from https://memory.loc.gov/cgi-bin/ampage?collId=llac&fileName=011/llac011.db&recNum=2 (Accessed March 28, 2019).
2   Ibid, 22.
3   Ibid, 24.

Buckner Thruston

1   Tufts Digital Collections and Archives, "Kentucky 1804 U.S. Senate," A New Nation Votes, http://elections.lib.tufts.edu/catalog/tufts:ky.ussenate.1804 (Accessed August 2, 2017).

2   Mason, Matthew E. "Slavery Overshadowed: Congress Debates Prohibiting the Atlantic Slave Trade to the United States, 1806–1807," *Journal of the Early Republic*, no. 20 (Spring 2000): 59–62.

3   To Amend the Resolution (8 STAT L. 214) that further consideration of treaty concluded at Tripoli on June 3, 1805, between the U.S. and the Bashaw Bay and subjects of Tripoli, be postponed until the next session of Congress, and to request the President to ascertain whether wife and children of Hamit Bashaw have been delivered to him, agreeable to the 3rd Article of preliminary Articles of aforesaid treaty; amendment to include the further condition that the wife and children of the Bashaw, and brother of the Bashaw of Tripoli, be delivered agreeably to the 3rd Article of said treaty.

4   9th Congress, April 12, 1806, Senate, #60, "To Ratify the Treaty Concluded at Tripoli on June 3, 1805, Between The U.S. and the Bashaw Bay and the Subjects of Tripoli," Govtrack, (Accessed 09/27/2019).

5   *Journal of the Senate of the United States of America*, Vol. 4, (Tuesday, December 17, 1805): 11. Retrieved from https://memory.loc.gov/cgi-bin/ampage?collId=llsj&fileName=004/llsj004.db&recNum=9&itemLink=r?ammem/hlaw:@field(DOCID+@lit(sj0041)):%230040001&linkText=1 (Accessed 09/27/2019).

6   Ibid.

7   *American State Papers, 9th Congress, 1st Session. Indian Affairs: Volume 1*, Pages 705–743, No. 113. Lewis and Clarke's expedition. https://memory.loc.gov/cgi-bin/ampage?collId=llsp&-fileName=007/llsp007.db&recNum=706 (Accessed 09/27/2019).

8   *Senate Executive Journal*, Tuesday, February 11, 1806. *Senate Executive Journal*, Tuesday, February 11, 1806; http://memory.loc.gov/cgi-bin/query/D?hlaw:1:./temp/~ammem_o4Lz::(Accessed March 28, 2019).

9   "A Century of Lawmaking for a New Nation: U.S. Congressional Documents and Debates," 1774–1875, *Annals of Congress, Senate, 9th Congress, 1st Session, 22*. https://memory.loc.gov/cgi-bin/ampage?collId=llac&fileName=015/llac015.db&recNum=6 (Accessed March 28, 2019).

10   Ibid, 41.

Henry Clay (First Term)

1   Heidler, David and Jeanne Heidler, *Henry Clay—The Essential American*, 61.

2   Heidler, David S. and Jeanne T. Heidler. *Henry Clay—The Essential American*, 57–61.

3   Heidler, David S. and Jeanne T. Heidler. *Henry Clay—The Essential American*, 64.

John Pope

1   Journal of the Senate of the United States of America, Vol. 4, p, 1, October 27, 1807. Retrieved from https://memory.loc.gov/cgi-bin/ampage?collId=llsj&fileName=004/llsj004.db&recNum=178&itemLink=r?ammem/hlaw:@field(DOCID+@lit(sj004175)):%230040179&link (Accessed 10/26/2019).

2   Ibid.

PART II

Henry Clay (Second Term)

1   Heidler, David S. and Jeanne T. Heidler. *Henry Clay—The Essential American*, 75–76.

2   Heidler, David S. and Jeanne T. Heidler. *Henry Clay—The Essential American*, 73.

3   Heidler David S. and Jeanne T. Heidler. *Henry Clay—The Essential American*, 83.

George M. Bibb

1   *Niles Weekly Register*, "Progress of Cholera," Vol. 43, (Nov. 10, 1832): 171.

2   Senate Vote #63 in 1832 (22nd Congress) To Recede from 23rd Amendment to H.R. 116 (App. MAY 5, 1832) making appropriations for the support of the U.S. for the year 1832, which Amendment eliminates the appropriation of $27,000 for outfitting a Minister to France. (P. 709-872). (Accessed 10/12/2019) https://www.govtrack.us/congress/votes/22-1/s63

3   *World Heritage Encyclopedia Edition*, "George M. Bibb" Project Gutenberg Self-Publishing Press (2019), Retrieved from http://gutenberg.us/article/WHEBN0000845670/Georgia%20M.%20Bibb (Accessed 10/12/2019).

John Rowan

1   *Kingfisher Daily Star*, "Author of 'Old Kentucky Home' Honored," Kingfisher, Oklahoma: July 31, 1906.

2   The *Susquehanna Democrat*, Wilkes-Barre, PA: September 25, 1829.

3   Heller, J. Roderick, *Democracy's Lawyer: Felix Grundy of the Old Southwest*. Louisiana State University Press, (2010): 23, 25.

4   Heller, J. Roderick, *Democracy's Lawyer: Felix Grundy of the Old Southwest*, 35.

5   Heller, J. Roderick, *Democracy's Lawyer: Felix Grundy of the Old Southwest*, 38.

6   Heller, J. Roderick, *Democracy's Lawyer: Felix Grundy of the Old Southwest*, 75.

7   *Journal of the Senate of the United States of America*, Vol. 14, 270–271. https://memory.loc.gov/cgi-bin/ampage?collId=llsj&fileName=014/llsj014.db&recNum=269&itemLink=D?hlaw:2:./temp/~ammem_JKd0::%230140268&linkText=1 (Accessed 9/6/2019)

8   Klotter, James C. *Henry Clay: The Man Who Would Be President*. (New York: Oxford University Press, 2018): 162.

9   Perrin, William Henry, Battle, J.H., Kniffin, G.C. *Kentucky: A History of the State, Embracing a Concise Account of the Origin and Development of the Virginia Colony; Its Expansion Westward and the Frontier Beyond the Alleghanies; The Erection of Kentucky as an Independent State and Its Subsequent Development*. 7th Edition, (Louisville & Chicago F.A. Battey, 1887): 512.

10   The *Courier Journal*, December 15, 1830.

11   The *Portsmouth Herald*, Portsmouth, New Hampshire: January 9, 1941, 4.

12   Note: Nullification would be the ability of a state to invalidate or nullify federal law as it applies to that state.

13   The *Courier Journal*, (From the Henderson Columbian) March 19, 1831.

14   *Burlington Weekly Free Press*, "From the Lexington Ky. Reporter," Burlington, Vermont: August 27, 1830. 2.

15   *Commercial Advertiser and Journal*, Buffalo, NY: July 1, 1840. 2.

16   *Vicksburg Daily Whig*, Vicksburg, Mississippi. July 20, 1843.

17   *Biographical Directory of the United States Congress, 1774-Present*; Rowan John. http://bioguide.congress.gov/scripts/biodisplay.pl?index=R000471 (Accessed 9/6/2019).

Jesse Bledsoe

1   Collins, Lewis, J.A. James, and U.P. James, *History of Kentucky*, Lexington: Henry Clay Press, (1968): 203.

2   *Journal of the Senate of the United States of America*, Vol. 9. p. 303 Retrieved from https://memory.loc.gov/cgi-bin/ampage?collId=llsj&filename=005/llsj005.db&recNum=295&itemLink=r?ammem/hlaw:@field(DOCID+@lit(sj005294)):%230050295&linkText=1 (Accessed 06/05/2019).

3   *Journal of the Senate of the United States of America*, Vol. 9, 306.

4   *Journal of the Senate of the United States of America*, Vol. 9, 407.

5   *Journal of the Senate of the United States of America*, Vol. 9, 595–596.

6   *Journal of the Senate of the United States of America* Vol. 9, 607-608, Retrieved from https://memory.loc.gov/cgi-bin/ampage?collId=llsj&filename=005/llsj005.db&recNum=582&itemLink=r?ammem/hlaw:@field(DOCID+@lit(sj005501)):%230050510&linkText=1 (Accessed 06/05/2019).

George Walker

1   Kleber, John E. eds. *Kentucky Encyclopedia*. Thomas D. Clark, Lowell H. Harrison, James C. Klotter, associate editors. (Lexington: University Press of Kentucky, 1992): 925.

2   "Recreating Washington DC's Lost Built Environment," Virtual Architecture Archaeology, 2013, http://washingtonarchitecture.blogspot.com/2013/03/blodgets-hotel-1793-1836. html. (Accessed March 01, 2017).

William Taylor Barry

1   Watson, Harry L. *Liberty and Power: The Politics of Jacksonian America* (New York, NY: Hill & Wang, 2006): 125.

Martin D. Hardin

1   A New Nation Votes-American Election Returns 1787–1825. Retrieved from https://elections.lib.tufts.edu/catalog/tufts:ky.ussenatespecialelection.1816 (Accessed 10/13/2019).

2   *Journal of the Senate of the United States of America*, Vol. 6. p. 29. https://memory.loc.gov/ cgi-bin/ampage?collId=llsj&fileName=006/llsj006.db&recNum=762&itemLink=r?ammem/ hlaw:@field(DOCID+@lit(sj006114)):%230060736&linkText=1.

3   *Journal of the Senate of the United States of America*, Vol. 6, 33.

4   *Journal of the Senate of the United States of America*, Vol. 6, 62.

5   *Journal of the Senate of the United States of America*, Vol. 6, 85.

6   *Journal of the Senate of the United States of America*, Vol. 6, 222.

7   *Journal of the Senate of the United States of America*, Vol. 6, 220.

8   *Journal of the Senate of the United States of America*, Vol. 6, 249.

John Jordan Crittenden (First Term)

1   *Journal of the Senate of the United States of America*, Vol. 7, p. 5. Retrieved from https://memory.loc.gov/cgi-bin/ampage?collId=llsj&filename=007/llsj007.db &recNum=4&itemLink=r?ammem/hlaw:@field(DOCID+@lit(s-j0071)):%230070002&linkText=1 (Accessed June 7, 2019).

2   *Journal of the Senate of the United States of America*, (Dec. 1, 1817): Vol. 7, 5–6.

3   "A Century of Lawmaking for a New Nation: U.S. Congressional Documents and Debates, 1774–1875; Annals of Congress, 7th Congress, 1st Session" p. 1, 11. Retrieved from https://memory.loc.gov/cgi-bin/ampage?collId=llac&fileName=011/llac011. db&recNum=2 (Accessed March 28, 2019).

4   Kirwan, Albert D. *John J. Crittenden Struggle for the Union*, Lexington: University of Kentucky Press: (1962): 33.

5   Kirwan, *John J. Crittenden Struggle for the Union*, 33–34.

6   Kirwan, *John J. Crittenden Struggle for the Union*, 35.

Isham Talbot

1   *Biographical Directory of the United State Congress, 1774 to the Present*. Talbot, Isham 1773–1836. Retrieved from http://bioguide.congress.gov/scripts/biodisplay.pl?index=T000017 (Accessed 12/18/2019).

2   *Journal of the Senate of the United States of America*, Vol. 6, 60, Retrieved form https://memory.loc.gov/cgi-bin/ampage?collId=llsj&fileName=006/llsj006.db &recNum=58&itemLink=D?hlaw:1:./temp/~ammem_iF1o::%230060 060&linkText=1 (Accessed 12/18/2019).

3   *Journal of the Senate of the United States of America*, Vol. 6, 75. Retrieved from https://memory.loc.gov/cgi-bin/ampage?collId=llsj&fileName=006/llsj006.db &recNum=58&itemLink=D?hlaw:1:./temp/~ammem_iF1o::%230060 060&linkText=1 (Accessed 12/18/2019).

4   *Journal of the Executive Proceedings of the Senate of the United States of America*, Volume 3, 82. March 4, 1817.

5 *Journal of the Senate of the United States of America*, Volume 10, 194–196. Retrieved from http://memory.loc.gov/cgi-in/ampage?collId=llsj&fileName=010/llsj010.db&recNum= 194&itemLink=D?hlaw:20:./temp/~ammem_IIpQ::%230100193&linkText=1 (Accessed 12/18/2019)

6 The *Argus of Western America*. Frankfort: January 31, 1822, 3.

7 Talbot, Isham. The *Argus of Western America*. November 12, 1821.

8 The *Argus of Western America*, Frankfort: May 26, 1824.

9 *Kentucky Reporter,* Lexington: December 29, 1827.

10 The *Frankfort Argus*, January 19, 1831.

11 *Biographical Directory of the United States Congress, 1774 to Present*; Talbot, Isham (1773–1837) Retrieved from http://bioguide.congress.gov/scripts/biodisplay.pl?index=T000017 (Accessed 12/18/2019).

PART III

William Logan

1 *Journal of the Senate of the United States of America*, Vol. 9. 5–6. Retrieved from https://memory.loc.gov/cgi-bin/ampage?collId=llsj&fileName=009/llsj009.db &recNum=4&itemLink=r?ammem/hlaw:@field(DOCID+@lit(sj0091)):%230 090001&linkText=1 (Accessed 06/03/2019).

2 Talbott, Tim. "Logan's Station," Explore Kentucky History, (Accessed March 20, 2017), http://explorekyhistory.ky.gov/items/show/572.

3 *Journal of the Senate of the United States of America*, Vol. 9, 403. (https://memory. loc.gov/cgi-bin/ampage?collId=llsj&fileName=009/llsj009.db&recNum=401&item-Link=r%3Fammem%2Fhlaw%3A%40field(DOCID%2B%40lit%28s-j0091%29%29%3A%230090001&linkText=1 (Accessed 9/13/2019).

4 William Logan to Pricilla Logan, Jan. 9, 1820, in Letters from Filson Historical Society. Referencing Secretary and Mrs.. John Q. Adams.

5 "Obituary," Letters from Filson Historical Society.

Richard M. Johnson

1 Reed, Billy. "Richard M. Johnson—An Engaging Non-Conformist," *Louisville Courier-Journal*, April 12, 1976.

2 Reed, Billy. "Richard M. Johnson," The *Courier Journal*, 1976.

3 *Journal of the Senate of the United States of America*, Vol. 9, 60. https://memory.loc.gov/cgi-bin/ampage?collId=llsj&fileName=009/llsj009.db&recNum=58&itemLink=r%3Fammem%2F-hlaw%3A%40field%28DOCID%2B%40lit%28sj0091%29%29%3A%230090001&link-Text=1 (Accessed 10/13/2019).

4 *History of Congress (Annals of Congress), Senate 16th Congress, 2nd Session*, 381–382. Retrieved from https://memory.loc.gov/cgi-bin/ampage?collId=llac&fileName=037/llac037. db&recNum=188 (Accessed 10/13/2010).

5 *American State Papers, Senate 20th Congress, 2nd Session*, Post Office Department: Vol. 1, 211–212. Retrieved from https://memory.loc.gov/cgi-bin/ampage?collId=llsp&file-Name=027/llsp027.db&recNum=216 (Accessed 10/13/2019).

6 *Journal of the Senate of the United States of America*, Vol. 15, 198. Retrieved from https://mem-ory.loc.gov/cgi-bin/ampage?collId=llsj&fileName=015/llsj015.db&recNum=197&item-Link=r%3Fammem%2Fhlaw%3A%40field%28DOCID%2B%40lit%28s-j0151%29%29%3A%230150001&linkText=1 (Accessed 10/22/2019).

7 "An Act to Authorize the Issuing of Treasury Notes," *Acts of the 26th Congress of the United States,* Statue II, Retrieved from http://legisworks.org/congress/26/session-2/chap-2.pdf , (Accessed Jan. 16, 2017).

8 Ebelen, Tom. "Crumbling landmark tells a 'challenging story' Now Historic Landmark Will Be Saved!" *Lexington Herald-Leader*. June 21, 2018. Retrieved from https://www.kentucky.com/news/local/news-columns-blogs/tom-eblen/article213579309.html (Accessed 01/17/2020).

9   Reed, Billy "Richard M. Johnson," The *Courier Journal*, 1976.
10   *Louisville Journal*, "From the *Bangor Republican*," Sept. 14, 1836.

Henry Clay (Third and Fourth Terms)
1   Remini, Robert V. *Henry Clay: Statesman for the Union*, W.W. Norton, (November 17, 1993): 360–370.
2   Remini, *Henry Clay: Statesman for the Union*, 373.
3   Heidler & Heidler, *Henry Clay*, p. 237.
4   Remini, *Henry Clay: Statesman for the Union*, 371.
5   Heidler & Heidler, *Henry Clay*, 237.
6   Remini, *Henry Clay: Statesman for the Union*, 377.
7   Heidler &Heidler, *Henry Clay*, 229.
8   Heidler & Heidler, *Henry Clay*, 242–245.
9   Remini, *Henry Clay: Statesman for the Union*, 409.
10   Remini, *Henry Clay: Statesman for the Union*, 415.
11   Remini, *Henry Clay: Statesman for the Union*, 436.
12   Remini, *Henry Clay: Statesman for the Union*, 446.
13   Heidler & Heidler, *Henry Clay*, 314–315.
14   Remini, *Henry Clay: Statesman for the Union*, 606.

PART IV:

John J. Crittenden (Second and Third Terms)
1   The *Courier Journal*, May 9, 1836.
2   Kirwan, Albert D. *John J. Crittenden: The Struggle for the Union*, (Lexington: University of Kentucky Press, 1962): p. 88.
3   Kirwan, Albert. *John J. Crittenden; "The Struggle for the Union*," 89.
4   Kirwan, *John J. Crittenden; "The Struggle for the Union*," 91.
5   Kirwan, *John J. Crittenden; "The Struggle for the Union*,"97–98.
6   Kirwan, *John J. Crittenden; "The Struggle for the Union*," 102–103.
7   The *Indiana Herald*, Huntington, Indiana: August 5, 1863.
8   United States Senate. Retrieved from https://www.cop.senate.gov/artandhistory/history/common/generic/VP_John_Tyler.htm (Accessed 11/13/2019).
9   Kirwan, *John J. Crittenden; "The Struggle for the Union*," 164–166.
10   U.S. Capitol Visitor's Center, "The Annexation of Texas," Retrieved from https://www.visitthecapitol.gov/exhibitions/artifact/senate-roll-call-treaty-annexation-between-united-states-america-and-republic (Accessed 11/15/2019).
11   The *Louisville Daily Courier*, March 8, 1845, 2.
12   *Journal of the Senate of the United States of America*, Vol. 37, .288. Retrieved from https://memory.loc.gov/cgi-bin/ampage?collId=llsj&fileName=037/llsj037.db&recNum=287&itemLink=r%3Fammem%2Fhlaw%3A%40field%28DOCID%2B%40lit%28sj0371%29%29%3A%230370001&linkText=1 (Accessed 11/15/2019).
13   Kirwan, *John J. Crittenden; "The Struggle for the Union*," 196.
14   Kirwan, *John J. Crittenden; "The Struggle for the Union*," 200–203.
15   Kirwan, *John J. Crittenden; "The Struggle for the Union*," 205–206.

James Turner Morehead
1   The *Louisville Daily Courier*, Dec. 30, 1854.
2   *Journal of the Senate of the United States of America*, Vol 34, 7. Dec. 6, 1842. https://memory.loc.gov/cgi-bin/ampage?collId=llsj&fileName=034/llsj034.db&recNum=3&itemLink=r?ammem/hlaw:@field(DOCID+@lit(sj0341)):%230340001&linkText=1(Accessed 04/25/2020)
3   *Louisville Morning Courier*, March 12, 1847.
4   *Louisville Daily Courier*, Sept. 15, 1852.

Joseph R. Underwood

1   After the financial panic of 1819, the legislature replaced the pro-creditor "Old Court" with a pro-debtor "New Court." With a change of legislature in the late 1820s, the "New Court" was abolished and the "Old Court" restored. 83–84.

2   *Journal of the Senate of the United States of America*, Jan. 24, 1852, Vol. 42, 111–112. Retrieved from https://memory.loc.gov/cgi-bin/ampage?collId=llsj& ilename=042/llsj042.db & recNum=110&itemLink=r%3Fammem%2Fhlaw%3A%40field%28DOCID%2B%40lit%28sj0421%29%29%3A%230420001&linkText=1 (Accessed 06/12/2019).

3   Phillips, Christopher. "The Fall of the House of Underwood," *New York Times*, March 3, 2012.

Thomas "Stonehammer" Metcalfe

1   *Louisville Daily Courier*, June 26, 1848.

2   Mathias, Frank F. "Thomas Metcalfe," *Kentucky's Governors*, Updated Edition, Edited by Lowell H. Harrison, (Lexington: The University Press of Kentucky, 2004): 33–37.

3   *Journal of the Senate of the United States of America*, January 23, 1849. 140. Retrieved from https://memory.loc.gov/cgi-bin/ampage?collId=llsj&fileName=040/llsj040.db&recNum=139&itemLink=D?hlaw:14:./temp/~ammem_DFw4::%230400139&linkText=1 (Accessed 08/26/2019).

Henry Clay (Fifth Term)

1   Heidler, David and Jeanne Heidler, *Henry Clay*, 437.

2   Remini, *Henry Clay: Statesman for the Union*, 716.

3   Remini, *Henry Clay: Statesman for the Union*, 715.

4   Remini, *Henry Clay: Statesman for the Union*, 726.

5   Remini, *Henry Clay: Statesman for the Union*, 728.

6   Heidler and Heidler, *Henry Clay*, 469–470.

7   Heidler and Heidler, *Henry Clay*, 473.

8   Heidler and Heidler, *Henry Clay*, 474.

9   Heidler and Heidler, *Henry Clay*, 476–478.

10 Heidler and Heidler, *Henry Clay*, 479–480.

11 Heidler and Heidler, *Henry Clay*, 491–492.

12 History, Art & Archives, "U.S. House of Representatives, Individuals Who Have Lain in State or Honor," Retrieved from https://history.house.gov/Institution/Lie-In-State/Lie-In-State/ (Accessed 11/02/2019).

13 Heidler and Heidler, *Henry Clay*, 484.

David Meriwether

1   *Journal of the Senate of the United States of America*, Aug. 6, 1852.Volume 43, 529. Retrieved from https://memory.loc.gov/cgi-bin/ampage?collId=llsj&fileName=043/llsj043.db&recNum=528&itemLink=r%3Fammem%2Fhlaw%3A@field%28DOCID%2B@lit%28sj0431%29%29%3A%230430001&linkText=1 (Accessed 11/04/2019).

2   *Journal of the Senate of the United States of America*, Vol. 44, 46. Retrieved from https://memory.loc.gov/cgi-bin/ampage?collId=llsj&fileName=044/llsj044.db&recNum=45&itemLink=r%3Fammem%2Fhlaw%3A@field%28DOCID%2B@lit%28s-j0441%29%29%3A%230440001&linkText=1 (Accessed 11/04/2019).

3   Fletcher, Noel Marie. *Taos News*, Retrieved from https://www.taosnews.com/stories/the-trials-and-triumphs-of-david-meriwether, 59665 (Accessed 11/04/2019).

PART V

Archibald Dixon

1   *Spirit of the Age*, Raleigh: September 27, 1853.

2   The *Courier Journal*, June 9, 1876, 3.

3   *Messenger-Inquirer*, Owensboro: October 11, 1934, 3.

4   Pettus, Gertrude. "The Issues in the Kentucky Constitutional Convention 1849–1850." 1941, 15.

5   Pettus, Gertrude. "The Issues in the Kentucky Constitutional Convention 1849–1850." 37.

6   The *Courier Journal*, "Election of Hon. Archie Dixon to the U.S. Senate", December 31, 1851.

7   *Journal of the Senate of the United States of America*, Vol. 4. 6.

8   *Journal of the Senate of the United States Senate*, p. 44 & 45. https://memory.loc.gov/cgi-bin/ampage?collId=llsj&fileName=044/llsj044.db&recNum=0&itemLink=r?ammem/hlaw:@field(DOCID+@lit(sj0441)):%230440001&linkText=1.

9   The *Sun*, ""Some New Books" (A book review) *The Missouri Compromise*," New York: February 12, 1899, 14.

10   *The Appendix to the Congressional Globe, 33rd Cong. 1st Session*, "The Nebraska-Kansas Bill,— Mr. Dixon" 140–145. Retrieved from https://memory.loc.gov/cgi-bin/ampage?collId=llcg&fileName=036/llcg036.db&recNum=151(Accessed 10/06/2019).

11   *The Appendix to the Congressional Globe, 33d Cong. 1st Session*, The Fugitive Slave Law—Mr. Dixon" 1024–1025. Retrieved from https://memory.loc.gov/cgi-bin/ampage?collId=llcg&fileName=036/llcg036.db&recNum=1031 (Accessed 10/06/2010).

12   Ibid, 1024.

13   The *Weekly Standard*, Raleigh: October 24, 1855.

14   The *Kentucky Tribune*, Danville: November 2, 1855.

15   The *Pantagraph*, "Dixon Endorses Douglas," Bloomington, IL: August 27, 1858.

16   The *Philadelphia Inquirer*, June 12, 1861, 4.

17   The *Courier Journal*, June 9, 1876.

John Burton Thompson

1   Mathias, *Kentucky's Governors*, ed. Lowell Harrison, 75.

2   *Daily Nashville Union*, Dec.15, 1851. 3.

3   *Senate Journal*, March 4, 1853.

4   The *Louisville Daily Courier*, April 26, 1854.

5   The *Louisville Daily Courier*, Dec. 20, 1854.

6   The *Louisville Daily Courier*, March 26, 1858.

7   The *Louisville Daily Courier*, Jan. 7, 1874.

John J. Crittenden (Fourth Term)

1   Remini, Robert, V. *Henry Clay: Statesman for the Union*, (New York: W.W. Norton & Company, 1991): 703.

2   Kirwan, Albert D. *John J. Crittenden; "The Struggle for the Union*," "Kentucky Interlude, Chapter 12," (Lexington: University of Kentucky Press, 1962).

3   Kirwan, Albert D. *John J. Crittenden; "The Struggle for the Union*," 284.

4   Remini, Albert D. *Henry Clay: Statesman for the Union*, 780–781.

5   Kirwan, Albert D. *John J. Crittenden; "The Struggle for the Union*," 269–270.

6   Kirwan, Albert D. *John J. Crittenden; "The Struggle for the Union*," 272–278.

7   Kirwan, Albert D. *John J. Crittenden; "The Struggle for the Union*," 279.

8   Kirwan, Albert D. *John J. Crittenden; "The Struggle for the Union*," 285.

9   *Journal of the United States Senate*, Monday December 3, 1855, Retrieved from https://memory.loc.gov/cgi-bin/query/D?hlaw:18:./temp/~ammem_H30a:: (Accessed March 21, 2017).

10   *Journal of the Senate of the United States*, Wednesday, December 12, 1855, Retrieved from https://memory.loc.gov/cgi-bin/query/D?hlaw:8:./temp/~ammem_H30a::.

11   Kirwan, Albert D. *John J. Crittenden; "The Struggle for the Union,"* 313.

12   *Senate Journal*, Retrieved from http://www2.ku.edu/~imlskto/cgi-bin/index.php?SCREEN=show_document&document_id=102869&thumbnailcount=8&SCREEN_FROM=show_document&submit=search&search=Kansas Nebraska%&startsearchat=15&searchfor=&document_id=102869&county_id=&topic_id=&selected_keyword= (Accessed May 16, 2017).

13   Barry, Robert T. "Kentuckians Who Made History." The *Courier Journal*, March 4, 1917.

14   *Burlington Weekly Free Press*, "Votes on the Kansas Bill," Burlington, Vermont: May 7, 1858.

15   The *Louisville Daily Courier*, "The Funeral Ceremonies of the Seven Unfortunates," June 28, 1858.

16   *Cincinnati Enquirer,* "Reception of Hon. John J. Crittenden," June 20, 1858.

17   The *Courier Journal,* "Senate Moved Into New Hall," January 4, 1909.

18   Kirwan, Albert D. *John J. Crittenden; "The Struggle for the Union,"* 347.

19   *Journal of the Senate of the United States of America,* Retrieved from http://www.memory.loc. gov/cgi-bin/ampage?collId=llsj&fileName=052/llsj052.db&recNum=48&itemLink=r?am-mem/hlaw:@field(DOCID+@lit(sj0522)):%230520003&linkText= (Accessed May 12, 2017). Vol. 52, 49.

20   *Journal of the Senate of the United States of America,* Vol. 52, , 68.

21   *Journal of the Senate of the United States of America,* Vol. 52, , 50.

22   *Journal of the Senate of the United States of America,* Vol. 52, 71.

23   *Journal of the Senate of the United States of America,* Vol.52, 78.

24   *Journal of the Senate of the United States of America,* Vol.52, 88.

25   *Journal of the Senate of the United States of America,* Vol 52, 94.

26   *Journal of the Senate of the United States of America,* Vol. 52, 98.

27   Kirwan, *John J. Crittenden; "The Struggle for the Union,"* 425–426.

28   The *Summit County Beacon,* January 10, 1861: The *New York Times'* telegraphy says: Washington Jan 8; "Important from Washington—Washington, Jan, 2; The Crittenden Compromise; Washington, Jan 6.

29   Kirwan, Albert D. *John J. Crittenden; "The Struggle for the Union,"* 420–421.

30   Kirwan, Albert D. *John J. Crittenden; "The Struggle for the Union,"* 436–438.

31   Kirwan, Albert D. *John J. Crittenden; "The Struggle for the Union,"* 438.

32   Kirwan, Albert D. *John J. Crittenden; "The Struggle for the Union,"* 439.

33   Crittenden, John J. *The Life of John J. Crittenden, With Selections from His Correspondence and Speeches. Edited by his daughter, Mrs. Chapman Coleman, Vol. II,* J.P. Lippincott. Philadelphia: 1871. p. 380–381.

Lazarus Powell

1   *Louisville Daily Courier,* June 16, 1856.

2   *Louisville Daily Courier,* July 14, 1860.

3   The *New York Times,* "The Kentucky Legislature," Oct. 2, 1861.

4   Harris, William C. "His Loyal Opposition: Lincoln's Border State Critics," *Journal of the Abraham Lincoln Association,* Vol. 31, 1, 2011, 1–7. Retrieved from http://quod.lib.umich.edu/j/jala/2629860.0032.103/--his-loyal-opposition-lincolns-border-states-critics?rgn=main;view=-fulltext. (Accessed Dec. 24, 2016).

5   *U.S. Senate Historical Office, United States Senate Election, Expulsion and Censure Cases: 1793–1990,* (Washington: Government Printing Office, 1995) 112–114. Retrieved from http://www.senate.gov/artandhistory/history/common/expulsion_cases/042LazarusPowell_expulsion.htm.

6   *Louisville Daily Courier,* Jan. 23, 1867.

7   *Louisville Daily Courier,* July 6, 1867.

John C. Breckinridge

1   *Daily Courier,* "Letter from Frankfort: Prelude—Harmony in the Democratic," Dec. 13, 1859.

2   *Daily Courier,* "Latest by Telegraph: Acceptance of Hon. John C. Breckinridge of the Nomination for the Presidency," July 11, 1860.

3   *Journal of the Senate of the United States of America,* March 4, 1861. Volume 52, 402, Retrieved from https://memory.loc.gov/cgi-bin/ampage?collId=llsj&fileName=052/llsj052.db&recNum=401&itemLink=r?ammem/hlaw:@field(DOCID+@lit(sj0269)):%230520402&linkText=1 (Accessed 9/13/2019).

4   The *Louisville Daily Courier,* April 16, 1861.

5   The *Senate Journal,* Dec. 4, 1861, 22–23.

6   The *Courier-Journal,* "Dust to Dust: Funeral Service-Over the Remains of Gen. John C. Breckinridge," May 20, 1875.

PART VI

Garrett Davis

1   The *New York Times*, Dec. 17, 1861.
2   The *New York Times*, May 31, 1861.
3   Astor, Aaron, "Disunion; Bluegrass Blues and Grays," The *New York Times*, May 7, 2011.
4   The *New York Times*, "Jefferson Davis and Garret Davis," March 28, 1862.
5   Klein, Philip S., *President James Buchanan, A Biography*, Sixth Printing of the First Edition, (Newtown, CT. American Political Biography Press, 2015): 409–410.
6   Hernon, Joseph M., *Profiles in Character: Hubris and Heroism in the U.S. Senate, 1789-1990*, (New York: M.E. Sharper, 1997): 72.
7   The *New York Times*, Jan.14, 1865.
8   The *New York Times*, "The Proposed Expulsion of Senator Davis," Jan. 28, 1864.
9   The *Louisville Daily Courier*, "Hon. Garrett Davis' Opinion Filed in Connection with the Impeachment Trial," June 17, 1868.
10   The *Cincinnati Enquirer*, Sept. 25, 1872.

James Guthrie

1   The *Louisville Daily Courier*, Oct. 19, 1859.
2   Bussey, Charles J. *James Gutherie: Kentucky Politician and Entrepreneur; Kentucky Profiles: Biographical Essays in Honor of Holman Hamilton*. Edited by James C. Klotter and Peter J. Sehlinger, The Kentucky Historical Society, (Frankfort: 1982): p. 65.
3   Johnson, Leland R and Parrish, Charles E. "Triumph at the falls: the Louisville and Portland Canal Louisville District U.S. Army Corps of Engineers", (Louisville: 2007): 90.
4   Kentucky Historical Society, "James Guthrie," Kentucky's Abraham Lincoln, Retrieved from http://www.lrc.ky.gov/record/Moments09RS/web/Lincoln%20moments%2016.pdf   (Accessed April 6, 2017).
5   *Louisville Daily Courier*, "The News," Jan. 23, 1866.
6   The *Louisville Daily Courier*, Jan. 26, 1866, 1.
7   Ibid.
8   The *Louisville Daily Courier*, Feb. 11, 1868.
9   The *Louisville Daily Journal*, Feb. 17, 1868.

Thomas Clay McCreery

1   The *Louisville Daily Courier*, Feb. 14, 1868.
2   The *Louisville Daily Courier*, March 8, 1868.
3   The *Louisville Daily Courier*, Sept. 30, 1868.
4   The *Louisville Daily Courier*, Sept. 30, 1868.
5   Patler, Nicholas, "Chapter 12: The Startling Career of P.B.S. Pinchback: A Whirlwind Crusade to Bring Equality to Reconstructed Louisiana" Matthew Lynch, editor. *Before Obama: A Reappraisal of Black Reconstruction Era Politicians, Volume 1: Legacies Lost: The Life and Times of John R. Lynch and His Political Contemporaries*. (Santa Barbara: Praeger, an Imprint of ABC-CLIO, LLC, 2012): 228.
6   The *Courier Journal*, Dec. 20, 1871.
7   *Louisville Courier Journal*, July 12, 1890.
8   Patler, Nicholas. *Before Obama: A Reappraisal of Black Reconstruction Era Politicians*, "Chapter 12."
9   Patler, Nicholas. Lynch, Matthew editor. *Before Obama: A Reappraisal of Black Reconstruction Era Politicians, Volume 1: Legacies Lost: The Life and Times of John R. Lynch and His Political Contemporaries*. Praeger, an Imprint of ABC-CLIO, LLC, Santa Barbara. 2012, Vol.1, 228.
10   The *Courier Journal*, July 12, 1890.
11   The *Courier Journal*, July 12, 1890.

John W. Stevenson

1 The *Louisville Daily Courier*, Sept. 9, 1867.
2 The *Courier Journal*, Feb. 14, 1868.
3 The *Courier Journal*, Sunday, Aug. 15, 1897, Section 2.
4 *Journal of the Senate of the United States of America*, Saturday, March 4, 1871(https://memory.loc.gov/cgi-bin/query/D?hlaw:2:./temp/~ammem_NJ4r:)
5 The *Cincinnati Enquirer*, July 11, 1872.
6 The *Cincinnati Enquirer*, March 31, 1876.
7 Gamm, Gerald and Smith, Steven S. "The Rise of Floor Leaders in the United States Senate, 1890–1915." A paper presented for the Conference on the U.S. Senate, (Rothermere American Institute, Oxford University, April 2–3, 2005).
8 The *Cincinnati Enquirer*, Saturday Dec. 23, 1876.
9 The *Cincinnati Enquirer*, January 15, 1876.
10 The *Cincinnati Enquirer*, June 8, 1883.
11 The *Cincinnati Enquirer*, "Hon. John W. Stevenson: Death of Another Great Democratic Leader," August 11, 1886.
12 The *Cincinnati Enquirer* August 14, 1886.

Willis Benson Machen

1 The *Courier Journal*, Feb. 17, 1859.
2 *Louisville Courier Journal*, Dec. 9, 1858.
3 The *Louisville Daily Courier*, Nov. 23, 1861.
4 The *Courier Journal*, "Ex-United States Senator W.B. Machen of Eddyville, Taken to the Hopkinsville Asylum," Sunday September 10, 1893, 3.

PART VII

1 *Encyclopedia Britannica*, "United States Presidential Election of 1876". Retrieved from https://www.britannica.com/event/United-States-presidential-election-of-1876/The-disputed-election (Accessed 11/9/2019).

James Burnie Beck

1 The *Cincinnati Enquirer*, "The Kentucky Senatorship," January 19, 1876.
2 The *Cincinnati Enquirer*, "KENTUCKY'S GRIEF: At Her Terrible Bereavement General Sorrow Caused...," May 4, 1890.
3 Ibid.
4 The *New York Times*, "Democratic Nominees for Congress—Their Status—Antecedents and Prospects—Significance of the Recent Senatorial Election, and of the forthcoming Democratic and Union State Conventions," *Correspondence of the New York Times*, Kentucky: February 11, 1867.
5 The *Courier Journal*, "SENATOR-ELECT BECK: What is Thought of Him Throughout the Country—Press Comments," January 22, 1876.
6 The *Cincinnati Enquirer*, January 19, 1876.
7 The *Cincinnati Enquirer*, "SENATOR BECK. The Life History of Kentucky's Statesman," Jan 16, 1886.
8 The *New York Times*, "WEDDING IN HIGH LIFE. An Interesting Social Event In Kentucky—Marriage of Major Goodloe, of the Marines to To The Daughter of Senator Beck," April 18, 1877.
9 The *New York Times*, "SENATOR BECK IS DEAD. He expires suddenly In A Washington Railroad Station," May 4, 1890.
10 The *New York Times*, "Singular Statement of Senator Beck," July 14, 1881.
11 The *Courier Journal*, "Mr. Beck's Successor," July 18, 1881.
12 Barry, Robert T. "Kentuckians Who Have Made History." The *Courier Journal*, August 19, 1917.
13 The *Courier Journal*, "Special to The *Courier Journal*," December 3, 1881.

14   The *Courier Journal*, "THE LEGISLATURE: Senator Beck Formally Elected to Succeed Himself," December 7, 1881.

15   The *Courier Journal*, December 15, 1881.

16   The *Courier Journal*, April 5, 1882.

17   The *New York Times*, "BLACKBURN, BECK & CO.—To Fight The President on the Silver Question," December 28, 1885.

18   The *New York Times*, September 1, 1888.

19   The *Courier Journal*, March 7, 1887.

20   The *Courier Journal*, April 13, 1887.

21   The *Courier Journal*, July 20, 1887.

22   The *New York Times*, "SENATOR BECK IS DEAD. He expires suddenly In A Washington Railroad Station," May 3, 1890.

23   The *Courier Journal*, April 4, 1890.

24   The *New York Times*, "THE SENATE IN MOURNING; JAMES B. BECK'S CHAIR AND DESK DRAPED IN BLACK. THE FUNERAL TO BE HELD IN THE CAPITOL AT 1 O'CLOCK TO-DAY—ACTION OF BOTH HOUSES." May 6, 1890.

25   The *Courier Journal*, May 9, 1890.

26   The *Courier-Journal*, "BECK IS BURIED: Under the Shadow of Henry Clay's Monument the Dead. . ." May 9, 1890.

27   The *New York Times*, "GEORGE W.T. BECK OF WYOMING DIES; Rancher and Oil Operator Is Stricken at 87—Last Head of Territory Council," December 3, 1943.

John Stuart Williams

1   The *Courier Journal*, January 17, 1878.

2   The *Courier Journal*, July 18, 1898.

3   *Chattanooga Daily Times*, "Civil War Album" January 8, 1962.

4   *Breckinridge News*, Cloverport, KY: October 10, 1883.

5   The *New York Times*, January 19, 1878.

6   The *New York Times*, August 24, 1878.

7   The *Courier Journal*, March 13, 1880.

8   The *New York Times*, March 13, 1880.

9   The *New York Times*, "Another Duel Averted" May 20, 1882.

10   The *Courier Journal*, February 7, 1882.

11   The *Courier Journal*, January 5, 1883.

12   The *New York Times*, January 5, 1884.

13   The *Courier Journal*, January 5, 1884.

14   The *Courier Journal*, January 16, 1884.

15   The *Courier Journal*, January 17, 1884.

16   The *Courier Journal*, February 6, 1884.

17   The *New York Times*, April 6, 1884.

18   The *Courier Journal*, November 8, 1891.

19   "Brief History of Naples, Florida" Retrieved from https://naplesfloridavacationhomes.com/brief-history-naples-florida/ (Accessed 11/23/2019).

20   The *Courier Journal*, July 18, 1898.

Joseph Stiles Blackburn

1   The *Courier Journal*, "Mrs. Mary Morris. Death of a Venerable Woman Whose Life Was Filled With Acts of Kindness to the Poor and Afflicted," October 19, 1884.

2   The *Courier Journal*, "Clifford Berryman, 80, Political Cartoonist, Dies," December 12, 1949.

3   *U.S. Congressional Record, 44th Congress Second Session*, March 1, 1877, V. Part 3, 2062.

4   The *New York Times*, "Another Duel Averted," May 19, 1882.

5   Tapp, Hambleton, and James C. Klotter, *Kentucky: Decades of Discord, 1865–1900*. Kentucky Historical Society, (University Press of Kentucky, 1977): 225.

6   Tapp, Hambleton, and James C. Klotter, *Kentucky: Decades of Discord, 1865–1900*, 225.

7   Tapp, Hambleton, and James C. Klotter, *Kentucky: Decades of Discord, 1865–1900*, 225.

8   Tapp, Hambleton, and James C. Klotter, *Kentucky: Decades of Discord, 1865–1900*, 212–213.

9   Tapp, Hambleton, and James C. Klotter, *Kentucky: Decades of Discord, 1865–1900*, 212–213.

10   Tapp, Hambleton, and James C. Klotter, *Kentucky: Decades of Discord, 1865-1900*, 251.

11   The *Courier Journal*, "Boyle—The Republican Standard Bearer for Senator," March 6, 1896.

12   The *Courier Journal*, March 6, 1896.

13   The *Courier Journal*, "The Long Struggle Ended At Last," April 29, 1897.

14   The *New York Times*, "The Field In Kentucky," September 28, 1896.

15   The *New York Times*, "Beckham Takes Control," February 4, 1900.

16   The *Courier Journal*, October 31, 1903; IMMENSE, Crowd At Open Meeting of the Democratic Club

17   Schlup, Leonard. "Joseph Blackburn of Kentucky and the Panama Question." *Filson Club Quarterly* 51, October 1977 p. 353–354

18   Schlup, Leonard. "Joseph Blackburn of Kentucky and the Panama Question." *Filson Club Quarterly* 51, October 1977, 354–355.

19   The *New York Times*, "Jos. C.S. Blackburn, Is Dead," September 3, 1919.

John G. Carlisle

1   Barnes, James A. *John G. Carlisle—Financial Statesman*, (Dodd, Mead and Company, 1931, Reprinted 1967): 7.

2   Barnes, James A. *John G. Carlisle—Financial Statesman*, 157–158.

3   Barnes, James A. *John G. Carlisle—Financial Statesman*, 164.

4   Barnes, James A. *John G. Carlisle—Financial Statesman*, 70–71.

5   Barnes, James A. *John G. Carlisle—Financial Statesman*, 182.

6   Ibid.

7   History, Art & Archives, United States House of Representatives, "Historical Highlights," Retrieved from https://history.house.gov/Historical-Highlights/1851-1900/The-McKinley-Tariff-of-1890/ (Accessed 11/30/2011).

8   Barnes, James A. *John G. Carlisle—Financial Statesman*, 182.

9   Barnes, James A. *John G. Carlisle—Financial Statesman*, 196.

10   Barnes, James A. *John G. Carlisle—Financial Statesman*, 197.

11   Barnes, James A. *John G. Carlisle—Financial Statesman*, 199–200.

12   The *Cincinnati Enquirer*, January 21, 1893.

13   Whitten, David O. "The Depression of 1893", *Economic History Association*, Retrieved from https://eh.net/encyclopedia/the-depression-of-1893/ (Accessed 11/30/2019).

14   The *Clarksburg Telegram*, Clarksburg, WV: March 8, 1895, 5.

William Lindsay

1   The *New York Times*, Feb. 15, 1893.

2   The *Inter Ocean*, Chicago: November 14, 1899.

3   The *New York Times*, Nov. 24, 1896.

4   The *New York Times*, August 14, 1896.

5   The *New York Times*, "Anybody Can Beat Bryan," May 1, 1900.

6   Ibid.

7   Ibid.

8   The *New York Times*, Aug. 10, 1902.

9   The *New York Times*, Feb. 8, 1934.

Part VIII

1   *Beatrice Express*, Beatrice, Nebraska: May 14, 1897.

2   The *Courier Journal*, February 29, 1908.

William J. Deboe

1 The *Cincinnati Enquirer.* "Deboe Names the Winners. Johnnie Myers to be Postmaster at Newport," May 9, 1897.

2 The *Cincinnati Enquirer*, February 8, 1898.

3 The *Cincinnati Enquirer*, July 20, 1899.

4 The *Courier Journal*, "Deboe's Men Go To Louisville to Help Taylor Pass Through Louisville," December 4, 1899.

5 The *Courier Journal*, "Deboe's Men," December 4, 1899.

6 The *New York Times*, January 3, 1900.

7 The *New York Times*, November 6, 1901.

8 The *New York Times*, "Senator Deboe Declines; Will Not Be Republican Candidate for Governor of Kentucky," July 14, 1902, 1.

9 The *Courier Journal.* "Is the Prepared Patronage Slate of Deboe SENATOR SEES THE PRESIDENT Settled That Sapp's Name Will Go To the Senate" (Washington May 26) May 27, 1897.

10 The *Courier Journal*, July 12, 1897.

11 The *Courier Journal*, June 29, 1899.

12 The *Courier Journal*, January 5, 1902.

13 The *Courier Journal*, February 26, 1898.

14 The *Courier Journal*, July 17, 1901.

15 The *Courier Journal*, March 9, 1901.

16 The *Courier Journal*, May 15, 1901.

17 The *New York Times*, January 4, 1903.

James B. McCreary

1 The *New York Times*, "McCreary Elected Senator," January 15, 1902.

2 The *New York Times*, "Ex-Gov. McCreary to be Senator from Kentucky," January 10, 1902.

3 The *Baltimore Sun*, "Mrs. James B. McCreary," December 13, 1903.

4 *Washington Post*, "James B. McCreary of Kentucky," June 1, 1906.

5 The *Saint Paul Globe*, "New Found Friend, Salisbury's Accession to Power As Viewed by Bi-Metallist, Preferred to Rosebery; Chairman M'Creary of the Foreign Affairs Committee, Likes the Change," June 25, 1895.

6 *Interior Journal*, "Hon, James B. McCreary, Some of the Things Our Congressman done," Stanford, KY: September 21, 1894.

7 The *Courier Journal*, "DEBATE ON: Four Senatorial Candidates On the Stump," Sept. 24, 1901.

8 *Nashville American* quoted in the *Interior Journal*, Stanford, KY: January 24, 1902, 2.

9 The *Courier Journal*, "IS PREPARED: To See Parker the Nominee For President SENATOR M'CREARY," May 12, 1904, 6.

10 The *Big Sandy News*, "Senator James B. McCreary," Louisa, Kentucky: December 8, 1905, 2.

11 The *Senate Journal*, Retrieved from https://www.senate.gov/artandhistory/history/common/generic/FarewellAddressBook.htm; (Accessed April 2, 2017).

12 The *Cincinnati Enquirer*, "What McCreary Expects," November 30, 1905.

13 The *Courier Journal*, "Gaines Speaks for M'Creary 'Says He Lifted His Voices For Farmers of Kentucky,'" November 1, 1906.

14 *Kentucky Irish American*, "M'Creary-Statesman Soldier and Patriot the Next Senator from Kentucky—Has Characteristics That Distinguish Sons of the Emerald Isle," Louisville: October 27, 1906.

15 The *Cincinnati Enquirer*, "PRESENCE: Of Ancient Enemies, Who Have Felt the Weight of the Beckham... SPECIAL DISPATCH TO THE ENQUIRER," Dec 19, 1907.

16 The *Courier Journal*, "Peace Society Will Banquet," March 20, 1909.

17 Ibid.

Thomas Paynter

1 The *Courier Journal*, "Paynter Received 59 of the 105 Joint Votes. 53 were Necessary for Election," Jan. 3, 1906.

2   The *Cincinnati Enquirer*, March 18, 1905.
3   The *Courier Journal*, "Paynter: Makes Public His Letter To Blackburn His Services on the Bench Needed Because of Illness of Judge Cantrill Issues Between Aspirants He Says Are Not So Great As To Require a Joint Discussion Which Might Hurt the Party in the Close Districts," April 12, 1905.
4   The *Courier Journal*, Aug. 7, 1907.
5   The *Cincinnati Enquirer*, Nov. 21, 1909.
6   The *Cincinnati Enquirer*, "Paynter Asks Justice for Kentucky Farmers and Arraigns the Tactics of Tobacco Combine," May 13, 1909.
7   Jackman, William James, and Jacob Harris, *History of the American Nation: A History of the American People*, (1911): 1552.
8   "The Election Case of William Lorimer of Illinois (1910;1912)," United States Senate, Retrieved from http://www.senate.gov/artandhistory/history/common/contested_elections/095William_Lorimer.htm. (Accessed April 12, 2017).
9   The *New York Times*, Feb. 2, 1913.
10   The *New York Times*, March 1, 1913.
11   The *Courier Journal*, June 28, 1914.
12   The *Courier Journal*, Nov. 10, 1915.
13   The *Courier Journal*, June 26, 1914.
14   The *Courier Journal*, June 26, 1914.

William O. Bradley

1   The *Courier Journal*, Feb. 29, 1908.
2   The *Courier Journal*, March 20, 1880.
3   The *Courier Journal*, March 9, 1901.
4   The *Courier Journal*, June 20, 1908.
5   The *Courier Journal*, Sept. 20, 1908.
6   The *Courier Journal*, Aug. 15, 1909.
7   The *Courier Journal*, June 2, 1910.
8   The *Courier Journal*, Feb. 9, 1912.
9   The *Cincinnati Enquirer*, June 12, 1912.
10   The *Courier Journal*, May 24, 1914.
11   The *Courier Journal*, May 24, 1914.

PART IX

1   The *Cincinnati Enquirer*, June 20, 1916.
2   The *Owensboro Messenger*, August 13, 1916.

Ollie M. James

1   Ollie M. James (Late a Senator from Kentucky) Memorial Addresses; Delivered in the Senate and the House of Representatives of the United States; Sixty-Fifth Congress Third Session; Proceedings in the House, February 2, 1919 (Washington: Joint Committee on Printing, 1920): 24.
2   The *New York Times*, Jan. 11, 1912.
3   Special to The *New York Times*, August 11, 1904.
4   The *Courier Journal*, "James Candidate for U.S. Senator: First District Congressman Makes Announcement would Succeed Paynter in United States Senate Not After Speakership," Sept. 23, 1910.
5   The *Courier Journal*, "James Campaign Expenses—Costs Kentucky's New Senator $2,832 To Land New Toga," Jan. 10, 1912.
6   Memorial Addresses, 68.
7   Klotter, James, C. *Kentucky: Portrait in Paradox, 1900–1950* "Politics the Damnedest—In Kentucky: 1900–1919, 223.
8   The *Courier Journal*, May 30, 1914.

9   The *New York Times*, "Senator James Eulogistic; Tells President He Is Called Again to Serve Nation and Mankind," Sept. 3, 1916.

10   Memorial Addresses, 113.

11   The *New York Times*, Aug. 29, 1918.

12   "Free Speech in War Time," United States Senate, Retrieved from http://www.senate.gov/artandhistory/history/minute/Free_Speech_In_Wartime.htm. (Accessed Feb. 7, 2017).

13   The *New York Times*, Aug. 29, 1918.

14   The *New York Times*, May 17, 1918.

15   The *Cincinnati Enquirer*, May 24, 1918.

16   The *New York Times*, June 1918.

17   The *New York Times*, June 26, 1918.

18   The *New York Times*, Aug. 29, 1918.

19   Ollie M. James Memorial Addresses, 7.

20   Ibid, 50.

21   Ibid, 11.

22   The *New York Times*, Dec. 11, 1921.

23   The *New York Times*, Sept. 18, 1961.

John N. Camden

1   The *Courier Journal*, May 31, 1914.

2   The *Courier Journal*, Nov. 11, 1912.

3   The *Courier Journal*, June 19, 1914.

4   The *Courier Journal*, Aug. 5, 1914.

5   The *Courier Journal*, April 26, 1908.

6   The *New York Times*, Aug. 17, 1942.

7   Ibid.

John C. W. Beckham

1   The *New York Times*, Feb. 4, 1900.

2   The *New York Times*, Feb. 4, 1900.

3   Finch, Glen. "The Election of United States Senators in Kentucky: The Beckham Period," *Filson Club History Quarterly*, Jan., 1970, 39.

4   Finch, "U.S. Senators in Kentucky," *Filson*, p. 40.

5   The *Courier Journal*, Jan. 20, 1908.

6   Libbey, James, *Alben Barkley: A Life in Politics*, (Lexington: University of Kentucky Press, 2016): 30–31.

7   The *Courier Journal*, November 3, 1914.

8   The *Courier Journal*, "Kentucky Senators Divide Patronage—Agreement Made and Post Masters for Several Cities Announced," June 20, 1915.

9   The *Courier Journal*, "Beckham Opens M'Lean Fight: Begins Democratic Campaign in Western Kentucky," Oct. 8, 1916.

10   The *New York Times*, "Senate Rejects 62 to 17, Tax of 73% on Profits—Heavy Vote Against Johnson Amendment Believed to Doom All Radical Proposals," Sept. 2, 1917.

11   The *Courier Journal*, March 20, 1919.

12   The *New York Times*, July 23, 1919.

13   The *New York Times*, July 23, 1919.

14   The *New York Times*, July 23, 1919.

15   The *New York Times*, July 2, 1920.

16   The *Courier Journal*, Nov. 1920.

17   The *Courier Journal*, Feb. 13, 1921.

18   Finch, Glenn, "The Election of United States Senators: The Beckham Period," *Filson Club Quarterly*, January 1970, 43.

19   Finch, Glenn, "The Election of United States Senators: The Beckham Period," *Filson Club Quarterly*, January 1970, 44.

George Brown Martin

1   The *Courier Journal*, "A Public Duty," Sept. 7, 1918.
2   The *Courier Journal*, "The Old Lady's Letterbox: Old Woman to Old Lady", September 7, 1918.
3   The *Cincinnati Enquirer*, Sept. 18, 1918.
4   The *Cincinnati Enquirer*, Sept. 18, 1918.
5   The *Courier Journal*, Oct. 6, 1918.
6   The *Courier Journal*, Sept. 28, 1918.
7   The *Courier Journal*, Dec. 18, 1918.
8   The *Courier Journal*, Jan. 8, 1919.
9   The *Courier Journal*, Feb. 5, 1919.
10   The *Courier Journal*, "Senator Martin to See Battlefields," Feb. 8, 1919.
11   The *New York Times*, June 23, 1932.
12   The *New York Times*, Aug. 10, 1932.

Part X

Augustus Owsley Stanley

1   *Kentucky Profiles—Biographical Essays in Honor of Holman Hamilton*, Edited by James C. Klotter and Peter J. Sehlinger, The Kentucky Historical Society, Frankfort: 1982, p. 155–179—article on Augustus O. Stanley Early Twentieth Century Democrat.
2   The *Courier Journal*, "The Old Lady's Letterbox: Old Woman to Old Lady," September 18, 1918, 4.
3   The *New York Times*, "Wilson Supports Stanley," September 22, 1918.
4   The *Courier Journal*, "Stanley Takes Oath of Office As U.S. Senator," May 20, 1919.
5   Ibid.
6   The *New York Times*, "Fight By Senators To Curb Rum Raids Dims Hopes," August 21, 1921.
7   The *New York Times*, "Deadlock Blocks Anti-Beer Measure," August 23, 1921.
8   The *New York Times*, "Warns Of Dry Laws As Peril To Nation—Senator Stanley of Kentucky," June 18, 1922.
9   *News and Observer*, "Speeches Feature Bankers' Meeting; Senator Stanley and W.H. Booth, of N.Y., Speak," Raleigh, NC: May 26, 1921.
10   *Kentucky Advocate*, "Bureaucratic Government," Danville: September 22, 1922.
11   The *New York Times*, "Pleads For Tolerance; Senator Stanley of Kentucky Speaks at Temple Emanu-El," April 30, 1923.
12   The *Courier Journal*, "Mother of Senator Stanley dies at 85," December 30, 1922.
13   The *Courier Journal*, "Stanley and Sackett Run Ahead For Nomination," August 3, 1924.
14   The *New York Times*, "Labor Chiefs Claim Primary Victories—Assert They Helped Defeat Shields in Tennessee and Aided Stanley in Kentucky," August 13, 1924.
15   The *Advocate-Messenger*, "Wealth of the Country Has Dwindled, Says Senator Stanley," Danville: September 24, 1924.
16   The *New York Times*, "Senator Stanley Hit By Washington Auto," February 25, 1925.
17   The *Courier Journal*, "No Vacancy," October 25, 1953.
18   The *Courier Journal*, "Stanley's Funeral To Be Today In Capital, Saturday in Frankfort," April 14, 1958.
19   The *Courier Journal*, "Stanley's Funeral To Be Today, Body Lies In State Capitol," April 16, 1958.
20   Pace, C.J. The *Courier Journal*, "Stanley's Belief," Louisville: September 7, 1958.
21   The *Courier Journal*, "A.O. Stanley Jr., dies; was late senator's son," September 9, 1979.

Richard P. Ernst

1   *Biographical Directory of the United States Congress—1774 to Present*, Ernst, Richard P. Retrieved from http://bioguide.congress.gov/scripts/biodisplay.pl?index=E000206.
2   The *Cincinnati Enquirer*, "MEN WE MEET," Nov 4, 1901.
3   The *Cincinnati Enquirer*, "R.P. Ernst To Be Candidate For Nomination For Senator," May 10, 1920.

4   The *Cincinnati Enquirer*, "RAMBLERS: Are To Return To Fold If Ernst Is Nominated For Senator," Jun 24, 1914.

5   The *Cincinnati Enquirer*, "REWARD: Faithful Work the Republican Ranks Is Sought By Ernst," Jun 9, 1914.

6   The *Courier Journal*, "Grayot sees trickery to beat Beckham," November 5, 1920.

7   Bell, Ulric. "Progressive Wagon Lures," The *Courier Journal*, November 12, 1922.

8   The *Courier Journal*, "Kentucky Gossip in the US Capital," June 25, 1922.

9   The *New York Times*, "ERNST FOR VOLSTEAD ACT," December 15, 1922.

10   The *New York Times*, "Text of President Harding's Bonus Veto Message," Sept. 20, 1922.

11   Weekly Town Talk, "Soldier Bonus Lacks 4 Votes, Dies In the Senate," Alexandria, LA: September 23, 1922.

12   The *Courier Journal*, "Ernst, Quin To Wage Fight In GOP Session," June 18, 1923.

13   The *Courier Journal*, "Dawson Nominated On The First Ballot—Kentucky Republicans Meet In Lexington," June 27, 1923.

14   "Adjusted Compensation Act Hearings," 1–73. Retrieved from https://www.finance.senate.gov/imo/media/doc/68HrgAdjusted.pdf (Accessed on February 27, 2017).

15   The *Cincinnati Enquirer*, "Motorcade Halts For Dinner-As Guest of Cincinnati and Neighbor Cities," October 9, 1925.

16   The *Courier Journal*, "Ernst Bloc Draws Ire of Women," January 3, 1925.

17   The *Courier Journal*, "Sackett May Preside Here At Convention," March 28, 1926.

18   Libbey, James K. *Alben Barkley—A Life In Politics*. (Lexington: University of Kentucky Press, 2016): 123.

19   The *Courier Journal*, "Radio Listings," October 26, 1926.

20   The *Courier Journal*, "Stanley Flays Ernst," October 31. 1926.

21   The *Courier Journal*, Highlights of Election, November 3, 1926.

22   The *Courier Journal*, "FALLS STAND OF SAMPSON IS ASSAILED," January 16, 1930.

Frederic M. Sackett

1   The University of Louisville's Speed Museum of Art and the J.B. Speed College of Engineering were established in his name by his wife after his death in 1912.

2   Klotter, James. *Kentucky: Portrait in Paradox, 1900–1950*, 281.

3   The *Courier Journal* October 4, 1924.

4   The *Courier Journal*, October 16, 1924.

5   Hartmann, M.J. Edward. Prohibition and Its Consequences To American Liberty, Secretary Anti-Prohibition League of Missouri (1923) 141. Quoting the *Congressional Record* of Sept., 23, 1921.

6   The *Courier Journal*, October 17, 1924.

7   The *Courier Journal*, September 10, 1924.

8   Klotter, James. *Kentucky: Portrait in Paradox*, 282.

9   Burke, Bernard V. "Senator and Diplomat: The Public Career of Frederic M. Sackett." *Filson Club History Quarterly* 61 (April 1987): 192.

10   The *New York Times*, December 22, 1928.

11   Burke, Bernard V. "Senator and Diplomat: The Public Career of Frederic M. Sackett." *Filson Club History Quarterly* 61 (April 1987): 192.

12   Burke, Bernard B. *Ambassador Frederic Sackett and the Collapse of the Weimar Republic, 1930–1933*, Cambridge University Press.

13   Ibid, 18.

14   The *Courier Journal*, Saturday December 14, 1929.

15   The *Courier Journal*, January 3, 1930.

16   Burke, *Ambassador Frederic Sackett and the Collapse of the Weimar Republic, 1930–1933*, 17.

Alben W. Barkley (First through Fourth Terms)

1   *News-Democrat*, Two Paducans," Paducah: December 1, 1912.

2   The *Courier Journal*, August 8, 1926, 55.

3   *Oakland Tribune*, Oakland, CA: July 17, 1949.

4   The *Nashville Banner*, Nashville: November 8, 1932, 9.

5   *Lancaster Gazette Eagle*, Lancaster, Ohio: August 27, 1936, 9.

6   The *Paducah News-Democrat*, June 28, 1928, 1.

7   Henderson, J. Howard. "Obstacles in Life of Alben Barkley Senatorial Nominee Are Revealed By Friends," The *Courier Journal*, August 8, 1926, 55.

8   The *Neosho Times*, Neosho, MO: January 6, 1927.

9   The *Daily Times*, Davenport, Iowa: September 6, 1927, 20.

10   The *Courier Journal*, August 8, 1926, 55.

11   Henderson, J. Howard. "Obstacles in Life of Alben Barkley Senatorial Nominee Are Revealed By Friends," The *Courier Journal*, August 8, 1926, 55.

12   The *Courier Journal*, August 8, 1926, 55.

13   The *Paducah Sun Democrat*, December 15, 1911.

14   Libbey, James K. *Alben Barkley—A Life In Politics*, (Lexington: University Press of Kentucky, 2016): 115–119.

15   Libbey, James K. *Alben Barkley—A Life In Politics*, 120.

16   Libbey, James K. *Alben Barkley—A Life In Politics*, 122.

17   Libbey, James K. *Alben Barkley—A Life In Politics*, 123.

18   Libbey, James K. *Alben Barkley—A Life In Politics*, 131.

19   Libbey, James K. *Alben Barkley—A Life In Politics*, 137–138.

20   The *Tribune*, Scranton, PA: June 28, 1932.

21   Libbey, James K. *Alben Barkley—A Life In Politics*, 166–167.

22   Libbey, James K. *Alben Barkley—A Life In Politics*, 167.

23   The *Messenger*, "Barkley Says Dollar Sound," Madisonville, Ky: December 14, 1933, 1.

24   Libbey, James K. *Alben Barkley—A Life In Politics*, 168–169.

25   Libbey, James K. *Alben Barkley—A Life In Politics*, 187–191.

26   Libbey, James K. *Alben Barkley—A Life In Politics*, 194–195.

27   Libbey, James K. *Alben Barkley—A Life In Politics*, 200.

28   Libbey, James K. *Alben Barkley—A Life In Politics*, 204.

29   Libbey, James K. *Alben Barkley—A Life In Politics*, 213–214.

30   Libbey, James K. *Alben Barkley—A Life In Politics*, 218–219.

31   Libbey, James K. *Alben Barkley—A Life In Politics*, 222.

32   Libbey, James K. *Alben Barkley—A Life In Politics*, 221–222.

33   The *Courier Journal*, February 27, 1944, 27.

34   The *Tennessean*, November 22, 1942, 17.

35   The *Santa Fe New Mexican*, Santa Fe: November 19, 1942.

36   Libbey, James K. *Alben Barkley—A Life In Politics*, 224.

37   Libbey, James K. *Alben Barkley—A Life In Politics*, 229–232.

38   Libbey, James K. *Alben Barkley—A Life In Politics*, 229–232.

39   *Long Beach Independent*, Long Beach, CA: July 19, 1948.

40   Ibid.

41   Libbey, James K. *Alben Barkley—A Life In Politics*, 254.

42   Libbey, James K. *Alben Barkley—A Life In Politics*, 222, 223.

43   The *New York Times*, May 1, 1956, 32.

John Marshal Robsion

1   The *Cincinnati Enquirer*, Nov. 9, 1930, 37.

2   1928 Presidential General Election Results, Retrieved from https://uselectionatlas.org/RESULTS/state.php?year=1928&fips=21&f=0&off=0&elect=0 (Accessed 10/15/2019).

3   Mason, Wilmer G., "Portraits of Political Personages John Marshall Robsion," The *Cincinnati Enquirer*, November 1, 1930, 13.

4   The *Courier Journal*, January 12, 1930.

5   The *Courier Journal*, "Robison Loses Office at Once" November 8, 1930, 26.

6   *Messenger-Inquirer*, Owensboro: January 29, 1930.

7   The *Courier Journal*, October 30, 1930.

8   The *Courier Journal*, Jan. 28, 1931.

Ben Williamson

1   *Biographical Directory of the United States Congress—1774 to Present*, Williamson, Ben Mitchell. Retrieved from http://bioguide.congress.gov/scripts/biodisplay.pl?index=W000550 (Accessed 12/16/2019).

2   Mason, Wilmer G. "Bonnet" - "Fingered by Vinson"—"Planning to Enter Kentucky Governor Race, Is Tip" "Action Would Eliminate Senator Williamson From Consideration Is Belief," The *Courier Journal*, Frankfort Bureau: December 31, 1930.

3   The *Baltimore Sun*, "Diverse Personalities Fill Unexpired Terms in the Senate," Sun Washington Bureau: December 21, 1930.

4   The *Kokomo Tribune*, "Several Business Men Retire From Congress" AP: March 3, 1931.

5   Ibid.

6   The *Cincinnati Enquirer*, "Kentuckian Affirmed as Director" "Ben Williamson Ashland Is Put In Charge of Finances—Also to Head State Electors In the State," September 13, 1936.

7   The *Cincinnati Enquirer*, "Williamson Rites Are Set; Philanthropist, Once Senator," June 25, 1941.

8   The *Courier Journal*, "Bridge Freed," August 10, 1941.

Marvel Mills Logan

1   International Order of Odd Fellows (IOOF) is a fraternal organization similar to the Masonic Orders. Membership was at its peak during the nineteenth-century up until the mid-twentieth century. They had lodges in many cities and towns and operated cemeteries for its members.

2   Oulahan, Richard V., The *New York Times*, Special to The *New York Times* "Kentucky Campaign Marked By Apathy; Democrats Assert Election of Judge Logan in Place of Senator Robsion Is Assured. Chances Seem In His Favor But More Efficient Republican Organization Is Striving to Rally Full Party Vote," October 26, 1930.

3   The *New York Times*, "19 New Members Chosen For Senate," November 9, 1930.

4   The *New York Times*, "Bingham Estate Taxed $345,403," December 25, 1918.

5   *Jefferson City Post Tribune*, "Crowd Hoots at At Long Probers in New Orleans—Counsel for Former Senator Broussard Cited for Contempt—Senator Logan Flays "Shameful Conduct" Short and Ugly Word Flies Around Room in Creole Capital," AP November 14, 1933.

6   Gableman, Edwin W., "Relief, In Kentucky Hit." The *Cincinnati Enquirer*, September 2, 1934, 6

7   Ibid.

8   *Kentucky Advocate*, "Senator M.M. Logan Sees Inefficient Set-Up In Kentucky's Relief," Danville: September 4, 1934.

9   The *New York Times*, "Odd Fellows Hear World Peace Plea," September 17, 1935.

10   *Kentucky Advocate*, "Senator M.M. Logan Makes A Powerful Appeal For The Ticket," Danville: October 26, 1935.

11   The *Cincinnati Enquirer*, "Third Federal Judge, Oked For State," June 16, 1936.

12   The *New York Times*, "Logan Leads Chandler's Man, Beckham, In Kentucky Returns on the Senate Race," August 2, 1936; by The Associated Press.

13   The *New York Times*, August 2, 1936.

14   Stokes, Thomas L. Scripps Howard Staff Writer, "M'Nary Enjoying Court Bill Fight," The *Pittsburgh Press*, July 8, 1937.

15   *Reno-Gazette Journal*, "Logan Will Vote For Compromise Court Plan," April 22, 1937.

16   *Kentucky Advocate*, "BOOM LOGAN AS SUCCESSOR TO SUTHERLAND; General Assembly Gives Endorsement To State's Junior Senator in Joint Resolution; CHANDLER OKS," January 11, 1938.

17   The *Gazette and Daily*, "AP Chandler Says Logan Begged For Judgeship," York, Pennsylvania: July 27, 1938.

18   The *Gazette and Daily*, "Chandler's Charge A Lie, Says Logan," York, Pennsylvania: July 27, 1938 AP.

19   The *Cincinnati Enquirer*, "To Honor Logan," October 5, 1939.

20   The *Advocate-Messenger*, Danville: October 4, 1939.

PART XI

1	The National World War II Museum. "U.S. Military By the Numbers," Retrieved from https://www.nationalww2museum.org/students-teachers/student-resources/research-starters/research-starters-us-military-numbers (Accessed 11/06/2019).

2	VA Benefits and Healthcare. "History and Timeline." Retrieved from https://benefits.va.gov/gibill/history.asp. (Accessed 11/06/2019).

Albert Benjamin "Happy" Chandler

1	Chandler, Albert B., Trimble Vince H., *Heroes, Plain Folk and Skunks: The Life and Times of Happy Chandler*. (Chicago: Bonus Books, 1989): 148.

2	The *New York Times*, "Chandler Ready To Go," December 9, 1941.

3	Reston, James, "Senator Favor Longer Service for Men in the Army," The *New York Times*, July 27, 1941.

4	*Anchorage Daily Times*, "Senators To Be Buckner Guests On Alaska Tour," August 11, 1942.

5	*Anchorage Daily Times*, August 7, 1942.

6	*Cincinnati Times Star*, "Charges By Brown Are Denied By Chandler," July 23, 1942.

7	*Pallidum-Item*, "Chandler Tops Opponent In Kentucky Vote," Richmond, IN: August 2, 1942.

8	Niiya, Brian, "Chandler Committee," *Densho Encyclopedia*, Retrieved from https://encyclopedia.densho.org/Chandler%20Committee/ (Accessed Oct 25, 2019).

9	The *New York Times*, "'East and West' New Blows Planned," May 23, 1943.

10	Chandler, Albert B., Trimble Vince H. *Heroes, Plain Folk and Skunks*, 167.

11	The *New York Times*, October 24, 1943.

12	Chandler, Albert B., Trimble Vince H.: *Heroes, Plain Folk and Skunks*, 151–152.

13	Riggs, Robert L., "No Real Labor Lack, Chandler Declares," The *Courier Journal*, February 27, 1945.

14	The *Baltimore Sun*, "Sen. Chandler Baseball Head," April 25, 1945.

15	The *New York Times*, "Chandler Urged to Quit his Post as U.S. Senator," September 27, 1945.

16	The *Courier Journal*, "Chandler Resignation Is Formally Accepted," November 1, 1945.

William A. Stanfill

1	The *New York Times*, Nov. 20, 1945.

2	The *New York Times*, Nov. 25, 1945.

3	Trussel, C.P., The *New York Times*, Feb. 5, 1946.

4	Crider, John H., The *New York Times*, April 19, 1946.

John Sherman Cooper (First Term)

1	Morris, Hugh, "Reece Predicts 4 Congress Seats for State G.O.P.—Stanfill May not Run for Senate; J.S. Cooper Mentioned as Candidate," The *Courier Journal*, May 7, 1946.

2	Riggs, Robert L., The *Courier Journal*, Oct. 6, 1946.

3	Schulman, Robert, *John Sherman Cooper—The Global Kentuckian*, (Lexington: University of Kentucky Press, 1976): 36–37.

4	Schulman, *John Sherman Cooper*, 36–37.

5	Schulman, *John Sherman Cooper*, 39.

PART XII

Virgil Munday Chapman

1	Papers of Harry S. Truman, 1949, 646–647.

2	Campbell, Tracy, *Short of the Glory: The Fall and Redemption of Edward F. Prichard Jr.* (Kentucky: University of Kentucky Press, 2004): 132.

3	Truman, Harry, *Public Papers of the Presidents of the United States: Harry S. Truman, 1948* (1963), 132–133.

4	Campbell, *Short of the Glory*, 129.

5	The *New York Times*, "Senator Chapman Dies After Crash," March 9, 1951.

6   The *Courier Journal*, "Isms in the US are Attacked by Chapman Opening Session of Farm Bureau Hears Senator," Nov. 21, 1950.

7   The *Courier Journal*, "Chapman Urges American Preparedness as Answer to 'Narrow Selfish, Ambitious Soviet Union,'" Sept. 5, 1949.

8   Campbell, *Short of the Glory*, 196.

9   The *Courier Journal*, "Senator Chapman Dies After Crash," March 9, 1951.

10   The *New York Times*, March 9, 1951.

Garrett Lee Withers

1   Brown, J.Y., "M. and F. Academy, Providence, KY," Kentucky Historical Society, Retrieved from http://www.kyhistory.com/cdm/ref/collection/Morgan/id/8397. (Accessed April 27, 2017).

2   Memorial Addresses Delivered in Congress; Garrett Lee Withers -Late A Representative And A Former Senator From Kentucky; Eighty-Third Congress-First Session (Stennis) U.S. Government Printing Office: Washington (1953).52.

3   Stark, Louis, "Truman's Powers Argued in Senate," The *New York Times*, June 10, 1949.

4   *Cincinnati Enquirer*, "Not Tieless Ty Tyler, But Senator Withers It is Who Appears Sans Cravat!" July 27, 1949.

5   The *Escanaba Daily Press*, Escanaba, MI: October 15, 1949.

6   The *New York Times*, Jan. 4, 1950.

7   The *New York Times*, Feb. 8, 1950.

8   The *Cincinnati Enquirer*, August 21, 1950.

9   The *Messenger-Inquirer*, Owensboro: March 1, 1949, 8.

10   The *New York Times*, Nov. 28, 1950.

Earle C. Clements

1   *Biographical Directory of the United States Congress, 1774 to Present*; CLEMENTS, Earle C. (1898-1985) Retrieved from http://bioguide.congress.gov/scripts/biodisplay.pl?index-=C000506 (Accessed 11/05/2019).

2   The *Courier Journal*, Sat. January 3, 1953, 10.

3   Edstrom, Ed, "Absenteeism Runs as High in 83d Congress As In the 82d, It Can Upset Narrow Margins," The *Courier Journal*, Friday January 30, 1953.

4   Hardin, John A. *Fifty Years of Segregation: Black Higher Education in Kentucky, 1904–1954.* (Lexington: University of Kentucky Press, 1997): 107.

5   The *New York Times*, "Happy's Way: Sodas and Soft Soap," Sunday August 14, 1955.

6   The *Courier Journal* editorial, Friday July 8, 1955.

7   Caro, Robert. *The Years of Lyndon Johnson: Master of the Senate* (New York: Alfred A. Knopf, a division of Random House, Inc. 2002): 680–681.

8   The *New York Times*, Friday, November 9, 1956.

9   *Biographical Directory of the US Congress*, Earle C. Clements, Retrieved from http://bioguide.congress.gov/scripts/biodisplay.pl?index=R000471 (Accessed 9/6/2019).

10   The *New York Times*, March 14, 1985.

11   Education. Ky, Retrieved from (http://education.ky.gov/commofed/mon/pages/march-23-2015.aspx).

Thomas R. Underwood

1   The *Courier Journal*, March 20, 1948.

2   The *Courier Journal*, March 18, 1951.

3   The *Courier Journal*, "Fayette County Sends Seventh Man to Senate—Thomas R. Underwood is the Seventh Resident of Fayette County to Serve in the United States," March 18, 1951.

4   The *Courier Journal*, June 21, 1925, 9.

5   The *Courier Journal*, March 18, 1951, 24.

6   The *Courier Journal*, "GOP's Cooper Drops from Governor's Race," March 18, 1951.

7   The *Courier Journal*, Oct. 29, 1952.

8   The *Courier Journal*, October 3, 1952.

9   Ibid.
10   The *Courier Journal*, Oct. 22, 1952.
11   The *Courier Journal*, Nov. 6, 1952.

John Sherman Cooper (Second Term)

1   The *Courier Journal*, Feb. 24, 1952.
2   Ibid.
3   The *Courier Journal*, "Good Choice for U.S. Senator, but There's a Lot to Consider," Feb. 29, 1952.
4   The *Courier Journal*, March 4, 1952.
5   The *Courier Journal*, Oct. 10, 1952, 12.
6   The *Courier Journal*, Oct. 10, 1952.
7   The *Courier Journal*, Nov. 6, 1952.
8   The *Courier Journal*, Nov. 7, 1952.
9   The *Courier Journal*, Nov. 27, 1952.
10   Riggs, Robert L. "Washington Bureau," The *Courier Journal*, Jan. 14, 1953.
11   The *Courier Journal*, Feb. 1, 1953.
12   The *Courier Journal*, "Cooper being on the Winning Team Isn't all Beer and Skittles," March 15, 1953.
13   The *Courier Journal*, May 10, 1953.
14   The *New York Times*, Sept. 18, 1953.
15   The *New York Times*, Nov. 30, 1953.
16   The *Courier Journal*, Dec. 19, 1953.
17   Schulman, Robert, *John Sherman Cooper—The Global Kentuckian*, (Lexington: The University Press of Kentucky, 1976): 59.
18   Schulman, Robert, *John Sherman Cooper—The Global Kentuckian*, 59.
19   Schulman, Robert, *John Sherman Cooper—The Global Kentuckian*, 59.
20   Schulman, Robert, *John Sherman Cooper—The Global Kentuckian*, 60.
21   Schulman, Robert, *John Sherman Cooper—The Global Kentuckian*, 61.
22   The *Courier Journal*, "Cooper Tells G.O.P. He's Running on His Record and What Ike's Done; Facts Faced, He Declares," Sept. 14, 1954.
23   The *Courier Journal*, Oct. 30, 1954.
24   The *Courier Journal*, Nov. 4, 1954.

Alben Barkley (Second Term)

1   Libbey, James K. *Alben Barkley—A Life in Politics*, (Lexington: University of Kentucky Press, 2016): 271–273.
2   The *Courier Journal*, Oct. 23, 1954.
3   The *Courier Journal*, Oct. 30, 1954.
4   The *Courier Journal*, Nov. 4, 1954.
5   *Wilmington Morning News*, Wilmington, Delaware: Tuesday, May 1, 1956, 6.
6   Libbey, *Alben Barkley*, 276.
7   Jordan, Paul R. *Journey from Beavercreek*, Xlibris, 20.

Robert Humphreys

1   The *New York Times*, Feb. 7, 1935.
2   The *New York Times*, June 22, 1956.
3   The *New York Times*, June 26, 1956.
4   *Biographical Directory of the United States Congress, 1774–Present*; Humphreys, Robert (1893–1977) (Accessed 08/25/2019).

Part XIII

John Sherman Cooper (Third through Fifth Terms)

1   The *Courier Journal*, "Kentucky Politics Now Has Everything" July 10, 1956, 6.

2   The *Paducah Sun*, September 19, 1956, 1.

3   The *Cincinnati Enquirer*, October 18, 1956, 1.

4   Morris, Hugh, "Official Returns Give President 95,740 plurality," The *Courier Journal*, November 23, 1956, 15.

5   The *Paducah Sun*, "Senator Get Many Requests for Positions", AP, February 17, 1957.

6   *Press and Sun Bulletin*, "GOP Regulars Back Dirksen—Cooper faces tough rowing," Binghamton, N.Y: December 31, 1958.

7   The *Courier Journal*, October 16, 1960.

8   The *Courier Journal*, February 23, 1991.

9   Morris, Hugh, "Cooper Sets New Record for Margin," The *Courier Journal*, November 10, 1960.

10   The *Courier Journal*, "Cooper, Wells, And Stitch Honored—WHAS Presents 'Man of Year' News Awards," January 2, 1961.

11   The *Tennessean*, "Senator Cooper Breaks Ground," Nashville: April 23, 1961.

12   Hall, Elmer, "Berea Mine Funds Seem Sure," The *Courier Journal*, July 13, 1963.

13   The *Philadelphia Inquirer*, September 29, 1964.

14   Spear, David, "Assassination Committee's findings receive criticism," Gannett News Service, The *Ithaca Journal*, January 6, 1979.

15   Dietz, Robert, C-J Staff Writer. "Senator Cooper Makes It Official, He'll Run Again," The *Courier Journal*, March 30, 1966.

16   The *Paducah Sun*, November 5, 1966.

17   The *Courier Journal*, "Cooper Backs Cook, Again Criticizes Nunn," AP May 22, 1967.

18   Greider, William, "Congressional Discontent—Vietnam in a Kentucky Mirror," The *Courier Journal*, October 8, 1967.

19   Pearson, Drew. "Cooper Offers LBJ New Advice," *The News-Messenger*, Fremont, Ohio.

20   Broder, David, "McIntyre won't back ABM plan," *Washington Post* Service *Washington Post Honolulu Star-Bulletin*, July 27, 1969.

21   The *Gastonia Gazette*, "Safeguard Foes Say They Smell Scent of Victory—Okay Is Given by Senate," August 13, 1970.

22   Schulman, Robert, *John Sherman Cooper, The Global Kentuckian*, (Lexington: The University Press of Kentucky, 1976): 101–102.

23   The *Dispatch* [Moline] November 13, 1971.

24   Toledano, Ralph de. "Can Congress Get Best of President?," The *Jackson Sun*, Jackson TN: January 5, 1973.

25   The *Courier Journal*, "Statesman renown for his integrity dies," February 23, 1991.

26   *Messenger-Inquirer*, "State, nation mourn loss of Cooper" from *Lexington Herald-Leader* Owensboro: February 24, 1991.

Thurston B. Morton

1   Frantz, Joe B. "Oral history transcript, Thurston Morton, interview 1 (I)", 2/26/1969, LBJ Library Oral Histories, LBJ Presidential Library, Retrieved from https://www.discoverlbj.org/item/oh-mortont-19690226-1-74-224. (Accessed November 29, 2019).

2   The *Courier Journal*, April 26, 1946.

3   Frantz, Joe B. "LBJ Library Oral History Transcript."

4   The *Courier Journal*, February 15, 1956.

5   The *Courier Journal*, November 10, 1956.

6   Frantz, Joe B. "Oral History p.2" Retrieved from https://www.discoverlbj.org/item/oh-mortont-19690226-1-74-224. (Accessed 11/29/2019).

7   Frantz, Joe B. Ibid, 6.

8   *Messenger-Inquirer*, Owensboro: June 29, 1960.

9   TV.com, "What's My Line," Retrieved from http://www.tv.com/shows/whats-my-line/episode-533-96917/ (Accessed 11/29/2019).

10   "To Pass H.R. 6675, the Social Security Amendments of 1965," GovTrack, Retrieved from https://www.govtrack.us/congress/votes/89-1965/s151. (Accessed April 27, 2017).

11   Frantz, Joe B. "Oral History," 25.

12   Frantz, Joe B. "Oral History," 25–28.

13   Frantz, Joe B. "Oral History," 28–29.

14   Frantz, Joe B. "Oral History," 29.

15   The *Cincinnati Enquirer*, February 24, 1968.

16   G Captain, "American Commercial Lines Chooses," Retrieved from https://gcaptain.com/american-commercial-lines-chooses/.

17   *St. Louis Post-Dispatch*, August 15, 1982.

Marlow W. Cook

1   The *Indianapolis Star*, AP "Haynsworth Forces Reply to Criticism" October 11, 1969.

2   Graham, Fred P., "Haynsworth Wins 10–7 Endorsement of Senate Panel," The *New York Times*, October 10, 1969.

3   *Congressional Record—Senate* November 21, 1969, 35396.

4   The *New York Times*, "A Major Setback" by Fred P. Graham; April 9, 1970.

5   C-SPAN, "MARLOW W. COOK "(ends at :50) Retrieved from https://www.c-span.org/video/?151128-1/bork-hearing-preview (Accessed 9/2/2017).

6   Madden, Richard L. "Cook Is Defeated In Kentucky Race," The *New York Times*, November 6, 1974.

Part XIV

1   The *New York Times*, April 19, 1978, 16.

Walter D. Huddleston

1   Kentucky Human Right Commission Hall of Fame, Retrieved from https://kchr.ky.gov/halloffame/Pages/hof05.aspx (Accessed February 19, 2018).

2   Vecsey, George, "Huddleston, Democrat Defeats Nunn for Kentucky Senate Seat", The *New York Times*, November 8. 1972. 24.

3   Bergen, Drew Von, "Washington's Unsettling For Freshman Legislator" *Fort Lauderdale News*, April 15, 1973, 6.

4   The *Indianapolis News*, "Vietnam Monument?" January 25, 1973, from the AP, 5.

5   The *Courier Journal*, "Huddleston Discusses War In Guard Talk," March 4, 1973, 30.

6   *Indianapolis Star*, "$6.2 Billion in the Vault—Lawmakers Find Fort Knox Not Empty After All," AP, September 24, 1974.

7   Senate Select Committee to Study Governmental Operations with Respect to Intelligence Activities. Retrieved from https://www.senate.gov/artandhistory/history/common/investigations/ChurchCommittee.htm (Accessed March 12, 2018).

8   Moat, Lucia, "Election '84: Midwest Battleground," *Christian Science Monitor*, September 20, 1984, Retrieved from https://www.csmonitor.com/1984/0920/092006.html. (Accessed March 12, 2018).

9   Chellgren, Mark R. AP, "McConnell Wins In Upset," The *Advocate-Messenger*, Danville, KY: November 7, 1984.

10   The *Cincinnati Enquirer*, "Senator Toasted," Retrieved from http://www.enquirer.com/editions/2002/06/18/loc_ex-senator_toasted.html (June 18, 2002).

11   Ice Cream Geek, "National Ice Cream Month: The Full Story" Retrieved from http://www.icecreamgeek.com/?p=1451 (Accessed March 12, 2018).

Wendell H. Ford

1   Clymer, Adam. "Wendell Ford, 90, Dies; Kentucky Senator Pushed Voting Rights." The *New York Times*, January 22, 2015.

2   The *Paducah Sun*, "Show of Support," September 18, 1974.

3   *Courier-Journal* Staff, "Walter "Dee" Huddleston" who lost Senate seat to McConnell, Dies." The Courier Journal, October 16, 2018.

4   Krebs, Emilie New Editor, The *Messenger*, Madisonville, Ky: October 25, 1978, 3.
         Billy Beer was a beer named after President Carter's younger brother Billy, who liked to drink
         beer while being interviewed at his business in Plains, Georgia.

5   During President Jimmy Carter's term (1977–1981) his younger brother Billy Carter had a
         store in Plains, Georgia, where he would often talk to the press while drinking beer. Someone
         got the idea to make a brand of beer in honor of the President's brother Billy Carter; there-
         fore, there was a "Billy Beer."

6   The *Courier Journal*, "Ford Has A Better Idea", July 5, 1975, 10.

7   Krebs, Emilie. The *Messenger*, Madisonville, KY: August 29, 1979, 1.

8   The *Courier Journal*, Ed Ryan, Chief of Washington Bureau; "Ford and Huddleston, 'just
         disagreed' on vote on Panama Canal Treaty," March 17, 1978.

9   Mapes, Jeff, "How California senator and congressmen voted in 1979," The *Petaluma Ar-
         gus-Courier*, January 9, 1980, 15.

10   C-Span, "'Control of the Senate'—Senator Wendell Ford talked about what it would mean
         if the Democratic party took control of the Senate," September 30, 1986. Retrieved from
         https://www.c-span.org/video/?150594-1/control-senate (Accessed December 7, 2018).

11   Brown, Mike, "Huddleston disagrees with CIA tactic," The *Courier Journal*, April 11, 1984, 10.

12   https://www.inaugural.senate.gov/about/past-committees/index.html#1993. (Accessed De-
         cember 12, 2018).

13   Garrett, Robert, "Sen. Ford steals a page from McConnell calls out the hounds in his latest
         TV ads," The *Courier Journal*, October 9, 1986.

14   Weintraub, Adam. The *Cincinnati Enquirer*, August 19, 1992.

15   Clymer, Adam. "Wendell Ford, 90, Dies; Kentucky Senator Pushed Voting Rights." The
         New York Times, January 22, 2015.

16   Roll Call, "Wendell Ford Longtime Kentucky Senator, Dies at 90" Retrieved from https://
         www.rollcall.com/news/wendell-ford-long-time-kentucky-senator-dies-at-90; posted Jan.
         22, 2015 at 3:53 p.m.

17   Anderson, Curt, "Congressional Debate Clouds Future for Tobacco Farmers," The *Paducah
         Sun*, AP, May 21, 1998.

18   Ford, Wendell H., "Debunking Myths About Tobacco," The *Courier Journal*, June 14, 1998, 41.

19   Campbell, Joy and Mayse James, "Legacy of Leadership—Ford left indelible mark on na-
         tion," *Messenger-Inquirer*, Owensboro: January 23, 2015.

20   S.Doc. 105-"Tributes Delivered In Congress" Retrieved from https://www.govinfo.gov/con-
         tent/pkg/CDOC-105sdoc31/pdf/CDOC-105sdoc31.pdf. (Accessed December 30, 2018).

Part XV

Addison Mitchell "Mitch" McConnell

1   Dyche, John David, *Republican Leader: A Political Biography of Senator Mitch McConnell*,
         Wilmington, (Delaware: Intercollegiate Studies Institute, 2009): 21-22.

2   Dyche, John David, *Republican Leader: A Political Biography of Senator Mitch McConnell*, 45–46.

3   Dyche, John David, *Republican Leader: A Political Biography of Senator Mitch McConnell*, 48.

4   Dyche, John David, *Republican Leader: A Political Biography of Senator Mitch McConnell*, 50.

5   Dyche, John David, *Republican Leader: A Political Biography of Senator Mitch McConnell*, 55.

6   Dyche, John David, *Republican Leader: A Political Biography of Senator Mitch McConnell*, 60.

7   Lawrence, Keith, *Messenger-Inquirer*, Owensboro: January 20, 1985.

8   Dyche, John David, *Republican Leader: A Political Biography of Senator Mitch McConnell*, 65.

9   Dyche, John David, *Republican Leader: A Political Biography of Senator Mitch McConnell*, 66.

10   Dyche, John David, *Republican Leader: A Political Biography of Senator Mitch McConnell*, 72.

11   The *Courier Journal*, "Bush expected to avoid picking a controversial running mate," June
         13, 1988.

12   Johnson, Bob, "McConnell's Bank Account for 1990 race holds $1 million," The *Courier
         Journal*, August 1, 1988.

13   Brown, Mike, "Hopkins asks McConnell's tobacco plan be rescinded," The *Courier Journal*, October 14, 1988.

14   Dyche, John David, *Republican Leader: A Political Biography of Senator Mitch McConnell*, 99–100.

15   The *Courier Journal*, "Citizens Flag Alliance (advertisement)" April 28, 1996, p. 29.

16   Dyche, John David, *Republican Leader: A Political Biography of Senator Mitch McConnell*, 112, 119.

17   The *Paducah Sun*, March 16, 1997.

18   Chen, Edwin, *Los Angeles Times*, appeared in The *Paducah Sun*, March 16, 1997.

19   The *Boston Globe*, October 20, 1999.

20   Cross, Al, "McConnell busier than ever in his role as fund-raiser," The *Courier Journal*, August 4, 2000.

21   Cross, Al, "What They Are Saying On the Picnic Grounds," The *Courier Journal*, September 2, 2001.

22   Carroll, James R, "Notes From Washington—Paul Puts Spotlight On Himself and History," The *Courier Journal*, May 23, 2010.
      Paul had stated he had problems with parts of the Civil Rights Act of 1964.

23   Espo, David. "GOP Asserts Strength, Targets Obama" *Democrat and Chronicle*, Rochester, NY: AP November 5, 2010.

24   Schreiner, Bruce and Alford, Roger. "McConnell and rivals take to the stage," *Messenger-Inquirer*, AP, Owensboro: August 4, 2013.

25   The *Cincinnati Enquirer*; "Ky. Senate race near dead heat; McConnell gains" July 20, 2014.

26   Raju, Manu & McCalmont, "McConnell defeats Grimes in KY," Politico, 11/04/2014 07:22 PM EST/Updated 11/05/2014 01:59 AM EST. Retrieved from https://www.politico.com/story/2014/11/kentucky-election-results-2014-mitch-mcconnell-defeats-alison-lundergan-grimes-112508 (Accessed January 31, 2019).

27   Beam, Adam. "Bevin, McConnell wait to meet" The *Paducah Sun*, AP, May 27, 2015.

28   Elving, Ron. "What Happened With Merrick Garland In 2016 And Why It Matters Now," NPR, June 29, 2018. Retrieved from https://www.npr.org/2018/06/29/624467256/what-happened-with-merrick-garland-in-2016-and-why-it-matters-now. (Accessed January 28, 2019).

29   GovTrack, Retrieved from https://www.govtrack.us/congress/bills/110/s1927 (Accessed February 4, 2019).

30   Politico, Trump Tightens Grip on Judges as McConnell wins 50th Circuit pick, 12/12/2019-https://www.politico.com/news/2019/12/12/trump-judges-mcconnell-circuit-082836 (Accessed 04/30/2020)

31   Snell, Kelsy, NPR, What's Inside The Senate $2 Trillion Coronavirus Aid Package" 03/26/2020 https://www.npr.org/2020/03/26/821457551/whats-inside-the-senate-s-2-trillion-coronavirus-aid-package (Accessed 04/30/2020)

32   McConnell Center, "McConnell Center About," Retrieved from http://louisville.edu/mcconnellcenter/about/. (Accessed January 28, 2019).

33   MacGillis, Alec. *The Cynic—The Political Education of Mitch McConnell*. (New York: Simon & Schuster Paperbacks, 2014): 127.

James "Jim" Bunning

1   *Minneapolis Star-Tribune*, "In Clinton's case, no rules exist on what evidence may be considered," MN: January 4, 1999.

2   The *Cincinnati Enquirer*, December 8, 2002, 18.

3   Zuckerbrod, Nancy. *Messenger-Inquirer*, AP, Owensboro: June 15, 2001.

4   National Security Archive, "Court Rules Delay in Presidential Papers is Illegal," October 1, 2007, Retrieved from https://nsarchive2.gwu.edu//news/20071001/index.htm (Accessed 10/24/2019).

5   Bunning-Bereuter-Blumenauer Flood Insurance Reform Act of 2004 (Public Law 108-264), Retrieved from https://www.nrcs.usda.gov/Internet/FSE_DOCUMENTS/nrcs143_009423.pdf) (Accessed April 28, 2018).

6   Fendrich, Howard. "Senators Jim Bunning and John McCain don't believe Major League Baseball will act," The *Springfield News-Leader*, AP, Springfield, MO.

7   McNeil, Neil and Baker, Richard A., *The American Senate—An Insider's History*, (New York: Oxford University Press, 2013): 346.

8   *Biographical Directory of the United States Congress, 1774–Present*, Bunning, James Paul David (1931–2017) Retrieved from http://bioguide.congress.gov/scripts/biodisplay.pl?index=b001066 (Accessed 10/24/2019).

Randal "Rand" Howard Paul

1   Phillips, Amber special to *Hartford Courant* from the *Washington Post*, November 26, 2017. A11.

2   The *Des Moines Register*, "Top 10 list of Rand Paul accomplishments," April 10, 2015.

3   Camia, Catalina. *USA Today*, March 7, 2013. Retrieved from https://www.usatoday.com/story/news/politics/2013/03/07/rand-paul-filibuster-longest-senate-thurmond/1970291/ (Accessed May 11, 2018).

4   Hunter, Jack, *Rare*. March 23, 2018. Retrieved from https://rare.us/rare-politics/issues/broken-bureaucracy/the-senate-passed-a-1-3-trillion-2232-page-omnibus-while-you-slept-did-anyone-bother-to-read-it-besides-rand-paul/ (Accessed May 11, 2018).

5   Phillips, Amber. "The drama of the overnight shut-down, hour by hour," The *Washington Post*, February 9, 2018.

6   Temple-West, Patrick, "Senator Paul stirs business ire over blocking tax treaties" Reuters. April 28, 2013. Retrieved from https://www.reuters.com/article/us-usa-tax-treaties/senator-paul-stirs-business-ire-over-blocking-of-tax-treaties-idUSBRE93R0A320130428. (Accessed May 12, 2018).

7   Senator Rand Paul. "About Rand," Senator Rand Paul's web page. Retrieved from https://www.paul.senate.gov/about-rand/legislation- (Accessed May 18, 2018).

8   The other two Republican senators voting "no" twice were John McCain of Arizona and Susan Collins of Maine.

9   Andrews, Wilson, "How Each Senator Voted on Trump's Cabinet and Administration Nominees," The *New York Times*, May 11, 2017.

10   *USA Today*, March 22, 2020.

ABOUT THE AUTHOR

Attorney Paul L. Whalen is a resident of Fort Thomas, Kentucky, and is past chair of the Kentucky Conference of the UMC Commission on Archives and History.

Whalen is a graduate of Lexington's Tates Creek High School. He has a degree in history from the University of Kentucky, JD from NKU's Salmon P. Chase College of Law, Diploma from the US Naval War College and Masters from Fort Hays State University.

INDEX